NATO at 70

Reflecting on North Atlantic Treaty Organisation (NATO) at 70, and the organisation's eventful history, this book challenges the traditional crisis-led approach that sees crises as key driving forces that pushed the alliance in radically new directions. It assesses the long-term development of NATO since its foundation.

Based on a wide range of case studies and on multinational archival research, the chapters in this book demonstrate the continuous effort of the NATO member states to build a shared political space and a common security thinking to enhance the Alliance resilience and deterrent function. The authors also correct the common tendency to focus on either the political or the military dimension of the Alliance. They show the deeply ingrained interdependence between the two and how their complexity has shaped the work, strategy, and development of NATO over time.

Thanks to its innovative approach and long-term scope, this volume offers new exciting insights into the history of the Alliance.

This book comprises articles originally published in *Cold War History*.

Linda Risso is Senior Research Fellow at the Institute of Historical Research at the University of London, UK. Her research focuses on the historical development of NATO and on the legacies of the Cold War on today's security and strategic thinking. She is the author of *Propaganda and intelligence in the Cold War: The NATO Information Service* (2014).

NATO at 70

A Historiographical Approach

Edited by
Linda Risso

Routledge
Taylor & Francis Group
LONDON AND NEW YORK

First published 2019
by Routledge
2 Park Square, Milton Park, Abingdon, Oxon, OX14 4RN

and by Routledge
52 Vanderbilt Avenue, New York, NY 10017

First issued in paperback 2020

Routledge is an imprint of the Taylor & Francis Group, an informa business

British Library Cataloguing-in-Publication Data
A catalogue record for this book is available from the British Library

ISBN 13: 978-0-367-66105-2 (pbk)
ISBN 13: 978-1-138-33297-3 (hbk)

Typeset in Minion Pro
by codeMantra

Publisher's Note
The publisher accepts responsibility for any inconsistencies that may have arisen during the conversion of this book from journal articles to book chapters, namely the possible inclusion of journal terminology.

Disclaimer
Every effort has been made to contact copyright holders for their permission to reprint material in this book. The publishers would be grateful to hear from any copyright holder who is not here acknowledged and will undertake to rectify any errors or omissions in future editions of this book.

Contents

Citation Information

The following chapters were originally published in the journal *Cold War History*. When citing this material, please use the original page numbering for each article, as follows:

Chapter 1
A nominal defence? NATO threat perception and responses in the Balkan area, 1951–1967
Dionysios Chourchoulis
Cold War History, volume 12, issue 4 (November 2012) pp. 637–657

Chapter 2
Out-of-area: NATO perceptions of the Third World, 1957–1967
Evanthis Hatzivassiliou
Cold War History, volume 13, issue 1 (February 2013) pp. 67–88

Chapter 3
Defeating the General: Anglo-American Relations, Europe and the NATO Crisis of 1966
James Ellison
Cold War History, volume 6, issue 1 (February 2006) pp. 85–111

Chapter 4
Propaganda on wheels: The NATO travelling exhibitions in the 1950s and 1960s
Linda Risso
Cold War History, volume 11, issue 1 (February 2011) pp. 9–25

Chapter 5
Cold War in the Aegean: Favouritism in NATO's Southeastern flank: The case of the Greek Colonels, 1967–74
Konstantina Maragkou
Cold War History, volume 9, issue 3 (August 2009) pp. 347–366

Chapter 6
'Footnoting' as a political instrument: Denmark's NATO policy in the 1980s
Nikolaj Petersen
Cold War History, volume 12, issue 2 (May 2012) pp. 295–317

Chapter 7

"A mass psychosis": The Netherlands and NATO's dual-track decision, 1978–1979
Ruud van Dijk
Cold War History, volume 12, issue 3 (August 2012) pp. 381–405

Chapter 8

General Lyman L. Lemnitzer and NATO, 1948–69: a deferential leader
Lawrence S. Kaplan
Cold War History, https://doi.org/10.1080/14682745.2018.1530633

Chapter 9

The NATO-Warsaw Pact competition in the 1970s and 1980s: a revolution in military affairs in the making or the end of a strategic age?
Diego A. Ruiz Palmer
Cold War History, volume 14, issue 4 (November 2014) pp. 533–573

Notes on Contributors

Dionysios Chourchoulis is an Adjunct Lecturer at the Hellenic Open University, Patras, Greece. His specialties include North Atlantic Treaty Organisation (NATO), the First and Second World Wars and the Cold War, twentieth-century history of the Balkans and the Mediterranean, modern and contemporary Greek history, and history of political and military blocs and alliances.

James Ellison is a Reader in International History in the Department of History at Queen Mary University of London, UK. He has specialised in the history of international affairs, focusing on alliance politics, conflict, and diplomacy after 1945.

Evanthis Hatzivassiliou is Professor of Contemporary History at the University of Athens, Greece. His areas of expertise are history, the Cold War, and the Soviet Union.

Lawrence S. Kaplan was the Director of the Lyman L. Lemnitzer Center for NATO Studies at Kent State University, USA (1979–92), and a Professorial Lecturer in American History at Georgetown University, Washington, D.C., USA (1993–2015).

Konstantina Maragkou is a Lecturer in European Studies and History at Yale University, New Haven, USA. Her research interests include twentieth-century world history and modern Greek history with special emphasis on Greece's foreign relations in the post-Second World War era.

Nikolaj Petersen is Professor Emeritus of International Relations in the Department of Political Science at Aarhus University, Denmark. He has written extensively on Danish foreign policy, Arctic politics, NATO and the EU, as well as foreign policy theory.

Linda Risso is Senior Research Fellow at the Institute of Historical Research at the University of London, UK. Her research focuses on the historical development of NATO and on the legacies of the Cold War on today's security and strategic thinking. She is the author of *Propaganda and intelligence in the Cold War: The NATO Information Service* (2014).

Diego A. Ruiz Palmer serves on NATO's International Staff in Belgium. From 1980–1991, he was an analyst on the staff of the National Security Study Memorandum 186 task force assembled under the authority of the Director of Net Assessment, Office of the Secretary of Defense, and US Department of Defense, to analyse NATO and Warsaw Pact force trends and operational strategies in Europe.

Ruud van Dijk is Assistant Professor of History in the Department of History at the University of Amsterdam, the Netherlands. His areas of expertise are the Cold War, history, security and defence, NATO, and Europe.

Foreword

Diego A. Ruiz Palmer

In 2019, NATO's member nations will commemorate the 70th anniversary of the signature of the North Atlantic Treaty in Washington, D.C., on 4 April 1949, by the 12 founding Allies. This will be a memorable opportunity for Europe and North America to celebrate the enduring nature and many accomplishments of the Atlantic Alliance and to rededicate themselves to the common purpose and community of values enshrined in the Treaty.

This anniversary volume brings together eight articles that were published in issues of the *Cold War History* journal between 2006 and 2014. They provide a rich menu of perspectives on NATO's evolution, challenges and record of success during the Cold War, from the Alliance's early years through the transformational implications of the fall of the Berlin Wall in 1989. NATO's unity and resolve contributed immensely to the peaceful reunification of Germany and of Europe. They also planted the seeds for enlarging the Alliance to the newly born independent nations and democracies of Central and Eastern Europe, over the next three decades, and for expanding its missions beyond collective defence to crisis management and cooperative security, in cooperation with some 40 partner countries across Europe and around the world.

The introductory chapter by Linda Risso, the book's editor, makes the case persuasively for a new look at multiple dimensions of the Alliance that have been largely neglected in NATO's Cold War historiography, namely the buildup among the Allies of a shared political space and common security thinking that provided the necessary underpinning for overcoming their divisions, and, furthermore, the strong interdependence between the Alliance's political and military components. This introduction sets the stage for an examination of several of the key issues that shaped NATO's Cold War agenda. These include the close partnership between the United Kingdom and the United States in the 1960s that helped steer NATO through the vicissitudes of France's stormy withdrawal from the Alliance's integrated military structure (by James Ellison); the often overlooked weight and influence of smaller Allies, such as the Netherlands in the 1970s (by Ruud van Dijk) and Denmark in the 1980s (by Nikolaj Petersen); the longer term impact on NATO of its enlargement to Greece and Turkey in 1952 (by Dionysos Chourchoulis); the implications for NATO of Greece's domestic politics between 1967 and 1974 (by Konstantina Maragkou); the practice among the Allies to view the so-called Third World through the often distorting Cold War lens (by Evanthis Hatzivassiliou); the role that was assigned to NATO travelling exhibitions in the 1950s and 1960s for reaching out to public opinion in an unconventional way (by Linda Risso); and, lastly, the determining influence of the competition between NATO and the Warsaw Pact in the 1970s and 1980s in shaping military postures that, at times, could have courted disaster, but that, in the end, NATO's steadfastness proved effective in taming.

As this book illustrates compellingly, while the Cold War has long been over, NATO's successful record between 1949 and 1989 of sustaining its political cohesion and military coherence through several international crises, and a few internal ones, holds many applicable insights for addressing effectively the current challenges to Euro-Atlantic security. For this, much gratitude is owed to the Editorial Board of *Cold War History* and to Linda Risso.

INTRODUCTION

Writing the History of NATO: A new agenda

Linda Risso

This year, NATO celebrates its 70th anniversary. The Alliance was launched in 1949 by 12 members to promote collective defence (article 5) and to foster political and defence cooperation among its members (article 2). Over time, NATO has expanded in more than one way. Today, it counts 29 members, and it has developed partnership agreements with more than 20 countries. Its strategic concept is based on a complex definition of 'security'. While collective defence remains at the core of NATO's mission, crisis management and cooperative security allow the Alliance to engage on multiple levels and to respond to a wide range of security challenges around the world. Contrary to what was the case in the Cold War, when NATO action was strictly limited to the territory of its member states, today engagement 'out-of-area' is an essential tool in projecting stability beyond NATO's borders. The Alliance aims to strengthen stability, resilience, and good governance on its periphery, thus strengthening its own security.[1]

As NATO's mission and strategic vision changed over the years, so has the work of historians. In the first decades, scholars focused predominantly on the Alliance's deterrence and defence functions and on how changing perceptions of the Soviet threat and of the military balance between the two blocs informed NATO's military strategy and force planning. In the geopolitical struggle between East and West, the Alliance was presented as a response to the Soviet threat and as a tool of American foreign policy in the stabilisation of Western Europe. The European allies, on their part, were eager to have a formal commitment that the United States would not abandon Europe to its fate and that it would continue to offer protection from both Soviet aggression and – at least initially – a resurgent Germany. Less attention was initially paid to how the Alliance evolved into a forum of political consultation and cooperation and to how it reacted to new political and economic challenges.[2]

Yet, during the Cold War, Western political leaders feared the disintegration of the West as much as an attack from the Soviet Union. In fact, in their eyes, the two challenges were not entirely separated. Not dissimilarly from today, during the Cold

[1] The official text of the NATO Strategic Concept 2010 is available at www.nato.int/cps/en/natohq/topics_82705.htm (Last accessed on 1 October 2018). Partnership agreements date back to 1994 with the Partnership for Peace Programme. Allies officially adopted 'Projecting Stability' as a guiding principle at the Warsaw Summit of 2016. It was expanded at the most recent 2018 Brussels Summit.

[2] Kaplan, Lawrence S., *NATO 1948: The Birth of the Transatlantic Alliance* (Plymouth: Rowman & Littlerfield Publishers, 2007).

War, NATO defence planners assumed that a Soviet offensive operation would likely be preceded by misinformation and propaganda campaigns to create confusion and distrust among the public and to foster anti-NATO opposition in key member states. Defence planners expected the tensions to create political turmoil that would offer fertile ground for military escalation. The 1957 NATO Strategic Concept (MC 14/2) included specific guidance about the threat of 'operations with limited objectives such as infiltrations, incursions or hostile local actions in the NATO area'.[3] Later, Nato's forward strategy included special provisions for the defence of the geographically exposed city of Kassel, which could be captured, occupied and then offered in exchange for West Berlin. Similar contingency planning was also in place for the defence of Denmark, Norway, Italy, Greece, and Turkey. Archival documents from the 1960s and 1970s offer countless examples of discussions on how to respond to Soviet psychological warfare and propaganda.[4] In all cases, solidarity among the members and a shared assessment of the Soviet threat were paramount. The Alliance's deterrent function was not credible without strong political cohesion among its members. Allied leaders therefore saw NATO as a tool to deter Soviet aggression as much as to maintain peace in the West.[5] Lord Ismay, NATO's first Secretary General, spoke aptly of a "Pax Atlantica".[6]

The end of the Cold War and the transformation of the Alliance initiated a debate among historians about the significance of NATO as a political forum that promotes cooperation among existing and with prospective members. In the recent decades, historians have attempted to bring together NATO's complementary functions of deterrence and defence on the one hand and cooperation and consultation on the other. Notions of a 'NATO system' started to emerge in the mid-1990s.[7] Not surprisingly, article 2 became the object of increasing scholarly attention. John Milloy has investigated the key role Canada played in pushing forward the article during the discussions on the wording of the Washington Treaty.[8] Andreas Wenger and Leopoldo Nuti have looked at the emergence of a common political culture to explain NATO's resilience during the 1960s and 1970s crises.[9]

Broadly speaking, looking at NATO as a political forum has allowed historians to move away from a narrow focus on the key members and to bring the smaller

[3] Text of MC14/2: www.nato.int/docu/stratdoc/eng/a570523a.pdf (Last accessed on 1 October 2018).

[4] Risso, Linda, *Propaganda and Intelligence in the Cold War: The NATO Information Service* (London: Routledge, 2014).

[5] This point has been made, among others, by Lawrence Kaplan in *The United States and NATO: The Formative Years* (Lexington, KY: The University Press of Kentucky, 1984).

[6] Lord Ismay, "Pax Atlantica". www.nato.int/docu/articles/1954/a54000a.htm (Last accessed on 1 October 2018). Originally published in *Unilever Magazine*, Winter 1954.

[7] Trachtenberg, Marc, *A Constructed Peace: The Making of the European Settlement, 1945–1963* (Princeton, NJ: Princeton University Press, 1999), 95–145.

[8] Milloy, John C., *The North Atlantic Treaty Organization, 1948–1957: Community or Alliance?* (Montreal, QA: McGill-Queen's University Press, 2006).

[9] Wenger, Andreas, Christian Nuenlist, and Anna Locher (eds.), *Transforming NATO in the Cold War: Challenges Beyond Deterrence in the 1960s* (London: Routledge, 2006); Nuti, Leopoldo (ed.), *The Crisis of Détente in Europe: From Helsinki to Gorbachev 1975–1985* (London: Routledge, 2008); Risse-Kappen, Thomas, *Cooperation among Democracies: The European Influence on US Foreign Policy* (Princeton, NJ: Princeton University Press, 1995).

countries into their framework of analysis. While never completely ignored, the study of the role of non-nuclear members really took off after the end of the Cold War. We now have a rich body of literature, which demonstrates clearly how different countries often shaped the strategic view and political discussions.[10] Several chapters included in this volume are good examples of this exciting new trend. Dionysios Chourchoulis and Konstantina Maragkou, for example, look at the Southern Balkans region and the case of Greece and the Balkans. Nikolaj Petersen and Ruud van Dijk discuss the case of Denmark and the Netherlands, respectively. Finally, Evanthis Hatzivassiliou investigates how during the Cold War the Alliance monitored communist infiltration in newly decolonised countries in Africa.

The second challenge sitting on the desk of NATO historians is to carry out a sustained examination of the historical development of the Alliance over time. Geir Lundestad has spoken of a 'crisis perspective' that dominates the literature on European–American relations in general, and of NATO in particular.[11] There is a tendency to look at NATO through the lens of crises. Historians often zoom in on times of geopolitical tensions to examine how the Allies overcame their differences and faced the challenge at hand. In this narrative, the Suez crisis of 1954 led to the Three Wise Men Report, the decision of De Gaulle to withdraw from the Integrated Allied Command led to Harmel Report in 1967, and the protest movements of the 1960s and 1970s led to the Ottawa Declaration of 1974. However, if historians do not study the political development of the Alliance in the long term, they miss the opportunity to see how crises bring to fruition what is in effect a steady and meticulous process of political cooperation and dialogue that goes on behind the scene in committees, working groups, and Council sessions on a weekly basis. It would have been much harder for the Alliance to survive the end of the Cold War if the members had not been able to rely on 40 years of continuous cooperation among military and political leaders and if they had not built mutual trust as well as military interdependence.[12]

While historians may have been cautious about providing a sustained historical account of the history of NATO, practitioners in the field have attempted to do so. In *Defence of the West*, for example, Stanley Sloan offers a rich analysis of the challenges NATO is facing today by looking back at its origins. Like many security experts, Sloan draws heavily on his own recollections and experience. He includes, for example,

---

[10] See, for example, the French case, which has been investigated extensively: Vaïsse, Maurice, Pierre Melandri, and Frédéric Bozo (eds.), *La France et l'OTAN*. (Brussels: André Versailles, 2012); Vaïsse, Maurice, La Grandeur: Politique étrangère du général de Gaulle (1958–1969) (Paris: Fayard, 2014); Bozo, Frédéric, Deux stratégies pour l'Europe: de Gaulle, les Etats-Unis et l'Alliance atlantique (1958–1969) (Paris: Plon, 1996); Heuser, Beatrice, and Kristian Stoddart, "Difficult Europeans: NATO and Tactical/Non-Strategic Nuclear Weapons in the Cold War," *Diplomacy and Statecraft* 28, no 3 (2017): 454–76.

[11] Lundestad, Geir (ed.), *No End to Alliance: The Unites States and Western Europe. Past, Present and Future* (London: Macmillan, 1998); Lundestad, Geir (ed.), *Just Another Major Crisis: The United States and Europe Since 2000* (Oxford: OUP, 2008); Johnston, Seth A., *How NATO Adapts: Strategy and Organization in the Atlantic Alliance Since 1950* (Baltimore: Johns Hopkins University Press, 2017).

[12] Schmidt, Gustav (ed.), *A History of NATO: The First Fifty Years*, 3 vols. (Basingstoke: Palgrave Macmillan, 2001). See also Militargeschichtlisches Forschungsamt (ed.), *Entstehung und Probleme des Atlantischen Bündnisses*, vols. 1–6 (Munich: Oldenbourg, 1998–2005).

valuable references to private conversations with key policymakers.[13] The information provided by Sloan and other experts is extremely relevant and offers excellent primary source material to historians investigating NATO's institutional history and culture.

The last few years have seen important new contributions that correct the tendency to focus on moments of crisis. The most recent book by Lawrence Kaplan has the merit of looking at the history of the Alliance in the long term, although the chapters still focus on 'key moments' of crisis.[14] The upcoming monograph by Tim Sayle does indeed offer a genuinely long-term examination of the political and institutional history of the Alliance, and it is a welcome contribution.[15] The chapter by James Ellison offers a good example of how today historians look back at well-known episodes in the history of the Cold War – in this case the Suez crisis – to examine the complex ramifications that the crisis had at the national level as well as how it affected bilateral and Alliance-wide relations.

There may also be a tendency to overestimate the importance of the end of the Cold War. The collapse of the Warsaw Pact and of the Soviet Union were clearly crucial events that shaped the geopolitical context in which the Alliance operated, and they radically transformed how their members saw the NATO and its function. Yet, there is a tendency to rely on a 'before and after' vision that discounts obvious continuities between the Cold War era and the post-1990 period. As argued above, if we consider the Alliance as a political forum then it is clear that the political solidarity among its members and the shared values of democracy, rule of law, and human rights that matured in the previous 40 years deeply shaped the discussions that took place in 1989 and 1900 and that allowed the Alliance to adapt and to take on a new role. Crucially, the principles established during the Cold War guided the actions of the Alliance in its response to international terrorism and in crisis management operations in the 1990s and early 2000s. They are still at the core of today's idea of 'projecting stability' through partnership agreements.

In a recent speech, Secretary General has spoken of the 'three ages of NATO': the Cold War, when the Alliance focused on deterring the Soviet threat; the period between 1990 and 2014 in which NATO engaged out of area and developed crisis management and peacekeeping capabilities; and finally, the post-2014 era in which new challenges like cyberwarfare and international terrorism are combined with a resurgent Russia on NATO's borders.[16] Historians currently working on NATO should therefore be more discerning about the heterogeneous nature of the post-Cold War period and examine continuities as well as ruptures.

---

[13] Sloan, Stanley R., *Defence of the West: NATO, the European Union and the Transatlantic Bargain* (Manchester: Manchester University Press, 2016).

[14] Kaplan, Lawrence S., *NATO Divided, NATO United: The Evolution of an Alliance* (Westport, CT: Praeger, 2004).

[15] Sayle, Timothy, *Enduring Alliance: A History of NATO and the Postwar Global Order* (Ithaca, NY: Cornell University Press, 2019).

[16] "The Three Ages of NATO: An Evolving Alliance. Speech by NATO Secretary General Jens Stoltenberg at the Harvard Kennedy School" 23 September 2016. www.nato.int/cps/en/natohq/opinions_135317.htm (Last accessed on 1 October 2018).

A third challenge in writing the history of NATO is to overcome the tendency to look at the political and institutional history of the Alliance as separated from its military dimension. Historians of international relations study one side, military historians the other, and the two are often held scrupulously separated. Yet, they are strongly interdependent, and they mutually influence each other to a point that has yet to be examined in a satisfactory account. Discussions on burden-sharing, the construction of an Alliance-wide military infrastructure, and the implications of nuclear deterrence are integral to the political history of the Alliance. Similarly, the members' own assessment of the security threats of the day and their own defence and security priorities shape directly the work of the Military Committee. The history of SHAPE and the evolving relationship between the Supreme Allied Commander and the Secretary General are often neglected by historians.[17] The chapter by Lawrence Kaplan on General Lemnitzer included in this volume is a good example of the need for further research on these lines. The chapter by Diego Ruiz-Palmer demonstrates the close cooperation between the work of the Military Committee, the Supreme Allied Commander, and the North Atlantic Council. Future historical research will have to bring the two sides closer together.

Science, NATO's third dimension, has often suffered a similar fate and has been treated almost as an entirely separate issue. Yet, the work of the Science Committee, the Committee on the Challenges of Modern Society, and – more recently – of the Science for Peace and Security Programme has been crucial in fostering links between NATO, academia, and civil society as well as in establishing cooperation with new partners. Luckily, recent scholarship has started to fill the gap. The imminent publication of Simone Turchetti's book on the Science Committee is welcome and builds on a rich body of recent scholarship.[18]

Similarly, NATO's action in the field of public diplomacy has been a crucial tool in connecting the Alliance with its own public and, after the end of the Cold War, with prospective new members. The chapter by Linda Risso demonstrates the richness of NATO's information programmes and the relentless attempt to connect with the wider public. While we now have a sustained account of the history of the Information Service, more work needs to be carried out – possibly in the form of case

[17] Ryan Hendrickson, a political scientist, barely scratches the surface of this important dimension. Hendrikson, Ryan C., *Diplomacy and War at NATO: The Secretary General and Military Action after the Cold War* (Columbia and London: University of Missouri, 2006).

[18] Turchetti, Simone, *Greening the Alliance: The Diplomacy of NATO's Science and Environmental Initiatives* (Chicago, IL: University of Chicago Press, 2018). See also Hatzivassilious, Evanthis, *The NATO Committee on the Challenges of Modern Society, 1969–1975: Transatlantic Relations, the Cold War and the Environment* (Basingstoke: Palgrave Macmillan, 2017); Risso, Linda, "NATO and the Environment: The Committee on the Challenges of Modern Society", *Contemporary European History* 25, no. 3 (2016): 505–35. For the role of the United States in fostering scientific cooperation see: Wolfe, Audra, *Freedom's Laboratory: The Cold War Struggle for the Soul of Science* (Baltimore: Johns Hopkins University Press, 2018); Krige, John, *American Hegemony and the Postwar Reconstruction of Science in Europe* (Cambridge: MIT Press, 2008).

studies – about how the information programmes were received by the national public and what effect, if any, they had.[19]

Historians must promote a holistic approach in which the interdependence between NATO's dimensions becomes clear, and it is evaluated in the long term. This is of course a massive task that can only be achieved through cooperation and cross-fertilisation among the various strands of research. A sustained history of NATO as a political and military alliance thus requires multinational archival research to examine the position of the member states as well as of the organisation's own papers to understand how the different viewpoints and interests found their place within the intergovernmental structure.

[19] Risso, *Propaganda and Intelligence.*

A nominal defence? NATO threat perception and responses in the Balkan area, 1951–1967

Dionysios Chourchoulis

This article deals with NATO strategy in the Balkans from 1951, when Greek and Turkish admission to the alliance was decided, to 1967, when NATO revised its strategic concept for the last time until the end of the Cold War, while another serious Greek-Turkish crisis over Cyprus erupted. The analysis places emphasis on the defence posture of the southern Balkans, regional correlation of forces and the evolution of NATO military strategy throughout the period under examination. Consideration is also given to the integration of the southern Balkans in the NATO command structure, the provision of aid to Greece and Turkey, and Greek-Turkish relations.

Geography and strategy in the Balkans

Allied military strategy in the Southern Flank region was influenced disproportionately by geography and this was always mirrored in the assessments of the NATO officials. The area of responsibility of Allied Forces Southern Europe (AFSOUTH) did not present a unified theatre and the development and implementation of comprehensive strategy was a herculean task.[1] The sea predominated over the land factor on the Southern Flank, which was compartmentalised in three theatres of operations where three separate land and air battles would be fought: northern Italy, the Balkans, and eastern Turkey. This article does not deal with NATO strategy and planning in the Adriatic and the Ljubljana Gap, as this constituted a separate front.

---

[1] John Chipman, 'NATO and the Security Problems of the Southern Region: From the Azores to Ardahan', in *NATO's Southern Allies: Internal and External Challenges*, ed. John Chipman (London & New York: Routledge, 1988), 9.

The coastal zone of the northern Aegean Sea linked Greece and Turkey and provided access to the Mediterranean. The western part of this zone, Greek Thrace was dominated by the mountains of southern Bulgaria, but was also too thin and lacked depth for effective defence. The principal land approach to Greece, and Salonika in particular, ran through the Axios (Vardar) Valley in southern Yugoslavia, while the secondary one ran from Bulgaria along the Strymon (Struma) River in Greek eastern Macedonia.[2] The terrain in Turkish Thrace was suitable for the application of an offensive high-speed manoeuvre operation towards the Straits; this major effort could be combined with one or more supportive amphibious and airborne operations through the Black Sea on beaches east of the Straits.[3] Descent of Soviet and Bulgarian forces to the Aegean (in conjunction with possession or neutralisation of Anatolia) would give the USSR access to the Mediterranean, greater freedom of operation against the Middle East, and would extend the Soviet bloc's air warning cover and the range of its air operation.[4] Furthermore, NATO officials acknowledged that the alliance would probably have to deal with additional sub-theatres in the southern Balkans: for instance, even in case of local war, Greek forces would have to withdraw from Western Thrace in the face of Soviet bloc superiority, thus leaving exposed the flanks of Turkish forces defending Eastern Thrace. Therefore, almost from the beginning, two separate battles would be fought in the Balkans, one in Greek Macedonia and another in Turkish Eastern Thrace and the Straits area.

During the 1950s and 1960s, the US Sixth Fleet, which was permanently stationed in the Mediterranean, constituted the most powerful allied (though not NATO assigned) force in the Southern Flank. By the end of 1951 atomic bombs had been deployed to its carriers. Initially, the potential targets were various Soviet bloc military facilities and war sustaining resources. Soon, the construction of smaller and lighter atomic devices, and other technological developments, gave to the Sixth Fleet's naval aviation the capability to launch tactical atomic airstrikes, as well as to perform conventional close air support, in order to blunt any Soviet bloc advances on NATO soil.[5]

The role and value of allied naval preponderance in the eastern Mediterranean, though significant, should not be overestimated. Control of the eastern Mediterranean alone was insufficient to defeat a Soviet bloc land campaign in Greek and Turkish Thrace: Greek and Turkish land and air forces could only count on very modest US/NATO support during the 1950s and 1960s.[6] Furthermore, one could justifiably doubt

[2] David Shlapak, Sam Gardiner and William Simons, *Sample Campaign Plans and Staff Assessments for NATO's Southern Region* (Santa Monica: RAND, 1989), 1.

[3] Ali Karaosmanoglu, 'Turkey and the Southern Flank: Domestic and External Contexts', in *NATO's Southern Allies*, 321.

[4] NATO Archives (hereafter: NATO/), M.C.14/1 (Final), *Report on Strategic Guidance*, December 9, 1952.

[5] Joel Sokolsky, *Seapower in the Nuclear Age. The United States Navy and NATO 1949–80* (London & New York: Routledge, 1991), 58–59; Dean Allard, 'An Era of Transition, 1945–1953', in *In Peace and War: Interpretations of American Naval History, 1775–1978*, ed. Kenneth Hagan (Westport & London: Greenwood Press, 1978), 300–302.

[6] John Chipman, 'Allies in the Mediterranean: Legacy of Fragmentation', in *NATO's Southern Allies*, 76.

the real capability of the Sixth Fleet's naval aircraft to contribute decisively to a NATO campaign in the eastern Mediterranean, at least during a crucial initial phase. At least until the mid-1960s, overall NATO air forces were relatively weak; while after this time the Soviets permanently stationed naval forces in the eastern Mediterranean. Therefore, in the event of war with the Soviet bloc, the US Chief of Naval Operations (CNO) and the Commander-in-Chief Southern Europe (CINCSOUTH) would most likely decide to withdraw the Sixth Fleet west of Sicily to avoid a Soviet air attack and prepare for a counterattack.[7] In such a context, the establishment and maintenance of NATO naval supremacy might prove irrelevant to the actual defence of mainland Greece, Turkish Thrace and the Straits, should deterrence fail and war occur. With the increased possibility of retaliatory nuclear strikes by the Sixth Fleet against the advancing Soviet bloc forces *within* Greek and Turkish territory, this made NATO's strategy in the Southern Flank unattractive to the Greeks and the Turks.

Early NATO military planning for the Balkans, 1951–54

From the beginning, NATO sought to integrate Greece and Turkey in the wider policy of containment to deter Soviet (or Bulgarian) aggression, but failed to develop and pursue a comprehensive and effective strategy in the Mediterranean, and particularly on the Balkan frontier. Several factors account for this. To a significant extent, geography determined strategy, while Greek and Turkish military weakness aggravated the predicament. However, these inherent difficulties were further exacerbated by the establishment of a complicated command structure in the Southern Flank, where two commands and ten sub-commands were finally set up in 1952–3.[8]

As regards the integration of Greek and Turkish forces to the NATO command structure, the NATO Headquarters Allied Land Forces Southeastern Europe (HALFSEE) was established in Izmir, Turkey, in September 1952, with the mission of exercising operational command of the field armies of Greece and Turkey in the event of war. The commander was a US lieutenant general. HALFSEE had no direct responsibility for sea and air operations. HALFSEE operated as a major subordinate command to Allied Forces Southern Europe (AFSOUTH) located in Naples, Italy. The Sixth Allied Tactical Air Force (SIXATAF), established in Izmir at the same time and commanded by a USAF major general, was charged with coordinating NATO air operations in Greece and Turkey. SIXATAF was not under the command of HALFSEE but operated directly under the command of Air Forces Southern Europe (AIRSOUTH) with headquarters in Naples; and AIRSOUTH was in turn directly under the command of AFSOUTH. Since the NATO Mediterranean naval command structure was independent from AFSOUTH and even more complex, no unity of

[7] John Iatrides, 'Failed Rampart: NATO's Balkan Front', in *NATO and the Warsaw Pact: Intrabloc Conflicts*, ed. Mary Ann Heiss and Victor Papacosma (Kent: The Kent State University Press, 2008), 63.

[8] Dionysios Chourchoulis, 'High Hopes, Bold Aims, Limited Results: Britain and the Establishment of the NATO Mediterranean Command, 1950–1953', *Diplomacy & Statecraft* 20, no. 3 (September 2009): 449.

command existed in the Southern Flank of the alliance. The problem was being exacerbated further, because there was no unity of command of the US military forces in the area. The relationship between HALFSEE and the US Military Missions in Greece and Turkey (JUSMAGG and JAMMAT – later JUSMMAT – respectively) was never entirely clear. An additional problem was that few Greek officers, and even fewer Turkish ones, were proficient enough in English to meet the increasing requirements of Greece and Turkey for staff officers serving in NATO headquarters, particularly at HALFSEE in Izmir. Therefore, at least during the 1950s, most of the workload was assigned to the American and British officers.[9]

It appears that the Greek and Turkish forces were never integrated properly in the overall NATO command structure and seemed to function more as national forces rather than as allied ones. Indeed, the NATO-assigned land and air forces of Greece and Turkey would be commanded by the regional land and air headquarters of the alliance in Izmir. However, local NATO commanders would have to command and control, but essentially not *coordinate* (although officially, the latter was supposed to be their main task) the Greek and Turkish forces: in case of war in the Balkans, a Soviet bloc offensive operation would cut these forces off, forcing them to fight different battles in separate sub-theatres; no contact between Greek and Turkish land forces would be maintained.

Soon after their admission to NATO in early 1952, Greece and Turkey held talks in an attempt to coordinate their defence plans and enhance their military position in the Balkans. Ideally, Athens and Ankara wished the conclusion of a tripartite Greek-Turkish-Yugoslav defence pact, which would also associate Yugoslavia with NATO's Southern Flank. Greece, Turkey and Yugoslavia had reasons to fear Bulgaria: due to its geographical position it could threaten all three countries; moreover, it was the most reliable Soviet ally and had the better equipped, and probably the better trained army in the region.[10] The Yugoslavs, for their part, were particularly interested in engaging in military talks provided that Turkey was prepared to place sufficient forces in Thrace; something that both Turkey and Greece were fully aware of, and in broad agreement.[11] In June 1952 the Turks argued that a NATO decision to defend Thrace would give Yugoslavia sufficient confidence to proceed with military cooperation with Greece and Turkey and would constitute a decisive deterrent against possible Soviet aggression. Once Turkey's western front had been secured, the Turks would be able to play their full part in Middle East defence.[12]

[9] Charles Fergusson, 'Problems of an International Military Headquarters', *Military Affairs* 23, no. 4 (Winter 1959–1960): 200–203.

[10] Evanthis Hatzivassiliou, *Greece and the Cold War: Frontline State, 1952–1967* (London: Routledge, 2006), 36; see for more, John Iatrides, *Balkan Triangle: birth and decline of an alliance across ideological boundaries* (The Hague: Mouton, 1968).

[11] *FRUS*, 1952–54, VIII, Ankara to State Department, 2 July 1952, 896; TNA/DEFE/5/40, COS(52)429, Defence of Thrace, August 11, 1952.

[12] TNA/DEFE/5/40, COS(52)429, Defence of Thrace, 11 August 1952.

However, NATO, American and British policy makers did not share the Greek-Turkish views on the defence of the Balkans. For instance, according to the British military,

> even with air parity, any attempt to hold Thrace would involve the major part of the Greek and Turkish armies. With the overwhelming superiority in armour that the Russians are likely to possess added to their probable superiority in the air we do not consider a successful defence of Thrace to be practicable. Any serious attempt by the Greeks and Turks to defend Thrace in the foreseeable future could only result in a military disaster. In addition, it is likely that any defence of the Middle East would be gravely jeopardized[sic].[13]

The US and British views on Balkan defence were finally reflected in the late 1952 report of NATO's Military Committee on the alliance's new strategic guidance, M. C.14/1(Final), and, in more detail, to a Standing Group study on Allied Command Europe's capabilities plan, two years later. In essence, northeastern Greece and the bulk of European Turkey would remain virtually undefended. Although the defence of Turkey was deemed necessary, much more attention was granted to the protection of eastern Turkey as part of the Middle East, and next, to that of the Straits area, than to Thrace. Obviously the main Turkish roles in the West's (not strictly NATO's) military planning were its considerable contribution to Middle Eastern, rather than Balkan, defence, and its use as a platform for the launch of strategic air offensives against the USSR and the Soviet bloc. Implicitly, the Balkan frontier constituted one of Supreme Allied Commander Europe's (SACUER) lowest priorities.[14]

NATO military authorities acknowledged that Greek Thrace and eastern Macedonia were virtually indefensible. They hoped that successful delaying action would permit completion of the mobilisation to halt a Soviet advance to the south of Greece. The security of coastal sea lines of communications (SLOCs) in the Aegean was extremely important; in wartime, 40% of the support for forces in northern Greece should use coastal sea lift, because of the limited road and rail capacity. However, the unsatisfactory air defence situation made this task extremely difficult. The most critical factor would be the close cooperation with Yugoslav forces. Should Soviet-Bulgarian forces (which were highly mechanised) advance in southern Yugoslavia, they could easily turn southwards via the Axios Valley outflanking the main Greek defence position along the Strymon River, then sweep across Greece and quickly destroy its ability to fight. Only if Yugoslavia combined its efforts with Greece had the latter a chance to resist for some time a combined Soviet-Bulgarian attack, which would possibly be comprised of 15 divisions and around 600 aircraft, thus being significantly preponderant over Greek (and other NATO) forces. Airfields and ports (including Piraeus and Salonika) would constitute potential targets for Soviet nuclear strikes, but it was estimated that the Soviets would probably prefer to seize them intact to sustain future operations in the Mediterranean theatre.[15]

---

[13] TNA/DEFE/5/41, COS(52)511, *Report on Defence of Thrace*, 18 September 1952.

[14] NATO/M.C.14/1 (Final), *Report on Strategic Guidance*, 9 December 1952.

[15] NATO/SGM-600-54, *Capabilities Plan ACE 1957*, 10 September 1954.

If it was implicitly acknowledged that mainland Greece was probably indefensible, NATO considered that a significant portion of Turkish territory could and should be defended and held. There were three focal points: the Straits, which constituted the only outlet to the Black Sea and a natural barrier; the central Anatolian Plateau; and the Iskenderun area in Southeastern Turkey. However, the main Turkish industrial and economic centres (Istanbul, Izmir and Bursa) as well as military facilities (bases around the Straits, the Izmir port and the Çiĝli air base complex) lay in northwestern and western Turkey. Therefore, this area should also be protected. The NATO planners did not regard the whole of the Turkish territory as defensible. The Soviets were expected to commit significant land, air, naval, amphibious and airborne forces to their campaigns against Turkey, and would probably strike on various fronts: Turkish Thrace and the Straits; the area east of the Bosporus; the northern Turkish coast; and northeastern Turkey. Soviet-Bulgarian forces might comprise a total of 31 to 33 divisions with 3300 tanks, and around 2500 aircraft (although it is not clear to what extent those figures reflected reality), while they would probably expend tactical nuclear weapons against Turkish forces, facilities and installations. At any rate, once again the cornerstone of NATO strategy was the extensive use of tactical nuclear weapons against Soviet bloc forces concentrating in Bulgaria and the Caucasus and advancing in Eastern Thrace and northeastern Turkey, and against Soviet beachheads established by amphibious or airborne forces on the northern coast; in addition, a major allied interdiction campaign against Bulgarian facilities and communication centres would be undertaken to disrupt Soviet bloc logistics.[16]

Nevertheless, it is highly doubtful whether the NATO strategy described above could have been implemented successfully and could have borne fruit, at least during the 1950s. The new NATO strategy (as described in M.C.48 document) did not provide yet for the actual equipping of allied forces with tactical nuclear weapons. Until the late 1950s Greek and Turkish forces had virtually no warheads or delivery means to implement the M.C.48 strategy. The only powerful nuclear element in the region was the Sixth Fleet and the relatively few US aircraft operating from US bases, which obviously would not be able to support land, air, naval and amphibious campaigns effectively in the three different sub-theatres of the Southern Flank. In addition, heavy reliance on nuclear weapons for the defence of the area in case of war would most likely lead to a nuclear holocaust: not only would the Soviets retaliate, but part of allied nuclear bombing would take place on Greek and Turkish soil. Therefore, as the military usefulness of the tactical nuclear weapons remained ambiguous their primary importance seemed to lie in their deterrent effect, rather than in their military utility.

Meanwhile, Greek-Turkish-Yugoslav negotiations to conclude a tripartite Balkan pact and parallel (though separate) US-UK-French efforts to affiliate Yugoslavia with the Western defence system, continued. But membership in NATO complicated the situation not only as regards the commitments that Athens and Ankara might be able

[16] Ibid.

to undertake towards Yugoslavia, but also concerning the guarantees that Washington, London and Paris were able, or willing, to provide. When in late 1952 the major NATO powers failed to integrate Yugoslavia into the Western defence scheme (after the failure of the 'Handy mission'), Tito opted for the conclusion of a regional pact with Greece and Turkey.[17]

In early 1953 tripartite military talks were initiated. The Yugoslav preference for the provision of some kind of automatic guarantee was rejected by both the Greeks and the Turks for fear that this would not be in conformity with their obligations to NATO. Nevertheless, the three countries reached an accommodation leading to the conclusion of the Greek-Turkish-Yugoslav Pact of Friendship and Collaboration, signed in Ankara on 28 February 1953. For the time being the Pact of Ankara was an entente, not an alliance. But even so, the Pact's conclusion, and the prospect of future military cooperation directly influenced the regional correlation of forces; particularly, since the Pact of Ankara was implicitly directed against the common regional enemy, Bulgaria.[18]

In June 1953 tripartite staff talks were resumed. Those lasted for several months. The defence of Thrace and Greek and Yugoslav Macedonia against attack by, or through, Bulgaria, was the focal point. A tripartite emergency plan was adopted as a basic document, providing general directives for the coordination of Yugoslav, Greek, and Turkish forces to defend Thrace and Macedonia.[19] For their part, the three Standing Group powers soon accepted that the conclusion of a Balkan military alliance could not be put off. Then, they sought to ensure that it would be accepted by Italy and the junior NATO allies and that the Balkan alliance would make 'a positive contribution to the political unity and military strength of the West' through practical cooperation with NATO.[20]

Finally, on 9 August 1954 the Treaty of Alliance, Political Co-operation and Mutual Assistance was signed in Bled, Yugoslavia. The Balkan alliance redressed the regional balance and led to the creation of a continuous and solid front in the Balkan Peninsula. Tripartite Balkan military cooperation could offer chances of effective defence of Greek and Turkish Thrace, mitigating to some extent the lack of a NATO forward defence in the region. Most importantly, the Soviets would have to undertake a major campaign and commit significant land and air forces if they wanted to advance to the western and southern Balkans in the event of local or general war. This was crucial in the context of the new NATO strategy; as the Soviet bloc would now have to concentrate significant forces on the Balkan front, valuable warning time would be offered to Greece and Turkey to mobilise their reserves, and to the United States to launch

[17] Iatrides, Balkan Triangle, 96–97; Beatrice Heuser, *Western 'Containment' Policies in the Cold War: the Yugoslav Case, 1948–53* (London and New York: Routledge, 1989), 170–171.

[18] Iatrides, Balkan Triangle, 103–104; David Stone, 'The Balkan Pact and American Policy', *East European Quarterly* 28, no. 3 (September 1994): 398–9.

[19] *FRUS* 1952–54, VIII, Athens to State Department, 28 November 1953, 634–5.

[20] TNA/FO/371/113222/WU1073/23G, FO to Ankara No.445, 12 July 1954; TNA/FO/371/113222/WU1073/14G, UK delegation to NATO to FO, 30 June 1954.

tactical nuclear weapons against enemy formations at a very early stage of the campaign, rather than deep in Greek and Turkish territory.

Nevertheless, the thorny issue of the cooperation and planning coordination between NATO (SHAPE, AFSOUTH or HALFSEE) and the Balkan alliance remained unsolved. Despite the conclusion of the Balkan alliance in August 1954, very little effective cooperation with NATO on military or other matters had taken place by late 1954. Western military interest lay chiefly in the defence of northern Yugoslavia to cover Italy (and not to the defence of Thrace and Greek Macedonia), and this aim could be best served by direct planning with Yugoslavia rather than by coordination of plans through the Balkan alliance. Things were further complicated due to the continuation of Italian-Yugoslav hostility over Trieste. Moreover, Greece, Turkey, and Yugoslavia managed to cooperate and form an alliance so long as the Soviet threat was acute and seemed imminent. As the international and regional environment changed after the summer of 1954, their rapprochement proved short-lived and ill-fated, in spite of the fact that, ironically, Italian-Yugoslav relations were restored in late 1954. Those flaws notwithstanding, the conclusion of the Balkan alliance was a major military asset for the West and its three signatories. Never before or after 1954, was the defence situation in the Balkans so favourable for the West.

Regional challenges and the evolution of NATO strategy in the Balkans, 1955–59

1955 was a watershed as regards the development of NATO military, and, particularly, political position in the Balkans. First of all, Yugoslavia soon began to downgrade the military aspects of the Balkan alliance and in mid-1955 the Soviet 'peace offensive' towards Belgrade eventually succeeded.[21] Equally significant were the outbreak of the Cyprus question and the rapid deterioration of Greek-Turkish relations after the violent disturbances in Istanbul and Izmir – against the Greek minority, and the Greek officers serving in HALFSEE, respectively.[22] That rupture soon slid into an open dispute between the Greeks, the Turks, and the British, as the Cyprus crisis was exacerbated further, and proved to be the key development during that period.

The Greek-Turkish rupture of the mid-1950s severely complicated the NATO position in the region: the traditional mutual distrust and enmity was revived and military cooperation between the Greeks and the Turks, either within the framework of the Balkan alliance or NATO, was suspended. From 1946–7 onwards, Greece and

[21] NATO/C-M(55)87, *Memorandum on Policy vis-á-vis the Soviets and the Education of NATO Public Opinion*, 14 October 1955; also, Iatrides, Balkan Triangle, 162–3; Svetozar Rajak, 'The Cold War in the Balkans, 1945–1956', in *The Cambridge History of the Cold War*. Vol. I, Origins, ed. Melvyn Leffler and Odd Arne Westad (Cambridge: Cambridge University Press, 2010), 216–217; Vladislav Zubok, *A Failed Empire. The Soviet Union in the Cold War from Stalin to Gorbachev* (Chapel Hill: The University of North Carolina Press, 2009), 99–100.

[22] Correspondent in Athens, 'Indignation in Greece. Turkish "Apathy" in Riots', *The Times*, 8 September 1955, 10; correspondents in Istanbul, Athens and Paris, 'Damage to Greco-Turkish Relations', *The Times*, 9 September 1955, 9.

Turkey were regarded as a strategic whole and this was the reason why both were admitted to NATO simultaneously. Greek-Turkish relations never returned to the cordial cooperation of the early 1950s. The threat of a Greek-Turkish conflict was looming on the horizon each time Greek-Turkish relations reached a crisis point over Cyprus. Indeed, Turkey threatened Greece (in 1956 and 1957) and this could hardly contribute to Greek-Turkish military cooperation within the framework of NATO. After 1955, NATO and the United States could not count on the existence of a solid front in the Eastern Mediterranean and the Balkans, but had to keep a delicate balance between Athens and Ankara. Without the shield of the Balkan alliance, Greece's defence problem was exacerbated.[23] During the same period Turkey adopted a new policy in the Middle East and played the leading role in the formation of the Baghdad Pact as a means to enhance the security of its eastern and southern frontier and increase its value as an ally to the West.[24] It could nevertheless not ignore that the situation had deteriorated at its Balkan frontier. The regional correlation of forces had been redressed in the Warsaw Pact's favour, and Turkey could easily be cut off from the West if Greece fell. Last but not least, the events of autumn 1955 marked the end of 'the golden era' of US-Greek relations. The seeds of anti-Americanism in Greece were sown exactly during this period.[25]

Meanwhile, in summer 1956 Greek-Turkish relations deteriorated significantly and the threat of war was aired.[26] The Greek government, now under Konstantinos Karamanlis, tried to bolster the country's position by starting to substitute the Balkan alliance with a bilateral Greek-Yugoslav cooperation.[27] As Tito responded positively, Greece sought to take advantage of its emerging 'special relationship' with Yugoslavia to counterbalance Turkey's weight (so clearly demonstrated in the affairs of the Middle East) and enhance its own position within NATO.[28] In the meantime, Greece and Yugoslavia continued to cooperate closely at the political-diplomatic and military levels during 1957–8, as both countries felt more or less isolated in a period of great international tension. The Greek-Yugoslav entente reached its peak in 1959.[29]

The second Greek response involved the strengthening of the military capabilities of the country. In 1957, the Greek leadership, in consultation with NATO and US

---

[23] Hatzivassiliou, *Greece and the Cold War,* 66–67.

[24] William Hale, *Turkish Foreign Policy, 1774–2000* (London: Frank Cass, 2000), 126, 128.

[25] Ioannis Stefanidis, *Stirring the Greek Nation: Political Culture, Irredentism and Anti-Americanism in Post War Greece, 1945–1967* (Aldershot: Ashgate, 2007), 191–6; James Edward Miller, *The United States and the Making of Modern Greece: History and Power, 1950–1974* (Chapel Hill: The University of North Carolina Press, 2009), 58.

[26] Konstantinos Svolopoulos (ed.), *Konstantinos Karamanlis: Archeio, Gegonota, kai Keimena* [hereafter: *Karamanlis*], Vol. 2 (Athens: Ekdotiki Athenon and Konstantinos Karamanlis Foundation, 1992–7), Memorandum on Karamanlis' conversation with US Ambassador Cannon on 12 July 1956, 128–9.

[27] *Karamanlis,* 2, Record of Karamanlis' statements on Tito's visit and Greek-Yugoslav negotiations on 27–29 July 1956, 134.

[28] NATO/C-R(56)70, Summary Record of North Atlantic Council meeting, 11 December 1956.

[29] Hatzivassiliou, *Greece and the Cold War,* 110–11, 113.

planners, undertook a military reform, reinforcing with additional equipment and personnel the Greek divisions covering northern Greece, and increasing their operational readiness. The actual defensive power of the army was almost doubled, while the air force and anti-aircraft defence was also strengthened. Significantly, for the first time the country also obtained the – minimal – means to counterattack, as the Greek Army was gradually able to form an armoured division (the XX). The reform took place partly due to reports that the operational readiness and combat capabilities of the Bulgarian armed forces had increased considerably, and that Bulgarian facilities and installations were designed to support additional, probably Soviet, forces, in case of conflict.[30] However, even this military reform did not give Greece the capabilities to repel a Soviet bloc attack.

Despite the deterioration of Greek-Turkish relations and the relative relaxation of Cold War tension, both Athens and Ankara continued to place great emphasis on NATO's military preparedness and on intra-allied cooperation in the political and economic fields. The problem was that they interpreted 'intra-allied cooperation' in strange ways: both meant that they were ready to cooperate with the United States, but not necessarily with one another. On the military level, NATO was still unable to raise sufficient conventional ground forces to enhance the credibility of deterrence against a Soviet invasion in Western Europe or the Southern Flank. On the other hand, the alliance could not rely exclusively on nuclear weapons. The military theorist Sir Basil Liddell Hart remarked that those made 'sense as a deterrent, but not as a defence – for put into use it means suicide'.[31] Therefore, a revised NATO strategic concept was agreed in April/May 1957 (the M.C.14/2), which recognised the possibility of Soviet aggression with limited objectives that should be dealt with without recourse to nuclear weapons, if possible.[32] Concurrently, Greece and Turkey undertook military reforms to improve the quality of existent forces and enhance their combat readiness, but it was obvious that their security problems were too complex to be addressed by military means alone. By that time it was becoming apparent that the flow of US hardware and funds was not sufficient to enable the Greeks and the Turks to modernise their obsolete equipment and at the same time expand their forces to reach the NATO-approved force levels. In the absence of a sound economic and industrial basis, both countries lacked the necessary resources to sustain effectively their defence establishments.

In early 1958 the alliance modified its strategy, adopting the M.C.70 document. In essence the new strategy provided for the nuclearisation of NATO assigned ground and air forces (that is, NATO 'Shield' forces, not merely the retaliatory – 'Sword' – ones) which would be equipped with tactical nuclear weapons.[33] Therefore, it threatened to erode

[30] NARA/RG59/781.5/1-3157, box 3726, Athens to State Department, 31 January 1957.

[31] Basil Liddell Hart, 'European Defence', *The Times*, 26 March 1957, 11.

[32] John Duffield, *Power Rules: The Evolution of NATO's Conventional Force Posture* (Stanford: Stanford University Press, 1995), 126–8.

[33] NATO/M.C.70, *A Report on the Minimum Essential Force Requirements*, 29 January 1958.

further NATO's conventional capabilities.[34] Moreover, this strategy, placing emphasis on modernisation of equipment and a higher state of readiness, entailed a considerable increase of defence expenditure, without commensurate increase of US economic and military aid. Greece initially declared its intention to maintain and build up additional forces in an effort to implement a forward defence, and, until 1959, to retain a relative balance with the Turkish forces.[35] NATO experts believed that such additional goals would probably exceed Greek capabilities, since the provision of additional US aid was unlikely. By the late 1950s, the Greek defence effort was supported, in approximately equal measure, by national resources and by external aid. National funds were allocated mainly to maintenance and operating expenditures, without being able to cover them fully; the rest was covered by Mutual Aid, which also financed almost the whole of the new material and equipment needed for the Greek rearmament.[36]

The situation in Turkey was worse. The Turkish effort to meet and even exceed NATO-approved force levels outstripped the ability of the national economy to support it. In 1958 the economic situation deteriorated rapidly and got out of control. Faced with bankruptcy, Ankara had no option but to agree in late July on a bail-out and a stabilisation programme imposed by an international consortium.[37] Then, as the Turkish Armed Forces relied exclusively on foreign aid for equipment, Ankara sought to achieve a considerable increase in external (that is, mainly US) assistance. By late 1959 the alliance assessed that 'if the NATO military requirements for modernisation and stock levels are to be met on time... additional aid must be made available on an unprecedented level'.[38] But such an increase in economic and military assistance was not forthcoming. Therefore, the new strategy as described in M.C.70 could not address the endemic problem of NATO members' (particularly the underdeveloped ones) inability to allocate the necessary resources to meet the approved force-goals.

Meanwhile, the successful launch of *Sputnik* in early October 1957 shocked the West as it appeared to undermine the validity of US nuclear deterrence. The Eisenhower administration responded by offering, during the NATO summit in Paris in December 1957, the deployment of US *Jupiter* or *Thor* Intermediate Range Ballistic Missiles (IRBMs) on allied territory. As regards the Balkan frontier, Greece eventually did not accept the IRBMs, as the whole issue was linked with other matters, such as the extent of US influence in Greece and NATO's attitude towards the Cyprus problem.[39] On the

[34] Duffield, *Power Rules*, 144.

[35] Hatzivassiliou, *Greece and the Cold War*, 76.

[36] NATO/C-M(59)94, Part II, *Report on the 1959 Annual Review – Greece*, 3 December 1959; NATO/C-M (58)141, Part II, *Report on the 1958 Annual Review – Turkey*, 6 December 1958.

[37] NATO/C-M(58)141, Part II, *Report on the 1958 Annual Review – Turkey*, 6 December 1958; also Erik Zürcher, *Turkey. A Modern History* (London & New York: I. B. Tauris, 2004 – New Edition), 229.

[38] NATO/C-M(59)94, Part II, *Report on the 1959 Annual Review – Turkey*, 3 December 1959.

[39] Theodore Couloumbis, *Greek Political Reaction to American and NATO Influences* (New Haven & London: Yale University Press, 1966), 111; Philip Nash, 'Jumping Jupiters: the US Search for IRBM Host Countries in NATO, 1957–59', *Diplomacy & Statecraft* 6, no. 3 (November 1995): 769, 773.

contrary, the Turkish ruling elite, in the absence of any local socialist or communist party, was enthusiastic for the deployment of IRBMs in Turkey. This would increase Turkey's leverage within NATO, secure the continuation of US economic and military aid, and provide the country with an effective deterrent to the Soviet threat. In autumn 1959 the United States and Turkey concluded the final agreement for the deployment of a squadron of 15 *Jupiter* missiles in the Çiĝli air base, near Izmir. The missiles would become operational in 1962.[40]

At the political level, the situation had become critical during 1958 because extensive violence flared throughout Cyprus, while Greece once more decided to withdraw from HALFSEE. The Secretary General, Paul-Henri Spaak, tried to mediate, but his initiative collapsed in late October 1958.[41] But then, in early 1959, when everyone feared the worst (for instance, a possible Greek drift out of NATO with unforeseeable repercussions), Greece and Turkey managed all of a sudden to reach a compromise solution; then, Britain also had to follow suit. Indeed, by mid-1958 the Menderes government had been weakened significantly by economic failure and declining domestic support. After the coup of July 1958 in Iraq, Turkey was becoming increasingly worried about its regional isolation and feared it would be cut off geographically from NATO and the West, if Greece left the alliance. Turkish fears were further exacerbated due to rising Cold War tension over Berlin in late November 1958. Therefore, in late 1958–early 1959 the Turkish leadership proved ready to accept a compromise solution over Cyprus.[42] In some sense, NATO ultimately served indirectly as a stabilising factor in the area.

1960–67: Towards the adoption of the 'flexible response'

The USSR and the Soviet bloc countries increased significantly their conventional military capabilities (not to mention the Soviet nuclear forces) in the 1960s. The Soviet armed forces began to operate a new generation of fighters and strike aircraft, improved their electronic equipment, expanded considerably their parachute and airborne units, formed a formidable fleet and, after the mid-1960s, deployed a strong Soviet naval squadron in the Mediterranean (which included a considerable submarine component). These developments, in conjunction with the still inadequate firepower, armour, mobility, air defences and early-warning systems of Greece and Turkey, meant that the threat facing the Balkan frontier grew during the 1960s. Even if a final conclusion for the validity of the above argument cannot be reached in the

[40] Nur Bilge Criss, 'Strategic Nuclear Missiles in Turkey: The Jupiter Affair, 1959–1963', *The Journal of Strategic Studies* 20, no. 4 (September 1997): 98–103; Nash, 'Jumping Jupiters', 774–6.

[41] Robert Holland, 'NATO and the Struggle for Cyprus', *Journal of Modern Greek Studies* 13, no. 1 (May 1995): 33–61.

[42] Hale, *Turkish Foreign Policy*, 127; Robert Holland, *Britain and the Revolt in Cyprus, 1954–1959* (Oxford: Oxford University Press, 1998), 293; Evanthis Hatzivassiliou, *Britain and the International Status of Cyprus, 1955–59* (Minneapolis: Minnesota Mediterranean and East European Monographs, 1997), 152.

absence of adequate Warsaw Pact sources, surely that was the threat perception in Greece, Turkey, and their NATO allies.

In the West, a debate started in the United States and NATO over the proper role of conventional forces and over a possible revision of US and NATO military strategy. The 'Flexible Response' military strategy represented a shift away from overreliance on nuclear weapons. Nevertheless, NATO was slow to formulate the new strategic concept, and formally adopted 'Flexible Response' in December 1967, when the North Atlantic Council approved M.C.14/3.[43] The new strategy had significant implications for the Balkan frontier: it placed greater emphasis on the need to increase conventional capabilities to respond to limited forms of conflict, but Greece and Turkey appeared incapable of raising and sustaining such forces at an adequate level.

In late 1960 the Greek military authorities sought to stress the need for an adjustment of NATO strategy on the Balkan frontier. They argued that the NATO strategic concept relied disproportionately on nuclear forces; the conventional forces were given an extremely passive role for the maintenance of allied territorial integrity. The Greek political and military leadership once again tried to downplay the role of nuclear weapons (strategic and tactical) and elevate the need for conventional defence. A corollary to that vision was the emphasis on the strategic importance of the Balkans as a platform for NATO to threaten the Soviet thrust in Central and Western Europe. The Greeks could hardly conceal their anxiety about the conventional superiority of the Warsaw Pact in the Balkans (that is, mainly of Bulgaria). Not only did they believe that a more balanced (conventional-nuclear) counteroffensive capability of CINCSOUTH would add significantly to NATO's deterrent capability in the region; they also claimed that the Southern Flank, and the Balkan frontier in particular, should be utilised 'as a base of departure for counter-offensive operations against their [Soviet bloc] soft underbelly'.[44] The Greeks stressed that, according to NATO assessments, in case of war approximately 25 enemy divisions would operate in the southern Balkans against eighteen Greek and Turkish divisions progressively built within three weeks. The Greek military authorities argued that the Soviet bloc would probably not be able to undertake two major operations against both Greece and Turkey (and presumably Yugoslavia). Therefore, Bulgarian, Soviet and any other Warsaw Pact forces would strike against one of them, while containing the other. But, 'under suitable conditions' and provided that Greek-Turkish forces would be 'improved for offensive action', the country not suffering the main effort could meet the situation actively, transferring the fight to Bulgarian soil within ten days. Thus the narrow Balkan bridgehead would be widened to cover firmly the critical

---

[43] Duffield, *Power Rules*, 151; Andreas Wenger, 'The politics of military planning. Evolution of NATO's strategy', in *War Plans and Alliances in the Cold War: Threat perceptions in the East and West*, ed. Vojtech Mastny, Sven Holtsmark and Andreas Wenger (London and New York: Routledge, 2006), 176–83.

[44] NATO/MCM-196-60, *General Frontistis' Memorandum on the Defense of the Balkans in accordance with the Forward Strategy Principles*, 27 December 1960.

area of the Straits, link effectively the Greek and Turkish defences and encourage Yugoslavia.[45]

Naturally, SHAPE flatly rejected any idea for an adoption of a strategy in the Balkans relying on major operations deep into Bulgarian territory; such an offensive forward strategy was neither politically acceptable – due to the defensive nature of NATO – nor militarily feasible under existing forces and the anticipated level of external assistance.[46] However, any further build-up was out of the question, particularly since Turkey (and, to a lesser degree, Greece) was facing serious financial difficulties and the US Congress was pressing the Kennedy Administration for the termination of US military aid. During the early 1960s, CINCSOUTH Admiral Charles Brown, and his successor, Admiral James Russel, urged the SACEUR, General Lauris Norstad, to convince the US leadership not to cut, or reduce, the American economic and military aid to Greece and Turkey. Both officers argued that any cuts would seriously impede the attainment of satisfactory operational standards of the Greek and Turkish armed forces, greatly undermining the defence posture of the Southern Flank.[47] For instance, the Greek and Turkish armies experienced great shortfalls even in ammunition (including bullets for the M-1 rifle) and spare parts: there were less than ten days of supply for all types of ammunition on hand (instead of a minimum of thirty days supply).[48]

Another factor was the constant Greek and Turkish fears that NATO would 'abandon' them in the event of a Bulgarian *local* attack.[49] To allay those worries, NATO military planners considered the possibility of adopting a forward defensive strategy along the Bulgarian borders. They admitted that under certain conditions that might be feasible, but Norstad himself pointed out that this problem 'was not one of concept, but one of money, manpower and material.' Several military measures should be taken for a successful implementation of a real forward defence, including the timely provision of allied amphibious and/or airborne forces, with air and logistical support, to reinforce local NATO forces in case of war. These were not forthcoming, though. NATO planners emphasised that Greece and Turkey could further enhance their military capabilities on the Balkan frontier, only so long as they continued to receive adequate military aid from the United States.[50]

---

[45] Ibid.

[46] NATO/MCM-164-61, *Memorandum for the Military Committee on Status Report on the Defense of the Balkan Area*, 6 December 1961.

[47] Dwight D. Eisenhower Library [hereafter: DDEL], Norstad Papers/Subject Files/box 95, Admiral Brown to General Norstad, 3 February 1961, and 12 December 1961; Admiral Russel to General Norstad, 4 February 1962; General Norstad to Admiral Russel, 5 February 1962.

[48] DDEL/Norstad Papers/Subject Files/box 95, Admiral Brown to General Norstad, 18 May 1961.

[49] Hatzivassiliou, *Greece and the Cold War*, 74, 77; Hale, *Turkish Foreign Policy*, 146.

[50] NATO/MCM-164-61, *Memorandum for the Military Committee on Status Report on the Defense of the Balkan Area*, 6 December 1961.

Therefore, throughout the 1960s the Greek political and military leadership remained anxious to enhance the army's armour, firepower and mobility to counterbalance Bulgarian superiority, which could prove *the* decisive factor in a sudden, short local conflict. Greek leaders (including Prime Ministers Karamanlis and Georgios Papandreou) sought to convince NATO and US military authorities that the implementation of forward defence strategy in Western Thrace was necessary. They tried, unsuccessfully, to achieve additional aid to strengthen the Greek army, or to secure an immediate intervention of allied forces in the area.[51] However, after 1962 US defence support aid to Greece (though not to Turkey) was terminated. American and NATO officials considered that Greece was economically successful and that it could sustain its defence effort by the provision of long-term loans, rather than economic aid. Although US aid in hardware continued, this could not enable Greece to attain NATO-approved force goals and qualitative standards.[52] In subsequent years, the Americans and NATO contemplated other measures to channel economic aid to Greece, but ultimately no substitute for US aid was found. On the contrary, US defence support aid to Turkey continued; the latter was struggling to overcome the economic crisis of the late 1950s, and the West had to keep it militarily strong.[53] Furthermore, Turkey, with an army of approximately 400,000 men, provided 'one of every five Nato soldiers in Europe'.[54] It also possessed the human resources to raise additional ground forces in the future.

During the early 1960s Turkey had similar anxieties to Greece. The most important issue, according to the Turkish policy-makers (civilian and military), was their concern over the 'new US strategic concept', as they put it, which appeared to differentiate between 'general war' and 'local actions'. The Turks expressed their worries to General Norstad and the US leadership about allied (basically US) response to a swift Soviet local action (either in Eastern Thrace or northeastern Turkey) which would present the West with a fait accompli. Furthermore, the Turkish leadership worried that Soviet bloc aggression against Turkey or Greece would be met by NATO only with conventional forces; but, a conventional response would not suffice to repel an attack, particularly in Thrace, where Turkish forces suffered from many deficiencies. In several instances General Norstad, and Secretary of State, Dean Rusk reassured the Turks that the United States and NATO would come to Turkey's support, as the 'NATO treaty does not differentiate between types of attack'. NATO and US commitment to defend any member was clear, so allied military assistance 'would be in[the] form of

[51] *Karamanlis*, 5A, Record of conversation between Karamanlis, Foreign Minister Averoff-Tossitza, and Lt. General Frontistis, with US Deputy Secretary of Defense, Gilpatric, Assistant Secretary of Defense for International Affairs, Nitze, and Chief of Staff of the Army, General Dekker, on 18 April 1961, 45; *Karamanlis*, 5B, Records of conversations between the Greek leadership and SACEUR Lemnitzer and Chairman of the JCS, General Taylor during their visit in Athens on 24 and 29 April, 1963, 617–20.

[52] Hatzivassiliou, *Greece and the Cold War*, 90–93.

[53] Correspondent in Ankara, 'Turkey Expects Massive Aid From West', *The Times* 16 March 1962, 9.

[54] Defence Correspondent, 'One of the Keys to World Power', *The Times*, 19 February 1962, 11.

conventional and/or atomic forces and would be appropriate to circumstances'; therefore, an attack on Turkey would lead to total war.[55]

The Turkish leadership also sought to receive as much military and economic aid as possible from the United States and the West in general. During the early 1960s Turkey tried to recover from the economic collapse of the late 1950s – and the subsequent political crisis – by undertaking political reforms and instituting austerity measures.[56] Meanwhile, the Turkish Armed Forces pressed for the adoption and implementation of a new military programme which would greatly enhance their conventional as well as tactical nuclear capabilities (for instance, the Turks asked for an early dispatch of as many *F-104G* aircraft as possible). As a result, in 1961–2 Ankara pleaded with NATO and US officials to increase the level of military aid, although the Turkish Military Assistance Programme (MAP) was the largest grant aid programme in NATO. The Turkish leaders argued that if aid remained at its current level, it would be 'impossible to carry out the tasks assigned to Turkey by SACEUR'. In April 1962 Inönü told General Norstad that the Turkish Army required increased mobility; the Navy modernisation; while the Air Force needed 'everything'. The US and NATO officials expressed their sympathy to Turkey, but in essence made clear that an increase in military and financial aid was unrealistic.[57] Furthermore, in April 1963, only a few months after the deployment of the *Jupiter* missiles in Turkey, the Americans withdrew the IRBMs from the country; they had already become obsolete and they would be replaced by *Polaris* submarines. US officials had considered removing the *Jupiters* before the eruption of the Cuban missile crisis in October 1962, but eventually these were removed only after the secret Kennedy–Khrushchev agreement that the missiles would be mutually withdrawn from Cuba and Turkey. As Turkish archival material is not available, it is difficult to assess to what extent the *Jupiter* affair undermine US and NATO credibility, since at that time the US officials denied any linkage between the Cuban missile crisis and the subsequent withdrawal of the *Jupiters*.[58]

In the mid-1960s, NATO began to put increasing emphasis on improving its capabilities on the flanks. The Balkans were among the critical areas under examination. NATO planners admitted that Shield forces by themselves could not effectively implement the forward defence concept either in the Southern or the Northern Flank.[59] The provision of adequate local forces constituted the best method

[55] *FRUS*, 1961–63, XVI, Paris to State Department, 14 May 1961, 699–701; Paris to State Department, 3 April 1962, 724–6; Dean Rusk to State Department, 15 December 1963, 765–7.

[56] Zürcher, *Turkey*, 244–7, 264–6.

[57] *FRUS*, 1961–63, XVI, Paris to State Department, 14 May 1961, 699–701; conversations between Chairman of the JCS, General Lemnitzer, and Turkish Chief of the General Staff, General Sunay, 14 November 1961, 714–7; conversation on Aid for Turkey, NATO Ministerial Meeting, 15 December 1961, 717–9; Paris to State Department, 3 April 1962, 724–6.

[58] Hale, *Turkish Foreign Policy*, 133–6; Philip Nash, *The Other Missiles of October: Eisenhower, Kennedy, and the Jupiters, 1957–1963* (Chapel Hill:, The University of North Carolina Press, 1997), 117–57.

[59] NATO/MCM-73-66, *Memorandum on the Possible Methods for Improving NATO Capabilities on the Flanks*, 14 July 1966.

of improving the defensive capability on the flanks (including the Balkan frontier), but it was obvious that military self-sufficiency was impossible. The essence of a sound defence strategy, serving to deter the enemy from aggression, was to defend the flanks 'by a combination of resolute local forces and rapidly intervening NATO and external forces, the latter including strategic nuclear forces'. The reinforcement of the Balkan frontier by the permanent reallocation of SACEUR forces did not appear a realistic option, because in general war the defence of Western Europe would be the top priority.[60]

As previously – and despite several operational limitations already mentioned – the US Sixth Fleet constituted the most powerful and flexible element for the defence of the Southern Flank. However, after the mid-1960s the growing strength of the Soviet fleet in the Black Sea and the Mediterranean (the *Fifth Eskadra*) complicated NATO planning in the whole area. Until then, NATO naval forces and the US Sixth Fleet could operate virtually unhindered across the Mediterranean and support, almost from the beginning, the land and air campaigns in the Balkans. From the mid-1960s onwards, the first task of allied naval forces in the Mediterranean in case of crisis or conflict would be the elimination, or at least the neutralisation, of the Soviet naval presence in the area.[61] Therefore, valuable time would be lost until allied naval forces and maritime aviation would be able to support Greek and Turkish land forces defending the Balkan frontier.

Support by mobile reserve forces appeared more probable; both national and Allied Command Europe (ACE) Mobile Force units.[62] At any rate, NATO planners assessed that a timely response and deployment of those forces to deal with a crisis was a prerequisite of effective deterrence, and would improve the prospects for successful defence.[63] In fact, with regard to a possible local incident in Greek Thrace, they argued that the timing of arrival of reinforcements from other NATO countries might be a more important factor than their actual numerical strength; such reaction would demonstrate clearly NATO's determination to defend allied territory against local aggression. For instance, the Sixth Fleet's US Marine Battalion Landing Team was able to deploy in Thrace in a very short period.[64] Other measures included the modernisation of local forces and the improvement of local infrastructure, particularly in Greek Macedonia and Thrace and in Turkish Thrace and the Straits.

[60] Ibid.

[61] NATO/MCM-37-68, *Memorandum for the Secretary General on the Appreciation of the Strategic Situation in the Southern region of ACE*, 30 May 1968.

[62] In 1966, from the ACE Mobile Force (AMF) two US divisions (one armoured) and four fighter squadrons were earmarked for deployment in the Southern Flank. However, at that time only one US airborne division and one US Marines Battalion from the Sixth Fleet were capable of timely deployment in the Balkans.

[63] NATO/MCM-73-66, *Memorandum on the Possible Methods for Improving NATO Capabilities on the Flanks*, 14 July 1966; TNA/DEFE/5/165, COS 25/66, *Contingency Planning – Hellenic Thrace*, 1 March 1966.

[64] NATO/MCM-67-66, *Memorandum on Contingency Study for Hellenic Thrace*, 3 June 1966.

Modernisation included timely replacement of obsolete or obsolescent equipment, conversion of infantry units to armoured or mechanised ones, and improvement of their general readiness. Similarly, improvement of military infrastructure and other facilities (such as signal communications and warning systems, as well as roads, ports and fortifications) would add considerably to national and NATO ability to support and reinforce local forces in case of crisis or conflict. However, NATO planners recognised that this situation stemmed from 'adverse economic factors', while no vehicle by which to extend economic assistance to Greece and Turkey was visible in the near future.[65]

The assumptions of another contingency study for Greek Thrace and eastern Macedonia took into account the Greek views, which, contrary to those of NATO, assumed that Bulgarian forces would act independently of Warsaw Pact support. That scenario envisaged a situation where, after two months of Bulgarian propaganda and psychological warfare activity, the Bulgarians announced that they would hold extensive manoeuvres in areas adjacent to Greek borders. Those manoeuvres could be a cover plan for mounting a conventional attack against northern Greece with all Bulgarian armed forces except those required for covering the Turkish and Yugoslav borders. The aim of the attack would be to descend to the Aegean Sea and capture the ports of Kavala and Alexandroupolis.[66]

NATO experts considered the various options available at that time. Their primary goals were to deter the enemy by clearly indicating NATO's firm intention and ability to defend its territory, but also to reduce the chances of war by misunderstanding, by keeping the tension as low as possible. The NATO military authorities acknowledged that, since Greek forces alone would not be able to deter a Bulgarian attack, additional forces consisting of the AMF (Land) would be required. In essence, though, they concluded once again that emphasis should be placed on nuclear weapons. It is also noteworthy that the study did not give due consideration to the potential Turkish contribution to the deterrence of a local Bulgarian attack on Greece. Turkey, though invited, did not participate in the Expert Group nor did it state its intentions regarding the contingency under study.[67] In fact, during 1966–68 the Turkish authorities clearly stated that they were unwilling to approve the views of NATO on Turkey's prospective force levels, particularly the naval and the air defence ones. Ankara also stressed the strategic importance of the Straits and the need to defend them effectively should war occur.[68] While in mid-1968 the Turks declared that the Straits constituted for Turkey 'the heart core of her survival', and that 'the Turkish Nation has to be ready to defend it with every sacrifice'.[69]

[65] NATO/MCM-73-66, *Memorandum on the Possible Methods for Improving NATO Capabilities on the Flanks*, 14 July 1966.

[66] TNA/DEFE/5/165, COS 25/66, *Contingency Planning – Hellenic Thrace*, 1 March 1966.

[67] Ibid.

[68] NATO/MCM-34-66 (Revised), *Memorandum on Turkish BRAVO Force Proposals*, 13 June 1966.

[69] NATO/MCM-57-68, *Memorandum on Plans for external Reinforcements for the Southern Region*, 2 August 1968.

Meanwhile, the significant deterioration of Greek-Turkish relations after the outbreak of the new Cyprus crisis in 1964 not only undermined bilateral coordination of planning along the common frontier in Thrace, but forced Athens to move modest forces to western Thrace to cover the region against possible Turkish attack. Therefore, Greek land forces, already overstretched and inadequate to repel a Bulgarian attack, were further dispersed to implement a forward defence against Turkey.[70] The Cyprus crisis of 1964, as well as that of 1967, brought Greece and Turkey to the brink of war, and had serious repercussions for the stability and defence posture of the Southeastern Flank. Both Greece and Turkey expressed their disillusionment, disappointment and regret at the US and NATO's role in the Cyprus crisis and the Greek-Turkish dispute. The Turks in particular resented President Lyndon Johnson's blunt interference in June 1964 against a Turkish military intervention in Cyprus. The Greeks eventually rejected the Acheson Plans of August 1964, while in late November 1967 the Greek junta was persuaded by Johnson's envoy, Cyrus Vance (as well as by NATO's Secretary General, Manlio Brosio), to yield to certain Turkish demands in order to avoid a clash over Cyprus.[71]

In any case, by 1967–68, years that constituted a turning point for NATO and the Southeastern Flank in particular, the alliance had not devised any effective strategy for the actual defence of the Balkan frontier (as well as the other flank areas), should nuclear deterrence fail. NATO military authorities admitted in April 1968 that 'the provision of external reinforcements for the flanks is a complex and difficult problem, which requires forces of appropriate size, composition and availability tailored to a wide range of contingency situations. Transportation, local infrastructure, logistic support, communications and the principle of cost sharing, must all be integrated into the solution'.[72] In fact, they never were. Hence the SACEUR, General Lyman Lemnitzer, assessed that in case of major aggression, Soviet bloc forces would advance deep into Eastern Thrace and reach the Straits within five or six days, unless tactical nuclear weapons were fully employed. He also pointed out that the weakness of the Greek defence positions and forces in Western Thrace would permit the enemy to outflank the Turkish ones.[73]

[70] Hatzivassiliou, *Greece and the Cold War*, 147.

[71] NATO/PO/64/688, Secretary General's 'Watching Brief' – Greek-Turkish Relations, 11 December 1964, and NATO/PO/67/873, Greek-Turkish Relations – Secretary General's Watching Brief, 8 December 1967. For Turkey, see for more Suha Bolukbasi, 'The Johnson Letter Revisited', *Middle Eastern Studies* 29, no. 3 (July 1993): 505–25, and Cihat Göktepe, 'The Cyprus Crisis of 1967 and its Effects on Turkey's Foreign Relations', *Middle Eastern Studies* 41, no. 3 (May 2005): 431–44. For Greece, see Sotiris Rizas, Enosi, Dichotomisi, Anexartisia: Oi Enomenes Politeies kai i Vretania stin Anazitisi Lysis gia to Kypriako, 1963–1967 [Union, Partition, Independence: the United States and Britain in search of a solution for the Cyprus question, 1963–1967] (Athens: Vivliorama, 2000), 158–60, 227–31.

[72] NATO/MCM-23-68, *Memorandum on A Concept for External Reinforcement of the Flanks*, 16 April 1968.

[73] NATO/MCM-37-68, *Memorandum for the Secretary General on the Appreciation of the Strategic Situation in the Southern region of ACE*, 30 May 1968.

Soviet bloc perceptions, intentions and capabilities are beyond the scope of this article, and Soviet bloc sources on military planning in the southern Balkans are very scarce. At this point it is nevertheless worth noting that, in the wake of the June 1967 Six Day War, a report of the Bulgarian Ministry of Defence assessed that the Bulgarian armed forces would be entirely unprepared to counter an 'Israeli-style' surprise attack from either Greece or Turkey. The most alarming flaws were the ineffective intelligence, the inadequate combat and mobilisation readiness of the army, and the weak anti-air defence. What is most surprising, though, is the report's conclusion that defence of the Greek-Bulgarian line constituted Bulgaria's Achilles' heel.[74] Taking into consideration the regional balance of forces, and particularly geography, this last conclusion was an exaggeration. While, obviously, neither the Greek nor the Turkish armed forces were able to perform as the Israeli ones.

Conclusion

This article argues that during the 1950s and 1960s NATO failed to implement a sound military strategy but nonetheless played a significant stabilising role in the region. This was probably because NATO nuclear deterrence worked, and thus its flawed military strategy was never put to the test, as Moscow would not be prepared to risk a world war for the sake of the Balkans; yet, if war came through a crisis (for example in Berlin), it was equally certain that the Balkans would become a field of hostilities. NATO planners acknowledged that mainland Greece could not be held, and Turkey could only partially be defended. This concept stemmed from NATO conventional inferiority, particularly in the Balkans, as well as from unfavourable geography and the primacy of Central Europe in Western defence planning. Furthermore, Greece and Turkey, the poorest members of NATO, were in no position to meet the high qualitative standards that NATO strategy required. Moreover, evidently both Athens and Ankara knew where real power lay and sought to rely primarily on the United States, rather than NATO, to safeguard their political independence and territorial integrity. Last but not least, NATO and US nuclear deterrence was not enhanced in the Southern Flank until after 1959 when tactical nuclear weapons were integrated in the Greek and the Turkish armed forces. This meant that militarily the Southern Flank remained the weakest spot of the Atlantic Alliance, and the situation did not change significantly during the 1960s.

On the contrary, NATO's success was remarkable at the level of grand strategy. The extension of the Atlantic Alliance to include Greece and Turkey filled a power vacuum and denied crucial regions and waterways to the Soviets: Cold War deterrence meant that, despite the apparent defence problems, the Soviet road to the Mediterranean was blocked, except in the case of total war. Full integration with the Western defence system tied Greece and Turkey with the West. This was a major accomplishment, if

[74] Vojtech Mastny and Malcolm Byrne eds., *A Cardboard Castle? An Inside History of the Warsaw Pact, 1955–1991* (Budapest: Central European University Press, 2005), 245–48.

compared with the course undertaken by many neighbouring countries, particularly on the eastern shores of the Mediterranean and in the Middle East. Last but not least, NATO membership and western deterrence arguably also played a stabilising role in the relations between Greece, Turkey and Bulgaria: in a Cold War context it was unthinkable for these states to initiate bilateral conflicts which had proved so common in the past. Greece and Turkey were members of a viable alliance, i.e., NATO, and Bulgaria a member of another one, the Warsaw Pact; not just three independent nations which might be involved in a military crisis over Thrace (or regarding Greece and Bulgaria, Macedonia). Any local situation could not be considered in isolation from the wider political, diplomatic and military framework. Similarly, if Greece and Turkey occasionally seemed to teeter on the brink of war over Cyprus after 1955, they could nevertheless hardly consider seriously expanding a possible bilateral conflagration in the island to their common land borders in Thrace.

Out-of-area: NATO perceptions of the Third World, 1957–1967

Evanthis Hatzivassiliou

This article discusses the reports of the NATO study groups on the situation in the Third World, from the aftermath of the Suez crisis until the 1967 reorganization of the alliance through the Harmel Report. These were the infamous 'out-of-area' issues which caused significant disagreements within the alliance. NATO analysis was dominated by the primacy of the Cold War: its major subject was 'Soviet penetration' of the periphery, rather than the problems of the global South as such. Arguably, this Cold War perspective prevented the NATO analysts from fully evaluating the dangers of the situation in the Third World.

Introduction: discussing perspectives

As one of the two major Cold War alliances, NATO, at least in principle, did not have to deal with the problems of the extra-European world: its responsibilities lay in the strictly defined 'NATO area', which had to be defended against a Soviet attack. Yet, by the mid-1950s the Western alliance came to realise that in the context of a long Cold War, it should carefully monitor the periphery, if only because the Soviets seemed to become particularly active there. Moreover, as the 1956 Suez crisis demonstrated, trouble in other parts of the globe could spark *intra*-NATO problems.

This article will discuss the findings of the NATO working groups on the Third World. The analysis will begin in 1957, when NATO civilian machinery was reformed, and new groups of experts were set up, such as the Committee of Political Advisers and the Committee of Economic Advisers; in 1959, a separate Committee on Africa, and in 1961 an *ad hoc* expert group on Latin America were created, while the advent of the Atlantic Policy Advisory Group (APAG) in 1962 added another body which studied the global Cold War. The article will focus on the main conclusions, rather than on the detailed parts of the reports dealing with individual countries. The analysis will end in 1967–8, when the Harmel Report led to a further restructuring of NATO administrative machinery, and to a new phase of intra-alliance political consultation. Thus, this is an article on NATO *perceptions* about the 'global Cold War', not an account of developments in the Third World as such.

These reports formed part of intra-alliance consultation, the strengthening of which was strongly encouraged by the Report of the Three in late 1956.[1] After 1957, the new Secretary-General, Paul-Henri Spaak, regarded political cooperation as 'the essential condition for the survival and progress of the Alliance'. He suggested that the distinction between 'questions arising within the Treaty area and questions arising elsewhere is largely artificial: it is the common interest and not geography which justifies consultation'. But Spaak went even further: he noted that in consultations about out-of-area problems, it would not be necessary to arrive 'in all circumstances [to] a specific expression of unanimity'; reservations would be acceptable.[2] This caused the discomfort of many alliance members, who regarded unanimity as an essential precondition for NATO's survival.[3] Evidently, the alliance's consultation deficit was among the reasons which led Spaak to resign in 1961. Yet, by then the NATO members accepted that their obligation to *consult* went beyond the narrowly defined NATO area; this did not entail an obligation to *act* on these issues. At any rate, out-of-area issues threatened to disrupt NATO cohesion: during the 1950s the Americans often refused to help the European powers deal with decolonisation, whereas in the 1960s the Europeans grew impatient (and sometimes alarmed) about US policy in Vietnam. Thus, the major priority of the alliance was to avoid exacerbating disagreements, rather than to present a comprehensive policy on these fields.[4] This also stands for the NATO reports on the Third World, which were *agreed minutes*, often drafted with an eye to paper over such disagreements.

---

[1] Winfried Heinemann, '"Learning by Doing": Disintegrating Factors and the Development of Political Cooperation in Early NATO', in *NATO and the Warsaw Pact: Intrabloc Conflicts*, eds. Mary Ann Heiss and S. Victor Papacosma (Kent, Ohio: The Kent State University Press, 2008), 43–57.

[2] Brussels, NATO Archives, International Staff, (hereafter NATO/) CM(58)138, 'Interim Report of the Secretary General on Political Consultation', 17 November 1958; CM(59)29, 'Annual Political Appraisal', 17 March 1959.

[3] See for example the discussion in the ministerial NAC in NATO/CVR(58)62, 16 December 1958.

[4] Geir Lundestad, *The United States and Western Europe since 1945: from "Empire" by Invitation to Transatlantic Drift* (Oxford: Oxford University Press, 2003), 142–167; Lawrence S. Kaplan, 'The Vietnam War and Europe: the View from NATO', and Fredrik Logevall, 'The American Effort to Draw European States into the War', in *La Guerre du Vietnam et l'Europe, 1963–1973*, eds. Christopher Goscha and Maurice Vaïsse (Paris: LGDJ, 2003), 89–102 and 3–16 respectively; John Kent, 'NATO, the Cold War and the End of Empire', and Frode Liland, 'Explaining NATO's Non-Policy on Out-of-Area Issues during the Cold War', in *A History of NATO: the First Fifty Years*, ed. Gustav Schmidt (Basingstoke: Palgrave, 2001), 1:141–152 and 1:173–189 respectively; Effie Pedaliu, 'Transatlantic Relations at a Time When "More Flags" Meant "No European Flags": America's War in South East Asia and its European Allies, 1964–68', *International History Review*, forthcoming.

The NATO reports on the Third World were meant to serve as background material for the biannual ministerial sessions of the North Atlantic Council (NAC). By the early 1960s, the ministerial NACs devoted much time on the Third World situation, but the *tour d'horizon* was a rather theoretical exchange: the NAC was not expected to make 'decisions' on these issues. The NATO studies were situation reports, and thus differed from the US National Intelligence Estimates: it was an accepted convention within the alliance that the experts should normally refrain from offering proposals for action. By the early 1960s most of the documents were drafted by expert working groups, with the participation of national officials, and were reviewed by the Political or the Economic Advisers. The authors were largely dependent on the availability of information and intelligence by the national delegations. US influence was strong, while the contribution of France, West Germany and Italy was also significant. On specific issues, in which they had special interests, smaller members also claimed a role. For example, Belgium and Portugal in the Committee on Africa, or Greece, Turkey, and Italy in the Middle Eastern reports; Turkey tried to participate in all working groups, including the Far Eastern and the Latin American ones.

However, it was Britain which played a major role in the NATO committee system.[5] The British wealth of experience in international deliberations and colonial affairs allowed them to lead the process of NATO analysis, especially in matters of the global South. Moreover, they needed to ensure that the NATO process would not affect adversely the non-member Commonwealth countries or British colonial policy;[6] that consultation would not lead to a 'fruitless' (and potentially risky) effort to devise a common NATO policy on out-of-area issues; and that NATO members were educated about the problems of the Third World.[7] Arguably, the presence of Lord Ismay, NATO's first Secretary-General (1952–7), and after 1958 of Evelyn Shuckburgh, the NATO Assistant Secretary-General on Political Affairs (chairing the Committee of Political Advisers), played a role in the relative prevalence of the British mentality and methods of analysis. British documents often include reports of the British experts who took part in the NATO meetings, offering information on intra-NATO disagreements which are missing from the sterilised NATO documents. British officials often noted, with barely concealed pride, that their draft had served as the working paper for the NATO reports.[8] Still, the alliance documents were not simply the reflections of British worldviews; they

[5] On Britain's influence in the NATO Committee on Information and Cultural Relations, see Linda Risso, '"Enlightening Public Opinion": A Study of NATO's Information Policies between 1949 and 1959 Based on Recently Declassified Documents', *Cold War History* 7, no. 1 (February 2007): 45–74.

[6] London, The National Archives (hereafter TNA/), FO 371/137956/65, Petrie (IRD) to Ewart-Biggs (FO), 16 October 1959; FO 371/131198/4, FO to UK delegation NATO, 23 December 1958; FO 371/151729/3, Boothby (FO) to Murray (NATO), 20 January 1961.

[7] See, among others, TNA/FO/371/137955/35, Brief, March 1959; FO371/141835/18, minute (Rothnie), 19 March 1959; FO 371/146519/37, minute (Boothby), 6 September 1960.

[8] See, among others, TNA/FO/371/137956/59, Shattock (NATO) to Watson (FO), 29 August 1959; FO 371/154730/23, East (CRO) to Faber (FO), 15 November 1961 (on Africa); FO 371/150863/9, minute (Rothnie), 15 February 1960 (Middle East); FO 371/155761/15, minute (Hankey), 21 November 1961; FO 371/162000/17, minute (Edmonds), 16 April 1962 (Latin America).

were products of an international process, and thus of compromise. As the Foreign Office noted on the first Far Eastern report

> although it is naturally not expressed quite in the way we would have written it if left to ourselves – as I suppose must always be the case with international papers of this kind – it is generally a reasonable statement of the situation.[9]

The subject of these reports was the Cold War in the periphery. By the mid-1950s, it was impossible for the two blocs of industrial countries to ignore the 'developing' (or as it was usually called at that time, 'under-developed') world.[10] Yet, the two alliances of the industrial North tended to view the needs of the Third World through their own Cold War lenses; the versions of modernity of West and East were not necessarily applicable in the South, although both the Americans and the Soviets (standard-bearers of ideologies with universalist pretensions) claimed – or believed – that they were.[11] The tendency to interpret the emerging North-South divide in terms of the East-West conflict was a serious impediment, and created a variety of dilemmas for the NATO analysts. Since NATO cared about the Cold War in the periphery, its reports formed part of a wider analysis on the capabilities of the Soviet enemy.[12] Indeed, until 1956, conflict in the Third World was briefly mentioned in the documents reporting on the Soviet Union itself. After 1957, concerned mostly with Soviet penetration of specific areas, the NATO experts produced a long series of *regional studies*. Reports on the Middle East started in 1957 (after the Suez crisis), on the Far East in 1958 (to deal with the ascent of the People's Republic of China), on Africa in 1959 (in anticipation of the projected decolonisation), on Latin America in 1961 (closely following the Cuban 'defection'). Thus, the undertaking of each group of studies was a response to the perceived transfer of Cold War antagonism in the specific region.

The primacy of the Cold War coloured NATO analysis. The rapid Soviet industrialisation and the outward-looking character of post-Stalin Soviet policies

---

[9] TNA/FO 371/133300/1, Benson (FO) to Cheetham (NATO), 28 November 1958.

[10] In NATO reports, the term 'Third World' was used for the first time in the 1963 documents, but the French referred to 'le tiers monde' in a memorandum that they submitted to APAG in 1962: NATO/AC/214 (a)-WP8, 15 October 1962.

[11] See the analysis of the American 'empire of liberty', the Soviet 'empire of justice' and the search of Third World leaders themselves in Odd Arne Westad, *The Global Cold War* (Cambridge: Cambridge University Press, 2007), 8–109; Robert J. McMahon, 'Eisenhower and Third World Nationalism: a Critique of the Revisionists', *Political Science Quarterly* 101, no. 3 (1986): 453–473; Mark Philip Bradley, 'Decolonization, the Global South and the Cold War, 1919–1962', in *The Cambridge History of the Cold War*, eds. Melvyn P. Leffler and Odd Arne Westad (Cambridge: Cambridge University Press, 2010), 1:464–485. See also John Darwin, *After Tamerlane: the Global History of Empire* (London: Penguin, 2007), 439: 'But the drift to cold war is only part of the story, and in many parts of the world not the most important part'. On a different analysis regarding the notion of the Cold War lens and the interactive nature of the East-West cleavage and the North-South divide, see Matthew Connelly, 'Taking Off the Cold War Lens: Visions of North-South Conflict during the Algerian War of Independence', *American Historical Review*, 105, No.3 (June 2000): 739–769.

[12] Evanthis Hatzivassiliou, 'Images of the Adversary: NATO Assessments of the Soviet Union, 1953–1964', *Journal of Cold War Studies* 11, no.2 (2009): 89–116.

posed a severe threat for the West: by the 1950s 'the Soviet model of national development [was] beguilingly attractive as a fast track to modernization'.[13] Moreover, the Soviet state-controlled trade fixed prices independently of the world market, insulated national from international markets and thus distorted international trade, on which the affluence of the West – its major advantage in the Cold War – depended.[14] Last but not least, contrary to the Soviet world with its solid, land-based heartland, the West was geopolitically more 'loose' and therefore more vulnerable: Soviet penetration of the global South threatened to disrupt Western communications or access to important materials. In this context, the realities of the Third World added a tremendous fluidity in a post-war world already undergoing rapid transitions.

Dealing with the Soviet economic ascent: the 'economic offensive of the Sino-Soviet Bloc'

Since 1954, NATO studies on the Soviet economy had stressed that its rapid growth would soon enable it to extend aid to the 'under-developed states', which might also view communism as a model for rapid development.[15] The post-Stalin Soviet effort to 'penetrate' the South caused particular concern to the NATO authorities. Thus, in December 1956 the short-lived Committee of Technical Advisers discussed a French scheme (the Pineau Plan) to set up an international organisation to administer aid to the periphery. Still, the NATO members opposed the idea of setting up new international machinery.[16] The US did not want to subject their global policy to the cumbersome NAC process, and Britain consistently stressed that it was impossible to agree to common NATO action, while the new states of the periphery distrusted the Western alliance. Consultation, however, was another matter. Although the Americans initially wondered 'what such countries as Portugal, Italy and Greece could contribute besides "views"', they finally agreed that periodical surveys of the 'economic offensive' would be welcome.[17]

Under Spaak's leadership, the Soviet economic activity in the periphery became the subject of systematic analysis by the newly-created Committee of Economic Advisers. As always, perceptions and terminology were crucial: the reports studied the 'Economic Offensive of the Sino-Soviet bloc', a phrase already used in Western, particularly Anglo-American, discourse revealing the West's feeling that it was facing an attack in parts of the globe in which, until recently, it had been unchallenged. It was

[13] Melvyn P. Leffler, *For the Soul of Mankind: the United States, the Soviet Union and the Cold War* (New York: Hill and Wang, 2007), 231.

[14] See, among others, Charles S. Maier, 'The World Economy and the Cold War in the Middle of the Twentieth Century', in *The Cambridge History of the Cold War*, 1:44–66.

[15] Hatzivassiliou, 'Images of the Adversary'.

[16] NATO/CM(56)142, 'Report on the Pineau Plan for Aid to Underdeveloped Countries', 18 December 1956.

[17] TNA/FO 371/120804/4, Coulson (Washington) to Wright (FO), 5 April 1956; FO 371/120804/16, FO to Washington Embassy, 29 April 1956; FO 371/120807/97, Steel (NATO) to FO, 28 June 1956.

also telling that the term 'the Sino-Soviet bloc' was not revised until 1963–4, even after it had become clear that the Sino-Soviet dispute was difficult to bridge. Ironically, at a time when Moscow and Beijing were clashing in the Third World,[18] the NATO analysts spoke of their 'joint' economic offensive, accepting the Cold War mentality regarding the similarity of dogs of any colour.

The 'Economic Offensive' reports stressed that the phenomenon posed 'a major political and strategic threat to the outside world', and was 'an integral element of total communist strategy'. The perceived offensive involved trade, aid, and technical assistance including education. It was noted that a bloc of totalitarian states could easily pursue political aims through its centralised economic/diplomatic initiatives, something which the sovereign nations and the free economies of the West were unable to do. Soviet trade was still small in volume (in 1957 it represented 2.5% of total world trade), but was 'designed so as to have the maximum political effect and concentrated on countries who are in need of economic assistance and trade outlets', as well as Soviet capital goods (August 1957). The Kremlin was offering long-term credits at low rates of interest, and arranged for the bulk purchases of raw materials from the 'under-developed countries', usually (or at least nominally) above market prices, thus tying up a large part of their surpluses, and ultimately distorting world trade. Equally selective was Soviet aid, which was directed towards a small number of strategically placed countries (Egypt, Syria, Yemen, India, Turkey, Indonesia, and after 1959 Cuba), and on 'spectacular' projects (the Indian steel mill or the Aswan High Dam). The Soviet bloc had carefully orchestrated its 'offensive', with each Eastern European country specialising in specific fields (for example East Germany in electrical equipment or ships, Poland in railroad rolling-stock and mining equipment, and so on). The Soviet arms trade involved obsolescent arms and secured in exchange important raw materials, and thus it was an economic and political gain for the Soviet bloc. The NATO experts also stressed the importance of Soviet technical aid to countries such as India, Burma, Afghanistan, and Egypt: the number of Soviet technicians abroad was estimated to have risen from 2000 in 1958 to 10,230 by late 1961. The training of Asian, African, and Latin American students (especially after the foundation of the Patrice Lumumba University in Moscow) was equally disquieting. Although the number of students was low, Soviet educational activity was highly selective to nationals of specific key countries, and included indoctrination.[19] The political threat of the 'economic offensive' was also

[18] Westad, *The Global Cold War*, 160–170. See also an interesting analysis in Jeremy Friedman, 'Soviet Policy in the Developing World and the Chinese Challenge in the 1960s', *Cold War History* 10, no. 2 (May 2010): 247–272.

[19] NATO/CM(57)116, 'The Economic Offensive of the Sino-Soviet Bloc', 21 August 1957; CM(58)97, 'Economic Offensive of the Sino-Soviet Bloc'16 June 1958; CM(59)103, 'The Economic Offensive of the Sino-Soviet Bloc', 8 December 1959; CM(60)4, 'The Sino-Soviet Bloc Economic Offensive in Underdeveloped Countries', 1 March 1960; CM(62)13, 'The Economic Offensive of the Sino-Soviet Bloc', 12 February 1962; CM(62)36, 'The Sino-Soviet Bloc Economic Offensive, 1954–1961: A Summary Review', 9 April 1962.

stressed by the Committee of Political Advisers: 'Moscow is clearly intent on demonstrating that no region of the world is now beyond its reach'.[20]

The tone of NATO reports became calmer after 1963–4, when signs appeared that Soviet economic growth was slowing down. The Soviet leadership adopted a more active posture in the Third World, which was described by the American delegation as the communists' 'principal target area'.[21] Yet, the NATO experts thought that the Soviets were less successful than previously feared. Moreover, since 1960 Shuckburgh, the Assistant Secretary-General on Political Affairs, had insisted that the emphasis on 'Soviet penetration' tended to lead to an exaggerated picture of Soviet success.[22] Thus, the title of the relevant reports changed to the more descriptive 'Communist Economic Activities' in the developing countries. Notably, the change of tone was due mostly to NATO's assessment of developments *in the Soviet economy*, not in the Third World as such.

These new reports noted that the Sino-Soviet dispute had affected the foreign aid policies of the two states, which now appeared competitive. Still, China was not yet able to challenge the Soviet Union in the developing world. Soviet aid was slowing down, probably due to the economic problems of the Soviet bloc: as the May 1963 report noted, the Soviets could not afford '"several Cubas" at the same time'. Moreover, 'in total value, Communist countries have thus far provided developing nations with more weapons and military goods than industrial equipment and tools for their economic expansion'. Still, the Economic Advisers stressed that technical assistance played an increasingly important role: the number of civilian and military technicians in the developing countries reached 15,800 in 1963 and 25,820 in 1966. The number of students from developing countries in the Soviet bloc reached 17,000 in 1963 and 36,000 in 1967 (of which 14,500 came from African countries). Thus the NATO experts noted that communist tactics in the Third World were becoming more sophisticated, remained politically targeted, and represented a major threat to the West.[23]

Monitoring the Middle East: from Suez to the Fifth *Eskadra*

The Middle East was a geopolitical special case for the Western alliance, since a crisis in that region (possibly also bringing Turkey, a NATO member, into the conflict) could spill over to the NATO area.[24] The Middle East was the first part of the Third World

[20] NATO/CM(60)38, 'Trends and Implications of Soviet Policy', 12 April 1960.

[21] NATO/APAG(65)4, Note by the US Delegation, 18 Mach 1965.

[22] TNA/FO 371/146509/17, minute (Shattock), 11 April 1960.

[23] NATO/CM(63)39, 'The Economic Offensive of the Sino-Soviet Bloc in the Less-Developed Countries', 31 May 1963. See also the documents entitled 'Communist Economic Activities in the Developing Countries', CM(64)67, 7 August 1964; CM(65)72, 15 September 1965; CM(67)55, 14 September 1967.

[24] On the special position of the Middle East in NATO planning, see Dionysios Chourchoulis, 'The Southern Flank of NATO, 1951–1959: Military Strategy or Political Stabilisation?', PhD thesis, University of London, 2011.

which the Kremlin sought to penetrate, through the 1955 arms deal with Nasser and its aid for the Aswan Dam project.

The Political Advisers stressed that Western ideas and technology had an 'unsettling' effect in that part of the world, upsetting the structures of traditional society. Arab disunity was a major problem: the Arab states were quarrelling among themselves, but there also were sharp social divisions within each country, and 'there is no consensus on the methods and ultimate purpose of government'. The Arab population was young, poor, and insecure about its prospects, while living standards were even expected to drop in some areas. Indeed, it was the effort of young and radical leaders to build modern states in the countries with the poorest populations, that created much pressure; for these leaders, the Soviet model could be attractive, especially since the Kremlin promised to provide aid without 'political strings'. Moreover, the Arabs saw Israel as a creation of Western imperialism, and this maximised Soviet opportunities for involvement. The Political Advisers insisted that the West's pursuit 'of sound and consistent policies in the Middle East is an essential element for success in reducing or eliminating Soviet influence there'.[25]

According to the Political Advisers, in the Middle East the Kremlin employed 'flexible and opportunist methods', supporting nationalism. The experts were particularly impressed by the absence of Soviet attacks on religion, and were puzzled by the (until then) unprecedented phenomenon of a Soviet policy not working through the medium of the local Communist parties or even tolerating their suppression. The Soviets were described as aiming to disrupt Western defensive arrangements such as the Baghdad Pact and Western bases, and cause trouble in the flow of Western oil supplies. Soviet trade gave to many Arabs the prospect of offsetting the disquieting Western domination; arms, especially, flattered the nationalist regimes and the army officers, 'for whom the gun is still the symbol of power' (December 1957). The Soviets mounted a huge propaganda campaign in the Middle East, increased or elevated the status of their diplomatic representation there, and offered support to the Arab cause at the UN. Still, the main Soviet gains were recorded in Egypt and Syria, which were oil-transit rather than oil-producing countries; the latter's interests lay primarily with their Western clients. The NATO experts did not expect the Soviets to risk war in the Middle East, but noted the risk of miscalculation. The Soviet penetration of Syria in 1957 was seen with much alarm, since it threatened to outflank NATO defences in Turkey and the Eastern Mediterranean, and destabilise pro-Western regimes in Lebanon and Jordan.[26]

Gamal Abdel Nasser was a major question mark. The Egyptian leader was not regarded as a Soviet puppet, but was perceived as being prone to adventurism, which (together with his economic problems) could increase his dependence on the Soviets.

[25] NATO/CM((57)63, 'The Middle East', 16 April 1957; CM(57)141, 'Situation in the Middle East', 2 December 1957; CM(57)147, 'Soviet Economic Penetration in the Middle East', 10 December 1957.

[26] *ibid.*

The Political Advisers had already noted the enormous impact of the Egyptian propaganda machinery, especially Cairo radio. The creation of the United Arab Republic (UAR) early in 1958 made the Egyptian leader very strong, at a time when his popularity in most Arab countries was significant. The Political Advisers now foresaw a polarised competition between the UAR and the pro-Western combination of Iraq and Jordan. In summer 1958, the British and the Americans blocked Nasserist attempts in Lebanon and Jordan, but a huge failure was recorded in the coup in Iraq, causing its withdrawal from the Baghdad Pact. Still, the emergence in Baghdad of a new centre of Arab nationalism was interpreted as a 'check to Cairo's expansionism'. The experts also appeared anxious about General Kassem's reliance on the communists in Iraq.[27]

After late 1959, a major change occurred. In the second half of the 1950s, some NATO members, such as Greece and Italy, had insisted that Cairo could not be lured into an anti-communist alliance, and neutrality was the maximum that could be achieved from Egypt.[28] The Political Advisers had timidly inserted similar views in their previous reports.[29] But now, the Americans started a cautious rapprochement with the Egyptian leader.[30] The NATO experts came out strongly in favour of such a policy, pointing out that Nasser had not, after all, become a Soviet stooge.

The Political Advisers stressed that the West should accept that 'a stance of "positive neutralism" corresponds to what the Arabs at present think they want'. Mostly, the Arabs seemed to have grown impatient with their 'Russian "princesse lointaine"', a trend which the West should carefully encourage. The experts vaguely referred to the collapse of the Baghdad Pact and the making of CENTO as an 'opportunity for re-organization'; this was partially because Canada and the Scandinavians (always reluctant to be drawn into Middle Eastern defence) objected to expanding the alliance's links with the Baghdad Pact.[31] However, the advent of a Soviet dilemma between its UAR and Iraqi connections was welcome to NATO. In April 1961, the Political Advisers noted that Nasser was still close to the Soviets, but added: 'There is no indication, however, that Nasser is consciously acting as an instrument of Soviet policy or that the UAR would, in the near future, accept a position of subservience to the USSR'. Thus, they even suggested that his model of neutrality could be acceptable

[27] See the reports 'The Situation in the Middle East', NATO/CM(58)71, 24 April 1958; CM(58)142, 28 November 1958; CM(59)25, 9 March 1959. See also AC/119-WP(59), 'The Soviet Role in the Middle East', 12 May 1959.

[28] Evanthis Hatzivassiliou, 'Greece and the Arabs, 1956–1958', *Byzantine and Modern Greek Studies*, 16 (1992): 49–82.

[29] NATO/CM(57)141, 'Situation in the Middle East', 2 December 1957.

[30] H. W. Brands, *The Specter of Neutralism: the United States and the Emergence of the Third World, 1947–1960* (New York: Columbia University Press, 1989), 296–303; Roland Popp, 'Accommodating to a Working Relationship: Arab Nationalism and US Cold War Policies in the Middle East, 1958–60', *Cold War History* 10, no. 3 (August 2010): 397–427.

[31] TNA/FO 371/141835/16, Shattock to Rothnie, 6 March 1959.

for other nationalist regimes in the region. Nasser's further weakening after the dissolution of the union with Syria strengthened this trend.[32]

From 1962 until the Six Day war, the NATO analysts argued that the Soviets were attempting, but not succeeding, to make further inroads in the Middle East. The normalisation of Franco-Arab relations following the Algerian settlement was greeted with relief. The overthrow of the Kassem government in Iraq in 1963 was seen as a major blow to the Soviet position. Thus, the Political Advisers argued that the West should maintain its policy of non-interference in intra–Arab disputes, ensure a balance of military power in the region, and try to prevent a new Arab–Israeli conflict, which would offer new opportunities to the Kremlin. The dispute over the waters of the Jordan river was regarded as particularly dangerous. The experts called for 'greater impartiality' in the Arab–Israeli dispute, since 'the West's great handicap in the Arab world is identification with Israel'. They did not want Nasser to win the conflict in Yemen, but also wished to avoid his clear defeat, which could force him to turn again to the Soviets. Arab nationalism was now seen as an uncontrollable force, but also potentially as 'a barrier to Communist expansion'.[33] NATO analysis reflected the Johnson Administration's reserve towards Nasser,[34] but things were very different compared to the almost open hostility of 1957–59.

In this context, the Political Advisers expected a deepening of intra-Arab disputes, and were surprised by the Six Day War. Initially, mirroring the US preference,[35] the Political Advisers hoped that the war 'offers perhaps the best opportunity in 20 years for making progress towards a lasting settlement'. Yet, soon afterwards, the absence of a settlement and the Soviet naval activity in the Mediterranean caused significant anxiety.[36] From 1968 onwards, new studies were undertaken, on the political, economic, and military situation in the Mediterranean, with a special emphasis on its southern shores. The Soviet challenge was seen as expanding, although the presence of the Soviet naval squadron was regarded as having political rather than military implications.[37]

---

[32] See the reports 'The Situation in the Middle East', NATO/CM(59)95, 23 November 1959; CM(60)37, 12 April 1960; CM(60)113, 5 December 1960; CM(61)27, 14 April 1961; CM(61)119, 30 November 1961.

[33] From the biannual reports on 'The Situation in the Middle East', see mostly NATO/CM(62)112, 4 December 1962; CM(63)31, 13 May 1963; CM(65)89, 16 October 1965; CM(66)101, 22 November 1966.

[34] Douglas Little, 'A Fool's Errand: America and the Middle East, 1961–1969', in *The Diplomacy of the Crucial Decade: American Foreign Relations during the 1960s*, ed. Diane B. Kunz (New York: Columbia University Press, 1994), 283–319. See also Guy Laron, 'Stepping Back from the Third World: Soviet Policy toward the United Arab Republic, 1965–1967', *Journal of Cold War Studies* 12, no. 4 (Fall 2010): 99–118.

[35] Peter L. Hahn, 'The Cold War and the Six Day War: US Policy towards the Arab-Israeli Crisis of June 1967', in *The Cold War in the Middle East: Regional Conflict and the Superpowers, 1967–1973*, ed. Nigel J. Ashton (London and New York: Routledge, 2007), 16–34.

[36] Reports 'The Situation in the Middle East', NATO/CM(67)19, 3 May 1967; CM(67)62, 23 November 1967; CM(68)20, 7 June 1968. See also CM(67)65, 'Trends and Implications of Soviet Policy', 29 November 1967.

[37] NATO/PO/68/98, Brosio to Permanent Representatives, 'The Threat to NATO in the Mediterranean Area', 15 February 1968; CM(68)15, 'Economic Activities of the Communist Countries in the

Committee on Africa: the challenges of a different type of society

Africa 'south of the Sahara' was studied by an ad hoc Committee, consisting of experts from Belgium, France, Germany, Italy, Portugal, Britain, and the US. Problems regarding this Committee became evident from the start. Thus, the Americans objected to the setting up of an ad hoc group, which differentiated Africa from other out-of-area cases, fearing that this was an experiment by Spaak aiming to harmonise the policies of the member states. The Americans told the British that they intended to 'sabotage Spaak's proposal', and were reassured only when the British convinced them that no common policy would emerge. On their part, the British strongly stressed that the West would lose Africa if it failed to understand the African point of view and the impetus of Africanism, or if it equated Africanism with Communism. However, other member states possessing African colonies (Portugal, Belgium, or France) did not want the alliance to discuss African nationalism (and therefore their own colonial rule), and insisted that 'NATO should not be encouraged to interest itself too closely in anything except Soviet penetration'. Early in 1959 the Italians caused a minor crisis by submitting a paper strongly criticising Belgian and Portuguese colonialism; after the latter's reaction, Spaak convinced the Italians to withdraw it.[38]

The first African reports, under the title 'Communist Penetration in Africa', focused on the social and economic conditions in the continent. Africa was seen as passing through a stage of 'transformation and ferment': the prospect of independence, the demands for industrialisation and development, the impact of Western education (but also the weakening of Western political influence due to decolonisation), and the influence of new ideologies radically changed the region. The prospect of development created new social groups, 'living on the margins of the industrial and commercial centres, severed from traditional institutions and open to new influences'. The formidable force of African trade unionism was directed against the rich, the white, and the imperialists. The appalling social conditions in a continent where national identities had not been fully developed and borders were largely 'artificial' created a fluid situation. Moreover, the presence of European minorities with a superior social status introduced an additional, inherently anti-Western factor. Mostly, in such social conditions and in a region where personal freedom was not a central concept, Western representative democracy was not necessarily appealing: authoritarianism was an indigenous tendency, and 'the new, centralising, "party boss" type of leader, at the head of a single party, tends to prove stronger than the tribal or religious leader'. In such a complicated situation of state-building from scratch (a 'revolutionary' situation),

Footnote 37 continued

Mediterranean', 14 May 1968; CM(68)16, 'Report on the Situation in the Mediterranean', 17 May 1968. See also Lawrence S. Kaplan and Robert W. Clawson, 'NATO and the Mediterranean Powers in Historical Perspective', in *NATO and the Mediterranean*, eds. Lawrence S. Kaplan, Robert W. Clawson and Raimondo Luraghi (Wilmington, Del: Scholarly Resources, 1984), 3–17.

[38] TNA/FO 371/131198/1 and 2, minute (Bruce), 20 November 1958, and Roberts (NATO) to FO, 25 November 1958; FO 371/137954/10, Roberts to FO, 14 January 1959.

there was little distaste for the Communist system: '[A]uthoritarian rule that succeeds in eliminating cultural backwardness, corruption and tribal divisions, and in bringing about rapid industrialization, will continue to be profoundly attractive in Africa'. The Soviet Union, a strongly centralised country with no colonial record in Africa, presented an attractive model.[39]

The experts noted that the Soviet leadership had adopted flexible tactics, mostly the infiltration of national parties and trade unions; the experts despaired of the Soviets' readiness to use even the social networks of sorcery for their ends. The Soviets had started studying Africa (new research centres appeared in the Soviet Union), and had intensified their diplomatic presence and propaganda: diplomatic missions rose from 40 to 63 within six months in 1960–61, while propaganda included six hour daily broadcasts by Moscow Radio, and transmissions by Bucharest and Beijing radios. The Moscow-Cairo ties, the impact of Cairo radio, and the Cairo-based Afro-Asian Solidarity Council were regarded, at least initially, as helpful to this Soviet drive. Yet, the NATO analysts stressed that the pan-African movement, though 'demonstrably open to Communist infiltration', had the potential to develop on independent lines. The experts argued that the West should provide aid, encourage the diversification of the continent's economy, and also accept the instinctive disposition of the new states towards neutralism. The cleavages of the Cold War were unimportant to Africans, and '[a]ny propaganda based on exposing the fallacies of Communism would have little or no appeal'. In an era of decolonisation, Western influence would naturally weaken, and the West should 'hold the relationship between Africa and the West until the tide turns'.[40]

In 1960–61, the major problem for the West was the Congo crisis, and the obvious opportunities that it presented for Soviet penetration. Yet, as numerous conferences were taking place in the continent, the experts also focused on the emergence of various groupings of African states: they noted that initially there was a polarisation between the Afro–Asian grouping and the pan-African movement, which was seen as more promising in providing a nationalist bulwark to Communist influence. However, by 1962 the experts were particularly heartened by the emergence of the so-called Brazzaville group (mostly West African states, including Nigeria) which advocated close co-operation with the European Economic Community (EEC). The emergence of a group of African 'moderate' states, the apparent distance that Nasser was taking from the Soviets and his own difficulties in claiming African leadership, and last but not least the evidence that Soviet policy in the continent was running into problems (mostly because the Soviet mentality scared African leaders) mark a turning point in NATO analysis. Thus, the experts noted that the Afro–Asians

[39] See the reports 'Communist Penetration in Africa', NATO/CM(59)32, 20 March 1959 and CM(60)43, 23 April 1960. See also CM(61)112, 'Communist Penetration in Africa', 23 November 1961.

[40] *ibid.* See also the reports 'Communist Penetration in Africa', NATO/CM(60)106, 28 November 1960; CM(61)35, 22 April 1961.

commanded a majority in the United Nations, but some of these countries often sided with the West.[41]

In the following years, reports were drafted by an expert working group. The experts kept stressing that the continent remained in a state of 'endemic instability', and was 'a priority target' of the Soviets. But the title 'Communist Penetration in Africa' was changed to the calmer 'The Situation in Africa', an indication of increased Western self-confidence. Despite the strengthening of the Soviet presence in the Horn of Africa and the appearance of the Chinese on the scene, the NATO analysts hoped that the Organization of African Unity (OAU) could settle regional disputes, and thus hinder Soviet interference. The greatest danger was now seen as coming from the long-term Soviet indoctrination of African elites and infiltration of trade unions, as well as from the situation in South Africa and Southern Rhodesia with its racist dimensions. However the racial question could hide various implications: as of 1967, a Portuguese reservation was constantly expressed with regard to Rhodesia, noting Portugal's 'neutrality' on that issue. Concern was also expressed in 1966 at the growing tendency for military rule in Africa, although the experts thought that the causes were local, and did not reveal a general pattern beyond disappointment at the dashing of hopes for economic development. In general, however, the experts believed that the West had held its ground in Africa. They did not seem to foresee the major upheaval of the following decades.[42]

Far East: the spectre of China and the torment of Vietnam

The Far East was not seen as a case of Communist 'penetration' of a Western-controlled area, for the very simple reason of the towering presence of the People's Republic of China.[43] The region was regarded as particularly vulnerable also because of the divided countries, the lack of ethnic backbone of the regional states, the presence of large Chinese minorities, rapid population growth, the ineffectiveness of non-Communist governments, and the appalling economic and social conditions. Mostly, the NATO Political Advisers failed accurately to assess the Sino-Soviet split, which violently disputed one of the West's unspoken assumptions: the notion of the Communist 'monolith'. In late 1958 (in the aftermath of the offshore islands crisis)

---

41 *ibid.*

42 NATO/CM(62)110, 'The Situation in Africa', 4 December 1962. See also the reports, with the same title, CM(64)23, 16 April 1964; CM(64)113, 28 November 1964; CM(67)21, 8 May 1967; CM(67)63, 24 November 1967; CM(68)18, 29 May 1968; CM(68)55, 5 November 1968. On military rule, see TNA/FO 371/187696/4, Bushell (NATO) to Brown (FO), 17 February 1966.

43 Chen Jian, *Mao's China and the Cold War* (Chapel Hill and London: The University of North Carolina Press, 2001); Lorenz Luthi, *The Sino-Soviet-Split: Cold War in the Communist World* (Princeton: Princeton University Press, 2008); Chen Jian and Yang Kuisong, 'Chinese Politics and the Collapse of the Sino-Soviet Alliance', in *Brothers in Arms: the Rise and Fall of the Sino-Soviet Alliance, 1945–1963*, ed. Odd Arne Westad (Washington DC: Woodrow Wilson Center Press, 1998), 275–277; Mingjiang Li, 'Ideological Dilemma: Mao's China and the Sino-Soviet Split, 1962–63', *Cold War History* 11, no. 3 (August 2011): 387–419.

the Political Advisers reported 'no sign of a weakening of the Sino-Soviet alliance'. In April 1960 they stressed that 'a breech between the two countries can be confidently ruled out for the foreseeable future', and in late 1960, after the split had come out in the open, they argued that 'no rupture of the alliance is to be expected in the foreseeable future'.[44] As late as November 1963, APAG noted that 'the two threats [Soviet and Chinese] were cumulative rather than mutually exclusive'.[45]

The enormous human and material resources of the PRC were the major theme of the Political Advisers until the early 1960s. The lack of information on the PRC – due to the unreliability of Chinese statistics but also to the absence of Western diplomatic representation in Beijing – tormented the NATO experts. It is telling that initially, they regarded the Great Leap Forward as a successful policy, and only gradually came to realise its failures. Even then, they were alarmed to note that the PRC was anyway developing faster than the *other* countries of the region. The experts also monitored the increasing international activity of the PRC, including its ambition to court the neutral Asian countries. Thus, the Political Advisers tended to regard India (and its version of neutralism) as an indispensable counter-weight in Asian politics: '[t]he policy of neutrality as visualised by India constitutes one of the elements of resistance to communist subversion' (April 1962). The other counter-weight to China was Japan: the West should recognise the country's importance and aspirations. The experts hoped that Chinese aggressiveness in Tibet in 1959 could alert the other Asian countries to the PRC menace. The Chinese success in the 1962 war against India impressed and alarmed the NATO analysts: 'There is an urgent need to convince Asians that the balance of power does not lie with Communist China'.[46]

By 1964 the Political Advisers finally acknowledged the Sino-Soviet split, but this did not solve their problem: NATO was clashing with the Kremlin, and the PRC was an even more extremist anti-Western force. The post-1964 reports constantly repeated that the Sino-Soviet dispute 'affects, but does not basically alter, the problems facing us in Asia'. The new Chinese nuclear potential was seen as having political rather than strictly military implications. The turmoil of the Cultural Revolution caused the PRC's short-lived eclipse in international affairs, but also worried the experts. The spring 1967 report included the impressive statement that it was 'desirable that Communist China should be brought out of her isolation', as its extremism could hide grave dangers. The Prime Minister, Chou En-Lai, was seen as aiming to 'protect the country's economic and technological development from the disruptive effects of Mao's political extremism'. On other fronts, India's conflict with Pakistan was regarded as 'a major set-back for the free world': the Soviet Union, by working for pacification

[44] 'The Situation in the Far East', NATO/CM(58)143, 5 December 1958; CM(60)42, 22 April 1960; CM (60)108, 30 November 1960.

[45] NATO/CM(63)84, 'Atlantic Policy Advisory Group', 15 November 1963.

[46] 'The Situation in the Far East', NATO/CM(58)143, 5 December 1958; CM(59)101, 3 December 1959; CM(60)42, 22 April 1960; CM(60)108, 30 November 1960; CM(61)33, 19 April 1961; CM(62)44, 17 April 1962; CM(63)26, 6 May 1963. See also the views of the Economic Advisers in AC/89-D.21, 'Economic Development in Communist China', 9 July 1958.

between India and Pakistan, had managed to impress Third World opinion. Moreover, the Political Advisers warmly welcomed Sukarno's effective fall in Indonesia (as a major blow to Chinese influence), and hoped that the country would now adopt a 'genuine, non-aligned neutrality'.[47]

As could be expected, analysis now focused on Vietnam. The Political Advisers, reporting on 'Trends and Implications of Soviet Policy' (their 'main' Soviet reports), estimated that the Kremlin regarded the Vietnam war as a manageable low intensity conflict, which the Soviets were content to let unfold. They did not believe that Beijing was trying to effect an expansion of the war.[48] The Far East situation reports argued that 'it remains a vital interest of the West to prevent a Communist victory in South Vietnam which would stimulate similar developments throughout South East Asia'. It is clear that the wording incorporated the domino theory regarding Vietnam. The reports insisted that the commitment of US ground troops had led to an amelioration of the military situation in South Vietnam, but did not affect North Vietnamese ability to 'maintain their forces' in the South (November 1966). The analysts mostly lamented the lack of cohesion of the anti-Communist forces in the country. This, rather than the military activity of the Viet Cong, was seen as the major Western problem. The 1968 Tet Offensive was regarded as important mostly because it impaired constitutional progress and the prospect of a viable South Vietnamese government, rather than because of its military implications.[49] However, recent bibliography stresses the European complaints about the 'consultation deficit' in NATO in the case of Vietnam, which by itself was a failure of the reports.[50]

Latin American uncertainties

The last set of regional studies, by an *ad hoc* expert group, started in late 1961 at US insistence.[51] The title was 'The Situation in Latin America' right from the start; evidently, the authors did not even want to think of Communist 'penetration' in the soft underbelly of the US. The Kennedy Administration's reformist ideas, projected by the US-led Alliance for Progress, were viewed as major priorities for the West.[52] Yet, during the initial discussions, disagreements also emerged: the French, Belgians, and

---

[47] Reports 'The Situation in the Far East', NATO/CM(64)79, 30 October 1964; CM(65)93, 23 November 1965; CM(66)45, 23 May 1966; CM(66)100, 22 November 1966; CM(67)27, 30 May 1967; CM(67)60, 20 November 1967; CM(68)17, 28 May 1968; CM(68)53, 25 October 1968.

[48] NATO/CM(65)32, 27 April 1965; CM(65)94, 26 November 1965; CM(66)129, 7 December 1966; CM (66)1, 'Atlantic Policy Advisory Group', 5 January 1966.

[49] Reports 'The Situation in the Far East', NATO/CM(64)79, 30 October 1964; CM(65)34, 29 April 1964; CM(65)93, 23 November 1965; CM(66)45, 23 May 1966; CM(66)100, 22 November 1966; CM(67)27, 30 May 1967; CM(67)60, 20 November 1967; CM(68)17, 28 May 1968; CM(68)53, 25 October 1968.

[50] Pedaliu, 'Transatlantic Relations'.

[51] TNA/FO 371/155759/1, Murray (NATO) to Ramsbotham (FO), 19 July 1961.

[52] On the intellectual origins of this approach see, among others, Michael E. Latham, *Modernization as Ideology: American Social Science and 'Nation Building in the Kennedy Era* (Chapel Hill: The University of North Carolina Press, 2000); Nils Gilman, *Mandarins of the Future: Modernization Theory in Cold War*

Dutch noted that the Alliance for Progress was a long-term plan, and could not address the immediate problem of Soviet penetration; the Italians thought that US promises for aid could even aggravate the situation by raising expectations; the Canadians proved too critical of US policy and hegemony in Latin America, and embarrassed all the others.[53]

The first reports noted that social disparities in Latin America were enormous due to the antiquated land tenure system, the unequal distribution of land, and the 'obstinate defence of their narrow interests' by small groups of rich landowners and businessmen. The parallel existence of a politically apathetic mass of Indians was also 'a dangerous question-mark for the future'. The population of the region was the fastest growing in the globe, while the appalling social conditions in the shanty towns bred desperation and 'prophets of reform or revolution'. Better communications led to an awareness of conditions in other parts of the world, and especially bred 'anti-yankeeism'. In such circumstances, the middle classes, 'often justifiably indignant at the grinding poverty around them', were attracted by the concept of revolution as a shortcut to development. Cuba was described as 'virtually a Communist state', whose defection from the West had 'thrown the inter-American system into disarray and made Latin America a vital arena in the Cold War'; the potential for 'fidelismo' was 'vast'. In other words, Latin America was viewed as a world in a crossroads: it could move towards either revolution or reform (the 'necessary peaceful revolution'). The reports expressly mentioned the hope that the danger of social upheaval could make reform acceptable to local reactionary elites, and would aid the emerging Christian and Social Democratic movements in the area. The Brazilian policy of independence (which was 'far from non-alignment in the Afro-Asian sense') was probably 'the best the West can hope for'. The reports often contained a strong plea for a more active European interest, economic as well as cultural and political: 'money alone is not enough to promote development or to arrest the spread of communism' (April 1962). The constant repetition of the plea was an indication that this European interest was not forthcoming. [54]

The experts welcomed the Soviet/Cuban defeat in the Cuban missile crisis, but noted that the situation remained unstable. They regarded Castro as ideologically closer to China than the Soviet Union, although they assessed that his dependence on Soviet aid would prevent him from siding with Beijing. Yet, the prospects of development, rather than Soviet/Cuban policies, would determine the future. In this context, the experts saw dangers both from the far Left, as well as from the far Right (the local military) which could arrest the pace of reform. Four military coups in 1963

Footnote 52 continued
America, (Baltimore: Johns Hopkins University Press, 2003). See also William O. Walker III, 'Mixing the Sweet with the Sour: Kennedy, Johnson, and Latin America', in *The Diplomacy of the Crucial Decade*, 42–79.

[53] TNA/FO 371/155761/15, minute (Hankey), 21 November 1961; FO 371/162000/17, minute (Edmonds), 16 April 1962.

[54] 'The Situation in Latin America', NATO/CM(61)123, 1 December 1961; CM(62)33, 6 April 1962; CM (62)108, 27 November 1962; CM(63)20, 17 April 1963.

(Guatemala, Ecuador, the Dominican Republic and Honduras) were seen as grave setbacks. Yet, in late 1963 the experts noted that 'there may be cases in which a military take-over could have immediate or short-term advantages [. . .] or, in the last resort be the only alternative to a total breakdown in law and order or a communist take-over'. By the mid-1960s, the experts were anxious about the revival of peronism in Argentina, but pinned their hopes mostly to the Christian Democratic experiment in Chile. The magnitude of hope that Chilean Christian Democracy stimulated can only be contrasted sharply with the inglorious, for Western democracy, outcome of 1973. Moreover, the reports noted with relief NATO attempts to undertake propaganda in Latin America, at a time when 'Communism continues to make significant inroads in Latin American intellectual circles'. [55]

By the mid-1960s, left-wing armed insurrections caused increasing concern: the experts saw an on-going Cuban 'assault' in the area (although the Soviets seemed to prefer peaceful penetration), including the holding of the Havana Tri-Continental Conference in January 1966. The challenge was becoming even more pressing by the 'transistorized revolution in communications', which aided radicalism. Despite Che Guevara's elimination in 1967, the NATO analysts continued to insist that the major problem for the West in Latin America was social rather than military: 'Guevara's legend will, with Castro's help, remain a powerful inspiration so long as the economic and social changes implicit in the goals of the Alliance for Progress are not achieved'.[56]

Beyond the regional: attempts to generalise

NATO reports did not put forward an overall assessment of the issue of neutralism. The monitoring of the 1961 Belgrade Conference which founded the Non-aligned Movement was left to national policies.[57] In the regional situation reports, one can find random comments, pointing to the unspoken assumptions of the NATO experts. Commenting on the Belgrade Conference, the Political Advisers did not appear impressed: 'Nothing particularly new emerged from this meeting', while the African experts complained that 'Afro-Asian solidarity finds little expression except within the organizations set up to assist movements aiming at emancipation or engaged in subversive activities'.[58] The NATO experts often felt that neutralism was unfair to the

[55] 'The Situation in Latin America', NATO/CM(63)76, 12 November 1963; CM(64)37, 27 April 1964; CM(64)86, 16 November 1964; CM(65)26, 23 April 1965; CM(65)91, 19 November 1965; CM(66)39, 11 May 1966; CM(67)23, 24 May 1967.

[56] 'The Situation in Latin America', NATO/CM(66)39, 11 May 1966; CM(67)23, 24 May 1967; CM(67) 64, 27 November 1967; CM(68)19, 11 June 1968.

[57] See Robert Rakove, 'The US and British Assessment and Response to the Inaugural Nonaligned Conference', and Jason Parker, '"What Might Come Out of This Bag of Eels": The USIA, Nonalignment, and the Babel of Belgrade', papers presented at the conference 'Non-aligned Movement (NAM) in the Cold War: A True Alternative?', Belgrade, 24–26 May 2012.

[58] NATO/CM(61)119, 'The Situation in the Middle East', 30 November 1961; CM(61)112, 'Communist Penetration in Africa', 23 November 1961.

West. Thus, in early 1962 they referred to the 'present strong current of Afro-Asian jingoism' directed against the West.[59]

Attempts to establish a more comprehensive picture can be found in the papers of another NATO body, the Atlantic Policy Advisory Group, formed in 1962. APAG's reports were not agreed minutes, but rather the chairman's account of a brainstorming process, and thus they could prove bolder than the findings of the other study groups. The 'Problems of Neutralism' were discussed in APAG's first meeting in summer 1962. The report did not deal with classic neutralism of the Swiss or Swedish type, but with the 'new and emotional' version of Asia, Africa, and Latin America. The experts agreed that the West should accept neutralism, and should draw 'a clear line of division between communist bloc countries and neutral countries, while keeping the dividing line between Western-committed and neutral states as blurred and fluid as possible'.[60] The truth was, however, that the blurring of the lines appeared more often in the opposite direction, namely between the Communist and the neutral spheres.

APAG insisted on the primacy of the economic factor. Reporting on NATO and the developing countries in late 1964 and in January 1966, it considered that the Third World was undergoing 'a significant process of diversification and even of disintegration', as the unifying force of anti-colonialism was being weakened, and the Sino-Soviet dispute introduced new factors in the global conflict. The West should take advantage of this trend, and encourage the new countries to pursue development. However, often Western private enterprises pursued maximalist demands, and intensified the distrust of the new states for Western investment.[61] Studying the new Soviet doctrine of 'wars of national liberation' in late 1966, APAG stressed that the West should facilitate economic and social progress, and avoid offering 'unconditional support to reactionary régimes'; emphasis should be given to 'the strength of national feelings and traditions as an antidote to Communism'.[62] These, however, were rather over-optimistic views in the years of Vietnam.

Out-of-area problems were also discussed in the Harmel Report of late 1967.[63] These were the subject of subgroup 4, under Professor C.L. Patijn. Subgoup 4 accepted that NATO could not act outside the area, but lamented the lack of harmony on out-of-area issues, and argued that only a global policy could secure the attainment of its aims:

> It may well be that the future prestige of the Western world is less dependent upon its power and wealth than upon its response to problems of human rights, racial

[59] NATO/CM(62)44, 'The Situation in the Far East', 17 April 1962.

[60] NATO/CM(62)94, 'Atlantic Policy Advisory Group', 28 September 1962.

[61] NATO/CM(64)128, 'Atlantic Policy Advisory Group', 2 December 1964; CM(66)1, 'Atlantic Policy Advisory Group', 5 January 1966.

[62] NATO/CM(66)142, 'Atlantic Policy Advisory Group', 20 December 1966.

[63] See among others, James Ellison, *The United States, Britain and the Transatlantic Crisis: Rising to the Gaullist Challenge, 1963–1968* (Basingstoke: Palgrave Macmillan, 2007), 108–116 and 170–178; Helga Haftendorn, *NATO and the Nuclear Revolution: a Crisis of Credibility, 1966–1967* (Oxford: Clarendon Press, 1996), 320–374; Andreas Wanger, 'Crisis and Opportunity: NATO's Transformation and the Multilateralization of Détente 1966–1968', *Journal of Cold War Studies* 6, no. 1 (Winter 2004): 22–74.

> relations and economic development [. . .] In their relations with the Third World the NATO members should clearly strive for more than anti-communism; they need a political strategy which will command respect and sympathy. Here again study in depth, consultation and co-ordination of policy are required.[64]

Yet, the Report mostly focused on East-West relations and the dual pillars of defence and détente. Relations with the Third World clearly formed the least 'important' part of the Harmel process.

Conclusions

The NATO reports on the Third World formed part of the West's attempt to react to incoming bad news. In the early 1950s the West controlled the periphery, and thus any Soviet move in the global South could only result in an absolute Soviet gain and a Western loss. Moreover, out-of-area issues usually produced strong discomfort in NATO. Disagreements occurred on too many issues, and involved the different perspectives of many countries.

Still, the NATO reports show more than the low level of political integration in the alliance. NATO analysis was based on a crucial unspoken assumption: the Cold War was not only a strategic conflict but also a *battle for legitimisation*, involving the economy and the ability of the social systems to cope with the problems of modernity. However, as far as the Third World was concerned, the terms of reference of these working groups obliged them to focus mainly on 'Soviet penetration'. The experts (or at least many of them) were cognizant of the need to go, at least to some extent, beyond the East-West cleavage when discussing the Third World. Yet, at least until the mid-1960s, the NATO experts themselves tended to assume that this battle for legitimisation, even in the Third World, involved the application of one of the two systems of the industrial North. This tended to reinforce the Cold War perspective of the reports. This Cold War perspective did not mean that NATO analysts *ignored* local circumstances in the Third World. It meant that there was a conceptual framework giving a *priority* to the Cold War, if nothing else because this was the lowest common denominator, on which all NATO members agreed – although it is correctly stressed that the Cold War lens was more evident in US, rather than in European attitudes.[65]

As could be expected, there are ample cases of silences in NATO reports. The absence of references to the burdened legacies of Western colonialism is telling. For example, it was correct to point to 'artificial borders' in Africa, but the reports did not elaborate on the causes of this problem. The reports on Africa 'south of the Sahara' were carefully designed to avoid intra-NATO discussion of (and therefore quarrels on) some of the most salient and embarrassing Western problems, such as Algeria and

[64] Harmel Report, sub-group 4, 'Developments in Regions Outside the NATO Area' (Patijn), NATO, http://www.nato.int/archives/harmel/harmel02.htm, assessed 12 February 2011.

[65] See for example, Kathryn C. Statler, *Replacing France: the Origins of American Intervention in Vietnam* (Lexington: The University Press of Kentucky, 2007), 285–286.

South Africa, with their multiple connotations about international affairs.[66] It is telling that the southern Mediterranean became a subject of study *only after the emergence of a Soviet naval squadron in the region*. Similarly, there was little if any analysis of the effects of the Suez crisis in Third World opinion, of the adverse anti-Western impressions created by the Congo crisis and the assassination of Patrice Lumumba, or of the near-disastrous effects of US conduct in Vietnam. Moreover, the emphasis on social and economic problems was only one side of the coin questionable Western methods regarding propaganda, special operations and counterinsurgency[67] were not covered in detail, as the Americans were reluctant to share information on their most sensitive covert operations with their NATO allies.

There is another 'dark' aspect of the NATO studies under review here. This article confirms that the mid-1960s was a turning point in the toleration of military dictatorships by the West.[68] By 1965, the view even appeared (in the Latin American reports) that 'in some instances military-controlled governments may, at least temporarily, be conducive to economic and social development'.[69] In 1968, fresh military coups in Latin America (Peru and Panama) led the experts to remark that the NATO countries should 'not necessarily view these events with too much disquiet', since the military had promised eventually to hold elections.[70] The NATO studies stressed the importance of economic and social conditions which would determine the future. They also noted the need for ensuring reasonable and stable prices for Third World commodities, which would allow these states to plan for the future. Yet, in the midst of a huge Western 'holding operation' in the Third World, there was always the temptation to accept 'temporary' deviations from Western principles. This was, perhaps, an inevitable result of the fact that, when the chips were down, the American/Western attitude 'bootlegged Bandung in Yalta bottles'.[71]

Despite the shortcomings of NATO analysis, an evolution took place. The initial alarmism of the 1950s did not lead to the reproduction of John Foster Dulles' aphorism about the 'immorality' of neutralism. Anyway, this alarmism was largely contained in the early 1960s, when (evidently influenced by the attitude of the Kennedy Administration), the experts argued that the West should come to terms with a *form* of neutralism. However, they never saw neutralism as a coherent 'bloc'; they understood it as a fluid state of affairs, divergent and depending on local conditions and regional backgrounds.

[66] See especially, Matthew Connelly, *A Diplomatic Revolution: Algeria's Fight for Independence and the Origins of the Post-Cold War Era* (Oxford: Oxford University Press, 2002).

[67] See, among others, Jeffrey H. Michaels, 'Managing Global Counterinsurgency: the Special Group (CI), 1962–1966', *Journal of Strategic Studies* 35, no. 1 (February 2012): 33–61.

[68] Michael E. Latham, 'The Cold War in the Third World, 1963–1975', in *The Cambridge History of the Cold War*, 2:258–280. See also NATO/CM(62)44, 'The Situation in the Far East', 17 April 1962; CM(63)76, 'The Situation in Latin America', 12 November 1963.

[69] NATO/CM(65)26, 'The Situation in Latin America', 23 April 1965.

[70] NATO/CM(68)57, 'The Situation in Latin America', 8 November 1968.

[71] Brands, *The Specter of Neutralism*, 9.

The relationship between nationalism and communism is a hotly debated issue. It is clear that US policies played a major role in 'constructing' the identity of the Third World, by applying a Cold War mentality not always applicable in local circumstances.[72] Yet, this article disputes the interpretation that the Americans 'in their own words, too easily confused nationalism with Communism'.[73] Indeed, recent research seeks more complicated interpretations, pointing to the interactive character of the relationships.[74] Moreover, nationalism was seen as a 'secure' bulwark to Communism in the social conditions of the *First or the Second* World. Although one should not confuse US and NATO analysis, it is important to stress that in large areas of the Third World, states lacked an ethnic/national backbone and strong national identities; in these conditions, nationalist discourse was an alternative form of populism, aiming to stimulate the nexus of state-building, social reform (unclear in content), state-controlled development, and personal rule by petty dictators. The NATO analysts were clearly afraid of the impetus and extremism of the latter sort of nationalism, especially since it appeared in areas with little tradition of Western representative democracy. Whatever the universalist American ideology of the 'empire of liberty' claimed, this kind of populism *could* turn to the Communist bloc.

This was the crux of the problem of Western analysis on the Third World. The model of US/Western 'soft power' was the Marshall Plan, as implemented in Europe in 1948–52. Although the NATO experts never said it in so many words, they clearly thought that a repetition of that exercise was impossible in the Third World, a large part of which lacked the necessary preconditions, such as national backbone, diversified economies, high-quality education, and a tradition of representative government. There were cases, for example South Vietnam, where the Americans did not have a credible political/social structure to support, and were trying to draw Cold War dividing lines 'in the sand'.[75] Indeed, the feebleness of the pro-Western forces in the Third World often emerged in the NATO reports as the West's greatest problem. This was why, following the first phase of an American-led liberal optimism (or 'innocence') in the 1950s and early 1960s, and as the challenges mounted and multiplied in the Third World, the huge Western 'holding operation' could easily degenerate into the crude realist dilemma of choosing between chaos and order.

---

[72] Westad, *The Global Cold War*, 110–157.

[73] See this view, among others, in Walter LaFeber *America, Russia and the Cold War, 1945–2006* (Boston: McGraw-Hill, 2008), 165.

[74] See, among others, Vanni Pettinà, 'The Shadows of Cold War over Latin America: the US Reaction to Fidel Castro's Nationalism, 1956–59', *Cold War History*, 11, no. 3 (August 2011): 317–339; Bevan Sewell, 'A Perfect (Free Market) World? Economics, the Eisenhower Administration, and the Soviet Economic Offensive in Latin America', *Diplomatic History*, 32, no. 5 (November 2008): 841–868; Nathan J. Citino, 'The "Crush" of Ideologies: the United States, the Arab World, and Cold War Modernization', *Cold War History* 12, no. 1 (February 2012): 89–110.

[75] David L Anderson, *Trapped by Success: the Eisenhower Administration and Vietnam, 1953–61* (New York: Columbia University Press, 1991), 200; Thomas Schwartz, *Lyndon Johnson and Europe: In the Shadow of Vietnam* (Cambridge, MA: Harvard University Press, 2003), 235

Still, by the mid-1960s, the Cold War-centred analysis tended to trigger crucial misunderstandings. The West seemed, for the moment, to hold its ground versus the Soviets, but it was in fact losing the psyche of the Third World. The NATO experts tended to focus on the former dimension rather than the latter. By 1967, APAG insisted that the problems of the developing countries 'are expected to become increasingly important in the 1970s'.[76] However, perhaps the NATO experts themselves did not fully realise the extent of the turmoil that emerged in the Third World in the decades to come; arguably, there lay new opportunities for Soviet policy as well.

[76] NATO/CM(67)38, 'Atlantic Policy Advisory Group', 26 June 1967.

Defeating the General: Anglo-American Relations, Europe and the NATO Crisis of 1966

James Ellison

Recent accounts of the resolution of the NATO crisis of 1966 have praised the role of Lyndon Baines Johnson and his administration. This article suggests that there was an Anglo-American dimension to the outcome of the crisis. It shows how the US government sought British assistance to defend the principles of Atlantic partnership and European integration and how the British readily and effectively responded. The result was Anglo-American cooperation to defeat de Gaulle's challenge. The two governments turned the crisis into an opportunity to reinvigorate NATO and to pursue national objectives. For the Americans, this meant the stabilization of US–European relations, particularly in regard to the Federal Republic of Germany. For the British, it meant the strengthening of Britain's position in NATO and its prospects for future EEC entry, and the reinforcement of Anglo-American ties against the backdrop of Britain's global retreat.

Introduction

At 12:50 p.m. on Monday 7 March 1966, the President of the United States, Lyndon B. Johnson, was warned that he would within an hour receive a letter taking 'a very hard line' from the French president, General Charles de Gaulle.[1] The letter did just that. De Gaulle announced in characteristically grand fashion that France proposed 'to recover the entire exercise of her sovereignty over her territory ... to terminate her participation in "integrated" commands and no longer to place her forces at the disposal of NATO'.[2] In effect, what the French president had done by serving this 'eviction notice' on the North Atlantic Treaty Organization (NATO) was to dispute the whole architecture of Atlantic relations and thus generate 'the most traumatic moment in NATO's history'.[3] De Gaulle threw into question the future of NATO and the Atlantic Alliance at a time when US–European relations were already badly strained by Western European doubts about America's involvement in the Vietnam war and American doubts about the loyalty of their European allies. The NATO crisis was an instant when, in the words of the Chancellor of the Federal Republic of Germany, Ludwig Erhard, 'the world could go apart'.[4]

The world did not go apart. De Gaulle's denunciation of military integration and his greater criticisms of the geopolitics of Western relations, principally that the United States should not have the monopoly on control even if it did have the monopoly on power, failed to win support.[5] NATO withdrew from France and France withdrew from NATO's integrated military command structure, although the French remained members of the Atlantic Alliance. In response, France's fourteen allies united in defence of NATO and used the opening created by the 1966 crisis to solve many of the problems that had troubled the Alliance since the early 1960s. Moreover, by December 1967 a full-scale review of NATO's purpose and function was completed in the Harmel Report which answered the questions raised by de Gaulle's letter about the organization's legitimacy in an era of détente.[6] De Gaulle had thus been isolated and then defeated and NATO had survived his challenge and emerged revitalized. Thomas Schwartz has recently attributed this accomplishment primarily to the statesmanlike diplomacy of Johnson which, he suggests, had positive ramifications for wider US foreign policy: 'it was the effective maintenance and nourishment of the alliance that allowed the United States to prevail peacefully in the Cold War, a successful chapter in American diplomacy that places the American experience in Vietnam in a different, and less dominating, perspective'.[7] Such a positive view of Johnson's leadership has been sustained by Andreas Wenger's analysis of NATO's response to de Gaulle: '[f]aced with de Gaulle's challenge, Johnson was willing to put in the effort to achieve a consensus within the alliance and to avert further fragmentation'.[8]

Both Schwartz and Wenger note that while the resolution of the NATO crisis was dominated by the US government under the skilful guidance of Lyndon Johnson, it was nevertheless a multilateral affair. Key allies from the 14 played leading roles in the management of NATO's response to France, not least the Belgians whose foreign minister, Pierre Harmel, was responsible for the 1967 review of the future tasks of the organization. Most significant, however, were the British and the West Germans. They enjoyed close relations with the Americans, held positions of relative authority within NATO, and, as will be seen, were central to the pressing issues of the day.[9] Indeed, the Federal Republic's status rose as a result of France's self-exclusion and thus demotion within the Alliance, a realignment acknowledged by *The Economist*, which wrote as the crisis began that the 'future skeleton of Nato is bound to be a tripartite arrangement between America, Britain and Germany with German views carrying far greater weight than they have done in the past'.[10] For these reasons, relations between the Federal Republic, the United Kingdom and the United States in the resolution of the NATO crisis have received specific and appropriate attention. By contrast, a distinct Anglo-American perspective, common to studies of the clashes with de Gaulle in the early 1960s, has not yet featured. This may be because the Anglo-American relationship seems less pertinent to NATO in the mid-1960s than it was previously, due to the multilateral nature of the dispute with France and the apparent correlation between ever closer American–West German relations and ever weakening US–UK relations. Such a view is not adopted here. Instead, this article argues that there was an Anglo-American dimension to the NATO crisis of 1966 which was central to dealing with de Gaulle's challenge and which had important repercussions for relations between the US and the UK.[11]

It is generally accepted that the Anglo-American relationship waned under Johnson and Harold Wilson, suffering its first major blow in the Labour government's refusal to commit even a token British force to fight alongside the Americans in Vietnam. The second came when the underlying asymmetry of Anglo-American relations present since World War II was fully revealed in a stark and debilitating light by the 1967 devaluation of the pound and the East of Suez decisions.[12] Despite these trials, the relationship endured and a recent account has provided a convincing interpretation of why by suggesting that while the importance of the relationship contracted in line with Britain's global stature, its quality remained.[13] The habit and practice of cooperation, especially between individuals and institutions, was sustained even though the size and scope of their activities was inevitably reduced. This view is confirmed by an analysis of the reactions of the Americans and the British to the NATO crisis and their collaboration in its settlement. As this article will show, the confrontation with de Gaulle created the conditions which had always produced Anglo-American cooperation: a shared interest in defeating a common enemy. For the Johnson administration, de Gaulle threatened to destabilize the established US formula for Western relations – Atlantic partnership and European integration – and in defending these principles the Americans sought British assistance. At the same time, they also encouraged the British to play the larger role in European affairs that influential elements in the US government had desired since the 1950s. The Wilson government responded energetically to American direction not least because the British similarly upheld Atlantic partnership and European integration, but also because they sought to capitalize on the unpopularity of France caused by de Gaulle's policies. In so doing, the objective was to enhance British influence in Europe, improve the chances of EEC membership and thus protect what remained of special relations with the Americans as Britain's global horizons contracted. Mutual interests thus produced conformity between the US and the UK on the tactics to neutralize de Gaulle and on the strategy of engaging in diplomatic alchemy to turn the NATO crisis into an opportunity for renewal. The Americans and the British therefore joined forces once more, but it would be a mistake to suggest that the result was seamless agreement. Cooperation had occurred in the past regardless of disagreement, a characteristic of the relationship which persisted as the Americans and the British focused their collaboration on the Atlantic Alliance and Europe in 1966.

This article begins by briefly considering events from de Gaulle's return to the presidency of France in 1958 up to his letter to Johnson in 1966. It then analyses American and British reactions to de Gaulle's challenge within the context of their policies towards Atlantic–European relations. Thereafter, it explores the points of contact between the Americans and the British in 1966 as they sought to use the occasion provided by France to solve festering problems in the alliance. Here, it concentrates on diplomacy within NATO; the nuclear sharing question; Britain's relationship with the EEC; the issue of UK–US–West German relations and the problem of foreign exchange costs for American and British troops stationed in the Federal Republic. Finally, it offers conclusions on the outcome of the NATO crisis and its significance for British foreign policy and Anglo-American relations.

De Gaulle's Challenge

The first move in the contest over NATO which reached its height in 1966 came on 17 September 1958 when de Gaulle attempted to break what he perceived as the Anglo-Saxon monopoly of the Atlantic Alliance by suggesting a tripartite directorate for the defence of the free world.[14] De Gaulle's central criticism of NATO, a criticism shared by many in France, was that it was 'hegemony disguised as Atlantic solidarity'.[15] For the French president, whose view of the world was deeply informed by his sense of history, this was unendurable; in de Gaulle's mind, America was Europe's 'daughter', not its master.[16] It has been suggested that de Gaulle's intent in proposing tripartitism was to provoke a negative reaction from the Americans and the British which in turn would provide him with a pretext for French withdrawal from integration in NATO. De Gaulle's admission that 'I asked for the moon' certainly suggests that he anticipated the rejection that came from the Eisenhower administration and the Macmillan government.[17] Even if he did not, permanent tripartite consultation failed to evolve and thus de Gaulle began slow divorce proceedings from NATO. The March 1959 withdrawal of France's Mediterranean fleet from the Supreme Allied Command and the June 1959 refusal to allow nuclear weaponry for US tactical aircraft to be stored on French soil were portents of greater actions in the 1960s. The first of these was de Gaulle's 14 January 1963 press conference. If the September 1958 memorandum had been when, in de Gaulle's words, he 'hoisted [his] colours', then the 1963 vetoes of Britain's first application for EEC membership and of John F. Kennedy's Grand Design for an Atlantic Community was when he sent a shot across the bows of the Anglo-Saxons.[18]

In this act, imbued with the grandeur that de Gaulle was seeking to recapture for France, it is possible to see how the issues of Europe and the Atlantic Alliance were entwined for the French president. De Gaulle's denial of Britain's application was motivated by a desire to protect French supremacy within the EEC, the institution which the French hoped would provide for their national renewal. Through his dismissal of Kennedy's Grand Design, de Gaulle sought to defend Europe's independence from American subjugation as the leadership of Europe was to be France's destiny once renewal was achieved.[19] These policies and their aims conflicted with the twin objectives of Atlantic partnership and European integration supported by the Americans, the British and the other members of the Atlantic Alliance.

The result was diplomatic dissension. President Kennedy's anger was exposed at a meeting of the National Security Council's Executive Committee 11 days after the double vetoes, when he said that the United States 'should look now at the possibility that de Gaulle had concluded that he would make a deal with the Russians, break up NATO and push the U.S. out of Europe'.[20] However, immediate retribution was not the product of this analysis, nor of that of the British government. Instead, while the fundamental foreign policies of Atlantic and European cooperation would be sustained, the tactics to deal with the main threat to them, President de Gaulle, evolved. There would be no retaliation; France would be treated as an ally, direct confrontation with de Gaulle would be avoided and the day for a new relationship with France under a new leader would be awaited.[21] In the meantime, Atlantic and European cooperation would be fostered where possible. Progress in European integration was prevented by de Gaulle's continued resistance to enlargement and the disruption caused by the French boycott of EEC institutions from June 1965. The consequent empty chair crisis, eventually resolved in January 1966, only strengthened the impression that de Gaulle was set on superimposing his formula for European relations upon the contrary vision of the Americans, the British and other European states.[22] Disarray in the EEC made it all the more necessary to strengthen NATO, and with it the Atlantic Alliance, as a way of countering de Gaulle. And it is here that the peak of his policy towards NATO is significant. If 1963 was a shot across the bows then 1966 was a broadside.

On 21 February 1966, de Gaulle announced in another one of his magisterial press conferences that France would seek to restore its sovereignty 'as regards soil, sky, sea and forces, and any foreign element that would be in France, will in the future be under French command alone'.[23] After a period of international uncertainty about when de Gaulle would act on this promise, the French president wrote his 7 March 1966 letter to Lyndon Johnson confirming, in essence, '[t]he indisputable fact ... that France wants everything French out of NATO and everything NATO – especially everything American – out of France'.[24] As one historian has put it, '[e]mbracing a worldview different from that animating American leaders, de Gaulle pursued policies that would have seemed challenging if practiced by an avowed enemy, but appeared intolerable in an ally'.[25] Given their particular experiences of de Gaulle, many in London and Washington may have wished that the embittered members of *Algérie français* had succeeded in their assassination attempt of August 1962, but rather quickly they became glad that de Gaulle's Citroën had been so bullet-resistant. In 1966, they sought to turn the challenge he posed to their advantage.

American and British Reactions to de Gaulle's Challenge

In *The Vantage Point*, Johnson recalled his meeting with de Gaulle at Kennedy's funeral and remarked that, in the face of the French president's constant criticism of his administration, 'I made a rule for myself and for the U.S. government simply to ignore President de Gaulle's attacks on our policies and the doubts he had raised about the value of our pledges'.[26] Ignoring de Gaulle publicly masked the Johnson administration's great preoccupation with the potential threat he posed to US conceptions of the Atlantic Alliance and US–European relations. In July 1965, in the light of the EEC's empty chair crisis, this was the focus of a report for the administration on 'Europe and United States Policy' produced by the State Department, the Department of Defense and the White House National Security staff. The report summarized US attitudes towards de Gaulle:

> The stature and capacity of General de Gaulle cannot be allowed to blind us to the divisive nature of his views and their baneful effects on our own interests. De Gaulle is not indulging in petty tactics but is dedicated to the national ambitions of a single state. The ultimate purpose of the present French Government is to establish the position of France as clearly superior to its European neighbours and freed of all commitments that limit France's ability to maneuver as De Gaulle wishes.[27]

The letter of 7 March only heightened such an appreciation of French intent, especially among those heavyweight State Department figures long schooled in relations with de Gaulle such as Dean Acheson, George Ball and 'Chip' Bohlen. These and other so-called 'theologians' or Europeanists were firm proponents of the Atlantic Alliance and European unity as the two pillars of the West and instinctively opposed de Gaulle's contrary beliefs.[28] Their attempt to urge Johnson to reply in kind to the French president has been well documented, most recently by Schwartz, who goes further than most in praising Johnson's measured and clear-headed response to de Gaulle.[29]

From 2 March, the State Department instructed its missions in NATO capitals that the US government's response to de Gaulle's 'messianic belief in the glory and importance of France' and his forthcoming actions against NATO was 'to lean over backward to be polite and friendly to France, to President de Gaulle personally, and to all French government officials ... we should continue quietly and firmly on our course, ignoring Gaullist objections ... while awaiting the day when a more friendly and cooperative government comes to power in France'.[30] Why this peaceable diplomacy given the hostile public reaction in the United States and the fact that Johnson had eventually to assume, in the words of the US ambassador to London, David Bruce, the character of 'a human thundercloud' to quash Acheson's arguments for a tough reproach against France?[31] Apart from the fact that Johnson personally had other issues of priority, first and foremost Vietnam, and thus sought to minimize the impact of de Gaulle's mischief, there was another determinant of American policy. It was the answer to a question put to Johnson by White House national security adviser, Robert W. Komer: 'Do we want a full-blown war with De Gaulle?'[32] The answer was no. Here, the administration had learnt '[t]he lessons of recent history' which suggested that it 'stop, look and listen before flinging down the gauntlet to De Gaulle'. A full-blown war with the French president would confirm his accusations of American dominance and lack of regard for its allies amongst whom there were significant concerns about the effects of continued US military actions in Southeast Asia. An acrimonious US–French dispute over NATO would also give rise to Soviet efforts to weaken the Atlantic Alliance. In February 1965, the US ambassador to

Moscow, Foy Kohler, had warned that 'the Soviets have entered on the current dialogue [with France] in order to exploit to the hilt de Gaulle's disruptive value; the opportunities must seem particularly tempting to the Soviets in view of the coincidence between Soviet and French views on certain key East–West issues – i.e., MLF [the Multilateral Force], Southeast Asia, the weakening of NATO, and the U.S. role in Europe'.[33] In March 1966, Kohler advised Washington that should de Gaulle proceed along envisaged lines on NATO, the Soviets 'will consider they are hitting [an] even larger vein of pay dirt than they initially expected and will attempt [to] derive every possible advantage therefrom'.[34] Their broad objective, according to Kohler, remained a European settlement which would include 'a general movement in Western Europe away from purely NATO arrangements'. In this connection, de Gaulle's planned visit to Moscow in June 1966 caused unease; the Americans and the British may have taken solace in their estimations that de Gaulle had less influence in Moscow than he believed, but the potential for public instability was patent.[35]

This analysis made a non-disruptive solution to the crisis in NATO vital to US interests. Consequently, and perhaps in an attempt to speak to Johnson's innate character, Komer reminded the president that '[c]ounsels of caution need not be those of cowardice' and in the case of de Gaulle, caution could bring returns. Isolating de Gaulle would be matched with turning the threat he posed into an opportunity by meeting his criticisms of the Alliance within the Alliance, and out-waiting him. This tactical response was also underscored by the belief of Francis Bator, another of Johnson's national security advisers on Atlantic affairs, that de Gaulle had 'no real cards. If we play our hand skillfully, we can manage to carry on with NATO without him. In many ways, he is like a lightweight jujitsu artist. All his leverage comes from our over exertion'.[36] To deprive de Gaulle of his leverage, there were two elements in the US government's 'prime objective' as a State Department circular telegram put in on 17 March 1966. The first was 'to maintain the unity of [France's] fourteen [NATO allies] in the face of the French assault'.[37] This would be done at the detailed level of the issues relating to French withdrawal from the integrated military command structure and the evacuation of NATO men and materials from France. It would also be done on a grand scale by addressing those questions which had dogged the Atlantic Alliance for some time alongside the issues raised by de Gaulle. Hence, the niggling but major question of nuclear sharing within the Alliance would need to be addressed. So would the reorganization of NATO to foster greater partnership amongst its members and to transform its role from one founded purely on defence to one which promoted East–West bridge-building.[38]

The second element of the government's 'prime objective' was 'to try to limit spillover [from the NATO crisis] to the European Communities'.[39] The Americans had been concerned since de Gaulle boycotted the EEC during the empty chair crisis that his EEC and NATO policies were linked. In October 1965, for example, the US ambassador to the Communities, John Tuthill, advised Francis Bator in the White House that '[t]he present crisis in the EEC can only be viewed in the context of de Gaulle's related objectives – in NATO and elsewhere. It [was] a manufactured crisis created for basically political purposes ... [de Gaulle's] continuing efforts to reshape Europe to his concepts'.[40] Immediately prior to the Luxembourg Compromise which resolved the EEC crisis, US Secretary of State Dean Rusk warned that the French 'have consistently seen [an] interrelationship between [the] EEC crisis and NATO. They probably calculate that [a] resolution of [the] EEC crisis on their terms, thereby weakening [the] German position in particular, would facilitate moves to restructure [the] alliance system more to their liking'.[41] Initially, therefore, the US government directed its posts in Europe to ensure that the NATO crisis was kept separate from the EEC for fear that its cohesion, and the related success of the Kennedy Round trade negotiations (eagerly awaited by the US government) might be jeopardized.[42] Isolation of the EEC from de Gaulle's activities in NATO, together with the continued internal strength of the EEC, especially in terms of the Federal Republic of Germany's insulation from French interference, were keen American concerns. It was in the pursuit of these objectives that the Americans would seek the cooperation of the British, who would prove to be willing partners given their particular experience of de Gaulle.

The speed with which the government of Harold Wilson prepared itself to intervene at the moment de Gaulle made his intentions public is indicative of its determination to meet his challenge. On 4 March, three days before de Gaulle's letter arrived in the White House, the Foreign Office sent a series of telegrams for the prime minister's approval. These held instructions for Britain's ambassador to NATO, Sir Evelyn Shuckburgh, to lead France's 14 NATO partners towards a British-inspired declaration in response to French actions and to begin the process of marginalizing de Gaulle.[43] In this diplomacy, implemented with President Johnson's assent on 8 March, we see the two principal elements of Britain's policy in reaction to de Gaulle in 1966: to isolate him and to show leadership in doing so.[44] By spring 1966, the motive for such a policy had become well established in the British government. As a Foreign Office report to Cabinet on de Gaulle's foreign policy over the next two years had put it in January: 'de Gaulle's policies are likely to be harmful to British interests'.[45] A succession of studies within Whitehall emanating from the Foreign Office, the Cabinet's Defence and Oversea Policy Committee (DOPC) and the Joint Intelligence Committee depicted de Gaulle as an opponent of Britain.[46] From February 1965 the Foreign Office began to link de Gaulle's policies with Britain's growing irrelevance to its Atlantic partners.[47] The barrier he presented to Britain's entry to the EEC and his exploitation of the leadership crisis in NATO and the problems surrounding the question of nuclear sharing highlighted Britain's weakness. Given the primacy of the Anglo-American relationship to Britain's economic and foreign policies and the longevity of the accepted view that Britain's relations with the United States were substantially dependent on the political role it could play in Europe, de Gaulle had the potential to undermine Britain's status and security: 'unless we can soon evolve a more effective relationship with Western Europe and the United States within the Atlantic framework Britain will cease to be a world power'. In March 1965, the foreign secretary, Michael Stewart, encouraged the prime minister to act: '[g]iven the headway which General de Gaulle is making, this is the time to resume our rightful place on the European stage and set about helping Europe towards a better relationship with the United States within the Atlantic Alliance'.[48]

Between March 1965 and March 1966 no such time presented itself to pursue a policy of boosting British influence in the Atlantic Alliance and Europe. In the two most significant areas, NATO nuclear sharing and Britain's policy towards European economic integration, there was no room for manoeuvre. Britain's Atlantic Nuclear Force (ANF) proposal did not gain the necessary support either in Washington or Western Europe and the Federal Republic's interest in a hardware solution to the long-standing multilateral force (MLF) impasse led the British to stall on this issue, rather than show leadership.[49] A combination of the Wilson government's own caution towards an active policy on EEC membership and the Community's internal problems during the empty chair crisis ensured that Britain also remained more or less motionless in this area of European relations.[50] Nevertheless, the necessity of making advances in NATO and towards the EEC was heightened throughout 1965 by successive studies pointing towards the ill effects on Britain's position in the Atlantic Alliance and Europe if nothing was done.[51]

This was the context of Britain's response to de Gaulle's actions towards NATO in March 1966. Very quickly, the government concluded that whilst the NATO crisis was a threat in that it could lead to political and military instability within the Alliance and thus the West, it was also an opportunity. As long as de Gaulle did not gain widespread support amongst NATO partners – and British diplomacy would be designed to prevent that by isolating France and giving the fourteen cohesion – the crisis could produce dividends for the Alliance and for Britain. The British did not dispute the fundamental criticism ranged by de Gaulle against NATO, in fact they agreed that the institution had become outdated and unprepared to meet the changed international atmosphere of the 1960s. They simply disliked his methods. Hence, they saw positive outcomes in a productive NATO response to de Gaulle which would see the organization streamlined and more economical, with an agreement on nuclear sharing and a new focus on détente as well as defence. They also saw occasion to counter de Gaulle and turn his actions to their own ends. Britain remained impotent in one area of European relations – economic integration – but it remained potentially dynamic in another: the Atlantic Alliance. By directing his policy towards NATO, the French president had freed the British to do what they could not do over the EEC, namely act and show leadership, and they could do so with American support and cooperation. As ministers agreed in the DOPC on 6 April 1966, here was 'an important opportunity to enhance our standing'.[52] Britain could strengthen its position in Europe by holding the fourteen together in NATO's response to de Gaulle. It could cooperate closely with the Federal Republic and the United States, thus responding to American wishes but also attempting to ensure that no special relationship between the West Germans and the Americans developed at Britain's expense. And it could make the most of what it saw as the inevitability of distance between de Gaulle and the Five within the EEC as a result of France's actions in NATO by presenting a stronger British influence in

European affairs, thus hoping to prepare the ground for a more active policy towards the Community in the future.[53] It was for these reasons that in his communications in March 1966 with President Johnson about France and NATO – or 'The General's rogue elephant tactics' as he put it – that Wilson emphasized that he saw them 'both as a threat and as an opportunity'.[54] His view was well received in Washington where a similar conclusion was reached. The French president had produced the ingredients for Anglo-American cooperation: a common enemy and shared interests. Both the Americans and the British had long-stored enthusiasm to deal with de Gaulle and both sought to protect NATO, the Atlantic Alliance and Europe from his influence. They had awaited a moment to act and it came in the post to Washington on 7 March 1966.

Turning a Crisis into an Opportunity

In the period running up to de Gaulle's letter to Johnson, the British sought to engage the Americans in bilateral preparations for a French attempt to destabilize NATO. The idea had first been raised in October 1965 by Rusk in a meeting between high level UK and US delegations amid mounting speculation that de Gaulle would make his move in spring 1966.[55] It featured again on 27 January when Rusk, Robert McNamara (the US secretary of defence) and George Ball (the US under secretary of state) met with Stewart and Denis Healey (the UK minister of defence).[56] Healey noted that the meeting's discussion about NATO force levels and the foreign exchange costs came at a time 'when we expect a de Gaulle initiative' and suggested Anglo-American contingency planning ahead of it. There was no manifest enthusiasm for this idea on the American side. Although Ball did not oppose 'invisible discussions' he added that 'the US did not want to create the appearance of an Anglo-American cabal in NATO'. The 'extreme sensitivity of the French and their disposition to use for their own ends any appearance of a US/UK initiative' made it 'unwise to push bilateral planning now, at least until French actions seem clearer'. Although this polite deflection had the air of the long-held American aversion to awarding the UK special status in US–European relations – a position argued firmly by Ball and other State Department Europeanists – the concerns raised were genuine and although pre-emptive contingency planning was off the agenda, collaboration once France had acted was not.[57] Thus when de Gaulle's intentions became clear in March, the Johnson administration did not immediately single out the British for special cooperation, keeping in close touch with the Dutch, the Italians and the West Germans as well.[58] As the crisis developed, however, the British assumed primary status, optimising where they could their reputation as an ally in Washington and in Western European capitals. Their ability to do so was assisted by their centrality to the main issues stemming from de Gaulle's letter, of which four were most significant: the immediate diplomatic response to France within NATO; the vexed issue of nuclear sharing within the Alliance; a possible British initiative on European economic integration; and the trilateral talks of 1966–67 between the Federal Republic, the UK and the US on the problematic issue of foreign exchange costs of troops stationed in West Germany. Anglo-American collaboration developed in each of these areas and, as will now be seen, produced both accord and discord in relations.

The Americans and the British reached the same conclusion about the immediate response to de Gaulle's actions. After a rapid exchange with the State Department, the Foreign Office instructed the British delegation to NATO that 'our line should be sorrow rather than anger, confidence rather than panic'.[59] Restraint was the key to repelling the French president's threat to the Alliance. Francis Bator's proposition that de Gaulle – 'the lightweight jujitsu artist' – would be disarmed by a lack of leverage had become accepted tactics.[60] The neutralization of de Gaulle was to be matched with the organization of France's fourteen NATO partners into a cohesive unit in defence of the organization. Achievement of this, according to a preliminary joint US Department of State/Department of Defense meeting on 6 March, would not be via 'a special US–UK approach to the problem'.[61] However, it served American interests well to encourage the British to take control in coordinating the official NATO reaction to France. On the one hand, the US government wished to ensure that the NATO crisis was not synonymous with a struggle between France and the United States and, on the other, the Americans hoped to enhance British involvement in Western European affairs, especially Anglo-German cooperation. Thus on 8 March, Rusk informed the US ambassador to NATO, Harlan Cleveland, of the government's 'strong desire to let the British take the lead' on a declaration they had drafted to be issued by the fourteen.[62] Following a NATO meeting on 18 March, the British declaration was accepted with the full support of the US government as the established position of the fourteen in response to a French *aide-memoire* which had elaborated upon de Gaulle's letter to Johnson.[63] The declaration enacted the strategy agreed between the Americans and the British by not singling out the French or referring to the crisis they had created but simply accentuating the achievements, purpose and strength of NATO and the Alliance:

> We are convinced that this organization is essential and will continue. No system of bilateral arrangements can be a substitute. The North Atlantic Treaty and the organization are not merely instruments of the common defence. They meet a common political need and reflect the readiness and determination of the member countries of the North Atlantic community to consult and act together wherever possible in the safeguard of their freedom and security and in the furtherance of international peace, progress and prosperity.

The British had been well prepared to lead the fourteen towards an agreed position. They initiated the process by readying the declaration in draft by 6 March 1966, the day before de Gaulle's move, and by tabling proposals for fourteen-Power machinery within NATO to oversee internal analysis and adjustment in light of France's withdrawal. Once the crisis had broken, they entered into close, regular discussions with the Johnson administration to ensure its agreement to Britain's tactical proposals and their swift implementation.[64] And, in pursuit of a leading role among the fourteen – a position they were encouraged to adopt by European governments – the British were ready to take direction from the Americans and adapt their proposals.[65] As NATO progressed towards a solution to the French challenge, the British continued to take a principal part in the diplomacy of the fourteen, and the US government, always eager to see Britain assume a greater role in Europe, approved. It should be noted that in doing so, the Americans had not abdicated their own dominant position in the Alliance. Indeed the US ambassador to London, David Bruce, raised early doubts about 'creat[ing] the impression that [the British] are representing us as intermediaries' and suggested that the administration 'give ample evidence to our allies through private diplomatic efforts that we are actively engaged and deeply concerned'.[66] The president himself agreed with the suggestion that the US had to signal its support for the Alliance and thus he did so privately and in public.[67] Yet Bruce's concerns did not alter the administration's policy of giving Britain the opportunity to adopt a central position in NATO's response to de Gaulle. While Johnson was happy to intervene on one level, his administration did not want to embroil itself in a bilateral dispute with the French and was thus satisfied by Britain's activities among the fourteen, which even Bruce admitted were 'militant and energetic'.[68] However, whilst this diplomatic aspect of the crisis proved positive for Anglo-American relations, the primary substantive issue – nuclear sharing – was more complicated.

De Gaulle's initiation of the March 1966 NATO crisis threatened to halt the very meagre progress that had been made by that time on the question of nuclear sharing. The issue had been a source of division and discontent in the Alliance since the Supreme Allied Commander, Europe, Lauris Norstad, had first suggested a multilateral atomic authority within NATO in 1960, an idea reformulated as the MLF by the Kennedy administration in 1961. Designed by the Americans chiefly to give the Federal Republic a legitimate role in the nuclear defence of the West but enmeshed with not-so-hidden agendas of depriving the British and the French of nuclear independence, the MLF became a symbol of impasse. It was not a welcome inheritance for the Johnson administration and remained one of the targets of de Gaulle's criticisms of the Alliance.[69] It was also an Anglo-American problem, as for many in Washington the British had never been helpful allies on this issue, resisting the principle of reduced status inherent in the nuclear sharing debate. Much of the rationale for the British proposal for the ANF in December 1964 had been to placate the Americans and the West Germans whilst retaining British nuclear independence.[70] Few, however, were mollified by the ANF and for much of 1965 the nuclear sharing question languished uncomfortably amid internal American vacillation between a hardware solution (multilateral control of nuclear weaponry) and a software solution (machinery for multilateral nuclear consultation), continued West German interest in a hardware solution, British intransigence and French criticism. And all the while, it prevented progress on a non-proliferation treaty with the Soviets, who were firm opponents of West German access to nuclear hardware.

There were always concerns that de Gaulle might seek to exploit the nuclear sharing deadlock to draw the Federal Republic out of the Alliance into a bilateral military agreement with France, and these were worsened in spring 1966 given the French president's self-appointed leadership of Europe in the pursuit of détente and his upcoming visit to Moscow in June. It also became an issue for urgent consideration for the US president because contemporaneously the State Department 'MLF-ites' pushed for a hardware solution and because the British government made its opposition to such a solution entirely clear.[71] Unless these contrary positions could be reconciled, the NATO crisis might confirm the rectitude of de Gaulle's accusations about the organization's inadequacies. From March to May 1966 the Johnson administration attempted to reconcile its differences on nuclear sharing with the White House National Security staff and the Department of Defense in favour of a software solution through Robert McNamara's Special Committee discussions in NATO and the Department of State's adherence to an MLF-type outcome.[72] Both sides recognized that '[t]he British have been playing a game' over nuclear affairs, as Rusk put it, but there was sympathy for British views about the impracticalities of a hardware solution and the probable costs in complicating or preventing a non-proliferation treaty with the Soviets.[73] Such views were sincerely held in London. From the outset of the NATO crisis the British government emphasized the opportunities it afforded for reform of the organization and moves towards détente with the East. A non-hardware solution to nuclear sharing was a key element in the achievement of both of those objectives. The nationalistic aspects of Britain's opposition remained pertinent, however, especially for Wilson, and early on the British government established that it would not be impelled by the NATO crisis into accepting a result which included hardware.[74]

Wilson made this point firmly in his 29 March letter to Johnson on the NATO crisis. The prime minister criticized de Gaulle's '19th century nationalism, his anti-American motivation and above all his bull in a china shop tactics', but suggested that 'it would be wrong to conclude from all this that all the General's thoughts are wrong-headed' and agreed that NATO needed to reform and progress.[75] It was against this background that Wilson outlined the British agenda points for this process, including NATO machinery issues, but principally regarding relations with the Federal Republic. Two things were paramount: first, the need to reach a fair agreement on foreign exchange costs for British troops stationed in West Germany, and second, that the only acceptable solution to nuclear sharing was consultative rather than hardware based. These were potentially hazardous issues for Anglo-German relations and for the Federal Republic's position within the Alliance. Should the West Germans be dissatisfied by the result of either or both issues, would they look more favourably on relations with de Gaulle's France? The crunch point was the May meeting between Wilson and Erhard and, ahead of it, Johnson reminded Wilson of the stakes in the game. With the outcome of the NATO crisis uncertain, the president warned that French actions and French political pressure on West Germany produced

> a grave danger that the Germans will over time feel that they have been cast adrift. A growing sense of uncertainty and insecurity on their part could lead to a fragmentation of European and Atlantic relations which would be tragic for all of us. On our part, we cannot risk the danger of a rudderless Germany in the heart of Europe.[76]

The answer was for the US, the UK and the Federal Republic to work together. It was also for the British not to press a non-hardware solution on Erhard.

The British were reserved in their meetings with Erhard in London on 23 May which were good natured and constructive. The nuclear issue was only discussed at foreign minister level by Gerhard Schröder and Stewart and they agreed that the first priority was to deal with the NATO crisis.[77] Johnson's fears about the effect of de Gaulle's actions on the Federal Republic proved unfounded at this stage: West German allegiance to NATO had been strengthened rather than weakened. Wilson was thus able to report that the meetings represented 'a high-point in our relations with Germany' and that he and Erhard had agreed that nuclear sharing was a 'secondary issue'.[78] Seemingly, the prime minister had responded to the president's requests over nuclear sharing. Actually, this was a low cost win for Wilson. He knew that the US government was undecided on this question, that Erhard did not want to push it, and that he had a more pressing concern: to secure greater offset payments from the Federal Republic. Johnson was satisfied with British diplomacy – 'it was really good and strengthening to know that your meeting with Erhard went well' he wrote. The issues remained unresolved but political relations were propitious for continued cohesion in response to de Gaulle. The British were in line, if not necessarily on message. In this regard, Johnson also noted in his letter to Wilson that he 'was very pleased to hear that you and Erhard had a good talk about your EEC situation'.[79]

The US government's 'prime objective' in responding to the NATO crisis had two elements, the first being to hold the fourteen NATO powers together and the second 'to try to limit spillover to the European Communities'.[80] Early concerns that 'de Gaulle's NATO policy [would] adversely affect French EEC objectives' and that the internal stability of the Community might be jeopardized by the NATO crisis were soon dispelled by agreement on all sides that spillover was in no one's interests.[81] Except the Americans, that is. In July 1966, the White House succumbed to pressure from the State Department to push the British towards a more active policy on European economic integration. The US government hoped to use the diplomatic/political atmosphere created by the NATO crisis – discord between the Five and France within the Community and a desire for enhanced British involvement in Europe – to increase the chances of a British initiative on the EEC which was in turn expected to galvanize the fourteen in NATO. The only problem was that the British themselves were not ready to make such a move.

The Europeanists within the State Department, led by Ball, had long promoted the benefits of British membership of the EEC. This was for the good of Europe, as Ball explained in his *Discipline of Power*, '[i]ntimate British participation in the affairs of the Continent could provide the necessary element of strength and solidarity; it could moderate . . . latent instabilities and provide a permanent balance, securing democracy in Europe'.[82] Providing 'a permanent balance' was a euphemism for the development of a European Community in which Britain could act as a proxy for American interests. The NATO crisis sharpened these arguments and the State Department Europeanists sought to capitalize on the final flowering of de Gaulle's divisive policies to press Johnson on Britain and the EEC. On 19 May 1966 in a memorandum for the president, the Policy Planning Council argued that the NATO crisis of 1966 was as crucial as that of 1947–50 and that '[t]he United States and the United Kingdom hold the keys to the present situation'. Whilst admitting that de Gaulle's hostility remained a barrier to British accession to the EEC, the Policy Planning Council nevertheless recommended that Johnson urge Wilson to declare explicitly Britain's determination to join the Community.[83] This would convince the EEC member states other than France and even many in France, 'that Britain identifies herself with Europe and the European desire to adjust the imbalance in the Alliance'. Amid the European policy debates in spring/summer 1966 in Washington, the State Department continued to press this line. Ahead of Wilson's visit in July, it presented a substantial report to the White House on a 'Presidential Push on Wilson toward U.K. Membership in the Common Market' which concluded that

> [i]n the long run the political gains from U.K. membership in the European Communities are in our interest. As in the short run, an unequivocal British willingness to join the Communities would significantly strengthen the Five in dealing with Gaullist France and indirectly help the fourteen hold NATO together, whatever the French do.[84]

Ball sent a further paper to Johnson three days later in which he added another consideration by playing on the administration's concern about current British economic weaknesses. 'We, on our part, should face the fact that it is basically unhealthy to encourage the United Kingdom to continue as America's poor relation, living beyond her means by periodic American bailouts', Ball contended. 'We must, in other words, redefine the so-called "special relationship" in terms consistent with the longer-range interests of both our nations'. British membership of the EEC would solve this problem and Ball told Johnson that Britain by itself was 'unlikely to adjust to the facts of a new world environment quickly enough to check a developing imbalance in European affairs that can be dangerous for all of us. She needs the stimulus of American leadership'.[85] By the morning of 29 July, the day of Wilson's visit to Washington, Johnson had received Ball's memorandum, a follow-up from Rusk and finally a note from his national security adviser, Walt Rostow, which added further weight to the State Department's recommendations.[86]

The records of the meetings between Johnson and Wilson reveal how the prime minister made it clear that whilst 'the time would come when the UK could enter the Common Market under satisfactory terms ... that time was not yet'.[87] In the after-gloom of recent meetings with French Prime Minister Georges Pompidou and Foreign Minister Maurice Couve de Murville where French opposition to British entry was made unquestionably clear, Wilson simply could not see an advance on British EEC policy as practical politics.[88] Foreign policy makers in Washington had not been alone in their consideration of the relationship between the NATO crisis and the potential development of Britain's relations with the Community. From the outbreak of the crisis, the issue was a live consideration in London also. On 5 April, for example, the

DOPC concluded that through their action against NATO, the French had created a gap which other countries in Europe would wish to be filled by a stronger British influence and that this meant Britain should determine its policy towards EEC membership.[89] On 6 April, in his influential report on Britain's future relations with Europe, Sir Eric Roll made the same point and re-stated well-established arguments about EEC membership strengthening Britain's foreign policy and the Anglo-American relationship.[90] It would not be until October 1966 and the Chequers meeting that the Wilson government decided upon its probe to determine whether British membership of the Community was feasible. Until then, there was agreement in London that in the face of French intransigence over the EEC, and the necessity of leading NATO through its crisis, Britain's priority in Europe ought to be the Atlantic Alliance rather than the European Community.[91] The probe decision marked the kind of advance in British policy towards the EEC that the Johnson administration had hoped for in July 1966 and it was received positively.[92] By October, however, the Americans were concerned that far from adding to the cohesion of Western Europe, the British were in fact risking its division over another area of Atlantic–European relations, namely the question of foreign exchange costs for troops stationed in the Federal Republic.

On 15 November 1966, Johnson received a letter from Wilson in which the prime minister elaborated on his government's new approach towards the EEC. Although Wilson stated that he did not think de Gaulle's view had 'changed one iota' with regard to Britain and the Community, he nevertheless noted that the world had altered around him and that if British policy succeeded, 'it [would] greatly strengthen not only Britain and Europe, but the West as a whole'.[93] The Americans shared these hopes, but in his reply to Wilson, Johnson spent one brief paragraph commending him on Britain's new EEC initiative – 'I am immensely heartened by your courageous announcement about joining the EEC' – and then eight on the necessity of success in the trilateral talks between the US, the UK and the Federal Republic.[94] The principal aim of these discussions (which began in October 1966 and would end in April 1967) was to solve the problem of US and UK demands for increased offset payments to cover the foreign exchange costs for American and British troops stationed in West Germany. The potential for disaster in these negotiations was dangerously high, involving as they did a US government under Congressional pressure to reduce forces in Europe, a British government compelled by economic weakness into an often intransigent negotiating position and West German governments reluctant to increase offset payments.[95] These risks were even higher in relation to the NATO crisis as Johnson's national security adviser Francis Bator warned: reductions in forces in Europe for financial reasons 'would confirm the impression that NATO is falling apart, that de Gaulle is right in saying that the British and Americans are unreliable and care more for their pocketbooks than for the safety of Europe'.[96]

The offset question and the trilateral talks were the main areas of concern in relation to the greater NATO crisis for Johnson because they affected not only foreign relations but also US domestic politics. Senator Mike Mansfield's Congressional Resolution of

31 August 1966, which called for substantial reductions in American forces in Europe, served only to intensify the pressure, especially as the Johnson administration had spent much of the summer of 1966 stalling the British government from cutting its forces in the Federal Republic.[97] Force levels were an aspect of the NATO crisis which the British quite literally could not afford to neglect given the costs to the balance of payments of the British Army of the Rhine (BAOR). From his first substantive communication to Johnson on the NATO crisis in March 1966 Wilson had raised the importance of the offset issue and the July 1966 sterling crisis only worsened the situation for the UK economy.[98] In August, the British raised proposals to cut the BAOR and within days the US government proposed the high level trilateral talks.[99] To underline the significance he attached to the safe passage of these talks, Johnson wrote to Wilson on 26 August stating that:

> I have become increasingly concerned during the past few weeks about the dangers of an unravelling in NATO which could easily get out of hand. With your urgent need to save foreign exchange in Germany, Erhard's budgetary and political difficulties …, my problems with our German offset and with the Congress on troops in Europe – all against the background of the General's antics – there is danger of serious damage to the security arrangements we have worked so hard to construct during the last 20 years.[100]

The political stakes were only increased when on 7 October 1966 Johnson made a wide ranging speech on US policy towards the Atlantic Alliance, Europe and détente in which he reaffirmed his country's allegiance to NATO and to ensuring the organization's continued vitality.[101] Yet still the British could not negotiate on anything other than the strictest principles – full offset payments from the Federal Republic – even though this troubled the trilateral talks. Ultimately, to enable the talks to reach a successful conclusion, the US government had to place $35million of additional defence orders with Britain, an amount equivalent to the costs of maintaining British forces in Germany at their current levels for six months.[102] In effect, Johnson bought Britain's continued involvement in the trilateral talks and in so doing prevented the offset question from creating the unravelling of NATO that he feared. In this area of the NATO crisis at least, the British had not been able to show much leadership but instead were part of the problems of the Alliance as well the solutions.

By the December 1966 NATO ministerial meeting a working situation between France and its NATO allies had been achieved and the crisis was over. The French had withdrawn from the military activities of the organization but remained members of the Alliance, despite refusing to guarantee their cooperation with NATO in a time of war. In response, the fourteen united in defence of the organization and no other state followed the French example. As an internal US government account of the crisis explained: 'While the long-range effects of the events of 1966 will depend on other developments and will not be discernable for some time, it was clear by the beginning of 1967 that the Alliance had weathered its confrontation with France in reasonably good order.'[103]

The experience of adjusting to France's withdrawal bred a new atmosphere of cooperation among the fourteen which was embodied by the intervention at the December meeting of the Belgian foreign minister, Pierre Harmel. It was his proposals for a far-reaching review of the role of the Alliance which eventually ensured one year later that de Gaulle's challenge to its purpose and vitality had been finally defeated.[104] NATO had adopted the appearance and machinery of an organization dedicated to détente as well as defence. Furthermore, in April 1967 the trilateral talks were concluded positively with a consensus between the US, the UK and the Federal Republic. And partly because of this, in December 1967 the nuclear sharing question was solved on the basis of a software solution in the form of the NATO Nuclear Planning Group, which in turn opened the way for the negotiation of the Non-Proliferation Treaty of July 1968. The only negative outcome for the objectives pursued by the Americans and the British from spring 1966 was that Britain's second EEC application was finally blocked by de Gaulle in November/December 1967. Yet even in its failure, there were, in the view of the US government, elements of success in that the British had shown themselves to be committed to the EEC and a non-Gaullist Europe.

Conclusion

As Frédéric Bozo has written, 'the 1966 rupture [in NATO] was above all a political rupture' rather than an operational one and it was ultimately played out as such.[105] In many respects, the resolution of the NATO crisis satisfied both sides. De Gaulle achieved the redefinition of France–NATO relations that he desired and the Americans and the British achieved the isolation of France that they aimed for, given the nature of the man in the Elysée Palace. Parallel with this achievement, NATO was strengthened rather than weakened by the experience, and the fourteen became a functioning unit.[106] Ultimately, however, it was de Gaulle who was the loser. Freedom from the subordination of integration, as he put it, did not enable him to lead Western Europe towards détente with the East. His June 1966 visit to Moscow revealed that he had less in common with the Soviets than the Americans and British feared he might, and that the Soviets were not as desirous of détente as he had hoped.[107] Yet despite de Gaulle's failure to win the leadership of Europe, it is widely accepted that he did the Atlantic Alliance a service by forcing the United States government to lead NATO reform and thus to redefine the organization's approach to détente.[108] And, as Schwartz has argued, Lyndon Johnson achieved a greater level of success as president in the development of this area of his foreign policy than in many others.[109]

Two further points need to be added to these judgements. The first relates to the fact that the Americans were not the only NATO member state to push the reform of the organization, even if they were the most powerful. As Wenger has suggested, the settlement of the NATO crisis was dependent on multilateral activity and European allies played major roles alongside the Americans.[110] Amongst them, it was the British who played a consistently significant part by prompting the Americans on reform, organizing the response of the fourteen from March 1966 and assisting NATO towards the solutions to its problems during 1966–67.[111] The second point is that Britain's influence and effect was partly the product of its own motivation but also partly a consequence of Anglo-American cooperation. Whilst always avoiding the impression of a US–UK 'cabal' (as Ball had put it in January 1966), the Americans encouraged and benefited from the activities of the British within NATO and in improving European relations in response to de Gaulle. The Johnson administration and the Wilson government were at one on the general principles of Atlantic partnership and European integration and opposed de Gaulle's attempt to grasp authority in the West to promote French influence in East–West relations. As a result, they worked together to protect NATO and to transform it into an institution which employed a multilateral approach to détente with the East.

In this regard, the interplay between the NATO crisis, the political atmosphere in Europe and Britain's relationship with the EEC is notable. Paradoxically, the NATO crisis had a positive impact on the general political atmosphere in Europe in 1966–67. The necessity of holding the Alliance together in the face of de Gaulle's actions acted as a check against harsh positions and a stimulus for conciliation in NATO. For example, although the progress on the nuclear sharing issue ultimately had much to do with the domestic political situation in the Federal Republic, it is clear that the British and the West German governments sought to ensure that their disagreements did not endanger the Alliance. Similarly, the development of Britain's second application for EEC membership was assisted by events in NATO. The crisis gave the Wilson government an opportunity to improve Britain's position with its Western European partners as a backdrop to its application for membership. The interaction that the Johnson administration had hoped would evolve did so with Britain playing a leading role in NATO and showing its ambition to join the EEC, thus helping to isolate de Gaulle and defuse the threat he posed to both institutions. Such a view is given a further dimension by the suggestion that the French eventually sought a constructive conclusion to the Harmel Exercise in NATO for fear of segregating themselves 'at a time when France's veto over Britain's entry in the EEC caused problems with London, Bonn and other capitals'.[112]

Britain's diplomacy during the NATO crisis of 1966 and thereafter through the institution's revitalization in 1967 was greatly influenced by the Wilson government's paradigmatic policy decisions to withdraw from East of Suez and adopt a European-based international position. Europe, as Saki Dockrill has suggested in her study of the political and military aspects of this recalibration of British priorities, 'played a major role in determining Britain's decision . . . Throughout all the defence debates in Whitehall between 1964 and 1968, Europe was always regarded as Britain's first priority'.[113] Analysis of Britain's reactions to the NATO crisis and the relationship between its policy towards the Atlantic Alliance and the European Community – indeed policy towards Europe as a whole – shows how the British government had begun the process of transition towards a European-centred position in the world which would come to characterize its foreign policy outlook in the 1970s and beyond.

In the face of the NATO crisis the British aimed to enhance their position in the Alliance in and of itself given the significance of the organization for Britain's international stature and its foreign and defence policies. The Wilson government also hoped that its diplomacy in NATO would bring dividends for a consequent movement towards the European Community and a general reorientation of Britain's foreign policy towards Europe and away from the world. This was always the policy of a Foreign Office set on riding 'the Atlantic and European horses in double-harness'.[114] It was also the policy of a prime minister who was committed to the Atlantic Alliance but who was not necessarily wedded, at the outset, to a second EEC application.[115] Wilson was also committed to the Anglo-American relationship, not least for Britain's economic survival. The improvement of relations between London and Washington was thus a key objective and the crisis in NATO provided occasion to work towards it. In dealing with the French challenge to the Alliance, the Johnson administration found an eager, welcome and useful partner in the Wilson government. It also approved of Britain's resurgent interest in gaining EEC membership from autumn 1966 and into 1967. It did not approve, however, of the contemporaneous British decisions to withdraw from East of Suez. Johnson's letter to Wilson of 11 January 1968 epitomizes the widespread disappointment in Washington:

> I cannot conceal from you my deep dismay upon learning this profoundly discouraging news. If these steps are taken, they will be tantamount to British withdrawal from world affairs, with all that means for the future safety and health of the free world. The structure of peace-keeping will be shaken to its foundations. Our own capability and political will could be gravely weakened if we have to man the ramparts all alone.[116]

Before long, anger within the Johnson administration over the timing of Britain's withdrawals subsided as the British began to fulfil the new European role many Americans hoped they would. In turn, the British hoped that this role would revitalize their foreign policy and economy and enable them to retain their status as the first ally of the United States. The opportunity to begin that process came with the NATO crisis in March 1966. Ironically, the British had General de Gaulle to thank for it.

Acknowledgements

The author would like to express his gratitude to the Arts and Humanities Research Council and the British Academy for their generosity in supporting the research upon which this article is based.

Notes

[1] Lyndon Baines Johnson Library, Austin, Texas (hereafter LBJL), Papers of Francis M. Bator (hereafter Bator Papers), Subject File, Box 27, Bator to President, 7 March 1966.

[2] *Foreign Relations of the United States, 1964–1968*, Vol. XIII (hereafter *FRUS* 1964–1968 XIII), doc.137.

[3] Kaplan, *NATO and the United States*, 96. On the foundation of NATO see Smith, *The Origins of NATO*; Wiggershaus and Foerster, *The Western Security Community*.

[4] National Archives and Records Administration, College Park, Maryland (hereafter NARA), RG59 DoS CF DEF4NATO Box 1587, Memorandum of Conversation (Erhard and McCloy), 17 April 1966.

[5] On de Gaulle, France and the NATO crisis, see Bozo, *Two Strategies*. Also see Soutou, "La France et la défense européenne," 21–46. On de Gaulle's foreign policy from 1958 in general, see Vaïsse, *La Grandeur*.

[6] On NATO in general see Kaplan, *NATO and the United States*, and Trachtenberg, *A Constructed Peace*, 95–402. On the 1966 NATO crisis and the 1967 Harmel Report see Bozo, "Détente versus Alliance"; Haftendorn, *NATO and the Nuclear Revolution*; Haftendorn, "The Adaptation of the NATO Alliance," 285–322; Wenger, "Crisis and Opportunity."

[7] This is the central argument of Schwartz, *Lyndon Johnson and Europe*, 5; also 229–30. Also see Schwartz, "Lyndon Johnson and Europe," 37–60. Schwartz has gone further than most in his praise of Johnson, see Brands, *The Wages of Globalism*, 86–121; Costigliola, "Lyndon B. Johnson," 173–210; Gardner, "Lyndon Johnson and De Gaulle," 257–78; and Kaplan, "The U.S. and NATO," 119–49.

[8] Wenger, "Crisis and Opportunity," 71 and 22–74 in general.

[9] Financial contributions to the NATO budget were one indicator of authority among allies. In 1965, the United States contributed 32 per cent, the French 13.96 per cent, the West Germans 13.92 per cent and the British 13.48 per cent. The next closest were the Italians (5.92 per cent) and the Canadians (5.87 per cent). Source: NARA RG59 DoS Lot72D139 Policy Planning Council Box 313, REU-73, 10.11.1966.

[10] *The Economist*, 1097, 19 March 1966.

[11] Schwartz, *Johnson and Europe*, 92–186 and Wenger, "Crisis and Opportunity," 22–74 have considered Anglo-American–West German relations in their accounts. Earlier studies pay little attention to the role played by the British; for example see Brands, *Wages of Globalism*, 86–121; Costigliola, "Lyndon B. Johnson," 173–210; Gardner, "Lyndon Johnson and de Gaulle," 257–78. To date, John Young is alone in the attention he pays to the Anglo-American relationship as an element of the Labour government's policies towards the Atlantic Alliance and détente. See Young, *The Labour Governments*, 115–41. Also see Hughes, "Harold Wilson" and White, *Britain, Détente and Changing East–West Relations*, 108–35. On the early 1960s see for example Ashton, *Kennedy, Macmillan and the Cold War*; Murray, *Kennedy, Macmillan and Nuclear Weapons* and Pagedas, *Anglo-American Strategic Relations*.

[12] For the most comprehensive study of the East of Suez decision see Dockrill, *Britain's Retreat*. On the Johnson/Wilson era see, for example, Bartlett, *"The Special Relationship"*, 107–26; Colman, *A "Special Relationship"?*; Dumbrell, *A Special Relationship*, 62–73; and Ellis, "Lyndon Johnson, Harold Wilson and the Vietnam War," 180–204.

[13] Young, *The Labour Governments*, 20–21. Also see in general Colman, *A "Special Relationship"?* and Dockrill, *Britain's Retreat*.

[14] *FRUS 1958–1960* Vol. VII, doc. 45.

[15] Jackson, *De Gaulle*, 98.

[16] John F. Kennedy Library, Boston, MA (hereafter JFKL), Papers of President Kennedy, National Security Files (hereafter Kennedy Papers, NSF), Countries, Box 72, David Klein to McGeorge Bundy, 18 April 1963.

[17] Jackson, *De Gaulle*, 97.

[18] de Gaulle, *Memoirs of Hope*, 202.

[19] Of the many studies of de Gaulle's foreign policy see, for example, Bozo, *Two Strategies*, 1–142; Giauque, *Grand Designs*, 126–223; Soutou, "La France et la défense européenne," 21–46; and, in general, Vaïsse, *La grandeur.*

[20] JFKL, Kennedy Papers, NSF, Meetings and Memoranda, Box 316, Bromley Smith, Summary Record of NSC Executive Committee Meeting No.38 (Part II), 25 January 1963.

[21] See, for example, The National Archives (Public Record Office), Kew, London (hereafter TNA), FO371/178922/W6/3, Butler to Harlech 187, 9 June 1964; TNA, FO371/177867/RF1022/115, FO to Certain of Her Majesty's Representatives 412, 3 July 1964; JFKL, NSF, Trips and Conferences, Box 239, President's European Trip June 1963, Background Paper, European and Atlantic Situation, 16 June 1963; JFKL, Kennedy Papers, NSF, Countries, Box72A, Bohlen, "Continuing Elements of de Gaulle's Foreign Policy," 7 August 1963.

[22] On the origins of the empty chair crisis, Ludlow, "Challenging French Leadership," 240–44. On its conclusion, Ludlow, "The Eclipse of the Extremes," 247–64.

[23] de Gaulle, *Discours et messages,* 19 ("Au total, il s'agit de rétablir une situation normale de souveraineté, dans laquelle ce qui est français, en fait de sol, de ciel, de mer et de forces, et tout élément étranger qui se trouverait en France, ne relèveront plus que seules autorités françaises").

[24] LBJL, Bator Papers, Subject File, Box 27, Acheson, Memorandum for the Secretary, 10 May 1966.

[25] Brands, *Wages of Globalism*, 87–8.

[26] Johnson, *The Vantage Point*, 24.

[27] NARA RG59 Lot File 67D516 Box 2, Ferguson to Rusk, 9 July 1965.

[28] See in general Winand, *Eisenhower, Kennedy.* Also, Ball, *The Past*, 208–18.

[29] Schwartz, *Johnson and Europe*, 92–139.

[30] *FRUS* 1964–1968 XIII, doc. 135.

[31] *FRUS* 1964–1968 XIII, doc. 166.

[32] *FRUS* 1964-1968 XIII, doc. 143.

[33] LBJL, Papers of Lyndon Baines Johnson, National Security Files (hereafter Johnson Papers, NSF), Country File, France, Box 177, Extract of February 6, 1965 cable from Ambassador Kohler, 9 February 1965. Also, LBJL, Johnson Papers, NSF, Country File, France, Box 171, CIA memorandum, "France's Dialogue with the Soviet Union," 21 May 1965.

[34] LBJL, Johnson Papers, NSF, Country File, France, Box 177, Bromley Smith to Johnson, 10 March 1966.

[35] For example, TNA, CAB129/124, C(66)16, 28 January 1966 and *FRUS* 1964–1968 XIII, doc. 172.

[36] LBJL, Bator Papers, Subject File, Box 27, Bator, Memorandum for the President, 8 March 1966.

[37] *FRUS 1964–1968* XIII, doc. 144.

[38] *FRUS* 1964–1968 XIII, doc. 157 and doc. 159.

[39] *FRUS* 1964–1968 XIII, doc. 144.

[40] LBJL, Bator Papers, Subject File, Box 26, Tuthill "The EEC and the NATO Crises," 19 October 1965.

[41] *FRUS* 1964–1968 XIII, doc. 127.

[42] *FRUS* 1964–1968 XIII, doc. 140. On the US government and the Kennedy Round, Zeiler, *American Trade and Power.*

[43] TNA, PREM13/1042, Wright to Wilson, 4 March 1966 and TNA, FO to UKDNATO 330–333, 6 March 1966.

[44] TNA, PREM13/1042, FO to UKDNATO 351, 8 March 1966.

[45] TNA, CAB129/124, C(66)16, 28 January 1966.

[46] TNA, CAB129/124, C(66)16, 28 Janury 1966; TNA, CAB148/27, OPD(66)44, 1 April 1966; TNA, CAB158/49, JIC(63)65, 18 July 1963; TNA, CAB158/61, JIC(66)13(Final), 17 June 1966.

[47] TNA, FO371/184288/6/12, Palliser, "British Foreign Policy," 9 February 1965.
[48] TNA, FO371/184288/6/13, Stewart to Wilson, PM/65/38, 3 March 1965.
[49] On Britain and the MLF, Schrafstetter and Twigge, "Trick or Truth?"; Young, "Killing the MLF?," 295–324.
[50] Parr, "Harold Wilson, Whitehall and British Policy," 81–104.
[51] TNA, CAB129/121, C(65)73, 11 May 1965; TNA, FO371/184289/6/28, Barnes, "Atlantic Alliance," 21 May 1965 and TNA, CAB129/122, C(65)119, 5 August 1965.
[52] TNA, CAB148/25, OPD(66)18th meeting, 6 April 1966.
[53] TNA, CAB148/27, OPD(66)44, 1 April 1966; TNA, PREM13/1043, Trend to Prime Minister, 4 April 1966; TNA, CAB148/25, OPD(66)18th meeting, 6 April 1966.
[54] TNA, PREM13/1043, Wilson to Johnson, 21 March 1966; LBJL, Johnson Papers, NSF, Head of State Correspondence, Box 9, Wilson to Johnson, 29 March 1966.
[55] LBJL, Johnson Papers, NSF, Country File, Europe and USSR, United Kingdom, Box 209, Memorandum of Conversation "France and NATO," 11 October 1965.
[56] *FRUS* 1964–1968 XIII, doc.126, Memorandum of Conversation, 27 January 1966.
[57] For an early example of the aversion see *FRUS, 1950*, Volume III, Paper Prepared in the Department of State, 19 April 1950: "In dealing with other Europeans, however, we cannot overtly treat the British differently and they should recognize that the special US–UK relation underlies the US–Europe relations, and that we do not consider close UK-European relations as prejudicial to the US–UK relations."
[58] LBJL, Bator Papers, Subject File, Box 27, Bator Memorandum for the President, 3 March 1966; TNA, PREM13/1042, Dean to FO 762 and 763, 3 March 1966.
[59] TNA, PREM13/1042, FO to UKDNATO 355, 8 March 1966. For FO-State Department exchanges, TNA, PREM13/1042, Dean to FO 780 and 781, 4 March 1966.
[60] LBJL, Bator Papers, Subject File, Box 27, Bator, Memorandum for the President, 8 March 1966.
[61] LBJL, Bator Papers, Subject File, Box 27, Memorandum of Conversation, 6 March 1966; TNA, PREM13/1042, Dean to FO 807, 7 March 1966. Also see LBJL, Bator Papers, Subject File, Box 27, Bruce to Rusk, 8 March 1966.
[62] *FRUS*, 1964–1968, XIII, doc. 139. See also TNA, PREM13/1042, FO to UKDNATO 351, 8 March 1966; TNA, PREM13/1043, Dean to FO 944, 19 March 1966.
[63] For the declaration, TNA, PREM13/1043, London Press Service "France–NATO," 18 March 1966. For the French *aide-memoire*, Ambassade de France, *French Foreign Policy*, 25–6.
[64] TNA, PREM13/1042, Wright to Prime Minister, 4 March 1966; TNA, PREM13/1042, FO to UKDNATO 330-333, 6 March 1966; TNA, PREM12/1042, Dean to FO 807, 7 March 1966.
[65] For European encouragement, see TNA, PREM13/1042, Shuckburgh to FO 91, 2 March 1966 and 97, 3 March 1966; also TNA, PREM13/1044, FO to Brussels 478, 20 April 1966 and TNA, CAB148/25, OPD(66)22nd Meeting, 27 April 1966. On British adaptation, TNA, PREM13/1043, FO to Washington 2951, 17 March 1966.
[66] LBJL, Bator Papers, Subject File, Box 27, Bruce to Rusk 4232, 8 March 1966.
[67] LBJL, Bator Papers, Subject File, Box 27, Bruce to Rusk 4232, 8 March 1966, undated handwritten note by Johnson. On Johnson's interventions, *FRUS* 1964–1968 XIII, doc. 148 and doc. 167; also see his speech to the Foreign Services Institute on 23 March: LBJL, Bator Papers, Subject File, Box 26, Text of the Remarks of the President, 23 March 1966.
[68] LBJL, Johnson Papers, NSF, Country File, France, Box 177, Bruce to Rusk 4437, 21 March 1966.
[69] On the US and the MLF, Winand, *Eisenhower, Kennedy and the United States of Europe*, 203–43; Costigliola, "Lyndon B Johnson," 173–210, 180–92, and Schwartz, *Johnson and Europe*, 39–46. On France and the MLF, Bozo, *Two Strategies*, 110–21.
[70] Young, "Killing the MLF?," 295–324.

[71] LBJL, Bator Papers, Subject File, Box 28, Bator, Memorandum for the President, 4 March 1966; LBJL, Johnson Papers, NSF, Head of State Correspondence File, Box 9, Wilson to Johnson, 29 March 1966.

[72] LBJL, Bator Papers, Subject File, Box 28, Bator to Johnson, enclosing Rusk Memorandum for the President, 12 April 1966; *FRUS* 1964–1968, XIII, doc. 159.

[73] LBJL, Bator Papers, Subject File, Box 28, Rusk Memorandum for the President, 12 April 1966.

[74] TNA, PREM13/1043, FO to Washington 3096, 22 March 1966.

[75] LBJL, Johnson Papers, NSF, Head of State Correspondence, Box 9, Wilson to Johnson, 29 March 1966.

[76] *FRUS* 1964–1968, XIII, doc. 168.

[77] TNA, PREM13/1044, Record of Conversation (Erhard/Wilson), 23 May 1966 and GCV(66)1st, 24 May 1966.

[78] LBJL, Johnson Papers, NSF, Head of State Correspondence, Box 9, Wilson to Johnson, 26 May 1966.

[79] LBJL, Johnson Papers, NSF, Head of State Correspondence, Box 9, Johnson to Wilson, 28 May 1966.

[80] *FRUS* 1964–1968 XIII, doc. 144.

[81] *FRUS* 1964–1968 XIII, doc. 152 and doc. 170. For the attitudes of EEC member states, see Ludlow, *The European Community*, chapter 4.

[82] Ball, *The Discipline of Power*, 88–9.

[83] NARA RG59 DoS Lot72D139 Policy Planning Council, Box 313, Memorandum for the President, 19 May 1966.

[84] *FRUS* 1964–1968, XIII, doc. 188; also NARA RG59 DoS CF EEC 3 Meetings, Sessions, Box 3292, Solomon and Stoessel through S/S to The Under Secretary, 19 July 1966.

[85] LBJL, Johnson Papers, NSF, Country File, Europe and USSR, United Kingdom, Box 209, Ball, Memorandum for the President, 22 July 1966.

[86] LBJL, Bator Papers, Subject File, Box 24, Rusk Memorandum for the President, 24 July 1966 and LBJL, Johnson Papers, NSF, Country File, Europe and USSR, United Kingdom, Box 209, Rostow to President, 29 July 1966.

[87] NARA RG59 DoS CF EEC 8 Structures & Functions, Box 3292, Memorandum of Conversation "UK and the Common Market," 29 July 1966 and LBJL, Johnson Papers, NSF, Country File, Europe and USSR, United Kingdom, Box 216, Bator through Moyers "Memorandum for the President," 29 July 1966. Also, TNA, FO371/190526/W2/52G, Killick to FO 2173, 27 July 1966.

[88] TNA, PREM13/1509, Record of a Conversation, 8 July 1966. On British policy towards the EEC, see Parr, "Wilson, Whitehall and British Policy," 105–225.

[89] TNA, CAB148/25, OPD(66)16th meeting, 5 April 1966.

[90] TNA, PREM13/905, Roll minute, 6 April 1966.

[91] TNA, PREM13/1044, Palliser to Wilson, 24 May 1966 and TNA, CAB148/69 OPD(O)(66)22Revise and OPD(O)(66)24Revise, both 29 July 1966. For the Chequers decision, TNA, CAB134/2705, E(66)3rd meeting, 22 October 1966.

[92] TNA, PREM13/909, Dean to FO 217, 29 October 1966; LBJL, Bator Papers, Subject File, Box 25, Leddy and Solomon to Secretary, 11 November 1966.

[93] LBJL, Johnson Papers, NSF, Head of State Correspondence, Box 10, Rostow to Johnson, 15 November 1966 enclosing Wilson to Johnson, 11 November 1966.

[94] *FRUS* 1964–1968, XIII, doc. 216.

[95] Schwartz, *Johnson and Europe*, 143–59. Ludwig Erhard was replaced by Kurt-Georg Kiesinger as chancellor in December 1966.

[96] LBJL, Bator Papers, Chronological File, Box 3, Bator, Memorandum for the President, 11 August 1966.

[97] Schwartz, *Johnson and Europe*, 121–2.
[98] LBJL, Johnson Papers, NSF, Head of State Correspondence, Box 9, Wilson to Johnson, 29 March 1966; TNA, CAB148/25, OPD(66)25th meeting, 18 May 1966 and OPD(66)36th meeting, 11 August 1966. Also, Zimmerman, "The Sour Fruits of Victory."
[99] LBJL, Johnson Papers, NSF, Country File, Europe and USSR, United Kingdom, Box 210, Memorandum of Conversation "British Proposals to Cut the Cost of the BAOR," 16 August 1966 and LBJL, Bator Papers, Subject File, Box 28, Memorandum of Conversation "British Plans to Reduce Military Spending in Germany," 25 August 1966.
[100] *FRUS* 1964–1968 XIII, doc. 198.
[101] *Public Papers*, 1125–30. Also, TNA, FO371/190534/W6/5 Dean to FO 189 and 190, 12 October 1966.
[102] *FRUS* 1964–1968, XIII, doc. 216; TNA, CAB128/41, CC(66)61st conclusions, 29 November 1966.
[103] NARA RG59 DoS Lot File 68D55 Entry 5302 NATO-General Box 12, "The France-NATO Confrontation of 1966 – A History," undated.
[104] Bozo, "Détente versus Alliance," 343–60; Haftendorn, "The Adaptation of NATO," 285–322; Wenger, "Crisis and Opportunity," 22–74.
[105] Bozo, *Two Strategies*, 167.
[106] Haftendorn, *NATO and the Nuclear Revolution*, 406–7.
[107] Bozo, "Détente versus Alliance," 359.
[108] Ibid., 348–9. Others make a similar point, for example Brands, *Wages of Globalism*, 88.
[109] This is the general argument of Schwartz, *Johnson and Europe*.
[110] Wenger, "Crisis and Opportunity," 72–3.
[111] For a similar view, White, *Britain, Détente and Changing East–West Relations*, 128–9.
[112] Bozo, "Détente versus Alliance," 355.
[113] Dockrill, *Britain's Retreat*, 218–19.
[114] TNA FCO41/2, Barnes to Hood, 7 December 1966.
[115] On Wilson and Britain's EEC policy see Parr, "Wilson, Whitehall and British Policy," 105–225, and Young, *The Labour Governments*, 142–65.
[116] LBJL, Johnson Papers, NSF, Head of State Correspondence, Box 10, Rostow to Johnson enclosing letter to Wilson, 11 January 1968.

References

Foreign Relations of the United States, 1950. Vol. III. Washington: United States Government Printing Office, 1977.

Foreign Relations of the United States, 1958–1960. Vol. VII. Washington: United States Government Printing Office, 1993.

Foreign Relations of the United States, 1964–1968. Vol. XIII. Washington: United States Government Printing Office, 1995.

Public Papers of the Presidents of the United States, Lyndon B. Johnson, 1966. Washington: United States Government Printing Office, 1967.

Ambassade de France, New York. *French Foreign Policy: Official Statements, Speeches and Communiqués 1966*. New York: Service de Presse et d'Information, 1967.

Ashton, Nigel J. *Kennedy, Macmillan and the Cold War: The Irony of Interdependence*. Basingstoke: Palgrave Macmillan, 2002.

Ball, George W. *The Discipline of Power: Essentials of a Modern World Structure*. Boston: Little, Brown & Co, 1968.

———.*The Past Has Another Pattern: Memoirs*. New York: W.W. Norton & Co, 1982.

Bartlett, C. J. *"The Special Relationship": A Political History of Anglo-American Relations since 1945.* London: Longman, 1992.

Bozo, Frédéric. "Détente versus Alliance: France, the United States and the Politics of the Harmel Report (1964–1968)". *Contemporary European History* 7, no. 3 (1998): 343–360.

———.*Two Strategies for Europe: De Gaulle, the United States and the Atlantic Alliance.* Oxford: Rowman & Littlefield, 2001.

Brands, H. W. *The Wages of Globalism: Lyndon Johnson and the Limits of American Power.* Oxford: Oxford University Press, 1995.

Colman, Jonathan. *A "Special Relationship"? Harold Wilson, Lyndon B. Johnson and Anglo-American Relations "At the Summit," 1964–68.* Manchester: Manchester University Press, 2004.

Costigliola, Frank. "Lyndon B. Johnson, Germany and 'the End of the Cold War'". In *Lyndon Johnson Confronts the World: American Foreign Policy, 1963–1968*, edited by Warren I. Cohen, and Nancy Bernkopf Tucker. Cambridge: Cambridge University Press, 1994.

Dockrill, Saki. *Britain's Retreat from East of Suez: The Choice between Europe and the World?* Basingstoke: Palgrave Macmillan, 2002.

Dumbrell, John. *A Special Relationship: Anglo-American Relations in the Cold War and After.* Basingstoke: Palgrave Macmillan, 2001.

Ellis, Sylvia. "Lyndon Johnson, Harold Wilson and the Vietnam War: A *Not* So Special Relationship?" In *Twentieth-Century Anglo-American Relations*, edited by Jonathan Hollowell. Basingstoke: Palgrave, 2001.

Gardner, Lloyd. "Lyndon Johnson and De Gaulle". In *De Gaulle and the United States: A Centennial Reappraisal*, edited by RobertO. Paxton, and Nicholas Wahl. Oxford: Berg, 1994.

de Gaulle, Charles. *Discours et messages. Janvier 1966–Avril 1969.* Paris: Plon, 1970.

———.*Memoirs of Hope: Renewal and Endeavour.* New York: Simon and Schuster, 1971.

Giauque, Jeffrey Glen. *Grand Designs and Visions of Unity: The Atlantic Powers and the Reorganization of Western Europe, 1955–1963.* Chapel Hill: University of North Carolina Press, 2002.

Haftendorn, Helga. *NATO and the Nuclear Revolution: A Crisis of Credibility.* Oxford: Clarendon Press, 1996.

———. "The Adaptation of the NATO Alliance to a Period of Détente: The 1967 Harmel Report". In *Crises and Compromises: The European Project 1963–1969*, edited by Wilfried Loth Baden Baden: Nomos, 2001.

Hughes, Geraint. "Harold Wilson, the USSR and British Foreign and Defence Policy in the Context of East-West Détente" Ph.D. diss, King's College London 2002.

Jackson, Julian. *De Gaulle.* London: Haus Publishing Limited, 2003.

Johnson, Lyndon Baines. *The Vantage Point. Perspectives of the Presidency 1963–1969.* New York: Holt, Rinehart & Winston, 1971.

Kaplan, Lawrence S. *NATO and the United States: The Enduring Alliance.* Boston: Twayne, 1988.

———. "The U.S. and NATO in the Johnson Years". In *The Johnson Years, Volume 3: LBJ at Home and Abroad*, edited by Robert A. Divine Lawrence: University Press of Kansas, 1994.

Ludlow, N. Piers. "Challenging French Leadership in Europe: Germany, Italy, The Netherlands and the Outbreak of the Empty Chair Crisis of 1965–1966." *Contemporary European History* 8, no. 2 (1999): 231–248.

———. "The Eclipse of the Extremes. Demythologising the Luxembourg Compromise." In *Crises and Compromises: The European Project 1963–1969*, edited by Wilfried Loth. Baden Baden: Nomos, 2001.

———.*The European Community and the Crises of the 1960s: Negotiating the Gaullist Challenge.* London: Routledge, 2006.

Murray, Donette. *Kennedy, Macmillan and Nuclear Weapons.* Basingstoke: Macmillan, 1999.

Pagedas, Constantine A. *Anglo-American Strategic Relations and the French Problem 1960–1963: A Troubled Partnership.* London: Cass, 2000.

Parr, Helen. "Harold Wilson, Whitehall and British Policy Towards the European Community, 1964–1967", Ph.D. diss. Queen Mary, University of London 2002.

Schrafstetter, Susanna, and Stephen Twigge. "Trick or Truth? The British ANF Proposal, West Germany and US Non-proliferation Policy." *Diplomacy and Statecraft* 11, no. 2 (July 2000): 161–184.

Schwartz, Thomas Alan. "Lyndon Johnson and Europe: Alliance Politics, Political Economy and 'Growing Out of the Cold War." In *The Foreign Policies of Lyndon Johnson: Beyond Vietnam*, edited by H. W. Brands. College Station: Texas A&M University Press, 1999.

———.*Lyndon Johnson and Europe: In the Shadow of Vietnam*. Cambridge, MA: Harvard University Press, 2003.

Smith, Joseph, ed. *The Origins of NATO*. Exeter: University of Exeter Press, 1990.

Soutou, Georges-Henri. "La France et la défense européenne du traité de L'Elysée au retrait de l'OTAN (1963–1966)." In *Crises and Compromises: The European Project 1963–1969*, edited by Wilfried Loth. Baden Baden: Nomos, 2001.

Trachtenberg, Marc. *A Constructed Peace: The Making of the European Settlement 1945–1963*. Princeton, NJ: Princeton University Press, 1999.

Vaïsse, Maurice. *La Grandeur: Politique étrangère du général de Gaulle 1958–1969*. Paris: Fayard, 1997.

Wenger, Andreas. "Crisis and Opportunity: NATO's Transformation and the Multilateralization of Détente, 1966–1968". *Journal of Cold War Studies* 6, no. 1 (2004): 22–74.

White, Brian. *Britain, Détente and Changing East–West Relations*. London: Routledge, 1992.

Wiggershaus, Norbert, and Roland G. Foerster, eds. *The Western Security Community: Common Problems and Conflicting National Interests during the Foundation Phase of the North Atlantic Alliance*. Oxford: Berg, 1993.

Winand, Pascaline. *Eisenhower, Kennedy and the United States of Europe*. Basingstoke: Macmillan, 1993.

Young, John W. "Killing the MLF? The Wilson Government and Nuclear Sharing in Europe 1964–66." In *Power and Stability: British Foreign Policy 1865–1965*, edited by Eric Goldstein, and B. J. C. McKercher. London: Cass, 2003.

———.*The Labour Governments 1964–70 Volume 2: International Policy*. Manchester: Manchester University Press, 2003.

Zeiler, Thomas. *American Trade and Power in the 1960s*. New York: Columbia University Press, 1992.

Zimmerman, Hubert. "The Sour Fruits of Victory: Sterling and Security in Anglo-German Relations during the 1950s and 1960s." *Contemporary European History* 9, no. 2 (2000): 225–243.

Propaganda on wheels: The NATO travelling exhibitions in the 1950s and 1960s

Linda Risso

Despite the restrictive terms of reference and a limited operative budget, in the 1950s and 1960s the NATO Information Service launched a series of successful propaganda campaigns. One of the most effective initiatives was the organisation of a series of travelling exhibitions which toured the NATO countries. By travelling through the countryside and small centres, the travelling exhibitions reached areas that had not yet been touched by any other propaganda campaign. This paper investigates the choice of themes and objects put on display, the organisational problems and the question of assessing the impact of such initiatives in an historical context.

The NATO Information Service (NATIS), later the Office of Information and Press and today the Division of Public Diplomacy, was launched in 1950. During the Cold War, NATIS's main task was to promote the North Atlantic Treaty Organisation among the publics of the member countries. In order to do so, it coordinated the activities carried out by the national governments in this field and it produced its own information material, such as posters, pamphlets, lectures and seminar series, films, newsreels and travelling exhibitions. NATIS therefore had the double task of fostering its own propaganda policy and of acting as a forum for the exchange of information among the national governments which carried out pro-NATO and more generally anti-communist propaganda in their own countries. Despite a few important exceptions, like the work of Valérie Aubourg on the NATO movies and of David Ellwood on the early attempts of NATO to launch its own propaganda machinery, little work on the history and activities of NATIS has been carried out, and the NATO archives remain largely under-researched.[1]

As demonstrated in this article, support for NATO within the Organisation's members was not consistent. In the 1950s, in many countries large sectors of public opinion were very critical about the need to divert huge portions of their national budgets away from reconstruction and towards defence and rearmament. In the climate of international détente that developed in the early 1970s, many questioned the need for a military alliance of this kind. Thus, NATO and the national governments put in place a series of information programmes to explain the need for NATO and for a common defence policy. Support for NATO was particularly weak in those countries – like Italy and France – with large and well organised communist parties, which opposed any plan for a common defence strategy at the European level and denounced NATO as yet another sign that the USA was planning to use its economic influence on Western Europe to strengthen its political grip on the Old Continent. It has already been demonstrated that the Soviet Union and the national communist parties were very effective in exploiting the fears of a new conflict among the western public and were able to take advantage of the numerous calls for neutrality and peaceful coexistence coming from various sectors of society, including the churches and the moderate political forces.[2]

The North Atlantic Treaty was signed on 4 April 1949 and all of the members completed the ratification process by the end of August 1949. In both France and Italy, however, ratification was dogged by fierce opposition. Maurice Thorez, leader of the French communists, focused his campaign on the delicate question of NATO compatibility with the Franco-Soviet Pact of December 1944. Thorez accused the government of selling off national sovereignty and independence to the US in an excess of anti-communist hysteria.[3] Likewise, in his parliamentary speeches, Palmiro Togliatti, leader of the Italian communists, asked for a policy of full neutrality and opposed the creation of NATO bases on Italian soil on the grounds that it undermined national sovereignty.[4] Communist opposition was in line with Moscow's criticism of any form of Western European rearmament and was centred on the need to respect the existing agreements between the Western Allies and the Soviet Union.[5] It is also worth noting that both French and Italian right-wing parties also opposed the treaty, claiming that it made European security dependent on the US, and the defence of national independence soon became synonymous with resistance to 'colonisation' by the Americans.[6] A similar point was also made by moderate political forces.[7]

The large and well organised anti-NATO front notwithstanding, the supporters outnumbered the opponents and the treaty was eventually ratified by all its members and NATO came into force in August 1949. Yet widespread mistrust and ignorance about the nature and scope of the Alliance persisted. Still in 1955, several years after the beginning of NATO's information activities, NATO officials had to admit that: 'Despite five years of effort on the part of the Information Division, national information services and voluntary bodies, knowledge about the structure and aims of NATO remains abysmally small, even in intelligent circles.'[8] Because only a very small portion of the public knew what NATO was and few had an interest in the its structure and aims, it was feared that communist propaganda could find fertile terrain in this widespread ignorance and undermine the defence effort of the whole organisation. For example, because it was true – as the communists claimed at the time – that the rearmament effort and the creation of NATO was absorbing a substantial amount of national resources that could have been otherwise employed to pay for reconstruction and modernisation projects, it was imperative to explain the reasons behind such politically sensitive decisions in order to maintain the public's support.[9] NATO officials and the national governments therefore initiated an intense campaign to spread the 'fundamental concepts constructive peace, solidarity and understanding between nations which are part of the aims of the NATO countries' using 'To the fullest the motion pictures, photographs, books, pamphlets, speeches and all other means at our command to disseminate and to repeat, over and over again, the truth about our purpose and our efforts to protect our liberties and our freedom, and to preserve peace'.[10]

The foundation of the NATO Information Service

The foundation of the Cominform in September 1947 allowed the Soviet Union, its satellite states and the national communist parties to carry out a coherent and energetic propaganda campaign against the West. The campaign benefited from the coordination of all information activities, generous funding and the possibility of exploiting the divisions between western powers as well as widespread sentiments of pacifism and neutralism. As demonstrated by scholars like Peter Kenez, the Soviet Union developed effective methods of mass mobilisation immediately after the 1917 revolution and devised numerous successful methods and techniques to mobilise large sectors of the public both at home and abroad through a series of agitprop operations, most of which were refined and re-launched after 1945.[11] In the eyes of British and American information agencies – which, after the Second World War, were the best organised and funded – it was imperative to promote a coherent response to the Soviets' anti-western propaganda. They believed that the establishment of permanent channels of consultation and the exchange of information about what each government was doing in the propaganda field were important first steps to produce an effective answer to the communist attacks.[12] At the beginning of August 1950, the NATO Council of Deputies approved the creation of the Information Service. Its tasks were to 'promote and coordinate public information in furtherance of the objectives of the Treaty while leaving the responsibility of national programmes to each country'.[13] The NATO Information Service became operative in November 1950 under the chairmanship of the Canadian Theodore F.M. Newton. At first, the new agency consisted of senior information staff contributed by member governments and operated through the existing national information agencies; later members of the

International Staff took up a more permanent role and ensured continuity. Initially, NATIS had no operative budget and limited means. With the exception of the United States, national delegations remained sceptical about NATIS and feared it might disrupt their national propaganda efforts.[14] Mutual distrust among the national delegations made the exchange of information all the more difficult and jeopardised the new agency's early activities.[15]

A step towards tighter collaboration was taken in 1953, when the council approved the merging of the existing Information Policy Working Group (IPWG) and the Social and Cultural Working Group (SCWG) to create the new Committee on Information and Cultural Relations (CICR) to assist NATIS. The relationship between these two bodies was very close. NATIS developed and coordinated multinational and national information programmes and was responsible to the NATO Secretary General for their implementation. During the Cold War, its activities were closely monitored by the CICR, which reviewed NATIS's output and practices and sent its recommendations for approval to the North Atlantic Council.[16] While NATIS consisted of members of the international staff, the CICR included representatives from each national delegation. The preparation, organisation and follow-up of the CICR's meetings were undertaken by the international staff acting in a secretarial and support capacity in addition to their day-to-day roles as programme managers and implementers. The representatives of the national delegations presented reports on the activities of their national governments in the field of pro-NATO and anti-communist propaganda and worked towards tighter coordination among the member states to ensure more coherent and consistent action. The CICR also reviewed the action, procedures and output of NATIS and made recommendations for improvements and cost-effectiveness.

In 1953, NATIS was also allocated financial support from the Civil Budget. Though modest, this contribution allowed NATIS to launch its first information programmes, which started with the creation of the NATO logo, still in use today. In 1953, NATIS launched its own press relations, editorial and special media sections.[17] NATIS's first step was to address the so-called 'opinion moulders' like journalists, trade union leaders, parliamentarians and academics. It organised official visits to NATO headquarters and tours of the NATO countries. Later, it expanded the range of its activities to include seminar series, lectures and summer schools, publication of specialised pamphlets, newsreels and films and travelling exhibitions. Following the recommendations of the CICR, NATIS addressed an increasingly wide spectrum of audiences and produced more targeted information material; great attention was paid to the younger generations, particularly university students.[18]

The travelling exhibitions, 1951–59

In an attempt to involve as large a portion of society as possible, NATIS and the national governments collaborated in the preparation of travelling exhibitions. At the beginning, these were small displays usually located in trailers and tents, where the public could see pictures of NATO headquarters, read figures about the rearmament progress and be reminded of the continuous danger of Soviet aggression. The success of these exhibitions was enhanced by the fact that they consisted of pictures and posters, with simple messages and figures and that they often included a large amount of information about the country where the exhibition was taking place. Another advantage was the fact that the wide use of pictures and drawings minimised translation, which was very costly and time-consuming. The idea of a travelling exhibition to explain to the public the origins and purpose of the North Atlantic Treaty goes back to May 1951. The scheme was worked out by the NATO Information Service with the technical assistance of United States Information Service.[19] The exhibition, which was housed in a large tent and four extendable trailers, had two themes: first, what NATO was about, and secondly, the role in NATO of the individual country where the exhibition was being shown. Numerous devices were used for attracting attention and for driving home the importance of NATO: photographs, graphic displays, moving devices, illuminated panels, maps, and the projection of films and newsreels.

The NATO travelling exhibitions followed the established model set by the propaganda campaigns designed to promote the Marshall Plan in Western Europe, which in turn replicated the Soviet attempt at promoting the achievements of the October Revolution through travelling exhibitions on trains.[20] Between 1948 and 1952, stationary and travelling exhibits on trains and ships had been part of the vast advertising campaign organised by the Economic Cooperation Agency. They included pictures, short films, newsreels, posters and pamphlets to explain the benefits of the Marshall Plan and argue that American generosity did not conceal any imperialist greed, as claimed by the communists.[21] Following the example of the Marshall Plan's exhibitions, the NATO mobile exhibitions combined the need to explain what NATO was about within the wider context of tighter transatlantic and European political and economic cooperation, without forgetting of course the need to defend Europe from the spread of communism. The first theme was hosted in Trailer 1; the exhibition began by recalling through photographs the happy days of summer 1945, when the West hoped for continued peace and worked to reconstruct western countries and their economies. Then, in the tent attached to the trailer, came the reminder of Soviet armed strength and of the acts of Soviet aggression between 1946 and 1948. Next, under the heading 'Answer to the Threat', exhibits showed how the NATO countries came together on equal terms for the defence of peace and freedom The exhibition illustrated NATO's military capability and explained the military framework of the organisation. At the same time, attention was drawn to the increasingly tighter political and economic cooperation between the member states beyond the purely military field. Trailers 2 and 3 were placed at the disposal of the government receiving the exhibition to explain the country's contribution to and position within NATO. In the 1950s, the content of the information material placed in the trailers and tents and of the publications distributed to the visitors focused on the Soviet Union as a military threat and on the fear of an imminent attack coming from the East. Thus, the need for rearmament and common defence was identified as the only way to protect western democracy, freedom and peace. Not surprisingly, therefore, military themes occupied a central position in all propaganda material.

The first exhibition was sent to Italy. At the Italian government's request, it was shown under the title of the 'Caravan for Peace'. Between February and August 1952, the 'Caravan' made a successful tour of the principal Italian cities (Naples, Rome, Florence, Genoa, Turin, Milan, Venice, Bologna and Bari) where it was seen by 1.5 million visitors. After some adaptation, the exhibition toured Greece and Tukey.[22] Upon recommendation of the Secretary General, in January 1953 the French government asked for the exhibition to be brought to France on its return from Turkey. A committee was set up to adapt the themes to French public opinion and the French version was called 'Exposition Atlantique: Défense de la Paix'. The national part of the exhibition covered the French defence effort as a whole and the French struggle against communism in Indochina as well as the French contribution to the Korean campaign.[23] In each of the four countries, the presence of the exhibition was the object of press articles and of extensive newsreel coverage, which was organised by the NATO Information Service in cooperation with the national broadcasting corporations. According to the final report, the NATO exhibition received extensive press coverage and 2.6 million publications were handed out to the visitors.[24]

Despite the clear success of this operation, however, in March 1953 the Information Service was advised that it could not expect further financial support for the project. In view of the costs involved, the NATO civil budget was unable to make extra contributions and it was therefore impossible to meet further requests.[25] The exhibition programme was suspended and it was left to the individual member states to take the initiative. Given the success of the exhibition in France, for example, the French government requested that a revised and smaller version of the Atlantic exhibition be made available to tour provincial towns and rural districts in France. This new exhibition, called 'Amitié Atlantique', laid more stress on the idea of an Atlantic community than on the notion of military defence and rearmament. The French government was responsible for financing the entire operation and the Information Service offered technical assistance.[26]

NATIS's budgetary crisis was due to the fact that in March 1954 the United States discontinued its voluntary contribution of half a million dollars per year to the Information Service.[27] Between 1949 and 1952, the Information Service had been assisted by the resources of the United States Information Service which, in the early days, enjoyed the financial backing of the counterpart funds available to the Economic Cooperation Administration (ECA) and, after 1948, to the Office of Policy Coordination under the Marshall Plan. The US funds had been vital for the foundation and early development of the NATO propaganda machinery. With the winding up of the Marshall Plan, however, there was a drop in direct support to NATIS. Thus, although the information budget for 1955 showed an increase over the budget voted in 1954, the overall amount of funds actually available to the Information Service fell dramatically.[28] Special projects, like the travelling exhibitions, were the first to suffer and more attention was given to publications and the HQ visiting programme, which were thought to offer better value for money.

In the meantime, some member governments – particularly the French and Italian – had realised the importance of counter-propaganda and offered more generous contributions, which softened the blow of the American withdrawal. Thanks to the support of individual member states, the travelling exhibitions could re-start. After having slowed down in 1953, they reached their peak in 1954 with 3.8 million visitors. In the summer of 1955, three mobile exhibitions toured Turkey, Italy and Denmark; they visited 75 cities and were seen by over a million people. Some 700,000 copies of various publications on NATO were distributed to the visitors.[29] In July, the British Atlantic Committee organised static exhibitions in London and Oxford entitled 'Partners for Freedom', which included an extensive section on NATO. Opened by HRH the Duke of Edinburgh, the exhibitions attracted considerable attention and were given ample space in the press.[30] By October 1957, seven mobile truck-trailer units were in use. Most of them had been donated by the USA government together with the appropriate exhibition equipment such as panels and display machinery.[31] Thanks to such generous contributions the mobile exhibition programme remained a success. More countries asked NATIS to organise the tours and the hosting governments often combined the mobile exhibition with a static one in the capital. In 1959, for example, while the NATO 'Britain and NATO' exhibition travelled across the UK, one static exhibition took place at the National Hall in Olympia; this last was visited by 17,000 people in two weeks.[32] NATIS also organised additional exhibitions on an ad hoc basis for special events like the Atlantic Treaty Association annual assembly or the armed forces exhibition in Aarhus.[33] In addition, four smaller exhibition panels were placed in the public area of NATO headquarters for the thousands of visitors touring the building every year to see.

The success of the travelling exhibitions in 1956–57 was part of an overall increase in the information effort of NATO following the budgetary crisis of 1953–54. The death of Stalin and the consequent climate of detente had made the education of the public more urgent. The Soviet call for peaceful co-existence had a strong echo in large portions of the public, well beyond the restricted sphere of communist militants. NATO officials feared that the new Soviet approach would 'encourage tendencies in the West which might undermine NATO, cause a degeneration of western military effort, and create a climate inhibiting the possible use of nuclear weapons by the West'.[34] The appointment of Paul-Henri Spaak as Secretary General in 1957 was crucial in this sense as it gave a boost to NATIS. Spaak believed that precisely because it blurred the line between communists and non-communists, the new Soviet strategy risked drawing uncommitted states into closer relations with the USSR and creating a rift among the NATO members. Spaak saw the Soviet 'peace offensive' as extremely dangerous and strongly supported NATIS, pushing for a more confident propaganda action.[35] At the same time, the review of the NATO Information Service output was made all the more urgent by the admission of West Germany into NATO in May 1955. The overwhelmingly neutralist German public opinion needed to be told about the need to have a strong NATO and, at the same time, large sections of the Western European public had to be reassured that a rearmed and sovereign Germany was not a threat to peace precisely because of its NATO membership. The 1954–55 period therefore marks a watershed in the history of NATIS, with more support coming from the Secretary General and from the member countries.

The new international situation and the need for a review of NATO's strategic concept was the focus of the Report of the Committee of the Three on Non-Military Cooperation in NATO (Three Wise Men Report), which was published in December 1956.[36] The report asked for more cooperation and consultation in political and economic matters, which led to the creation of the Committee of Political Advisers and Committee of Economic Advisers. For the purpose of this article, Chapter V of the Report (Cooperation in the Information Field) is of great importance. It recommended closer and more coordinated action and asked for more funds to be made available to the Information Service, particularly for translation purposes. Following the recommendations of the 1956 Report, the Conference of National Information Officials suggested replacing the strictly military-based themes widely used in the early 1950s with a new focus on the economic and social integration promoted by NATO, a view shared by the CICR.[37] The scope of NATO information policies should be widened both in terms of the themes used as well as of the targeted audiences. It was vital to target the 'opinion makers' without losing sight of the wider public, particularly the younger generations, who were becoming increasingly sceptical about the need for NATO. The NATIS experts suggested therefore that the overall language used in all information material become more positive and constructive. NATO's information material should move away from strictly defined military themes (Article 5) and portray NATO as a means to foster the economic and cultural ties among its members (Article 2). The new NATIS material should explain that the signing of the North Atlantic Treaty had brought peace in Europe and stopped Soviet expansion. Most importantly, the Conference of National Information Officials advised NATIS to make clear that Western expenditure on defence did not undermine the economic recovery of Western Europe by diverting funds towards rearmament, a point forcefully made by the communists. The new propaganda material should illustrate the dramatic economic progress in countries like Italy and West Germany and show the high standard of living enjoyed throughout the Alliance.[38]

The approval of the 1956 report meant that NATIS had to adapt the themes and approach of all its information material. In the films, newsreels and publications, NATO began to be described more convincingly as an Atlantic Community and although information on military defence was still provided in the background, more emphasis was placed on economic and political cooperation. As far as the exhibitions were concerned, it was recommended that the organisers place posters promoting NATO alongside those portraying the successes of the Organisation for Economic Co-operation and Development (OECD), the European Recovery Programme and the emerging Common Market. This juxtaposition was intentional and was designed to persuade the viewers that NATO was part of a wider plan to improve economic relations between its members. At the same time, the travelling exhibitions were adapted to suit the education of the troops and more material on the political and cultural dimensions of NATO was added to the military data. In 1957 the first truck designed to tour military bases visited British forces stationed in West Germany.[39] The following year a special exhibition for Allied air bases in Europe: two Royal Canadian Air Forces (RCAF) bases in West Germany and 15 United States Air Forces bases in Europe (USAFE) in France and West Germany, where it was visited by 17,000 people. One exhibition was sent to the Allied Forces Southern Europe (AFSOUTH) base in Naples.[40] At the same time, the larger exhibitions for the wider public were slower in adapting as the changes approved by NATIS required the production of a large quantity of new information material to be put on display.

At the end of 1959, the CICR reviewed the use of the mobile exhibitions and opted for smaller and more manageable units; the vans were either sold or sent to be refurbished. The decision was due to the fact that operational costs connected with updating the mobile exhibition trailers were relatively high for the NATIS budget. The Information Service did not have a graphics section and the mounting of any new exhibition required the employment of consultant designers, which was very expensive. The Service was never in the position to appoint a dedicated exhibition and visual aid officer and the work was to be carried out by the photo officer. Unable to update the information material put on display in the travelling exhibition, NATIS decided to suspend the exhibition programme until such an update was feasible.

The NATO mobile information centres, 1960–69

Despite the budgetary and organisational problems, the CICR and NATIS recognised the value of the exhibitions. It was decided to move the exhibitions away from a set of trailers and tents, which required staff to assemble them, and to use instead a small van, which would be a self-contained unit for the transport and exhibition of information material. Thanks to the profits made by the sale of the old vans and by the generous contributions of the French government and the USIS, which had made the trucks available in the first place, the operation was possible despite the limited NATIS budget.[41]

The new NATO mobile information centres (NMIC) were originally designed for audiences which could not be reached by other means, particularly in regions often neglected by other media (like the south of Italy or the Greek islands). One NMIC was designed to be used in southern countries and could include open-air film shows. The other van toured Northern Europe. In the much more confined space of 10 metres by 2.5 metres, the information centres could be used as mobile classrooms seating 40 people. Both vans were equipped to show movies and to host lectures and question and answer sessions.[42] The NMIC also included a graphic display which explained the organisation of the Alliance, again with a particular emphasis on the country hosting the exhibition. The mobile information centres were sent to smaller towns, often in conjunction with trade fairs, armed forces days and air shows so as to maximise attendance and impact. The centre stayed for a period ranging from one week to three months. In 1961, NMIC was put to the test and it spent one week in Gibraltar and one week in Naples in connection with the tenth anniversary celebrations of AFSOUTH. Then it toured Portugal for three months and Greece for an additional five months.[43] According to the report of the Portuguese representative, the NMIC was a very effective information tool, particularly in the countryside and small centres, where people had not yet been reached by means of common propaganda. The tour was announced daily on the radio and reports appeared in the local and national press.[44] The NMICs continued their tours successfully throughout the 1960s and the annual reviews of NATIS output show that a consistently high number of people visited the centres and that requests for new tours from member governments were sustained.

In the same period, NATO's information policy benefited from the internal restructuring of NATIS, which took place in 1963. All information activities were divided into two sectors: the Media Operation Service, in charge of the production of all information material (television, films and radio section; publications and photos section; editorial and documentation section) and the Public Affairs Service, in charge of promoting and stimulating activities in support of NATO (visits and lectures section; youth and education; armed forces education). The Media Operation Service reviewed the themes and audiences of its information material and the director of information, Raban Graf Adelmann, recommended that the new material concentrate on 'widening the scope of the present output by including more subjects of a non-military character'.[45]

In 1969, after discussions in the Information Committee, it was agreed to reduce the NMIC from two to one and eventually to cease the operation altogether. Although the two vans were very popular and demand remained steady, this method of briefing was considered to be the least cost-effective among those used by the Information Service at the time. With a population of 500 million in the Alliance, individual oral briefing had a limited impact, which was almost impossible to measure. The use of the NIMC in villages and schools could have only a negligible effect in moulding the public of the Alliance as a whole. On the grounds of cost-effectiveness, it was decided that this type of operation should be replaced by a policy of mounting an exhibition in connection with large events, like trade fairs, with a ready-made audience on an ad hoc basis. One van was therefore put out of commission and sold; the remaining van was joined by a mini-bus and was used to carry additional display panels and served as both information centre and mobile exhibition centre.[46]

The cuts suffered by the NMIC programme were part of the overhaul of the NATIS output which was put in place by the new director of information, John Price, who was appointed in November 1967. The appointment of Price took place around the same time of the publication of the Harmel Report on the 'Future Tasks of the Alliance'.[47] Both events exerted new pressure on NATIS. The Harmel Report advocated strong defence along with new diplomatic relations with the Eastern Bloc and called on the NATO members to use the Alliance in the interests of detente. As far as NATO's information activities were concerned, the Harmel Report stated that public support for the Alliance's defence efforts was vital to the accomplishment of the task ahead and that it would be important to bring home to public opinion the rationale underlying NATO strategy and the Alliance's efforts to preserve the balance of security between East and West. Public support for the defence effort was an essential factor in the credibility of NATO's deterrent and this support had to be made clearly visible. Without public support, any military operation would be meaningless. Effective modernisation of the defensive system, rearmament and any defensive policy and military operation could only be achieved with public involvement and full support. Without it, according to the Harmel Report, the deterrent value of NATO would be seriously undermined. The approval of the report therefore brought a review of the NATO information effort which coincided with the appointment of the new director of information.

It is worth mentioning that before joining NATIS, Price had worked for the Information Research Department, an agency within the Foreign Office in charge with anti-communist propaganda. Price was a very energetic and effective director of information and his first decision was to visit all the NATO capitals and to look for new ways to improve coordination between NATIS and the national information agencies.[48] The appointment of Price coincided with the launch of the Information Working Group (AC/123 series), which was operative from 1969 and 1973. The Working Group carried out a detailed examination of the NATIS output and suggested changes and cuts to make the Information Service more effective. Following the recommendations of the WG, Price proceeded to a substantial reshaping of the activities of the NATO Information Service. He agreed to significant cuts including, as it has been said, the NATO mobile information centres. The *NATO Letter* too was cut back from a monthly to a bi-monthly publication and it acquired a new focus on the day-to-day work of NATO, including an 'open forum' with discussion in which the authors could speak in a personal capacity about the activities of NATO and the challenges it faced. In the name of increased cost-effectiveness, films and documentaries became a central part of NATIS's communication effort. The new Media Operation Service produced fresh material, most of which was targeted to the younger generations, who did not have any experience of the war and did not recall the years when East/West tensions were at their peak and therefore remained doubtful about the need for NATO. Equally important was Price's work towards better coordination with the network of voluntary organisations in support of NATO. To that end, he asked for an increase in the Special Fund, which was used to support the activities of such organisations. NATIS was to focus on the younger generations, who seemed critical of all military alliances, a concern expressed by Pierre Harmel himself on several occasions.[49] The review also re-launched the annual Conference of the National Information Officials, which had been interrupted in 1960. The conference followed the same procedure it had adopted in the 1950s and facilitated the exchange of information and ideas while ensuring a tighter level of coordination between NATIS and the national information agencies of the NATO countries.[50]

Conclusions

The ratification of the North Atlantic Treaty by all its signatories left large sectors of the public in several member countries unconvinced about the need for a common defence policy and for rearmament. While in the USA and Britain the level of dissent was minimal, in other countries – as, for example, Italy and France – scepticism spread beyond the restricted sphere of communist militants and involved right-wing as well as moderate political forces and intellectuals. The western communist parties as well as the Cominform were therefore able to exploit widespread distrust and support for neutralism and pacifism and to attack NATO and the western defence stance with relative ease. Public support for NATO had therefore to be strengthened through a series of information programmes put forward by the national governments and by NATO itself. Of these programmes, the travelling exhibitions were a rather successful example. The programme thrived in the 1950s and 1960s. Despite the budgetary crisis that hit the Information Service in 1954–55, the exhibitions survived and proved to be a successful initiative. The examination of the travelling exhibition programme raises three questions about the Information Service's changing working practices and priorities.

First, there was a consistent delay between the time when the Security Council issued new guidelines about NATO's priorities in the field of political propaganda and the time when NATIS was in a position to produce the appropriate information material to reflect such shift. More often than not, by the time NATIS was in such a position, the Council's priorities had already moved on and a new version of the information material had already become necessary. The peaceful image of NATIS, for example, was clearly defined in the NMIC that toured Europe in the 1960s but far less so in the travelling exhibitions of the late 1950s, even though the Council had agreed to review the core message of NATIS propaganda material immediately after the publication of the Three Wise Men Report (1956). A closer look at NATO internal procedure may help explain this delay. The NATO Council would start by looking at surveys of public opinion and at studies of the impact of the current information programmes run by NATIS and by the member states. The Council and each national representative would then make comments and suggestions for improvement. The suggestions of the Council and of the national delegations would then be passed on to NATIS for comments. After having heard back from NATIS and the CICR, the Council would approve the final information programme. NATIS would then review the information material according to the new line approved by the Council and organise the production of the new material. The whole process could take up to two years. In times of crisis, two years can be a long time and very often NATIS material was outdated even before leaving the headquarters.

Second, the travelling exhibitions were only one of the many information programmes run by NATIS in the first 20 years of its activities. Despite their success and the continuous requests coming from the member states, the programme was suspended in 1969 in the name of cost-effectiveness. By the mid-1960s, the production costs of short films and newsreels had been substantially reduced and for the first time the new Media Operation Service could take charge of the production and distribution without relying heavily on the contributions and operational help of the member states, namely the USA. Although NATIS occasionally outsourced the production of the short films, they could now oversee the whole process and saw it as a more manageable in-house operation.[51] Thus, the new media allowed NATIS to reach a far larger audience with far fewer organisational problems than those imposed by the travelling exhibitions, which were therefore shelved.

Finally, the thorny question of how the exhibitions – as well as all the NATIS information material – were received and what impact they exerted on the public remains open. The recent media reception theories have not yet provided a convincing set of tools to answer this question and the archives still seem to be the best sources of information.[52] The NATO archival material gives details about the number of people who visited the exhibitions as well as of the visitors that toured the HQ. NATIS also kept a record of all the publications (and their translations) that were produced each year and how they were distributed. Similarly, it is possible to find numbers relating to the subscriptions to the *NATO Letter* and the rough estimates of how many people saw the NATO movies and newsreels. Yet it is one thing to know the number of visitors who saw an exhibition and another to assess what impact such experiences had on the public and to what degree they were successful in persuading the visitors that NATO was a project worth supporting. Following requests from NATIS, national governments periodically compiled questionnaires. Yet not every national delegation submitted them and it is difficult to gain a coherent picture from these documents. Even when NATIS tried to gain a more detailed picture, its effort was to no avail. In 1957–58, the CICR set up a special working group to assess to what extent the members used the information material sent by NATIS. The result of the survey was disappointing as it revealed that in several countries there was no actual redistribution network and that on some occasions the material remained in the corner of a forgotten office.[53] Between 1969 and 1973, the Information Working Group carried out an extensive survey of all the NATIS information material and concluded that the impact that such material exerted on the public could not be evaluated.[54] Reception of the information programme is perhaps the most difficult question a researcher can tackle in this kind of research. The collation of different sources helps gain a broad picture of the success of the information programmes but a precise assessment may remain beyond our grasp.

Notes

[1] Both Ellwood and Aubourg have contributed chapters on these topics in Aubourg, Bossuat, and Scott-Smith, *European Community, Atlantic Community*; Risso, '"Enlightening Public Opinion"'.

[2] Blackmer and Tarrow, *Communism in Italy and France*; Kriegel, *Les Communistes français dans leur premier demi-siècle*; Courtois and Lazar, *50 ans d'une passion française*.

[3] *Journal Officiel de la République Française. Débats parlementaires. Assemblée Nationale.* 28 July 1949.

[4] An example is available in Togliatti *Discorsi Parlamentari*, 405–41.

[5] 'Mutual Aid Treaty' signed by Churchill and Molotov in May 1942 and the 'Treaty of Alliance and Mutual Assistance' signed in December 1944 by General de Gaulle. Both treaties prohibited the signatories from taking part in any alliance that could be a threat to the other. These war-time treaties provided a powerful weapon for Soviet propaganda against NATO.

[6] De Gaulle, *Discours et messages*, 272–5.

[7] Nenni, *Tempo di guerra fredda*, 91.

[8] CICR: Information programme for 1956, 9 February 1956, NATO Archives, AC/52-WP/14; NATO Conference on Information Policy; 8 February 1955, AC/87-R/1; Survey by the Secretary General of Progress during the Period 1 May 1955 to 30 November 1955, 6 December 1955, CM(55)122.

[9] A good example of this is in 'Summary Record of a Meeting of the Council of Deputies held at 13, Belgrave Square, London, SW1, on Monday, 26 February 1951', 27 February 1951, NATO Archives, DR(51)13.

[10] CICR, Note by the Chairman, 26 August 1953, NATO Archives, CM(53)118. The same point is reiterated in NATO Information Conference, Note by the Assistant Secretary General for Political Affairs, 9 February 1953, NATO Archives, CM(53)6.

[11] Kenez, *The Birth of the Propaganda State.*

[12] Defty, *Britain, American and Anti-Communist Propaganda*; Aldrich, *The Hidden Hand*; idem, 'Putting Culture into the Cold War'. For a detailed examinaiton of the Anglo-American preparatory talks, Risso, '"Enlightening Public Opinion"'.

[13] 'Summary Record of the 7th Meeting Held on the 3rd August 1950, at Lancaster House', 3 August 1950, NATO Archives, DR(50)7; 'Summary Record of the 8th Meeting held on the 4th August 1950, at Lancaster House', 4 August 1950, NATO Archives, DR(50)8; 'Information Service', 11 August 1950, NATO Archives, DD/17.

[14] 'The NATO Information Service', 20 November 1950, NATO Archives, DD/186.

[15] 'NATO Conference on Information Policy: Development of Information since 1950', Report by the Director of Information, 24 January 1955, NATO Archives, AC/87-D/6; 'NATO Functions in the Field of Propaganda and Counterpropaganda', Report by the Assistant Secretary General for Political Affairs, 29 November 1952, NATO Archives, CM(52)115. For a detailed reconstruction of the origins of NATIS, Risso, '"Enlightening Public Opinion"'.

[16] During the Cold War, other committees and ad hoc working groups operated within and alongside NATIS. Among the most interesting ones was the Conference of National Information Officials; the Information Policy Working Group (1952–53, AC/24 series); the Political Committee (1957–64, AC/119 series); the Joint WG on Information Policy and Cultural Cooperation (1953–74, AC/52 series); the Atlantic Policy Advisory Group (1962–74, AC/214A); and the Working Group on Problems connected with 'Psychological Warfare' (1960–61, AC/186).

[17] 'Summary Record of a Meeting of the Council held at the Palais de Chaillot, Paris, on Wednesday, 1 July 1953', 2 July 1953, NATO Archives, CR(53)33; CICR, Note by the Chairman, 26 August 1953, NATO Archives, CM(53)118; CICR, 'Proposed NATO information activities in 1954', Note by Director of Information, 29 September 1953, NATO Archives, AC/52-D/17; Risso, '"Enlightening Public Opinion"'.

[18] Full details in Risso, '"Enlightening Public Opinion"'.

[19] CICR, 'NATO Atlantic Exhibition, 1952–1954. Italy, Greece, Turkey, France', Report by the Director of Information, 3 September 1954, NATO Archives, AC/52-D/54.

[20] Kenez, *The Birth of the Propaganda State*; Gorsuch, 'Soviet Youth and the Politics of Culture during NEP'.

[21] Ellwood, '"You too can be like us"'; Bischof and Stiefel, *Images of the Marshall Plan in Europe.*

[22] In Greece, it visited Thessaloniki and Athens (September–November 1952), where it was seen by 755,148 people. In Turkey (January–March 1953) it stopped in Ankara, Izmir and Istanbul and it was seen by almost half a million people. CICR, 'NATO Atlantic Exhibition, 1952–1954', NATO Archives, AC/52-D/54.

[23] It stopped in Strasbourg, Lille, Paris, Lyon, Marseille, Toulon, Nice, Bordeaux, Rennes, Nantes and Le Havre (September 1953–June 1954). The total number of visitors during the French tour was just above 1 million. CICR, 'NATO Atlantic Exhibition, 1952–1954', NATO Archives, AC/52-D/54.

[24] Ibid.

[25] Ibid.

[26] Ibid.

[27] 'NATO Conference on Information Policy', 8 February 1955, NATO Archives, AC/87-R/1.

[28] 'NATO Conference on Information Policy: Development of Information since 1950', Report by the Director of Information, 24 January 1955, NATO Archives, AC/87-D/6. For the examination of how the provisions of the Marshall Plan were used to finance the information activities of various CIA-led programmes, see Scott-Smith, *The Politics of Apolitical Culture*, 70–71. It is worth pointing out that despite the interruption of its voluntary contribution, the USA continued to support NATIS indirectly. Summary Record of the 34th Meeting of the Council held at the Palais de Chaillot, Paris, on Wednesday, 17 November 1954', 19 November 1954, NATO Archives, CR(54)43.

[29] 'Report by the Secretary General of progress during the period 1 December 1955 to 1 April 1956', 26 April 1956, NATO Archives, CM(56)54.

[30] 'Survey by the Secretary General of Progress during the period 1 May 1955 to 30 November 1955', 6 December 1955, NATO Archives, CM(55)122; CICR, 'Proposed information programme for 1956', Note by the Director of Information, 1 December 1955, NATO Archives, AC/52-D/144.

[31] The capital equipment was valued at approximately 90 million francs. CICR, 'NATO Information Activities in 1958', Note by the Director of Information, 22 October 1957, NATO Archives, AC/52-D/267.

[32] 'Report by the Secretary General of Progress during the Period 1st July to 31st December 1958', 18 March 1959, NATO Archives, CM(59)29.

[33] 'Report by the Secretary General of progress during the period 1st July to 31st December 1959', 26 April 1960, NATO Archives, CM(60)47; CICR, 'NATO Information Activities in 1958', Note by the Director of Information, 22 October 1957, NATO Archives, AC/52-D/267.

[34] 'Trends and Implications of Soviet Policy', Report by International Staff, 3 December 1956, NATO Archives, CM(56)133; 'Summary Record of a Meeting of the Council held at the Palais de Chaillot, Paris, on Saturday, 27th February 1954', 5 March 1954, NATO Archives, CR(54)6.

[35] 'Countering Soviet Propaganda Themes', 26 April 1960, NATO Archives, PO/60/502.

[36] Official text available on the NATO website: http://www.nato.int/cps/en/SID-4581F841-BE8FB761/natolive/official_texts_17481.htm (accessed 8 January 2010).

[37] 'Implementation of the Recommendation made by the Committee of Three', Note by the Deputy Secretary General, 10 January 1957, NATO Archives, CM(57)3.

[38] 'Conference of National Information Officials', 1 March 1960, NATO Archives, RDC/60/44; 'Information Programme for 1956', Report by the Chairman of the Committee on Information and Cultural Relations, 20 February 1956, NATO Archives, CM(56)18.

[39] CICR, 'NATO Information Activities in 1958', Note by the Director of Information, 22 October 1957, NATO Archives, AC/52-D/267.

[40] 'Report by the Secretary General of progress during the period 1st July to 31st December 1958', 18 March 1959, NATO Archives, CM(59)29.

[41] 'Report by the Secretary General of Progress during the Period 1st July to 31st December 1959', 26 April 1960, NATO Archives, CM(60)47; CICR, 'Meeting held on Thursday, 5 October 1961', Action sheet, 11 October 1961, NATO Archives, AC/52-R(61)22.
[42] 'Survey of the NATO Information Output, 1969', NATO Archives, AC/123-D(70)1, p. 272; and leaflet 'The NATO Mobile Information Centre' published by NATIS in 1961.
[43] CICR, 'Proposed 1962 Information Programme', Note by the Director of Information, 11 September 1961, NATO Archives, AC/52-WP(61)49; CICR, 'Second Mobile Information Centre', Note by the Director of Information, 11 September 1961, NATO archives, AC/52-WP(61)49/1.
[44] CICR, 'Meeting held on Thursday, 5 October 1961', Action sheet, 11 October 1961, NATO Archives, AC/52-R(61)22.
[45] CICR, 'Information Policy: Proposed General Lines to be Followed in Information Activities in 1965', Note by the Director of Information, 15 April 1964, NATO Archives, AC/52-D(64)1.
[46] These changes meant a 50% cut in the budget, from 1.8m Belgian francs to 0.9m. CICR, 'Proposed 1969 Information Activities', Note by the Director of Information, 5 November 1968, NATO Archives, AC/52-D(68)3; 'Survey of the NATO Information Output, 1969', NATO Archives, AC/123-D(70)1, 272–5.
[47] Official version available on the NATO website: http://www.nato.int/cps/en/SID-C6A160A2-9498A202/natolive/official_texts_26700.htm (accessed 8 January 2010).
[48] CICR, 'Activities of the NATO Information Service, January 1968–June 1968', Note by the Director of Information, 5 September 1968, NATO archives, AC/52-D(68)2; Price left NATIS on 19 May 1972, AC/52-R(72)2.
[49] CICR, 'Proposed 1969 Information Activities', Note by the Director of Information, 5 November 1968, NATO Archives, AC/52-D(68)3; 'Summary Record of a Meeting of the Council held at Reykjavik on Monday and Tuesday, 24th and 25th June 1968', 9 August 1968, NATO Archives, CR(68)30.
[50] CICR, 'Activities of the NATO Information Service: July 1968 to December 1968', Note by the Director of Information, 3 March 1969, NATO Archives, AC/52-D(69)1.
[51] NATIS often worked in cooperation with the Dedo Weigert Film Company in Munich.
[52] Thompson, 'Reception Theory'; Bruhn Jensen, *Handbook.*
[53] 'Interim Report by the Committee on Information and Cultural Relations', 8 July 1958, NATO Archives, AC/52-D(58)34(Final).
[54] 'Survery of the NATO Information Output, 1969', NATO Archives, AC/273-D(70)1; 'The NATO Information Service Survey Output, 1970', NATO Archives, AC/273-D(71)1; 'The NATO Information Service Survey Output, 1970', NATO Archives, AC/273-D(72)1.

References

Aldrich, Richard J., ed. *British Intelligence, Strategy and the Cold War, 1945–1951*. London: Routledge, 1992.

———. ed. *The Hidden Hand: Britain, America and Cold War Secret Intelligence*. London: John Murray, 2001.

———. ed. 'Putting Culture into the Cold War: The Cultural Relations Department (CRD) and British Covert Information Warfare'. *Intelligence and National Security* 18, no. 2 (2003): 109–33.

Aubourg, Valérie. 'Organising Atlanticism: The Bilderberg Group and the Atlantic Institute, 1952–63', in *The Cultural Cold War in Western Europe 1945–1960*, ed. Giles Scott-Smith and Hans Krabbendam, 92–105. London: Frank Cass, 2003.

Aubourg, Valérie, Gérard Bossuat, and Giles Scott-Smith, eds. *European Community, Atlantic Community*. Paris: Soleb, 2008.

Bischof, Günter, and Dieter Stiefel, eds. *Images of the Marshall Plan in Europe. Films, Photographs, Exhibits, Posters*. Innsbruck: Studien Verlag, 2009.

Blackmer, Donald L. M., and Sidney Tarrow, eds. *Communism in Italy and France*. Princeton, NJ: Princeton University Press, 1975.

Bruhn Jensen, Klaus, ed. *A Handbook of Media and Communication Research: Qualitative and Quantitative Methodology*. New York: Routledge, 2002.

Courtois, Stéphan, and Marc Lazar, eds. *50 ans d'une passion française: De Gaulle et les Communistes*. Paris: Balland, 1991.

De Gaulle, Charles. *Discours et messages: Dans l'atteinte, 1946–58*. Paris: Plon, 1970.

Defty, Andrew. *Britain, American and Anti-Communist Propaganda, 1945–1953: The Information Research Department*. London: Routledge, 2004.

Ellwood, David. '"You too can be like us": Selling the Marshall Plan: American Propaganda during the European Recovery Program'. *History Today* 48 (October 1998): 33–9.

———. 'The Propaganda of the Marshall Plan in Italy in a Cold War Context', in *The Cultural Cold War in Western Europe 1945–1960*, ed. Giles Scott-Smith and Hans Krabbendam, 225–36. London: Frank Cass, 2003.

Gorsuch, Anne E. 'Soviet Youth and the Politics of Culture during NEP'. *Social History* 17, no. 2 (1992): 189–201.

Kenez, Peter. *The Birth of the Propaganda State: Soviet Methods of Mass Mobilisation, 1917–1929*. Cambridge: CUP, 1985.

Kent, John, and John W. Young. 'The "Western Union" Concept and British Defence Policy, 1947–48', in *British Intelligence, Strategy and the Cold War, 1945–1951*, ed. Richard J. Aldrich, 166–92. London: Routledge, 1992: .

———. 'British Policy Overseas: The "Third Force" and the Origins of NATO. In Search of a New Perspective', in *Securing Peace in Europe, 1945–1962*, ed. Beatrice Heuser and Robert O'Neill, 41–61. London: Macmillan, 1992.

Kriegel, Annie. *Les Communistes français dans leur premier demi-siècle, 1920–1970*. Paris: Du Seuil, 1985.

Lashmar, Paul, and James Oliver. *Britain's Secret Propaganda War, 1948–1977*. Stroud: Sutton, 1998.

Nenni, Pietro. *Tempo di guerra fredda: Diario, 1943–1956*. Milan: SugarCo, 1974.

Risso, Linda. '"Enlightening Public Opinion": A Study of NATO's Information Policies between 1949 and 1959 Based on Recently Declassified Documents'. *Cold War History* 7, no. 1 (February 2007): 45–74.

———. 'A Difficult Compromise: British Plans for a Common Anti-communist Propaganda Response in Western Europe, 1948–1958'. *Intelligence and National Security* (forthcoming).

Scott-Smith, Giles. *The Politics of Apolitical Culture: The Congress for Cultural Freedom, the CIA, and Post-war American Hegemony*. New York: Routledge, 2002.

Scott-Smith, Giles, and Hans Krabbendam, eds. *The Cultural Cold War in Western Europe, 1945–1960*. London: Frank Cass, 2003.

Thompson, Martyn P. 'Reception Theory and the Interpretation of Historical Meaning'. *History and Theory* 32, no. 3 (October 1993): 248–72.

Togliatti, Palmiro. *Discorsi Parlamentari, 1946–1964*. Rome: Camera dei Deputati, 1984.

Warner, Geoffrey. 'Britain and Europe in 1948: The View from the Cabinet', in *Power in Europe? Great Britain, France, Italy and Germany in a Post-War World, 1945-1955*, ed. Josef Becker and Franz Kipping, 27–44. Berlin: De Gruyter, 1986.

Wilford, Hugh. *Calling the Tune? The CIA, the British Left and the Cold War*. London: Frank Cass, 2003.

Cold War in the Aegean

Favouritism in NATO's Southeastern flank: The case of the Greek Colonels, 1967–74

Konstantina Maragkou

The aim of this paper is to analyse the effect of the Cold War era on a historic event with serious consequences for Greece, namely the Greek Colonels' regime, which lasted between April 1967 and July 1974. Greece, due to its strategic position, served as guarantor of stability in NATO's southeastern flank, a benefit that the alliance considered indispensable to its strength, therefore impossible to compromise. In the light of this consideration, NATO tolerated, to put it mildly, the dictatorial, albeit pro-NATO regime that the Greek Colonels imposed on Greece on 21 April 1967. This paper will attempt to account for NATO's reactions to the Greek regime and the factors dictating them – a small, albeit indicative, peripheral segment of the puzzle of the global antagonism between the West and the East during the Cold War era.

At the dawn of 22 April 1967, Greece was entering one of the darkest phases in its modern political history. The night before, a group of middle ranking army officers, led by Colonel George Papadopoulos, Brigadier Stylianos Pattakos, and Colonel Nikolaos Makarezos staged a military coup, with the use of a NATO-instigated plan, called Prometheus. Their coup was bloodless and successful and resulted in the imposition of military rule until July 1974.

Not only the forcible way in which they took power, but also a number of methods that they implemented following their assumption of power – including the enforcement of martial law, suspension of parliamentary government, abolition of democratic freedoms, and arrest of opposition leaders and a few thousand potential dissidents – proved that, although their regime was quite idiosyncratic, it had indisputably adopted repugnant dictatorial elements. It did therefore result in causing public outcry at the international arena and casting doubt over the continuation of Greece's diplomatic relations with a number of countries and international organisations.

It has been often claimed that the policy of the West towards the military regime that plagued Greece for seven long years could not be examined outside the Cold War context. This allegation is undoubtedly well grounded, in view of Greece's significant geo-strategic position, which had resulted in NATO's deep appreciation of Greece's cooperation for the maintenance of stability in its southeastern flank. Before proceeding with the examination of NATO's attitude towards the unconstitutional regime of the Colonels, it is worth succinctly presenting the associated strategic benefits that Greece afforded to the Alliance, as well as its most powerful member, the United States of America.

At the time when the Colonels came to power, Greece had 1000 kilometres of common frontiers with three communist countries,[1] was quite close to the USSR, provided an essential link to the Turkish flank, which guarded the eastern access to the Mediterranean from the Black Sea, and was the gateway to the Mediterranean for any enemy attacking from Bulgaria.

The Mediterranean Sea, in which Greece possesses a dominant position, borders the Allied areas of western and southern Europe and the strategic areas of the Middle East and North Africa. The control of the Mediterranean Sea was essential to permit Allied naval forces to make use of their intrinsic flexibility.[2] Its importance was also intensified by the fact that it was 'the most intensely used maritime corridor of the world',[3] also due to the Mediterranean–Persian Gulf connection and the transport of oil. As a British Joint Intelligence Committee summarised it in 1967 'Greece's position in the Mediterranean is important vis-à-vis the Middle East and North Africa in relation to the prevention of Soviet expansion and communist penetration, the protection of material interests, the preservation of transit facilities, both military and civil by sea and air'.[4]

In the light of these axioms, which lay at the heart of the West's approach to the region, Britain first and then the United States, after having substantially contributed to the defeat of the Communists during the Greek civil war in the late 1940s, strove for the signing of the treaty of Greece's accession to NATO in 1952. As a result, Greece officially became a vital part of the southern region of NATO's Allied Command Europe (ACE), whose scope was to form a barrier between the countries of the Warsaw Pact and the Mediterranean–Middle East regions.

From the end of the fifties onwards, Greece's strategic position had assumed additional gravity in view of the perennial trouble spots the Mediterranean and the

Middle East were threatening to become. During the Cold War era, the Mediterranean seemed like a 'crowded lake where a massive Soviet fleet probed the rim for opportunities to exploit and expand Soviet influence':[5] and the greater the conflicting aspirations of the two superpowers were becoming in the Mediterranean, the higher importance was attached to Greece's cooperation.

Antagonism in the Mediterranean reached its zenith in the 1960s. The Soviets, in view of their weakness in naval strength as revealed by the 1962 crisis in Cuba, decided to establish a strong naval presence in the Mediterranean capable of posing a viable challenge to the supremacy of its American and NATO competitors. In the light of the perceived threat that the expanding Soviet fleet's incursions were posing in the Mediterranean for NATO, having access to naval bases in Greece was deemed crucial.

In addition to the aforementioned factors, NATO members and Britain in particular had a strong interest in maintaining a close relationship with Greece, also because of its certain interests in Cyprus. These included a NATO communications station that carried air defence and command material, a shared radar with Britain, and a NATO relay station. In fact, NATO's communication station in Cyprus was considered as a '[v]ital and probably irreplaceable part of the NATO air defence and command network',[6] whereas its planned relay station was 'said to be no less valuable'.[7] As it was summarised by the British Cabinet's interdepartmental working group on Cyprus:

> In general terms, our [British] military presence in Cyprus enhanced NATO's position in the Eastern Mediterranean by securing a strategically valuable site from Russian penetration; and by providing surveillance and certain irreplaceable intelligence facilities which help to reduce the freedom of action of Russian maritime and air forces, the loss of which could be very serious.[8]

Another catalytic factor related to Turkey, which in tandem with Greece, was considered among the staunchest members of the Alliance, contributing 750,000 troops to it.[9] Many opined that if Greece were lost to NATO, or even badly weakened military, Turkey would be isolated from the rest of the Alliance and subject to increasing pressures from the Soviet Union. It was deemed significant therefore that Turkey should not be faced with the possibility of an open flank in case of aggression against it by the Warsaw Pact.

Moreover, Greece's membership was vital not only vis-à-vis the southwards challenge represented in the Mediterranean by the Soviet naval squadron, but also the northwards threats in the form of an attack through Macedonia or Thrace. A local action by Bulgaria upon the narrow stretch of Greek land along its southern borders could result in two unwelcome developments on the grounds of the Bulgarian forces' undisputed superiority. First, Greek forces would be cut off from the Turkish forces and secondly Bulgaria would secure an exit to the Mediterranean for the whole Eastern bloc. This was particularly aggravating in view of the fact that Bulgaria had become the most loyal satellite of the Soviet Union.

Moreover, there were another two recent developments within NATO that resulted in putting more emphasis on avoiding creating a confrontation with Greece too. The first factor was the growing anti-NATO sentiment in some of the Northern allies; especially in Denmark and Norway internal political developments had strengthened anti-NATO socialist and extreme left political elements. The second disrupting factor was linked to De Gaulle's initiative to cancel France's membership of NATO in 1966. France's withdrawal from NATO's military wing had put considerable strains on the alliance as it resulted in the liquidation of all NATO installations.

Other various places for rest and rehabilitation for NATO forces were diminishing. NATO had to deal with the effects of the loss of the Arab ports and the inadequacy of the Turkish ones. At the same time, Italy was limiting landing rights and Spain prohibiting any landing in Gibraltar. In light of all the aforementioned developments, the significance of maintaining the *entrée* to the Greek ports had never seemed as essential as it coincidentally did at the time when the Greek Colonels came to power.

Finally, another lurking fear had for some time seriously troubled the minds of the NATO allies. More specifically, it was feared that Russia might take over Yugoslavia, once the ageing Tito was off the scene. Greece was an important factor in this, as it was felt that if Greece was expelled from NATO, then Yugoslavia would collapse. Consequently, keeping Greece on board and on good terms was part of the defence mechanism against Russia, against whose ambitions, Greece together with its Balkan Pact neighbours, namely Turkey and Yugoslavia, formed a land barrier.

In view of the above strategic preoccupations and the effort placed by Britain and the US upon maintaining Greece's cooperation with NATO throughout the Cold War years, NATO's tolerance of the infamous Colonels' regime seemed rather expected. After all, regimes as fanatically anti-Communist as the Greek one were perceived as harmoniously serving the alliance's *raison d'être.*

The Alliance's dependence on Greek cooperation in the context of maintaining stability in its southeastern flank was a factor that was manipulated skillfully by the troika of the Greek Colonels. In light of the international outcry that their coming to power had generated, it did not take them long to realise that their friendly predisposition towards NATO was their most effective leverage in their attempt to obtain their much-desired international legitimisation. This was particularly important as the unconstitutional way, in which they had assumed control of Greece had given rise to growing waves of international obloquy.

In view of this realisation, the Colonels for their part ascertained on several occasions that their pro-NATO feelings did not escape the Alliance's attention. Brigadier Stylianos Pattakos, the second most powerful coup plotter and executor, newly appointed Minister of Interior Order and spokesman of the new regime, tried to make clear that the Colonels were advocates of all things the West held dear, first and foremost their strong allegiance to NATO. This was accurately summarised in one comment made on the day following the coup by Pattakos to the US air *attaché*, which run as follows: 'the coup was designed to ensure domestic tranquility, loyalty to the

King and allegiance to NATO and the West as a whole, as well as to unify the people'.[10] In other words, the first omens received hinted that the new ruling establishment of Greece was in accordance with the West's wishes. As it was reported in the second telegram sent by the American Embassy in Athens to the State Department on the actual day of the coup, the new rulers 'have reaffirmed loyalty to NATO'.[11]

In the immediate aftermath of the Colonels' coming to power, Greece's unconstitutional rulers had shown strong commitment to suppressing Communist elements through imprisonment, censorship, the establishment of concentration camps at the island of Yaros, and proclaiming their fierce hostility towards communism on numerous occasions. In their first statement, they justified their *coup* principally on the grounds that it was needed in order to thwart a possible communist takeover. Although, the extent to which communism posed a real threat to Greece is highly debatable, it was nonetheless useful for the Alliance to know of the new regime's polemical stance against it.

In fact, such was the importance of keeping Greece in the Alliance that a fair number of people held the West's role in the Colonels' rule not only compromising, but even worse, instigating too. It was on the grounds of NATO's, and most specifically the US's, uncompromising hostility towards all Communist or Communist-tolerant elements in Greece that many believed that there was a degree of foreign intervention in the planning and/or execution of the coup. The Colonels' coming to power had averted the percolating threat, as perceived especially by the US government, of pro-Communist and anti-NATO Andreas Papandreou, Greece's '*enfant terrible*',[12] gaining power as a result of his father's party's forecasted victory at the 28 May elections. Several additional factors, such as the past precedent of American and British direct involvement in Greek affairs as well as the staging of the coup with the use of a NATO-instigated plan, which was called Prometheus and was devised in the case of a communist threat, significantly contributed to the spreading of such allegations.

However, on the basis of wide-ranging indications, it seems rather unlikely that the Western flank of NATO had any direct contribution to the Colonels' coming to power. The possibility of direct intervention mainly by the US was indeed put on the table on not a few occasions. Nevertheless, the decision, which was reached, favored the policy of non-intervention.[13] Instead, a suggestion for a 'wait and see' policy was brought forward, according to which the US was not to exert any influence prior to Greek internal developments and would only in the immediate aftermath decide its stance towards them. Provided that this was a frank assessment – it needs to be borne in mind that the zenith of the Cold War did not encourage the documentation of highly secretive operations – the US, hence NATO at large, did not contribute in any tangible way to the Colonels' forcible assumption of power.

Although it seems unlikely that any NATO member individually or the Alliance collectively had any role to play in the Colonels' coming to power, the Alliance avoided manifesting any objection, to the permissible extent, to the undemocratic nature of their regime. In the immediate aftermath of the regime's establishment to power, most individual NATO country members, including the US and Britain, froze their dealings with the new regime, albeit shortly, in an effort to acquire a better grasp of the unknown triumvirate's intentions. Immediately after the coup, the US suspended the delivery of major items of military aid to Greece, including aircraft, tanks, helicopters, armored personnel and mortar carriers, artillery equipment, and tank ammunition amounting to the value of $56 million.

However, the idea of creating hurdles to the Alliance's dealings with Greece was never supported by either the US or Britain. On the day following the coup, one representative of NATO stated that the Alliance considered the April coup as an internal affair and NATO's telecommunication web in Greece continued to operate as normal. In a continuous attempt at maintaining stability in NATO's southeastern flank, the Americans immediately after the *coup* pushed the line that JUSMAGG[14] should pursue its normal contacts with the Greek Colonels' regime. In addition, it was recommended that there should not be any change in the venue of international conferences scheduled for Greece as a politically punitive measure, as these negative actions could be counter-productive.

Prevailing hard politics considerations, particularly relevant to the two most prominent NATO members, did not allow any room for risking loosing Greece's cooperation with NATO. Besides, Greece was not the only undemocratic member of the Alliance, as Portugal, an even longer standing anomaly, had been one of NATO's founding members. However, the case of Greece was considered by many as a more serious breach of Article 2, in that the country was deprived of its democracy whilst being a member of NATO.

Another discrepancy within the Alliance was caused by Turkey's periodic failures to meet the democratic criteria for membership, due to the imposition of military dictatorships in 1960 and anew in 1971. Turkey, which had entered NATO in 1952 served as the other guarantor of the organisation's vital eastern anchor, controlling the straits leading from the Black Sea to the Mediterranean and sharing a border with Syria, Iraq, and Iran. Turkey, just like Portugal beforehand and Greece later on, was never expelled on the grounds that their strategic significance was difficult to compromise.

Polemic reactions to the regime became frequent on behalf of the Scandinavian members of NATO, which promptly expressed the wish that the question of suspending Greece's membership to NATO be discussed in due course. More specifically, the Dutch members of Parliament complained about the fact that a NATO contingency plan was used by the coup plotters without the prior consent of the Alliance. However, only the governments of Denmark and Norway decided to proceed with the matter further. In fact, Denmark insisted on the inclusion of the Greek issue in the agenda of NATO's ministerial meeting on 1 May. The meeting was postponed, as a result of NATO's General Secretary's initiative following the threat of Greece's withdrawal from the Alliance. The immediate and intensive diplomatic efforts resulted in convincing Denmark not to raise the issue during the Ministerial meeting. Instead the Danish government was confined to distributing among the participants a *communiqué* condemning the assumption of power in Greece by the Colonels and expressing the hope of the country's rapid democratisation.

The Scandinavian countries' political leaderships based their objections on the grounds that, aside the fact that the regime had an anti-Communist stance it also had a thoroughly undemocratic nature. This dimension became particularly aggravating in light of the Alliance's multifaceted scopes, which did not centre only on safeguarding its members against Communism, but also protecting their democratic liberties. The Preamble to the North Atlantic Treaty clearly affirmed the determination of the parties to safeguard the freedom, common heritage, and civilisation of their peoples founded on the principles of democracy, individual liberty, and the rule of law. Thus, many NATO countries admitted that 'the existence of an undemocratic regime in any member of the North Atlantic Alliance serves to weaken the Alliance as a whole'.[15] In other words, it seemed rather paradoxical that NATO should number among its members regimes like the newly emerged in Greece, which had not come to power through democratic procedures and against which there were pending allegations of lack of respect for the rule of law and its citizens' individual liberties.

Nonetheless, the main NATO allies, for fear of losing Greece's vital cooperation instantly decided not to upset the Colonels' ideologically incompatible regime by publicly opposing it. The Greek propagandists retorted that the Colonels' coup had saved Greece from communism and that their subsequent policies were designed to achieve the very purpose set out in the Treaty. The line, which the US and Britain adopted within NATO was that the new Greek government deserved the right of being allowed reasonable time to live up to its promises of rapid return to democratic rule. The strategic position of Greece was critical and the loyalty of the Greek rulers to the US and NATO unquestioned; hence these considerations overrode any political misgivings regarding the regime. The inflammable situation in the Middle East, the size of the Soviet fleet in the Mediterranean, and the inadequacy of other bases in the area were adduced in support of this view.

It should be always borne in mind that 1967, the year when the Colonels came to power, witnessed many Cold War peaks. Those were of particular concern to NATO and resulted in the increased appreciation of Greece's proximity to this vulnerable area. In fact, it can be argued that Cold War rivalries in the Mediterranean region significantly favoured the new rulers. In other words, the regime had fortuitously come to power at a time when a plethora of international developments taking place at areas geographically related to Greece heightened its value as an ally and put pressure on the NATO allies to endorse it in order to maintain Greece in their anti-Communist camp.

This became particularly obvious, when less than two months after the Colonels came to power, the Six Day War occurred in June 1967. It gave the first serious indication that the Soviets might wish to be involved in the Mediterranean, as during that crisis they deployed for the first time their surface fleet to challenge the influence of US sea power in a region away from the Soviet Union itself.

This Cold War incident proved in the officials' eyes how important Greece was in a very tangible way. During the crisis, the Greek government permitted the United States 'overflights, base rights and blanket [...] use of Crete's landing facilities for the sixth fleet'.[16] Furthermore, thousands of Americans were evacuated from the affected areas and landed in Athens, where they were taken good care of by the Greek regime. At the onset of the fighting, Brigadier Pattakos seized the opportunity immediately by calling the American Ambassador in Athens and offering Greece's assistance to the Americans in whichever way needed. After that, the Americans found it increasingly difficult to cut the bridges of cooperation with the Greek regime. In one of the memoranda composed for President Johnson shortly after, it war clearly pointed out that 'we have in Greece facilities [declassified text, one line] they have increased in values since the Arab–Israeli war' and that 'that war underlined the importance of Greece to US interests'.[17]

The extent to which Greece's collaboration was appreciated by the UK too, the other senior member of the Alliance, becomes manifest in George Thompson's comment made during a meeting with the Greek Minister of Foreign Affairs on 12 September 1967. According to him, 'the United Kingdom attached high importance to relations with Greece both bilaterally and within the Atlantic Alliance'.[18] He also added that his government 'considered it essential to maintain an integrated NATO organisation both as a deterrent and as offering the basis for further *détente* in East/West relations'.[19]

As the months elapsed and the regime's fake pretentions started to show signs of tarnish, a number of NATO members increasingly demanded that Greece's membership be placed under review. In an orchestrated attempt with the Americans to avoid the inclusion of the Greek issue in the December 1967 ministerial agenda, the British argued that to raise the question of Greece's membership would serve only to disrupt the functioning of the alliance. The British, like the Americans and unlike the Italians and the Scandinavians, who firmly supported an initiative to discuss the suspension of Greece from NATO, dearly wished to avoid the eruption of a debate that could evolve against NATO's interest in maintaining excellent relations with Greece. Their main reasoning evolved around their conviction that defence and NATO aspects should be kept separate from their general feelings towards the present regime in Greece. As it was reiterated, despite the realisation that 'as to the situation in Greece itself, the Colonels were bad', it was felt that 'if we pushed the Greek regime into a revolutionary situation, we might be faced with a successor regime with new and dangerous doctrines about NATO'.[20]

One claim, which was repeatedly used, held that the North Atlantic Treaty did not specify that membership of NATO should be restricted to democratic governments. Another argument employed was that punitive actions taken against the government of Greece at an international level, would probably serve the purpose of rallying the Greek public behind the *coup* group, thus fostering introverted nationalism. It was also believed that the Greek people's reaction against such sanctions would be all the more intense because of the fact that no NATO action was taken against Turkey in 1960, when the country was under similar conditions.

To the relief of Britain and the US, the question of Greece's membership to NATO was not raised at the ministerial meeting in December 1967, or indeed at any ministerial meeting thereafter. Commenting on the reasons behind this, the American government concluded the following:

> we believe passage of time, recognition of special relevance of Greece to NATO security at time of Soviet build-up in Eastern Mediterranean, and general desire to project image of united alliance at December meeting have produced a tacit agreement to keep the silence.[21]

Not even the Greek King's failed abortive coup staged from Northern Greece with the help, albeit rather ill-prepared and administered, of the royalist Air Force and Navy, managed to influence dramatically NATO's dealings with the Greek leadership. It is worth mentioning that parallel to the King's abortive coup, the 14th NATO ministerial meeting was taking place in Belgium. The following day, after the confirmation of the failure of the King's attempt and his subsequent flight into exile, the Italian Foreign Minister, Fanfani, openly raised the option of adopting some sort of drastic action against the Colonels' regime, even to the extent of expelling Greece from the Alliance.

Although, Fanfani's initiative was endorsed by some countries and enthusiastically backed by the German foreign Minister Brandt and the Danish Foreign Minister, Dean Rusk, the American Foreign Minister, managed to mute the initiative and instead confined the Alliance to bypassing any general debate, while expressing mild sympathy about the recent developments. The American Ambassador in Athens, Phillips Talbot, commented that 'any discussion within NATO, along the lines that could develop as a result of Fanfani's initiative, would strike at the junta's *amour propre* and thus reinforce the younger officers, who wished to push Papadopoulos towards a Franco-type regime, away from close association with the NATO'.[22] Besides, as Denney, Deputy Director of INR, reasoned, with Portugal a founding member of NATO, and with the Turkish coup of 1960 a matter of record, it seemed rather late in the day to try to give significance to preambular rhetoric.[23]

In fact, this very development, proves how reluctant NATO, mainly through its most powerful member's manipulation, was to even explore the possibility of any punitive actions against the Colonels' regime. This unwillingness becomes ever more aggravating in light of the fact that the King's counter coup on 13 December 1967 was the first serious incident, which challenged the Colonels' self-devised legitimisation theory, on the grounds that, upon coming to power, they did not challenge the institution of the Head of the Greek State. In other words, even when the quasi-constitutional facade of the Colonels collapsed following the King's flight into exile, NATO's attitude towards the Colonels did not change, epitomising therefore the claim that its interaction with the regime was not based on the Alliance's ideological foundations.

In this event's immediate aftermath, most foreign governments', as well as international organisations', dealings with the Colonels' regime froze for a few weeks, especially amidst wide-ranging calls for Greece's international marginalisation. Not long after nonetheless, Ambassador Talbot communicated to Assistant Secretary Lucius Battle on 19 January 1968 that 'indicators picked up in past 24 to 36 hours have given us uneasy feeling that revolutionary committee [has] been lathered into intense nervous excitement and frustration over NATO boycott and that fuse could be burning perilously close to flash point of verbal explosion against the alliance'.[24] The latter consideration was indeed catalytic. It was consequently recognised that the US could not 'squeeze much more out of withholding "recognition"' as they saw a 'real danger that continuing the hard line might push Papadopoulos towards his more radical supporters, who do not want to turn Greece over to civilians or have the King back, and who even talk of quitting NATO'.[25]

As US Defence Secretary Clifford eventually admitted, rather bluntly, in May 1968, 'the obligations imposed on us by the NATO alliance are far more important than the kind of government they have in Greece'.[26] He concluded his rationale by stating that 'if our military aid to our allies was determined by the kind of government they maintain at the moment, then NATO would disintegrate'.[27] So concerned was NATO's mainstream with maintaining Greece's close cooperation that, as *The Times* reported, on 23 September 1968, 'Northern Greece, one of the most sensitive areas of western defence, is to be visited tomorrow by the NATO Military Committee, the supreme military authority of the alliance'.[28]

At this point, it is worth mentioning that of indispensable importance to NATO's stance towards the Colonels was the prevailing American views on the matter. The United States concluded with Greece in October 1953 a military facilities agreement that 'authorised the construction, development, use and operation of military and supporting facilities in Greece necessary for the implementation of, or in furtherance of, approved NATO plans'.[29] The established and expanded facilities following this agreement 'strengthened the NATO forces in the area, provided important communication links, a staging area and supply depots for US and NATO air and naval forces and permitted surveillance and monitoring of the activities of Soviet forces in the Eastern Mediterranean'.[30] They also served the purpose of safeguarding NATO interests not only vis-à-vis the Soviet threat, but also those raised by Middle Eastern and North African countries; for instance, from 'the base at Hellenikon in Athens, surveillance planes had carried out flights over Libya, whereas the base at Iraklion monitored communications from Libya and the Middle East'.[31]

In light of this, the US government, more than any other NATO member, had a particularly strong interest in terms of the NATO-associated benefits in safeguarding the country's normal interactions with NATO. It is common currency that the US foreign policy at the time placed much more emphasis on the security and military considerations and was largely contextualised in the light of the West's hostility with the Soviet Union. Furthermore, the strategic benefits, which the Colonels' regime granted to the US, extended not only to the traditional areas of mutual defence interest against Soviet expansionism, but also those Middle Eastern areas of concern to the US. In view of this, the American officials tended to view NATO merely as an utterly significant strategic equation, to which Greece was quite an essential component, and seem to disregard any ideological discrepancies.

Several international developments in the second part of 1968 confirmed the importance of being on good terms with Greece reinforced the Alliance's determination. The invasion of Czechoslovakia by the Red Army on 20 August in an attempt to eliminate efforts to disassociate the country from Soviet influence came as a shock to NATO and served as a powerful reminder of the omnipresent Communist threat. Utmost importance was therefore attached to eliminating the danger of Communism spreading into neighboring countries. This event did not contribute any less than the significant strengthening of the Communist Parties in neighbouring Italy and Cyprus. Therefore, it can be argued that the events in Czechoslovakia, just like the six-day war in June 1967, brought about NATO's unrestricted backing to the regime resulting in tremendously boosting its grip on power. So provocative was the allied unwillingness even to examine the possibility of Greece's expulsion from the Alliance, that the Norwegian Premier expressed regret at the fact that 'we have allies in NATO who are not willing to observe the fundamental rules of human rights'.[32]

Keeping Greece within the Alliance was considered even more necessary also due to the disdain shown by Colonel Qadafi, soon after he forcibly came to power in 1969, of the conventions that allowed for American bases at the Wheelus Field and British ones at El Adem in Libya. Additionally, towards the end of 1969, a number of intelligence reports sent from Athens drew attention to the fact that the authorities in Moscow were predisposed to having 'relations as cordial as the [Greek] regime will allow'.[33] This was a line that the Soviets seemed keen on in view of the increasingly thorny issues the Greeks faced in their relations with Western organisations, predominately the Council of Europe. Several particularly problematic developments affecting Greece's relations with the West included the forced withdrawal of Greece from the Council of Europe in December 1969. The estrangement became more intense following the adoption on 20 October 1969 by the Plenum of the Parliamentary Assembly of NATO by 26 votes to 4 (with two abstentions), of a draft resolution expressing for the first time the most severe condemnation of the military regime.

The aforementioned intelligence reports were particularly alarming as they quoted Soviet proneness to support the regime, if Greece were to leave NATO and close the bases of its alliance partners. Although there was realisation that due allowance should be made for exaggeration, the expressed fears gained credibility from such developments as 'the recent signing of a new trade agreement and the laying of the cornerstone for a power plant to be built by the USSR'.[34]

Despite that a *rapprochement* between the Greek regime and the Soviet Union seemed unlikely it was believed that if the Greek regime was put into a revolutionary situation, the emerging regime would most probably resemble the one that followed the replacement of Neguib by Nasser in Egypt. Taking 'French leave' from the military side of the alliance was a prospect, which was always seriously feared. It was felt that if the Greek Colonels stopped hosting alliance exercises in Greece, participating in

NATO military committees, and cooperating in meeting NATO needs in Greece, the credibility of the NATO deterrent in its southeastern flank would be impaired.[35] Besides, Greece could simply try to bring counter pressure to bear by introducing new, unfavourable conditions into the use of the facilities used by NATO and the US; for instance, demanding the payment of rent for facilities would be enough of a harassing activity, which could be taken without any sharp break.

It was therefore concluded that Greece had to be convinced to remain within the NATO camp as an irreplaceable part of the alliance's attempt to hold back the Soviets in the Middle East. Emphasis was placed on encouraging Greece to remain an active and cooperative member of NATO and not be pushed towards a Gaullist policy of autonomy. The allied agony over not alienating Greece from the alliance was expressed on 1 April 1969 by British MP Briggs-Davidson in the following way, 'Will the Right Honourable Gentleman depreciate as very dangerous indeed anything tending to weaken the contribution of Greece to NATO?'[36] The reply he received from the government representative was the following:

> We remain firmly opposed to action taken against Greece in NATO, in which Greece occupies a key position of the South Eastern flank. Any attempt to interfere with Greek participation in NATO would be strongly opposed by, among others, the United States, German and Turkish Governments, and would have a politically divisive effect within the alliance in addition to its military implications.[37]

Additionally, as Eldon Griffiths, another British MP, put it: 'I personally hope that they [the Ministers] will not [. . .] suspend Greece'.[38] His argument ran as follows: 'Greece is a member of NATO and a bulwark of our southeastern flank, which is today threatened not only by the Red Army in Rumania, Bulgaria and Hungary but by the growing threat of the Soviet fleet'.[39] To further illustrate this, Griffiths added the following:

> It is essential for the security of every nation represented in this Assembly that the Greek Navy and the Greek air force should remain at NATO's disposal. Anything that were to cast doubt on NATO's commitment to Greece, or that jeopardised the confidence and enthusiasm of the Greek nation for the Atlantic Alliance, could put at risk the best interest of every one of our countries. To suspend Greece in a fit of self-righteousness would be to cut off our noses to spite our faces.[40]

By the end of the 1960s, the incessant Soviet drive for political hegemony in the world had become clearer than ever. The Soviets had continued their effort to spread communism, threaten NATO's lines of communication and disrupt the Western trade. They had expanded their activities both in quality and quantity towards those ends and their tactics had become far more sophisticated.

Furthermore, the competition between NATO and the Warsaw Pact to secure the support of governments in North Africa and the Middle East had been aggravated. Effective political warfare against the West's position was particularly noticeable in the so-called progressive regimes of the Middle East, including Morocco, Algeria, the Sudan, and Somalia. Italy had cajoled the Allies into accepting the return of Palmiro

Togliatti, one of the greatest communist tacticians and ideologists. At the same time in Greece, the Soviets were trying to capitalise and exploit the Greek rulers' dissatisfaction with the West.

As a result of these challenges, one of the first memoranda drafted upon Nixon's assumption of power in the US in 1969 drew attention to the following:

> In the Maghreb and Arab world the objective has been clearly a massive strategic attempt to neutralise and ultimately replace American power in the Mediterranean and to outflank the NATO area, thus dealing a decisive blow against the basic defence posture of the West. Its activities in Somalia, the Sudan and black Africa appear as supporting efforts to this strategic thrust. In each of these cases, there is a pattern of Soviet planning and tactics, indicating a concept of time phasing carefully related to local conditions – cultural, political, economic, etc constituting obstacles and providing opportunities. But the goal in each case is the same – to weaken American influence, to neutralize American power, to create a Soviet presence, to build the roots and posture relevant to progress toward the ultimate goal – an extremist regime, in turn a preface to a fully aligned communist regime.[41]

In the light of the increased uncertainty in strategic terms, it was concluded that not only Greece should not be alienated from the alliance, but, on the contrary, its relatively weakened military ought to be strengthened. By that time, it was assessed by the US Bureau of Intelligence and Research that 'the NATO alliance had taken on a new importance in the light of Soviet military and political penetration in the eastern Mediterranean'.[42] Furthermore, the Alliance's leadership seemed convinced about the necessity of not endangering NATO's stability on the grounds that 'actions against Greece in NATO would not necessarily help the Greek people, but would undermine the security of the southeast flank of NATO, thus putting at risk democratic ideals and parliamentary institutions on a scale far greater than Greece'.[43]

So important had NATO considerations become, as a result of the recent events in Central and Eastern Europe, that the American government announced on 22 September 1970 the partial resumption of deliveries to Greece of grant Military Aid Programme items, which were suspended shortly after the Greek *coup* in April 1967. The approved items included two minesweepers, some combat, trainer aircraft, and ammunition and were 'valued at about $20 million or equal to roughly two-fifths of value of all major items suspended to date'.[44]

The rationale, which the US presented in support of its decision, was justified on the grounds that 'it was an anomaly that Greece remained obligated under Article V of the NATO agreement to defend NATO territory, while the necessary arms deliveries were being withheld'.[45] The decision was reached 'on the premise that a friendly and capable presence in Greece is vital to our interests', a realisation which led to the decision that 'we must address ourselves seriously to the question of maintaining our ally's capabilities'.[46]

As it was recommended also by a report drafted by the British Ambassador about the Greek Armed Forces at the end of December 1970, the allies should not overlook the country's shortage of equipment and spare parts stemming from the suspension of the United States' military assistance. The report brought attention to the fact that the country's difficulty in maintaining any effective fighting units would become even more profound, if its NATO allies continued to deny Greece arms for a further indefinite period. The British agreed that 'we [the British government] should provide the Greeks with adequate means of external defence: particularly after Czechoslovakia, this was essential to NATO security and to our own'.[47] It was also frequently reiterated that their present policy of allowing 'the sale to Greece of arms that she could reasonably be expected to require in order to fulfill her NATO role, and prohibit only the supply of those arms intended to repress the civilian population',[48] should continue uninterrupted.

From the resumption of MAP deliveries and throughout the remaining time of the Colonels, NATO policy towards them did not change dramatically. The challenge of keeping up Greece's capabilities in NATO was recurrent as more regional developments consistently 'underscored the strategic importance of Greek territory, sea lanes, and facilities for maintenance of NATO interests'.[49] For instance, the Greek authorities had agreed to stage operation 'Fig Hill' for Jordanian relief through the Athens airport during the civil war in Jordan. At the same time, it was recorded that 'in November 1970 alone, units of the sixth fleet made more than 250 calls to Greek ports'.[50] Furthermore, observations like those noting Soviet pilots operating directly against Israelis in UAR air space underlined the critical importance of the Greek role in the defense of US and NATO interests in the Eastern Mediterranean.[51]

Among the principal supporters of NATO's unrestricted conduct of business with the Colonels and the resumption of MAP were, along with the US government, also the governments of Britain and Germany. On many occasions, the American officials commented on their joint demarches with the aforementioned countries in the Scandinavian and Benelux capitals to stress the need to avoid raising the issue of Greece in NATO. However, at least twice a year, NATO meetings were held in the shadow of a threatened quarrel over Greece, as there were two conflicting groups of member states formed concerning the issue of the Colonels' regime suitability for NATO.

This was particularly relevant at the time of the resumption of MAP, as it was feared that the American initiative could leave 'a deep and ugly scar upon the NATO and American image'.[52] However, the pro-Greece NATO members were able by hard work to muffle the actual NATO discussion of the Greek issue in Rome [in December 1970], and the NATO meeting was not seriously disturbed as a result.[53] In fact, all preceding and subsequent NATO ministerial meetings passed without serious incidents, as pressure for expelling Greece from the Alliance had significantly abated in response to several Cold War developments. Both the Greek representatives at NATO and their opponents were finding tactful ways of preventing an open clash.

During the seven years that the regime lasted in power, NATO visits and exercises on Greek soil continued unrestricted, with few occasional abstentions. The 'Sunshine Express', a September 1967 NATO exercise, secured the overall participation, despite the initial unwillingness of the British, Belgian, and Italian delegations to take part. Another exercise, the 'Olympic Express', took place in 1969, although the Italian government refused to send troops to participate in it. In addition, in October 1971, the scheduled NATO science committee meeting took place in Athens and a month later Joseph Luns, NATO's Secretary General, paid an official working visit to Greece, in a series of visits to the member states of NATO.

Despite the fact that no official opposition against Greece's membership was expressed during NATO's ministerial meetings, the fact remained that most NATO countries were sharply critical of Greece as well as confronted with domestic controversy on the question. Direct confrontations within NATO were avoided, but there were occasions, when a number of awkward incidents took place.

For instance, the European Atlantic Action Committee on Greece, which was founded under the chairmanship of Sir Hugh Greene in the summer of 1971, promulgated a declaration calling for 'effective action within the EEC and NATO for the restoration of democracy in Greece'.[54] The members of the Committee lobbied delegates to the Ministerial meeting in December 1971 and gave a press conference on the issue, with no tangible results nonetheless. Although the campaign did receive a substantial boost in September with the adoption by NATO's Assembly of a resolution urging governments and member of the Alliance to press for the restoration of democratic freedom in Greece, the official mechanism of NATO seemed untouched by the calls. As it was repeatedly claimed 'pressure in NATO is unlikely to accelerate the restoration of democracy and could even delay it'.[55]

By 1973, the Soviet naval presence in the Mediterranean had reached its zenith. On average, 'each day fifty-eight vessels were in operation in the area'.[56] Furthermore, developments like the Arab–Israeli Yom Kippur War in October 1973, contributed to further appreciating Greece's significance. It was therefore hardly surprising that even the Scandinavian countries, until then the staunchest opponents of the Greek regime, cooled down their opposition noticeable, particularly after feeling that they had applied pressure sufficient to satisfy their public and parliamentary opinion.

Additionally, the 1970s were quite turbulent for the cohesion of NATO. Several issues generated uncertainty including the Soviet Union's intentions, Europe's commitment to its own defence, uncertainty over America's future role, and the strategic and political implications of changes in the global military equation. In addition to this, Greece posed another serious challenge for the alliance due to the suppression of individual liberties, the lack of a genuine popular base for the regime, and the fissures between the government and the military. Concerns over the security of the Eastern Mediterranean were increasing as fears were expressed over the inabilities of the key elements of the Greek armed forces; those were either demoralised or could not in good conscience support a government which had arrogated the liberties of their fellow citizens. At the same time, the American officials noted that their relations with their NATO allies had suffered from the fact that 'NATO's European members consider the scope of the Alliance geographically limited to the area of the Atlantic community as defined in the treaty'.[57]

In addition to the aforementioned concerns, another two factors had come into play. First, at the beginning of the 1970s, the Alliance showed strong determination in achieving progress regarding the attainment of *détente*, making this its main priority at the expense of many other issues. Secondly, the Alliance was being subjected to even greater amounts of pressure demanding Greece's expulsion, as the Greek regime was becoming increasingly authoritarian. Besides, as it looked like the Greek dictatorial regime would not last much longer, there seemed to prevail no need to engage further with it.

In light of the above, the concluding part of the military dictatorship, especially after the overthrow of Colonel George Papadopoulos by the hardliner Brigadier General Dimitris Ioannides in November 1973, witnessed a mild cooling of relations between NATO and Greece. The rather low profile celebration of the NATO's 25th Anniversary in Athens on 8 April 1974, was rather representative of the lukewarm atmosphere which prevailed in the NATO–Greek relations from the beginning of 1974 until the final demise of the unconstitutional regime in July.

As a major concluding remark the stance of the individual NATO members vis-à-vis Greece should be summarised. The following was generally true for most part of the duration of the Greek Colonels' regime. France and Turkey appeared to share no concern about the nature of the Greek regime. The French in particular were carrying out business as usual with the regime, including arms sale, just like the Canadians did, albeit only initially. The British and the West Germans did not wish to cause a rift in NATO by expelling Greece from the Alliance, but certainly felt less comfortable with the Colonels' regime than their aforementioned colleagues. Likewise, the Belgians, despite the fact that they had expressed unhappiness with the Greek regime, lacked any zeal for taking any measures against it within NATO. The smallest members of NATO, namely Luxembourg and Iceland, exhibited a very low profile in connection with the Greek problem.

The governments of Norway, Denmark, Sweden, the Netherlands, and Italy, on the other hand, despite being centrist or right-centre in character, persistently pushed for raising the matter of expelling Greece from the Alliance. They did not necessarily wish to precipitate a rupture in NATO, but felt obliged to express their opposition to the Greek regime vigorously due to the vast amounts of public and parliamentary pressures to which they were subjected. However, the expulsion of Greece from the Council of Europe in December 1969 provided a safety valve for them, and from then followed a more conciliatory stance with the other members of the alliance.

In other words, behind the scenes virtually every NATO country was unhappy about the Greek regime. Although a number of awkward incidents did take place resulting from calls to expel Greece, direct confrontations were avoided, no official opposition against Greece's membership was expressed during NATO's ministerial meetings, and no drastic measures were taken against it.

Another major conclusion is that the regime was the beneficiary of a series of external events in the Mediterranean Sea and on the European continent that had re-emphasised Greece's strategic importance to the NATO alliance and counteracted the distaste of many NATO members for its undemocratic nature and practices. Although NATO officials generally agreed that a dictatorial regime was not ideal for Greece, they still thought that, under the circumstances, the fear of its possible replacement by a Communist regime, which would have been disastrously irresponsible towards NATO, excluded the possibility of opposing the current one.

Consequently, over time the initial awkwardness felt during regular NATO ministerial meetings, due to growing opposition of public opinion, generally softened. The working relationships among the delegations and the NATO headquarters were apparently little affected by Greece's domestic political conditions, as the day-to-day business with the Greek delegation was conducted smoothly.

This of course constitutes a serious discrepancy with the Western world's generally proclaimed attachment to democratic principles. More specifically, NATO showed a much greater degree of tolerance in juxtaposition to all other international organisations and foreign governments towards the regime that emerged from the April 1967 coup. In fact, it seems rather plausible that had it not been for NATO's need to safeguard Greece's membership, the Western governments would have almost certainly adopted a more robustly polemical stance against the Greek military regime, probably even contributing to its earlier demise.

In a nutshell, the importance of Greece for NATO and the consequent leniency showed by the Alliance towards the infamous regime was the main reason for which the regime was never seriously attacked by the western countries. It is undisputed that the Alliance was not content with the regime's practices; however, the need to safeguard itself against the potential threat the Soviets were posing in the Mediterranean surpassed any moral considerations. This should not have come as a surprise as this was the main, if not the only, concern of the Alliance and its most powerful member, when it came to deciding its stance towards the Colonels.

Interestingly enough, such was the degree of tolerance showed by NATO that during the early stages of *metapolitefsi* (the post-Colonels democratisation era), NATO had a negative influence on the formation of democratic political parties and on the Greek public opinion. In fact, NATO's soft attitudes towards the Colonels' regime provided the foundation stone, eventually complimented by the disillusionment, which resulted from the inaction of NATO during the Turkish invasion of the Northern Part of Cyprus in July 1974, on which the Greek Prime Minister Konstantinos Karamanlis based his popular decision to withdraw Greece from NATO's military command structure soon after he came to power in 1974.

Acknowledgements

I am heavily indebted to the A.G. Leventis Foundation and the Hellenic Observatory for hosting my Leventis Research fellowship, which facilitated the writing of this article. A special token of gratitude is also owed to NYU's Remarque Institute and the LBJ Library, whose hospitality and generosity made the collection of material from the American sources possible. Last, but not least, sincere thanks go to Professor John Iatrides for reading through my final draft and making constructive comments.

Notes

[1] Veremis, 'Greece and NATO: Continuity and Change', 237.
[2] MC 48/3 (Military Decision), NATO Strategy Documents, 1949–1969, 11–12.
[3] Snyder, *Defending the Fringe*, 7.
[4] British National Archives (NA), CAB 158/66, 1967 Reports, Memos, Cabinet JIC series, Soviet policies in the Middle East and North Africa and their likely development.
[5] Stavrou, *Mediterranean Security at the Crossroads*, 2.
[6] James, *Keeping the Peace in the Cyprus Crisis of 1963–64*, 51.
[7] Ibid.
[8] NA, FCO 46/1018, Annex, Draft Memorandum by the Secretary of State for Foreign and Commonwealth Affairs, GEN 187(73)5, Cabinet, Interdepartmental Working Group on Cyprus, Cyprus: Financial claims and facilities, Secret, 14 November 1973.
[9] CSIA European Security Working Group, 'Instability and Change on NATO's Southern Flank', 150.
[10] Lyndon Baines Johnson Library (LBJ), NSF, Country File, Middle East, Memos & Miscellaneous, VOL III, Intelligence Memorandum, Subject: Military takeover in Greece (Situation Report Number 2 – 1130 EST), CIA, Directorate of Intelligence, 21 April 1967.
[11] LBJ, NSF Country File, Middle East, Box Number 126, The White House, Memorandum for the President, Subject: The Greek Coup as of 9 a.m., W.W. Rostow, Confidential, 21 April 1967.
[12] LBJ, NSF, Country File Middle East, CIA Intelligence Memorandum, Directorate of Intelligence, The situation in Greece, No 1255/67, Secret, 6 July 1967.
[13] Maragkou, 'The Foreign Factor and the Greek Colonels', 438–9.
[14] The Joint US Military Aid Group (JUSMAGG), whose ranks swelled to 595 personnel at its peak during the Cold War, played an important part in channelling over 5 billion dollars in Marshall Plan post-war and Cold War security assistance aid to Greece between 1947 and 1977, helping to make Greece the single-largest recipient of Western aid in all of post-war Europe. Despite Greece's problematic post-war history, this aid is largely credited with holding Greece within the embrace of Western Europe, despite the economic collapse of literally all of Greece's Cold War-era communist neighbours.
[15] NA, PREM 13/3246, Prime Minister PM/70/9, Greece: Prime Minister's talks in Washington, 22 January 1970.
[16] *Hellenic Review* 1, no. 4 (September 1968), 12.
[17] LBJ, NSF Country File, Middle East, Memorandum for the President, Dean Rusk, Subject: Normalization of US–Greek relations, 21 July 1967.
[18] NA, FO 371/185666 Record of a Meeting held at the Greek Ministry of Foreign Affairs on 12 September 1966, between the Chancellor of the Duchy of Lancaster and the Greek Minister of Foreign Affairs, Confidential, Foreign Office and Whitehall Distribution 12 September 1967.
[19] Ibid.
[20] NA, PREM 13/3246, GMV (70) 2d meeting extract, Confidential, 3 March 1970.
[21] American National Archives and Records Administration, College Park, MA (NARA), Department of State, Central Files, POL Greece, Telegram, NATO 74, US Mission NATO to Secretary of State, Secret, 23 October 1967.
[22] NARA, Department of State, Central Files, POL 23–9 Greece, Telegram, Athens 3188, Talbot, Confidential, 16 January 1967.
[23] NARA, Department of State, Central Files, POL 23–9 GR, Research memorandum REU-68, Subject: Western Europe and Canada confront the Greek situation, George C. Denney to Rusk, Confidential, 27 December 1967.

[24] NARA, Department of State, Central Files, POL 16 Greece, Telegram, Athens 3238, Talbot, American Embassy in Athens to Secretary of State, Secret, Immediate, 19 January 1968.
[25] LBJ Library, NSF Memos to the President, Walt Rostow, Vol. 57, 16–24 January 1968 [2 of 2], Memorandum to the President, Subject: Reply to the Greek Prime Minister, 19 January 1968.
[26] NA, FCO 9/214, Extract from the *New York Herald Tribune,* 25 May 1968.
[27] Ibid.
[28] *The Times,* 23 September 1968, 6.
[29] Valinakis, 'The US Bases in Greece', 9.
[30] Ibid.
[31] Ibid., 11.
[32] Treholt, 'Europe and the Greek Dictators', 214.
[33] NARA Department of State, Central Files, POL Greece–USSR, Director of Intelligence and Research, Intelligence Note 878, Subject: USSR–Greece: Moscow wants good relations with present regime, INR-George C. Denney to the Secretary, Secret/No foreign dissemination, 30 December 1969.
[34] Ibid.
[35] NARA, NSSM 116, POL 1 Greece–US, Briefing Memorandum, J.J. Sisco, NEA, to Under-Secretary, Subject: Policy towards Greece, Secret, 19 March 1971.
[36] Parliamentary Records, House of Commons, Vol. 781, c. 231, 1 April 1969.
[37] NA, FCO 9/885, R.H.G. Edmonds to Bendall, Memorandum on policy towards Greece, Confidential, 6 January 1969.
[38] *Greek Report*, February 1969, 16.
[39] Ibid.
[40] Ibid.
[41] NARA, NSC Files, Nixon Presidential Material, Memorandum, Henry Tasca to The US President, Subject: some aspects of Soviet objectives and tactics in the Mediterranean, Secret, 30 December 1969.
[42] NARA, POL Greece–US, Intelligence Note, Bureau of Intelligence and Research, Greece: Rapprochement with US, Secret, No Foreign Dissemination, 2 November 1970.
[43] Parliamentary Records, House of Commons, Vol. 793, c. 1139, 16 December 1969.
[44] NARA, Department of State, Central Files, DEF 19-8, US–Greece, Telegram 257714, Dept of State to American Embassy in Athens, Confidential, Priority, 18 October 1968.
[45] NARA, Department of State, POL Greece–US, Attachment, Action Memorandum from NEA (Sisco) to the Secretary of State, Secret, 10 August 1971.
[46] NARA, Central Files, Department of State, DEFE 19 US–Greece, Telegram Athens 6505, Tasca American Embassy Athens to Department of State, Subject: US Military Assistance for Greece, Secret, 1 December 1970.
[47] NA, CAB 148/35, OPD (68) 16th meeting, 12 September 1968.
[48] NA, FCO 9/871 Record of a meeting on policy towards Greece: The supply of arms to Greece, Confidential 19 June 1969.
[49] NARA, RG 59, DEF 19 US–Greece, Telegram, Athens 6505, Tasca American Embassy Athens to Department of State, Subject: US Military Assistance for Greece, Secret, 1 December 1970.
[50] Ibid.
[51] NARA, RG 59, DEF 19-8 US–Greece, Telegram, Athens 2105, Tasca, American Embassy Athens to Secretary of State, Secret, 30 April 1970.
[52] NARA, DEF 19-8 US–Greece, Memorandum, Joseph J. Sisco NEA to the Secretary, Department of State, Subject: Arms Shipments to Greece, Secret, No dissemination, 5 June 1970.
[53] Ibid.

[54] NA, FCO 9/1392, Letter, R. L. Secondé to Mr Wiggin and Mr Goodenough, Greece and NATO, Confidential, 13 December 1971.

[55] Ibid.

[56] Winrow, *Dialogue with the Mediterranean,* 54.

[57] NARA, Department of State, Central Files, Telegram, American Embassy Athens to Department of State, Subject: Suggestions for strengthening détente and building peace, Secret, 3 January 1974.

References

Primary sources

Unpublished:
American National Archives and Records Administration, College Park, Maryland.
British National Archives, Kew, London.
Lyndon Baines Johnson Presidential Archives, Austin, Texas.

Published:
Parliamentary Debates, House of Commons & House of Lords.

Periodicals

The Times, London, (1967–1970).
Hellenic Review, ed. Helen Vlachos, (London, monthly, 1968).
Greek Report, ed. Panayotis Lambrias, (London, monthly, 1969).

Secondary sources

CSIA European Security Working Group. 'Instability and Change on NATO's Southern Flank'. *International Security* 3, no. 3 (1978–79): 150–77.

James, Alan. *Keeping the Peace in the Cyprus Crisis of 1963–1964.* London: Palgrave, 2002.

Manthoulis, Roviros. *I Diktatoria ton Syntagmatarchon* [The Dictatorship of the Colonels] [Televised Documentary]. ET1 (Hellenic Television 1).

Maragkou, Konstantina, 'The Foreign Factor and the Greek Colonels' coming to power on 21st April 1967'. *Journal of Southeast European and Black Sea Studies* 6, no. 4 (2006): 427–43.

MC 48/3 (Military Decision). Measures to implement the strategic concept for the defence of the NATO area. NATO Strategy Documents, 1949–1969, 6 May 1969.

Snyder, Jed F. *Defending the Fringe – NATO, the Mediterranean and the Persian Gulf.* Boulder, CO: Westview, 1987.

Stavrou, Nicholaos A., ed. *Mediterranean Security at the Crossroads: A Reader.* Durham, NC: Duke University Press, 1999.

Treholt, Arne. 'Europe and the Greek Dictators', in *Greece under Military Rule,* ed. Richard Clogg and George Yannopoulos. London: Secker & Warburg, 1972.

Valinakis, Yiannis, 'The US Bases in Greece: The Political Context', in *US Bases in the Mediterranean,* ed. Thanos Veremis and Yannis Valinakis. Athens: ELIAMEP, 1989.

Veremis, Thanos. 'Greece and NATO: Continuity and change', in *NATO's southern Allies: Internal and external challenges,* ed. John Chipman. New York: Routledge, 1988.

Winrow, Gareth M. *Dialogue with the Mediterranean: The role of NATO's Mediterranean Initiative.* New York & London: Garland Publishing Inc, 2000.

'Footnoting' as a political instrument: Denmark's NATO policy in the 1980s

Nikolaj Petersen

The intensification of the Cold War in the 1980s bred tensions within both the NATO alliance and its member states. Criticism of NATO's policy was pronounced among the social democratic parties in Northern Europe and found extraordinary expression in Denmark during the so-called footnote period of 1982–88. Here a coalition of centre-left opposition parties was able to control NATO policy by way of parliamentary resolutions which forced the government to take increasingly critical positions in NATO, mainly by 'footnoting' communiqués. The government chose to 'live with' footnoting in order to keep power. The result was domestic strife, allied criticism and a policy which moved Denmark away from NATO's mainstream.

The problem

The intensification of the Cold War in the 1980s bred tensions between the United States and its European NATO allies as well as within the individual member states over the right balance between alliance solidarity and political autonomy. In theoretical terms, Glenn Snyder's alliance dilemma[1] was sharpened, pitting political groupings (mostly governments) who feared 'abandonment' if alliance solidarity was weakened against those who feared 'entrapment' by the Reagan administration's harsh policies, if they did not protest. Prominent among these critics were the social democratic parties of Northern Europe, including Denmark where the alliance dilemma came to full blossom. During the so-called footnote period of 1982–88 a coalition of opposition parties, headed by the Social Democrat Party, managed to control official NATO policy via parliamentary resolutions. These obliged the government to take in critical positions in NATO by 'footnoting' communiqués. Hence the term *fodnotepolitik*. The government chose to 'live with' this in order to stay in power. The result was domestic strife, allied criticism and a policy which moved Denmark away from NATO's mainstream.

After the Cold War political strife continued over the footnote period. No fewer than four successive reports have been officially commissioned to find the truth, or rather the 'right' truth about Denmark's policies in the Cold War years.[2] The driving forces were the Liberal leader Uffe Ellemann-Jensen, who bore the brunt of footnoting as Foreign Minister in 1982–93, and especially Anders Fogh Rasmussen, Prime Minister 2001–09 and currently Secretary-General of NATO, in whose view the footnoting of the 1980s ranks with collaboration with the German occupiers during World War II as the most despicable episode in recent Danish history.[3] This denunciation of footnoting is part of the ideological underpinning of Denmark's activist foreign policy in the 2000s, notably its involvement in the 'War on Terror' in close cooperation with the United States. As a bonus, it has also proved a convenient disciplining instrument vis-à-vis repentant Social Democrat 'footnoters'.

A *précis* of footnoting

A preliminary delineation

Given the controversial nature of *fodnotepolitik* it is imperative to be precise about its contents and ramifications. In Danish as in German the term *politik* covers both 'politics' and 'policy', and *fodnotepolitik* therefore refers to both a specific political process, 'footnote politics', and its output, 'footnote policy'. 'Footnoting' literally means attaching (critical or dissenting) comments to an official document, but in an expanded sense it refers to open dissent to NATO positions, whether expressed in formal footnotes or not, and whether manifested in NATO itself or in other contexts.

The article first provides a *précis* of the two components of *fodnotepolitik*. Then follows a discussion of its background in international and domestic politics and a detailed history of this singular episode in Danish foreign policy. Finally, its impact on Denmark's post-Cold War policy is discussed.

Footnote politics

Footnote politics introduced a new way of coalition formation and foreign policy making in the *Folketing*, Denmark's unicameral parliament. Until the 1980s national security policy rested on a broad consensus between the so-called Atlantic parties, i.e. the Social Democrats, Liberals and Conservatives, with the Social Democrats in a hegemonic position. This had shown in the 1950s when Denmark's NATO policy was qualified by two reservations, initiated by social democratic governments, namely a ban on the permanent stationing of allied forces in Denmark (1953) and a ban on the introduction of nuclear weapons in Denmark (1957), both 'under present circumstances'. In both cases the Liberals and Conservatives had protested, but acquiesced for strategic reasons, primarily to prevent the formation of a security policy majority to the left, centred round the Social Democrats and the semi-neutralist Social Liberals. In the 1960s and 1970s the tripartite Atlantic coalition continued and was occasionally widened to include the Social Liberals. This took place on the same basis as before: The Social Democrats were allowed to call the tune, most visibly in an active detente policy, as long as they did not question alliance solidarity.

What happened in the 1980s was old fears coming true: the collapse of the Atlantic consensus and the consolidation of an 'alternative' security policy majority of centre-left parties in the *Folketing*. This situation evolved after the appointment in September 1982 of a minority government of Conservatives (whose leader Poul Schlüter stayed on as Prime Minister until 1993), Liberals, and two small centre parties. The government counted on support from the Social Liberals on domestic issues, but on security policy issues they were in opposition. This made possible the formation of an 'alternative majority' of Social Democrats, Social Liberals, People's Socialists and Left Socialists.

Over the next six years this formation used the whole gamut of parliamentary procedures to control official NATO policy by asking questions, arranging hearings in the Foreign Policy Committee, proposing parliamentary decisions, and (in particular) by demanding frequent interpellation debates. These debates could be called by any group of MPs and were usually wound up by the adoption of a resolution (*dagsorden*) which enjoined the government to follow a certain policy line and often also prescribed how. Most debates were called by the two socialist, anti-NATO parties.

According to the Danish Constitution Art. 20, foreign policy is a government prerogative, except that parliamentary consent is required for engaging in war and ceding territory. The only other qualification is Art. 19 to the effect that the government shall seek the counsel of the parliamentary Foreign Policy Committee before major foreign policy decisions. Even though neither such counsel nor parliamentary resolutions are legally binding, they are so in practice according to the principle of parliamentarism. Until the Schlüter government changed it, Danish parliamentarism meant that no government would accept a clear defeat in the *Folketing* without resigning or calling an election. Now the Schlüter government chose to accept repeated defeats and to 'live with' representing policies in NATO which it was dead against. As long as the Social Liberals kept their hands under the government, the alternative majority could vote the government *down* on specific issues, but not vote it *out* of office.

Footnote policy and its implementation

Over the years footnote policy meant a gradual change of Danish NATO policy, which by 1988 had veered significantly from NATO's mainstream. The most prominent case of this creeping process concerned NATO's 'dual-track' decision of December 1979 to deploy 572 medium-range (INF) missiles in Western Europe as from December 1983, failing an arms control agreement with the Soviet Union.[4] But new issues were added, such as the US Strategic Defense Initiative and NATO's tactical nuclear weapons. Other dissenting positions were taken in the UN General Assembly on nuclear freeze, no first use, and a comprehensive nuclear test ban. The promotion by the parliamentary majority of the idea of *Norden*[5] as a nuclear-free zone was a further irritant. Footnote policy climaxed in 1988, when the *Folketing* adopted a resolution on new conditions for port calls by allied naval vessels, which threatened to unleash a major crisis in Denmark's alliance relations. This government now finally called a general election, which came to mark the end of the alternative majority.

Footnote policy was thus mainly confined to nuclear weapons policy, while other security policy issues were less affected, most notably Greenland's role as an important US defence post.[6] Nor was defence policy directly affected, even though Denmark's performance did not escape US criticism.[7]

The defining method of implementation prescribed by the alternative majority was footnoting communiqués from NATO meetings to the effect that Denmark reserved its position on a certain question. But the 'footnote' could also consist of a reference to the Danish position in the communiqué itself. Over time these prescriptions became ever more concrete, e.g. by directing the government to 'work for' (or 'work actively for') specific positions in NATO or to express dissent on certain lines in NATO or elsewhere. Common to these prescriptions was a demand for visibility, i.e. a public documentation that the instruction had been heeded. The reason was two-fold. First, footnote policy was highly symbolic with visibility as a primary goal. Secondly, the opposition was manifestly distrustful of the government's will to act loyally upon its prescriptions. Especially, it distrusted Foreign Minister Uffe Ellemann-Jensen (Lib.), and with some reason.

The setting

The international background

Footnoting had external as well as domestic causes. The worsening East–West relations and the resulting pressure for NATO cohesion after the mid-1970s challenged social democratic feelings of ownership to European détente, which derived from Denmark's active participation in the CSCE process. As a result the party grew critical of the general course of US foreign policy under Jimmy Carter and still more under Ronald Reagan.

In the early days NATO's dual-track decision of December 1979 was the most conspicuous instance of the pressure for alliance cohesion. A new chapter opened in 1981 when the Reagan Presidency added new strain to alliance consensus by its harsh Cold War rhetoric, confrontational diplomacy and rearmament efforts.[8] By the time Anker Jørgensen's Social Democrat government quit office in September 1982, relations with Washington had soured considerably.[9]

It is important to note that the Danish Social Democrats were not alone in having difficulties with the course of US and NATO policy. In January 1981 the social democratic parties from Norway, Denmark, the Netherlands, Belgium and Luxembourg set up an informal forum, called *Scandilux*, for the discussion of NATO's INF programme and other nuclear issues. The French Socialist Party and the British Labour Party were associated with the group together with the German SPD whose security policy *Vordenker*, Egon Bahr, became its 'mentor'. *Scandilux*'s importance to the Danish party was threefold. It provided a platform for the exchange of information and ideas which accelerated the party's change of policy. It bestowed legitimacy on this change process. And it gave internal status to those who took part in its discussions. The Danish input in *Scandilux* was not significant, but contrary to the other parties, which also lost power in 1981–82, it remained in at least partial control over official foreign policy. Denmark thus became a sort of test lab for the *Scandilux* parties.[10]

The domestic background

The tightening of US and NATO policy would probably, *ceteris paribus*, have strained Denmark's position in NATO anyway. But things were not equal, as the Social Democrat Party had begun a revision of its security policy in the late 1970s. What was presented as a 'sharpening' (not a change) of long-held positions, had domestic roots besides the external ones discussed above.[11] First, the party leadership, Anker Jørgensen (Prime Minister 1972–73, 1975–82), Kjeld Olesen (Foreign Minister 1979–82) and Lasse Budtz (parliamentary foreign policy spokesman 1979–87), changed views individually and as a group. By the late 1970s Anker Jørgensen began to vent his view of nuclear weapons as 'the Devil's work'.[12] He was also critical of the dual-track decision and never accepted (some would say: understood) its rationale.[13] In the early 1980s he openly questioned the necessity of military balance, and in 1982, shortly before his resignation, he told a perplexed French journalist, that 'We are members of NATO, but I repeat I am absolutely against nuclear weapons'.[14] Anker Jørgensen was the decisive figure, but Foreign Minister Kjeld Olesen, originally a NATO stalwart, gradually followed suit. Finally, Lasse Budtz, a left-wing proponent of an independent, 'social democratic' foreign policy, became the kingpin in the parliamentary game, which began in September 1982.

The party's change of policy also reflected a shifting balance between moderates and leftists among its MPs after the election in October 1979 had returned a number of young, left-leaning MPs. While they never constituted a group majority, their dedication was high, and as the party leadership was receptive to their arguments, the moderate majority usually caved in. The first instance was the party's decision that Denmark should try to steer its own dissenting course at the NATO ministerial meetings in December 1979, where the INF deployment was up for decision.

The first 'footnote situation' therefore arose when Foreign Minister Olesen went to Brussels with a proposal to postpone the decision for up to six months while the Soviets' willingness to initiate arms control talks with the United States was tested.

If this proposal failed to gain support, he was at least to have 'something' included in the communiqué. As expected, the proposal got a short shrift, and the Minister had to fight hard for an oblique reference to it in the communiqué. Having secured this, he accepted the decision without any formal reservations.[15]

From this point and until Anker Jørgensen's government resigned in September 1982, it increasingly emphasised the arms control track, that is, the possibility to negotiate away or drastically reduce the need for a NATO deployment. Therefore it was soon frustrated by what it saw as the Reagan administration's lack of will to negotiate. And while the government formally adopted the so-called zero solution eventually proposed by President Reagan in November 1981, it was willing to accept a Western zero for a significant reduction of SS-20s.

This led to the first 'genuine' footnote in a meeting in NATO's Nuclear Planning Group (NPG) in April 1982. Shortly before, President Brezhnev suggested a compromise formula, which Prime Minister Jørgensen – against the express warning of the Ministry of Foreign Affairs[16] – termed 'agreeable' in a press statement.[17] No other NATO leader welcomed the proposal, and the Danish Ambassador to Washington was summoned before Deputy Secretary of State Walter Stoessel to receive a demarche.[18] At the NPG meeting Defence Minister Poul Søgaard argued that the Soviet proposal was a small step in the right direction, so he could not subscribe to a wholesale rejection of it. The crux of the matter was of course that he could not disavow his Prime Minister. So he set a footnote which was camouflaged as a disagreement over the right forum for commenting on the Soviet proposal.[19]

The main battles 1982–88

The formation of the 'alternative majority'

The 'real' footnote period began a few months later, after the formation of Poul Schlüter's (Cons.) government with Uffe Ellemann-Jensen (Lib.) and Hans Engell (Cons.) as Foreign and Defence Ministers, respectively. Between 7 December 1982 and 14 April 1988 the *Folketing* adopted a total of 23 security policy resolutions against the will of the government. For tactical reasons the government parties abstained on nine of them and even voted for a couple of opposition resolutions for the sake of domestic peace.[20]

These resolutions reflected the continued hardening of the Social Democrats' position on nuclear policy, but were also part of the general fight for power between government and opposition. The Social Democrats were now willing to exchange the traditional Atlantic consensus for cooperation with the left-wing parties, despite resistance among the party moderates. However, the moderate 'custodians' as they were called, caved in, especially as it turned out that the government did not consider its defeats serious enough to risk a general election. This gave the two socialist and anti-NATO parties an unprecedented opportunity to gain influence, which they used to the full in what party leader Gert Petersen (People's Socialist) called 'an aggressive cooperation policy with offensive pressure upon the Social Democrats'.[21] They did so by calling frequent interpellation debates where they presented draft resolutions which took their cue from Social Democrat statements, and which were eventually adopted in amended versions proposed by Lasse Budtz on behalf of the Social Democrats.

Footnoting was vehemently criticised by the government parties. They bemoaned the lapse of Atlantic consensus and criticised Anker Jørgensen for having abandoned the 'staunch' pro-NATO policies of his predecessors, Hans Hedtoft, H.C. Hansen and J.O. Krag.[22] The emerging chasm between the two sides was further widened in a polarisation process in which the government parties also sharpened their security policy profile. Before 1979 the Liberals had been a rather 'soft' pro-Atlantic party, not far to the 'right' of the Social Democrats and 'softer' than the Conservatives.[23] But now the party moved to a tougher pro-NATO position, which was reinforced when Foreign Minister Ellemann-Jensen became party chairman in 1984. The Liberals were now positioned to the right of the Conservatives, whose leading figures, Prime Minister Schlüter and Defence Minister Engell, proved less concerned about the alternative majority than the Foreign Minister. But as a whole, the government parties now emphasised alliance solidarity more strongly than before and sought to move closer to NATO's mainstream.[24]

Nonetheless the government chose to 'live with' the reign of the alternative majority for nearly six years. Why? Primarily because economic reform was considered more important than the largely symbolic concessions over foreign policy. Another argument for clinging to power was that it gave the government a certain latitude in the implementation of the directives. Besides, calling a 'NATO election' was risky, as public opinion rather seemed to side with the opposition than with the government. The dual-track decision had been unpopular with 43% of the population (only 31% for in 1979), and remained so as the deployment date in December 1983 approached; in the summer of 1983 58% were against and only 24% for deployment.[25]

The evolving footnote policy: the INF battle 1982–83

The Social Democrats tightened their grip on security policy during the first eight months of the Schlüter government. In October 1982 the first shot was fired, when Anker Jørgensen – inspired by the Norwegian Labour Party – demanded a suspension of Denmark's contribution to the INF part of NATO's Infrastructure Programme. The sum in question was only 46 million Danish kroner, but the government saw it as a serious threat to alliance solidarity and complained that the Social Democrats now reneged on their prior commitments to the financing of INF infrastructure.

When the *Folketing* debated the question in December 1982, the Social Democrats phrased their draft resolution so that the two socialist parties would not vote for it. At the same time, they threatened to vote for the stronger wording proposed by these parties if the government side defeated the party's own draft. Faced with the threat of what eventually became the alternative majority, and having been reassured that it could make those payments which the previous government had authorized, the government parties abstained in the vote with the odd consequence that the resolution was carried by only 49 votes (the Social Democrats themselves) against 13 (the right-wing Progress Party), while 90 MPs abstained.[26] The resolution was heavily criticised in NATO despite the government's attempt to downplay its importance and its assurances that Denmark continued to support the dual-track decision and the Western negotiation position, i.e. the zero solution.[27]

At the same time a second front was opened, namely Denmark's voting practice in the UN General Assembly. Here Sweden and Mexico had tabled a joint draft resolution which would freeze existing nuclear stocks, which the government was inclined to vote against together with other NATO members. However, after receiving the threat of a no confidence vote it abstained, and the next year, in 1983, it was obliged to vote *for* the resolution.[28]

Having broken the ice, the Social Democrats' attempt to direct official policy gained momentum. Returning in January 1983 from a *Scandilux* meeting former Foreign Minister Kjeld Olesen sketched a 10-point programme, which was converted into *Folketing* resolutions over the following years. Among its demands were: support for a nuclear freeze; rejection of 'President Reagan's zero solution'; a new Western INF initiative; no Western INF deployment against a further reduction of SS-20; the inclusion of the British and French strategic missiles in the Western count; and continuation of the INF negotiations beyond 1983 without deployment. Finally, the programme commented favourably on the idea of a Nordic nuclear-free zone.[29]

The next step in the evolution of footnote policy concerned the zero solution. On 8 February 1983 the Social Democrats introduced a draft resolution enjoining the government to work for supplementing the zero solution with 'a realistic alternative' to the latest Soviet 'offer'. Furthermore, it should work for such reductions of the Soviet SS-20s that would make a Western deployment superfluous, and support 'realistic efforts' to establish nuclear-free zones on both sides of the iron curtain.[30]

By now the government had itself begun to discuss the merits of a so-called 'interim solution', which would not require the total removal of the already deployed SS-20s. On 3 February a new government policy was proclaimed, according to which the zero solution remained the best, but NATO should be open to other outcomes and demonstrate an open and active will to negotiate.[31] The internal discussions in an ad hoc 'rocket committee' consisting of Prime Minister Poul Schlüter, his protégé Defence Minister Hans Engell, and Foreign Minister Uffe Ellemann-Jensen revealed significant differences between the Foreign Minister and his two Conservative colleagues.[32] The Prime Minister did not believe that NATO's INF missiles would be deployed and warned against positioning Denmark to the right of President Reagan. According to him the Danish position should be 'reasonable flexibility without disloyalty'. While Ellemann-Jensen accepted the need for flexibility, he expressed no preference for a specific outcome.[33] As a consequence the government voted for the Social Democrat draft resolution on 8 February. This time the reception in NATO was mild, as several other member states were moving in the same direction.[34]

In the follow-up Ellemann-Jensen emphasised the need to take European public opinion into consideration, so as to avoid a trans-Atlantic split. As he told US Assistant Secretary of State Kenneth Dam on 23 March, the essence of the INF question was 'the fight for Europe's soul'.[35] The US proposal on 30 March of an interim agreement on the reduction, not elimination of INF missiles on both sides was therefore received with satisfaction.

The government's reaction so far to the Social Democrat initiatives was motivated by a desperate wish to avoid the consolidation of a permanent alternative majority. But by May the last dike burst. On 26 May the Social Democrats presented a draft resolution in the *Folketing* which enjoined the government to present four detailed proposals at the upcoming NATO ministerial meetings: NATO should be prepared to negotiate beyond 1983; NATO should refrain from deployment as long as negotiations continued; French and British strategic missiles should be included in the East–West balance; and finally the aim should be such reductions of SS-20s which would obviate NATO's need for INF deployment.

There were strong doubts in the Social Democrat parliamentary group which the leadership countered by arguing that these were points to which the party was already committed.[36] In the *Folketing* Lasse Budtz emphasised Denmark's duty to counteract the arms race and a new cold war, and assured, in a remark prearranged with the Foreign Minister, that the resolution lay within the bounds of the dual-track decision. Even though the government doubted this, the assurance was important as it allowed it to state that Denmark's support of the INF programme was unimpaired. But otherwise the government was alarmed by the resolution. Prime Minister Schlüter proclaimed that 34 years of cooperation had come to an end, and that Denmark now risked being seen as a second-class member of the Alliance, as NATO's 'crank'. The government would vote against the resolution, he said, but respect it by presenting it in NATO – though without giving up its right to explain its own views.[37]

How to present the resolution in NATO once again revealed rifts in the government. Prime Minister Schlüter and Defence Minister Engell argued that in order to avoid new confrontations the resolution had to be mentioned in the communiqués from the forthcoming ministerial meetings in NATO. On the other hand, Foreign Minister Ellemann-Jensen argued that as the resolution allegedly lay within the dual-track decision, the usual procedure in NATO should be followed, leaving it to the alternative majority to topple the government if it would and could. However, the Prime Minister resolved that some kind of a footnote would probably be required.[38]

The end result was a paragraph in the relevant NATO communiqués that the ministers (Engell and Ellemann-Jensen) had repeated Denmark's support for the dual-track solution, but also mentioned the *Folketing* resolution. It proved difficult to reach this result, and there was much criticism of the two ministers.[39] The government's handling of the situation did not receive much praise back home, either. The opposition missed a proper footnote and doubted that the government had represented its view effectively and loyally. This pattern was to repeat itself over the following years.

Now the course was set towards a total collapse of government–opposition relations and of Denmark's support for the INF programme. The government fought in vain against this by counselling flexibility towards the Americans and appeasing the opposition by publicly declaring the May resolution part of government policy along with the dual-track decision.[40] But neither party was susceptible to persuasion. On 5 November the *Folketing* adopted a fresh resolution, which directed the government to work 'actively' for the May resolution and to call for a meeting in the NATO Council before deployment.[41] The government obliged, only to meet a flat no. Later in November the beginning of INF deployment occasioned a serious clash between the government and the alternative majority.

Tempers ran high, and at a closed meeting in his constituency on 21 November the battered Foreign Minister reportedly referred to the footnote resolutions in a way which could be interpreted as disdain for the *Folketing* as an institution. While the Minister claimed to have been quoted incorrectly by the press, the socialist parties now filed a motion of no confidence in him. He was eventually saved by the Social Liberals, but Prime Minister Schlüter had to concede officially that the government could not continue if acting against a *Folketing* resolution or majority counsel in the Foreign Policy Committee.[42]

At the same time the final INF drama unfolded. On 1 December a new parliamentary resolution demanded that the government should 'clearly' oppose INF deployment in the upcoming NATO meetings with the argument that the negotiation process was not exhausted. Furthermore, this point should be clearly mentioned in the communiqué. During the debate Mr Budtz claimed that detente and disarmament now lay in ruins and that the military balance had shifted since 1979, so that there was no longer any military need for NATO's INF deployment. In this way he avoided disavowing the 1979 decision as such. Foreign Minister Ellemann-Jensen also deplored the fact that deployment had become necessary, but repeated his main argument during 1983, that what was put up could be taken down again.[43] In the following NATO meeting he fought hard for a formula he could accept, but finally had to add the dreaded footnote to the effect that Denmark clearly dissociated itself from the ongoing INF deployment. This caused widespread dismay among the NATO ministers mixed with some understanding that the Foreign Minister acted under duress.[44]

This outcome of the long-running INF saga left a certain fatigue in its wake. INF disappeared from the domestic agenda, while the government duly continued to footnote references to the programme in NATO until a wording was found in December 1986 which did not require a footnote. One year later, in December 1987, the signing of the Washington Treaty which banned all INF missiles served as an ironic comment to the previous debate in Denmark.

SDI and other battles 1984–87

Having prevailed in the domestic INF battle, the Social Democrats sought to consolidate their hold by tabling a new draft resolution in May 1984. It became known as the 'omnibus' resolution, because it took up a number of issues that had been placed on the backburner or were new. The new front issue was the idea of a Nordic nuclear-free zone. This was an old Soviet concept, which had first entered the Nordic debate with the Finnish Kekkonen Plan of 1962 and then been re-launched in 1980/81 by the Norwegian Labour Party. Past Danish governments had routinely dismissed the idea because of its incompatibility with NATO's Flexible Response strategy. However, it was now embraced by the rapidly growing Danish peace movement,[45] and gained ground in the Social Democrat Party as well, where Anker Jørgensen became its primary spokesman.

In the omnibus resolution of May 1984 the central, somewhat convoluted demand was that the government should work for Denmark to remain nuclear-free in peace, crisis and wartime by promoting the nuclear-free zone within 'a larger European context' and guaranteed by the Soviet Union and the United States. This was a tall order, indeed impossible, as the United States was dead against the zone idea and the Soviets reluctant to commit themselves.[46] Besides, the resolution raised other demands such as the resumption of the INF talks, a freeze on the modernisation of short-range nuclear weapons systems, a general freeze of all nuclear forces, a total nuclear test ban, no-first-use, a ban on chemical and biological weapons, etc. Many of these demands were in conflict with Flexible Response, most clearly no-first-use.[47]

Foreign Minister Ellemann-Jensen responded in the *Folketing* debate on 3 May that the draft resolution could have been much worse, and that the government agreed with several of its elements, such as 'the proposal to ban nuclear detonations and nuclear deployment in space'.[48] The Minister stated that the government parties would abstain in the vote, but also expressed his hope for a restoration of a broad consensus on the basis of the resolution. Anker Jørgensen responded amiably that the government now seemed to be approaching the Social Democrats' position. A certain rapprochement was in the air.[49]

One month later Svend Auken, Social Democrat political spokesman and deputy chairman, proposed a procedure for restoring consensus. He recognised the weakness of parliamentary resolutions as foreign policy instruments and asked the government to provide an analysis of principles and problems in Danish security policy, which could then be discussed in an ad hoc committee.[50] The government eagerly grabbed the invitation and set up a civil servants' working group to provide a report. The so-called Dyvig Report of November 1984 appealed to both sides: to the Social Democrats to rejoin the former consensus and to the government parties to give more emphasis to détente and disarmament, so as not to obstruct an inter-party compromise.[51] Very little came out of the exercise, however. The political ad hoc committee was duly appointed, but none of the parties was ready to give the necessary concessions. The government saw the committee talks as a means to guide the Social Democrats back into the fold, while the latter saw them as a means to commit the government to the policies of the omnibus resolution.

One reason for this failure was bitter strife over the Strategic Defense Initiative (SDI), which had grown out of President Reagan's vision of making nuclear weapons 'impotent and obsolete'. The alternative majority expressed its negative (but mistaken) view of SDI in the 'omnibus' resolution, and Foreign Minister Ellemann-Jensen was originally also concerned about its consequences for the strategic balance, a concern which was also voiced in the Dyvig Report.[52] Gradually the Foreign Minister took a more agnostic stand, however. In March 1985 he professed to the *Folketing* that it was unknown whether or not SDI was the way to remove or reduce the nuclear threat. The debate ended with the adoption, against the no-votes of the government parties, of a Social Democrat draft resolution to the effect that Denmark was against deployment of weapons in outer space and against 'participation in research and development' into them. Even though opposition leaders assured that the resolution only banned Danish participation in SDI research, the government voted against, probably out of deference to President Reagan's pet idea.[53]

Simultaneously Defence Minister Engell sat in an NPG meeting where US Secretary of Defense Caspar Weinberger unexpectedly requested an allied endorsement of the SDI research programme and of the US invitation to NATO Europe to join it. While Engell duly put the customary INF footnote, he accepted – in close consultation with Prime Minister Schlüter – a reference in the communiqué which gave the requested support. At Engell's insistence, the Europeans were only asked to 'consider' joining, however.[54]

The Defence Minister had not promised Danish participation, but the opposition reacted forcefully by suspending discussions in the ad hoc committee and calling for another parliamentary debate which strengthened the previous resolution with a general censure of SDI research, not just of Denmark's participation in it.[55]

The episode sent the Danish–American relationship to rock bottom. Ever since the dual-track decision in 1979, but especially after the Reagan administration took over, the US administration had been dissatisfied with the Danish course of action. The Schlüter government sought to improve relations when it took over, but even though President Reagan reacted affably to the first footnote resolutions by remarking that such were the conditions of democracy,[56] the government could not avoid a growing US irritation over the reign of the alternative majority. In November 1983 Eigil Jørgensen, the grand old man of Danish diplomacy, was sent to Washington as Ambassador with the express mission to improve relations after the INF debacle. In June 1984 he reported rather alarmingly that the US had now formed an opinion of Denmark as a free-riding ally on its way to dissociating itself from the Western security community.[57] Tensions erupted in a dramatic encounter between US Secretary of State George Schulz and Ellemann-Jensen in Washington on 20 April 1985. Schulz started by criticising the Danish refusal to take part in SDI research. He found it incomprehensible that countries which had criticised the US preoccupation with nuclear weapons now criticised a defence concept which aimed at doing away with them. Ellemann-Jensen countered that the United States put too much pressure on NATO and asked whether the US preferred a united or a split alliance. Schulz bluntly rejected this argument. Denmark's policy differed not only from that of the United States, but from most other European countries as well. 'If all Europeans were like you, there would be no NATO', he exclaimed, and Denmark should be under no illusion that the United States would come to the rescue for the third time, if the European countries were like Denmark.[58]

The real addressee of this sermon was not the hapless Foreign Minister, who afterwards had the satisfaction of forwarding the message to the Foreign Policy Committee back home. On the other hand, as Schulz told Prime Minister Schlüter when he paid an official visit to Washington in September 1985, the government was ultimately responsible for the foreign policy of the country.[59] But now that the Americans had made their point, relations improved. As for SDI it seems that Ellemann-Jensen's warning had some effect, as the United States did not press the issue in NATO for more than a year. The Danish SDI footnote was not required until May 1986.[60]

The crunch 1988

In December 1986 Ellemann-Jensen defiantly declared the footnote period over,[61] and for more than a year the *Folketing* refrained from adopting new resolutions against the government's will. On 8 December 1987 the divisive INF issue was finally laid to rest with the signing of the Washington Treaty. But at the same time an esoteric issue, allied port calls, once again conjured up the spectre of footnote policy. As mentioned, Denmark had declared itself nuclear-free 'under present circumstances' back in 1957. Ten years later, in 1967, Prime Minister J.O. Krag laid down an official port call policy which was adhered to for the next 20 years, namely that Denmark would not remind allied governments of Denmark's nuclear policy in connection with port call permissions, but assume that the allied governments knew and respected this policy.[62]

US port calls in the summer of 1987 inspired the Socialist People's Party to table a draft decision in parliament, which called for a more restrictive policy.[63] This put pressure on the Social Democrats, whose leadership was painfully aware of the risks involved. In September both Lasse Budtz and Svend Auken warned the parliamentary group against a crisis like the one between the United States and New Zealand,[64] and the party's initial position was therefore noncommittal. But at the first hearing of the draft decision on 27 November 1987 Budtz stated that port call permissions should explicitly refer to Denmark's nuclear-free status and the expectation that nuclear weapons were not carried onboard. The government was totally opposed, fearing a crisis which would endanger Denmark's position in NATO.[65] After its first reading the issue was remitted to the parliamentary Defence Committee before its second and final reading some time in the spring of 1988. Soon after, on 7 December, the first US reaction came in a stern message to Defence Minister Bernt Johan Collet,[66] and the American concern was undoubtedly also voiced when Secretary Schulz met with Ellemann-Jensen and Auken the following week.

It is not clear what made the Social Democrats abandon their original reserve. One factor was an uneasy relationship between Auken, the newly elected party chairman, and Budtz, as well as Auken's difficulties with controlling a fractioned parliamentary group. Another was that Norway had recently adopted a slightly stricter formula, according to which port call permissions were given 'according to the conditions which apply to port calls of warships in Norway'. On the other hand, the Norwegian Labour Party was sceptical of the formula, which the Social Democrats presented in the Defence Committee on 22 March 1988. According to this, visiting naval vessels should be informed of the Danish policy; '[a] precondition for receiving permission is therefore that visiting warships know and respect this [policy]'. The formula was presented as a continuation of Krag's line, but in reality it was rather far-reaching in seemingly putting responsibility for observance on the individual ship and its captain.[67] Three days later US Ambassador Terrence Todman expressed his strong critique in a meeting with Svend Auken who responded that the party was under considerable pressure and that there was no change of policy substance.[68] When the two men met again on 28 March the Ambassador was armed with an instruction to the effect that the United States could not accept any undermining of the 'neither confirm nor deny' principle,[69] and that if port calls were to be conditioned upon observance of and respect for 'anti-nuclear policies', the United States would cancel ship visits to Denmark. Svend Auken responded emotionally that now he knew how it was to be in Budapest receiving directives from the Soviets.[70]

While the proposed parliamentary decision continued to be discussed in the Defence Committee, the process was short-circuited by an interpellation debate on 14 April 1988. This caused the government to contact both the State Department and leading Social Democrats in order to explore a compromise formula which both could accept. What followed was an incredibly complicated and high-risk game. On 11 April Schlüter and Ellemann-Jensen met with party chairman Svend Auken and Svend Jacobsen, Chairman of the *Folketing* and a moderate Social Democrat, and according to Ellemann-Jensen the four agreed that a 'NATO election' should be avoided and that both parties should now think about a compromise.[71] But the next day tempers ran high in the Social Democrat party group, where both Auken and Budtz gave very negative evaluations of the government's will to compromise.[72] On the same day, 12 April, the government instructed Ambassador Jørgensen to canvass a compromise proposal with the State Department.[73] The next day, 13 April, a formal compromise text in the shape of a draft parliamentary resolution which had been 'provisionally' agreed with Svend Auken and Lasse Budtz that same morning was forwarded to Washington for comment. According to this text the *Folketing* was to confirm Denmark's nuclear-free status, including its 'land territories, waters and harbours', and to enjoin the government 'to inform other countries about this Danish position'. Furthermore, the text of the specific letters of permission would use the Norwegian formula. Late that night the State Department gave 'a cautious green light'.[74]

In the 'provisional agreement' Auken and Budtz apparently conceded that the government could present the text as a draft resolution in the *Folketing* debate, and that the Social Democrats would accept, though not formally endorse it. However, the deal was not laid before the following Social Democrat party meeting, still on 13 April, where leading members, including Anker Jørgensen and Lasse Budtz, talked against compromising the party's position. After the meeting Auken informed Prime Minister

Schlüter that the party would table its own draft resolution. But he also expressed his expectation that the government draft would be adopted, as the Social Liberals could accept both drafts, and as the government draft would be voted upon first according to normal procedure.[75] Next morning Auken phoned the Prime Minister and confirmed their common understanding.[76]

In the first of several party meetings on the day of debate, 14 April, Svend Auken argued that the party would have no 'decency' if it did not vote for the government draft, which after all tightened the existing policy. He also reminded the group that it still had a fall-back position in the continuing discussions in the Defence Committee.[77] Auken's recommendation was backed up by the party's parliamentary executive committee and laid before the parliamentary group during the lunch recess. Here, however, it met strong criticism from several members, including Anker Jørgensen, and Auken's tactical game was toppled when Lasse Budtz informed the group that the Social Liberals were indifferent as to the voting sequence. This opened a possibility of having the Social Democrat draft voted on first by using a clause in the parliamentary rules of procedure, which allowed a vote on the voting sequence if demanded by 17 MPs.

As the group rallied round this idea a 'deeply desperate' Svend Auken[78] put his name first on the petition list while – as a last resort – he appealed to the Prime Minister to persuade the Social Liberal leader Niels Helveg Petersen to vote against changing the voting sequence, but in vain.[79] This would have killed the sequence proposal and secured the passage of the government draft. However, the Social Liberals abstained in the sequence vote and voted subsequently for the Social Democrats' draft. The unexpected and unwanted outcome was therefore that the *Folketing* adopted a resolution to the effect that the government should 'inform visiting warships' about the Danish policy.

The government had been defeated once more and reacted by stating that it now intended to study the reactions of the NATO allies and reflect on 'whether it would be possible to keep our membership in NATO completely unimpaired'. It would inform the *Folketing* within 10 days of its decision. This was quite a risky tactic compared to calling a general election right away, because it smacked of soliciting allied interference. However, several ministers, among them the normally combative Foreign Minister, feared that an election would be equally risky, given public opinion.[80]

As far as it is possible to ascertain, no instruction was sent to embassies abroad asking for comments, but the Prime Minister's message in the *Folketing* was enough to indicate this interest. It is also known that Foreign Minister Ellemann-Jensen spoke with George Schulz and presumably other NATO leaders after the debate without warning against interference.[81] The United States and Britain did comment publicly on the question, though mainly in hypothetical terms. Thus, George Schulz warned against implementing the resolution in a way that was incompatible with the 'neither confirm nor deny' doctrine, as this would undermine NATO deterrence and have extremely serious consequences for Danish–American defence cooperation.[82] The British government commented in similar terms, as did NATO Secretary General Lord Carrington.

After four days the government called an election on 'Denmark's continued full membership' in NATO, referring to the reactions from countries which according to NATO's Rapid Reinforcement Plan would be the primary suppliers of reinforcements to Denmark, that is the United States and Britain.

The election on 10 May resulted in losses for the parties of the alternative majority, but two mandates short of a majority shift.[83] Instead the Social Liberals, who had long been disillusioned about the alternative majority, defected and joined the Conservative and Liberals in a new government coalition. Footnote politics was no longer possible, and at the same time the rapid decline of the Cold War made its continuation pointless. As a result the Social Democrats soon oriented themselves towards a resumption of the traditional consensus.

The aftermath

As it happened, the end of the Cold War was the prelude to an active Danish foreign policy in the 1990s under the banner of 'active internationalism', Ellemann-Jensen's phrase, or 'engaged internationalism', a concept coined by the new government, a centre-left coalition led by the new Social Democrat leader, Poul Nyrup Rasmussen. In practical terms this change meant little, as the Rasmussen government (1993–2001) continued and consolidated the pursuit of a liberal international order which Uffe Ellemann-Jensen had initiated.

After 2001 and in the wake of 9/11 a new Liberal–Conservative government led by Anders Fogh Rasmussen (Lib.) stepped up the activist aspect of the new foreign policy and gave it a sharp military profile. Thus Denmark took on a hefty burden in the Afghanistan and Iraq wars in close cooperation with the Bush administration. This was part of a deliberate showdown with the small power tradition in Danish foreign policy, which had been a reflection of the political dominance of Social Democrats and Social Liberals in the preceding century. Denmark should now be a 'strategic actor' on the world scene.[84] Another manifestation of this break with the past was a head-on confrontation with the political left over the footnote period. As Anders Fogh Rasmussen wrote in 1997, it was 'fantastic, that those persons, who committed intellectual and moral treason, have actually avoided being held responsible for their words and deeds. ... [This] treason consisted of leading circles in our society behaving as if there were no difference between friend and foe'.[85] Finally, as we have seen, a keen interest in the historiography of the Cold War led to repeated interventions in favour of an interpretation which has been termed 'right revisionism'.[86] This brought the government into sharp conflict with the mainstream of Danish Cold War historians.

Conclusion

The Danish footnote policy of the 1980s was an eccentric response to a problem which affected many NATO member states. Europeans, and especially Social Democrats and Socialists meeting in *Scandilux*, had difficulties with accepting the reintroduction of Cold War practices by the Carter and – with a vengeance – the Reagan administration. While President Reagan talked about the 'evil empire', these parties now tended to see the Soviet Union as a conservative, reactive power, which might in time be integrated in a European security structure via the notion of Common Security.[87]

It so happened that all *Scandilux* parties fell from power during 1981–82. But the Danish Social Democrats continued to command a security policy majority from the opposition benches. This was possible because the Social Liberals allowed it, and because the government did not dare to call their bluff, namely that the alternative majority was no *regierungsfähig* ('government capable') formation. But footnote policy was in keeping with public opinion, which explains why the government for a long time shied away from calling a 'NATO election'. As we have seen, the NATO election in May 1988 was only a partial success.

Driving from the back seat naturally limited the levers at hand. Basically there was only one: the blunt instrument of parliamentary resolutions, which could only provide an imprecise road map for the driver to follow. This gave the government an important leeway. At the same time vision was limited from the back seat with the result that the policy of the alternative majority increasingly fed on itself, out of sync with developments and operating in a 'strategic no-man's-land'.[88] The port call debacle of 1988 was the most conspicuous example of this irrelevancy.

How did this come about? Ellemann-Jensen's standard explanation is petty harassment tactics on the part of the Social Democrats. To be sure, 'turkey hunting', i.e. indiscriminate shooting at any moving government target, was popular among the frustrated opposition politicians, but there was more to it than that. Footnoting had both external and internal causes. Basically, it was a reaction to the renewed pressures of the second Cold War for alliance cohesion and support for a confrontational US policy. This pressure was felt particularly strongly among North European Social Democrats who continued to hanker for detente and arms control in the *Scandilux* grouping. The alternative 'right revisionist' thesis of footnoting as an appeasement of Soviet pressure remains to be documented.[89]

The *Scandilux* forum served to inspire and stiffen the response of the Danish Social Democrats, but equally important was internal party dynamics. In particular, a sceptical view of nuclear weapons deepened towards the end of the 1970s into a near-rejection among party leaders like Anker Jørgensen and Lasse Budtz. At the same time the shifting balance between moderates and left-wingers among the party's MPs placed the moderates in a squeeze.

These developments were well under way when the party went into opposition in September 1982. The party now got caught in two dynamic relationships – with the parties of the alternative majority and with their erstwhile partners, the government parties. The formation of the alternative majority exposed the party to influence from the Socialist People's Party and the Left Socialists, who cleverly exploited their unprecedented chance to influence official policy. Their greatest 'feat' was to drag the cautious, but divided Social Democrats into the port call debacle. This was a Pyrrhic victory, however, which spelled their return to powerless opposition.

The Social Liberals were the 'enablers' of footnote politics by their divided loyalty. The party's role within the alternative majority was, however, ambiguous: it voted for its resolutions, but also prevented it from endangering the government's life. The party's behaviour on 14 April 1988, when it sealed the government's defeat by abstaining on the sequence vote, has hardly found a satisfactory explanation yet.

The government parties and especially the Liberals criticised the Social Democrats for veering away from the dependable policies of its former leaders and lambasted their 'desertion', both of the national interest and of alliance responsibilities. But, as mentioned, the party cleavage also reflected a polarisation process which moved the government parties away from the previous consensus. However, at the end of the day their main interest was to stay in power, and, despite all bitterness, this kept the government parties from playing hardball over the country's NATO policy.

This was reserved for the aftermath and served to bolster the transition to an ambitious interventionist foreign policy. The real losers of this game were the Social Democrats. As Bo Lidegaard has recently observed, 'while the footnotes probably did little harm abroad, they served to erode the domestic strength of the Social Democrat Party and, for years to come, considerably weakened its ability to influence key decisions within Denmark's foreign and security policy'.[90]

Notes

[1] According to Snyder, 'The Security Dilemma', the alliance dilemma consists of the choice between alliance solidarity and relative independence. The former choice involves the 'good' of avoiding abandonment and the 'bad' of possible entrapment by the alliance leader. The latter choice involves the 'good' of political autonomy and the 'bad' (risk) of abandonment. For an application to Danish NATO policy, see Petersen, *Denmark and NATO*.

[2] The first report, on Greenland during the Cold War (DUPI, *Grønland*) was commissioned from the Danish Foreign Policy Institute in 1995 and delivered in early 1997. In the sequel, former Foreign Minister Uffe Ellemann-Jensen (Lib.) demanded a follow-up report on the Warsaw Pact's nuclear plans against Denmark and its contacts with Danish politicians. The demand for a historical investigation focused on the 'internal threat' was repeated by the new Liberal leader Anders Fogh Rasmussen in 1998–99 when the *Folketing* set down a commission to investigate the activities of PET, the internal intelligence service, during the Cold War, but was only partially met (Rasmussen's foreword to Haarder, *Hvem holdt de med?*). The PET Commission took until 2009 to give in its report (*PET-kommissionens beretning*). In the meantime the non-socialist parties renewed their pressure for a historical investigation and succeeded partially in 2001, when the Poul Nyrup Rasmussen government commissioned a report from the Danish Foreign Policy Institute, DUPI (later: DIIS). But the opposition parties remained critical of the remit and expanded it when they came to power in late 2001. The focus now shifted from the external threat to the internal aspects with a concentration on the footnote period and the 'internal threat' from party and organisation contacts with Warsaw Pact authorities. When the four-volume report (DIIS, *Danmark*) was published in 2005, it failed to live up to expectations, however, as it took a rather balanced view of the footnote period and failed to disclose foul play with the enemy by the opposition parties. Consequently

the report was denounced as only 'preliminary' by the Liberal and Conservative government parties and their ally, the Danish People's Party, and a new temporary Centre for Cold War Research was set up to provide an alternative report. The report which is due in 2011, was entrusted to Professor Bent Jensen, a long-time advocate of a 'right revisionist' interpretation of Danish foreign policy and a leading critic of the DIIS Report as well as of the PET Report, when it was published in 2009 (see Petersen, 'Kampen'; Villaume, 'Confronting').

[3] Speech at the University of Copenhagen 23 September 2003, Prime Minister's Office, http://www.stm.dk.

[4] These missiles – the *Pershing II* ballistic missile and the *Tomahawk* cruise missile – were originally termed LRTNF (Long-Range Theatre Nuclear Forces), but were renamed INF (Intermediate Nuclear Forces) in 1981. Here INF is used throughout.

[5] *Norden* connotes the five Nordic countries: Denmark, Norway, Sweden, Finland and Iceland.

[6] In the 1980s this role centred round the Thule early warning radar, the hub of the US Ballistic Missile Early Warning System (BMEWS). Attempts by the socialist parties to question the modernisation of the radar in the mid-1980s failed to win the support of the Social Democrats. Petersen, *Europæisk og globalt engagement*, 334–45; Minutes of the Social Democratic Parliamentary Group. Folketingets Arkiv, Copenhagen (SD), 20 January 1987.

[7] See e.g. exchange of letters between US Secretary of Defense Harold Brown and his Danish colleague Poul Søgaard, January–May 1980, in *Dansk Udenrigspolitisk Årbog* (1980): 261–5.

[8] Petersen, *Europæisk og globalt engagement*, 237–40. In DIIS, *Danmark*, this is the main explanation of footnote policy. This analysis focuses heavily on the US 'clandestine war' on the Soviet Union in the early 1980s and such occurrences as the *Able Archer* exercise in October 1983. These activities were not commonly known, however, and certainly not by the Danish opposition parties. On the external vs. internal explanations of footnote policy, see Borring Olesen, 'Noter'.

[9] Petersen, *Europæisk og globalt engagement*, 237–40. The Americans were especially irked by Anker Jørgensen's tendency to draw parallels between the situations in Poland, Turkey and El Salvador. Secretary Alexander Haig's deputy, Lawrence Eagleburger, twice complained in person to Ambassador Otto Borch, who concluded, in a personal letter to Permanent Secretary Eigil Jørgensen on 3 May 1982, that he now met an unusual degree of scepticism towards Denmark in Washington (Washington amtel 539, 3 May 1982, General Files of the Ministry of Foreign Affairs. Rigsarkivet, Copenhagen (UM) 5.D.32.a).

[10] The regular Danish participants were Lasse Budtz as leader of the delegation, Foreign Minister Kjeld Olesen, and Prime Minister Anker Jørgensen (see Petersen, 'Scandilux').

[11] The most detailed analysis of doctrinal developments in the Social Democratic Party is Boel, *Socialdemokratiets*.

[12] *Aktuelt*, 18 April 1978.

[13] The dual-track decision had an official as well as an unofficial rationale. The official rationale focused on the need for a stronger coupling between the United States and Europe while the unofficial rationale aimed at improving the nuclear balance in Europe.

[14] Interview with Pierre Lellouche in *Le Point*, 26 April 1982.

[15] Petersen, *Europæisk og globalt engagement*, 194–21; DIIS, *Danmark*, vol. 3, 77–104.

[16] Letter Permanent Secretary Eigil Jørgensen to Foreign Minister Kjeld Olesen, March 1982, UM 105.I.40.e/3.a.

[17] Press statement 18 March 1982, *Dansk Udenrigspolitisk Årbog 1982*, 227.

[18] Washington amtel 353, 20 March 1982, UM 105.I.40.e/3.a.

[19] Petersen, *Europæisk og globalt engagement*, 279–80.

[20] See Table in Petersen and Svensson, *Valgenes*, 37.

[21] Petersen, *Inden for systemet*, 311.

[22] Hedtoft was Prime Minister 1947–50 and 1953–55; Hansen from 1955 to 1959, and Krag 1962–68, 1971–72.

[23] See Mariager, 'Den brede enigheds'.

[24] Poul Villaume has a different interpretation, as he claims that the Social Democratic opposition was basically triggered by Ellemann-Jensen's determination to turn Denmark into a core country in NATO (see his 'Confronting', 43).

[25] *Dansk Udenrigspolitisk Årbog 1979*, 372; *Dansk Udenrigspolitisk Årbog 1983*, 429

[26] Interpellation debate 7 December 1982, *Folketingstidende 1982–83* (Parliamentary Records, Debates), Forhandlinger, col. 2864ff.

[27] Ellemann-Jensen on press conference, 10 December 1982, Danato reptels 713 and 718, 13 and 14 December 1982, UM 105.G.152.

[28] Petersen, *Europæisk og globalt engagement*, 298–9.

[29] Speech at party conference in Silkeborg, 28–29 January 1983; *Dansk Udenrigspolitisk Årbog 1983*, 216–17.

[30] *Folketingstidende 1982–83*, Forhandlinger, 8 February 1983, col. 5566ff.

[31] Uffe Ellemann-Jensen on TV, 3 February 1983; *Dansk Udenrigspolitisk Årbog 1983*, 218f.

[32] The committee was proposed by Foreign Minister Ellemann-Jensen in an effort to rein in the two Conservative ministers. He was not at that time member of the government's 'inner cabinet' (Ellemann-Jensen letter to Prime Minister Schlüter, 3 January 1983, UM 105.I.40.e/3b. Cf. Ellemann-Jensen, *Fodfejl*, 129–31).

[33] Reports on meetings in the 'rocket committee', 20 January and 2 February 1983, UM 105.I.40e/3b; Schlüter in Minutes of the Conservative Parliamentary Group, Folketingets Arkiv, Copenhagen (KF), 2 February 1983.

[34] Petersen, *Europæisk og globalt engagement*, 302–3.

[35] Conversation Prime Minister Schlüter, Foreign Minister Ellemann-Jensen and Assistant Secretary of State Kenneth Dam, 23 March 1983, UM 105.I.40.e/3a.

[36] SD 26 May 1983.

[37] *Folketingstidende 1982–83*, Forhandlinger, 26 May 1983, col. 11922ff; SD, 26 May 1983; Budtz, *Brudstykker*, 119ff.

[38] Meeting in the 'rocket committee', 27 May 1983. UM 105.I.40e/3b.

[39] Communiqués from DPC meeting 1–2 June 1983 and NATO Council meeting 9–10 June 1983, *Dansk Udenrigspolitisk Årbog 1983*, 343ff.; Engell's statement in DPC 2 June, UM 105.G.153; Ellemann-Jensen's statement in NATO Council, UM 105.105.I.40.e/3a; Danato reptel 376, 27 June 1983, UM 105.G.153.

[40] Prime Minister Schlüter chose his opening speech to the new parliamentary session to proclaim the May resolution part of government policy (*Folketingstidende 1983–84*, 1; samling, Forhandlinger, 4 October 1983, col. 18ff.).

[41] *Folketingstidende 1983–84*, 1, samling, Forhandlinger, 5 November 1983, col. 1355ff.

[42] *Folketingstidende 1983–84*, 1, samling, Forhandlinger, 3 December 1983, col. 2641ff.

[43] *Folketingstidende 1983–84*, 1, samling, Forhandlinger, 1 December 1983, col. 2553ff.

[44] Foreign Ministry notice, 8 December 1983, UM 105.G.154; Texts in *Dansk Udenrigspolitisk Årbog 1983*, 292, 293.

[45] See Krasner and Petersen, 'Peace'; Hein Rasmussen, *Sære alliancer.*

[46] The Social Democratic Party sent a high-ranking delegation to Moscow in October 1984 for consultations on the zone proposal with the CPSU, but had to return empty-handed.

[47] Text in Petersen, *Europæisk og globalt engagement*, 312.

[48] Both proposal and comment demonstrated a lack of elementary knowledge as the placement of nuclear weapons in space had been outlawed since 1966.

[49] *Folketingstidende 1983–84*, 2, samling, Forhandlinger, 3 May 1984, col. 5265ff.

[50] *Politiken*, 6 June 1984. The proposal was inspired by a similar compromise in Norway between the Labour Party and the non-socialist government. See *Innstilling fra utenriks- og konstitutionskomiteen nr. 225*, Stortinget, Oslo.

[51] *Dyvig-rapporten 1985*; Faurby, 'Sikkerhedspolitisk consensus', 70.

[52] Petersen, *Europæisk og globalt engagement*, 329–31.

[53] *Folketingstidende 1984–85*, Forhandlinger, 26 March 1985.

[54] In a subsequent meeting in the Foreign Policy Committee on 12 April 1985. Prime Minister Schlüter explained that a footnote would have been a manifestation of defeat, and that by avoiding it Denmark had been able to influence the wording of the NATO communiqué. See Minutes of the Parliamentary Foreign Affairs Committee (UPN) (Foreign Policy Committee), 12 April 1985, UM 3.E.92.

[55] *Folketingstidende 1984–85*, Forhandlinger, 14 May 1985, col. 9944ff.

[56] See Petersen, *Europæisk og globalt engagement*, 242.

[57] Depeche X/1984 in Washington amtel 891, 15 June 1984, UM 5.D.32.a.

[58] Washington amtel 609, 22 April 1985, the Foreign Minister's talking points for press conference 20 April 1985, both UM 5.D.32.b; UPN 25 April 1985, UM 3.E.92.

[59] Washington amtels 1321 (11 September 1985) and 1337 (12 September 1985), UM 5.D.32.b; UPN, 13 September 1985, UM 3.E.92.

[60] Petersen, *Europæisk og globalt engagement*, 333–4.

[61] UPN (Foreign Policy Committee), 17 December 1986, UM 3.E.92.

[62] DIIS, *Danmark*, vol. 3, 447.

[63] This was a different procedure from the one usually used by the alternative majority. Over the years, the favourite vehicle of footnote politics had been interpellation debates in the Folketing, concluded by the adoption of a resolution. These debates normally lasted a couple of hours, were quite informal without committee work and often concluded with improvised draft resolutions. The procedure around parliamentary decisions is much more formal and the outcome more binding than resolutions. The procedure is initiated by presenting a text, which then has two plenary hearings with a committee stage in between. Instead of a single afternoon such proposals may be on the agenda for a whole parliamentary season.

[64] The United States had broken off defence cooperation with New Zealand in 1985 after NZ demands for guarantees against port calls of naval ships carrying nuclear weapons.

[65] *Folketingstidende 1987–88*, Forhandlinger, 27 November 1987, col. 2871ff.

[66] Collet's notice on talk with Ambassador Todman 7 December 1987, UM 55.Dan.10. Collet had succeeded Engell as Defence Minister in 1987.

[67] SD 22 March 1988; *Information*, 23 March 1988.

[68] Notice by Per Poulsen-Hansen, head of NATO Office; Ministry of Foreign Affairs, 25 March 1988, UM 55.Dan.10.

[69] 'Neither confirm nor deny' the presence of nuclear weapons was an ingrained doctrine with the US and British navies.

[70] Budtz in *Information*, 21 April 1988, Heltberg, *Hvor der handles*, 90, 12 April 1988.

[71] In meeting in the Liberal parliamentary group, 14 April 1988, at 15.45. Minutes of the Liberal Parliamentary Group. Venstre, Søllerød (V), 14 April 1988.

[72] SD, 12 April 1988.

[73] Umtel 263 to Washington, 12 April 1988, UM 55.D.10.

[74] Umtel 267 to Washington, 13 April 1988; Washington amtel 538, 13 April 1988, both UM 55.Dan.10.

[75] The normal procedure in interpellation debates where various competing draft resolutions were presented, was that the draft which appeared to have the largest backing, would be voted upon first.

[76] SD, 13 April 1988; Auken in Larsen, *Auken*, 160; Heltberg: *Hvor der handles*, 90ff.; Schlüter, *Sikken et liv*, 321ff; Kristiansen and Larsen, *Niels Helveg Petersen*, 187; Schlüter in KF, 14 April 1988 at 15.45.
[77] SD, 14 April 1988.
[78] Auken's own characteristic of his mood in interview with DIIS, November 2004 (DIIS, *Danmark*, vol. 3, 298).
[79] Subsequently Svend Auken has maintained that he fell into a trap deliberately set up by the Prime Minister and Niels Helveg Petersen, the Social Liberal party leader. See his review of Ellemann-Jensen, *Fodfejl*, in *Politiken*, 11 November 2004.
[80] *Aktuelt*, 15 April 1988.
[81] Uffe Ellemann-Jensen in Foreign Policy Committee 17 December 1991 and 17 January 1992, UM 3.E.92.
[82] Umtel 314 to Danato, 15 April 1988, UM 55.D.10.
[83] I have calculated that the NATO issue moved a few percent of the voters from the opposition to the government side. The losses of the alternative parties – 7 mandates – did not accrue to the four government parties, which stayed at 70 mandates, but to the rightist Progress Party. After the election the alternative majority still commanded a slim majority in the *Folketing* of 89 against the government's 86 mandates (Petersen, 'Sikkerhedspolitikken')
[84] Rynning, 'Denmark as a Strategic Actor'.
[85] *Berlingske Tidende*, 27 February 1997. The article singled out Anker Jørgensen as the most prominent representative of this view.
[86] 'Right revisionism' explains Denmark's footnote policy as appeasement of the Soviet Union or worse on the part of the Danish Social Democrats and leftist forces. This understanding is close to the political programme of the Fogh Rasmussen government (see Petersen, 'Kampen').
[87] According to the concept of Common Security which had been developed by Egon Bahr in the so-called Palme Commission in 1982, security can only be found through cooperation with the enemy, not by one-sided armament.
[88] Comment in DIIS, *Danmark*, vol. 4, 96 on the proposed Nordic nuclear-free zone.
[89] Jensen, *Tryk og tilpasning*.
[90] Lidegaard, *A Short History*, 318–19.

References

Boel, Erik. *Socialdemokratiets atomvåbenpolitik*. Copenhagen: Fremad, 1988.

Borring Olesen, Thorsten. 'Noter og fodnoter. En diskussion af indenrigspolitikkens primat i efterkrigstidens danske udenrigspolitik', in *Nye fronter i Den kolde Krig*, ed. C. Due-Nielsen, R. Mariager and R. Schmidt, 87–113. Copenhagen: Gyldendal, 2010.

Budtz, Laase. *Brudstykker–Erindringer*. Copenhagen: Fiskers, n.d.

Dansk Udenrigspolitisk Årbog 1979–88, ed. C. Thune (1979–88) and N. Petersen (1982–88) Copenhagen: DUPI, 1980ff.

DIIS. *Danmark under den kolde krig. Den sikkerhedspolitiske situation 1945–1991*. 4 vols. Copenhagen: Dansk Institut for Internationale Studier, 2005.

DUPI. *Grønland under den kolde krig*. 2 vols. Copenhagen: Dansk Udenrigspolitisk Institut, 1997.

Dyvig-rapporten. *Danmarks sikkerhedspolitiske situation i 1980'erne*. Copenhagen: SNU, 1985.

Ellemann-Jensen, Uffe. *Fodfejl. Da Danmark svigtede under den kolde krig*. Copenhagen: Gyldendal, 2004.

Faurby, Ib. 'Mod en ny sikkerhedspolitisk konsensus?', in *Dansk Udenrigspolitisk Årbog 1986 Dansk Udenrigspolitisk Årbog 1979–88*, ed. C. Thune and N. Petersen, 56–81. Copenhagen: DUPI, 1980ff.

Haarder, Bertel, ed. *Hvem holdt de med?* Copenhagen: Peter LaCours Forlag, 1999.
Hein Rasmussen, Søren. *Sære alliancer. Politiske bevægelser i efterkrigstidens Danmark.* Odense: Odense University Press, 1997.
Heltberg, Bettina. *Hvor der handles. Erindringsbilleder.* Copenhagen: Gyldendal, 1996.
Jensen, Bent. *Tryk og tilpasning. Sovjetunionen og Danmark siden 2. verdenskrig.* Copenhagen: Gyldendal, 1987.
Krasner, Michael, and Nikolaj Petersen. 'Peace and Politics. The Danish Peace Movement and its Impact on National Security Policy'. *Journal of Peace Research* 23 (1986): 155–73.
Kristiansen, Michael, and Thomas Larsen. *Niels Helveg Petersen. Manden og magten.* Copenhagen: Børsen, 1996.
Larsen, Thomas. *Auken. En familiefortælling.* Copenhagen: Møntergården, 1990.
Lidegaard, Bo. *A Short History of Denmark in the 20th Century.* Copenhagen: Gyldendal, 2010.
Mariager, Rasmus. 'Den brede enigheds ophør. Om baggrunden for det sikkerhedspolitiske opbrud i begyndelsen af 1980'erne – og noget om Socialdemokratiets exceptionalisme i dansk samtidshistorie'. *Historisk Tidsskrift* (2005): 553–83 and (2006): 646–75.
Petersen, Gert. *Inden for systemet – og udenfor.* Copenhagen: Aschehoug, 1998.
Petersen, Nikolaj. 'The Scandilux Experiment: Towards a Transnational Social Democratic Security Perspective?' *Cooperation and Conflict* XX (1985): 1–23.
Petersen, Nikolaj. *Denmark and NATO 1949–1987.* Oslo: Forsvarsstudier, 2/1987.
Petersen, Nikolaj. 'Sikkerhedspolitikken og 1988-valget', in *To folketingsvalg. Vælgerholdninger og vælgeradfærd i 1987 og 1988*, ed. J. Elklit and O. Tonsgaard, 305–27. Aarhus: Politica, 1989.
Petersen, Nikolaj. *Europæisk og globalt engagement 1973–2006.* Dansk Udenrigspolitiks Historie. vol. 6. 2nd ed. Copenhagen: Gyldendal 2006.
Petersen, Nikolaj. 'Kampen om Den Kolde Krig i dansk politik og forskning'. *Historisk Tidsskrift* 109 (2009): 154–204.
Petersen, Nikolaj, and Palle Svensson. 'Valgenes politiske sammenhæng', in *To folketingsvalg. Vælgerholdninger og vælgeradfærd i 1987 og 1988*, ed. J. Elklit and O. Tonsgaard, 22–51. Aarhus: Politica, 1989.
PET-kommissionens beretning. 16 vols. Copenhagen: PET-kommissionen, 2009.
Rynning, Sten. 'Denmark as a Strategic Actor? Danish Security Policy after 11 September'. *Danish Foreign Policy Yearbook 2003*, 23–46.
Schlüter, Poul. *Sikken et liv.* Copenhagen: Aschehoug, 1999.
Snyder, Glenn. 'The Security Dilemma in Alliance Politics'. *World Politics* 36 (1984): 461–95.
Villaume, Poul. 'Confronting the "Small State Syndrome": Danish Post-Cold War Foreign Policy and the Use of Cold War History', in *The Cold War and the Politics of History*, ed. J. Aunesluoma and P. Kettunen, 37–60. Helsinki: Edita, 2008.

"A mass psychosis": The Netherlands and NATO's dual-track decision, 1978–1979

Ruud van Dijk

When NATO took its so-called dual-track decision on Theatre Nuclear Weapons in December 1979, the Dutch government, while joining the decision, declared that it would not decide on the deployment of the Dutch share of the new weapons for another two years. With the help of new documents from Dutch archival collections, this essay examines the reasons behind this decision by the centre-right Van Agt government. It shows that there was great reluctance in parliament, but also in the cabinet, to contemplate the coming modernisation. In order to survive politically and keep the Netherlands within the NATO fold, the Van Agt government tried to align NATO's decision as closely with Dutch policy as possible while seeking majority support in parliament for its proposed compromise solution. The essay provides new detail on both efforts, including the response of allied governments to the Dutch reservations.

I. Introduction

When East-West détente came under pressure in the second half of the 1970s, tensions within the Western alliance also increased. The battle over the so-called 'Euromissiles' can be seen as both a result of this process and one of its major manifestations.[1] Nowhere in Europe was NATO's 1979 dual-track decision–to deploy 572 new intermediate-range nuclear missiles in Western Europe, should negotiations with the Soviet Union over this category of weapons fail–more controversial than in the Netherlands. In 1981, historian Walter Laqueur would liken West European reluctance to implement the dual-track decision to a disease: *Hollanditis*.[2] Anti-nuclear sentiments among the Dutch public found strong echoes in parliament in the late 1970s, making it impossible for the centre-right coalition government of Christian Democrats (the Christen Democratisch Appel, CDA) and centre-right liberals (Volkspartij voor Vrijheid en Democratie,VVD) fully to underwrite the NATO plan. At the alliance's Brussels meeting on 12 December, Defense Minister Willem Scholten stated therefore that while accepting the need for a response to Soviet deployments in this area, the Dutch government could not commit itself yet to deploy its share of the new missiles. Instead, it would decide in two years, after evaluation of the results of proposed negotiations over these weapons, often referred to as belonging to the 'grey area'. [3]

'Grey area' refers to categories of nuclear weapons between strategic arsenals on the one hand, and battlefield weapons on the other hand. Causing considerable concern with West European leaders such as West German Chancellor Helmut Schmidt, these weapons were not part of either the Strategic Arms Limitation talks (SALT) between the United States and the Soviet Union, or the East-West talks on conventional weapons in Europe (MBFR). In the course of the 1970s, the Soviet Union appeared to be building a lead in this category in Europe (deployment of its new, intermediate-range nuclear missile, the SS-20, began in 1976), on top of its lead in conventional forces, particularly tanks. Against the background of U.S.-Soviet agreements on a strategic balance, this caused concerns among European governments about a possible 'de-coupling' of US and West European security interests, or at least the perception of this. Both for military and political reasons, therefore, the Western alliance by the middle of the decade was exploring ways to address these discrepancies in this area of what were also called Theatre Nuclear Weapons (TNF). The possible production and deployment of the anti-tank Neutron bomb (or Enhanced Radiation Reduced Blast granate (ERRB)) was one aspect of this debate (conducted in 1977–1978 inside the alliance, in public opinion, and, between East and West through Soviet interference with the public debate in the West); the nuclear missiles central to NATO's dual-track decision of December 1979 were another.[4]

December 1981 came with negotiations just having commenced between the United States and the Soviet Union, so The Hague postponed again. In June 1984 there followed another delay, and it was not until November 1985 that the Netherlands became the last of the participants in the NATO scheme definitively to accept deployment. Thanks to the 1987 Intermediate Nuclear Forces (INF) treaty, the missiles, envisioned to arrive in 1988, never entered Dutch territory.

Public aversion to what many Dutch saw as an escalation of the arms race had much to do with the various postponements. More directly responsible was Dutch politics; particularly the fact that for various reasons a parliamentary majority for an unequivocal decision to deploy could not be found prior to November 1985. Finally there were the various Dutch cabinets between 1979 and 1985. On the one hand, they maintained that they were caught between a desire (shared, ironically, by a majority of the population) to be a reliable member of the Atlantic alliance, and the unmistakable widespread opposition in the Netherlands against the introduction of the new missiles. Accepting the dual-track decision while taking extra time to sort out Dutch participation was actually the best one could do under the circumstances, the argument ran, and scenarios more disadvantageous for NATO unity were certainly possible given the state of Dutch politics. On the other hand, reversing the nuclear arms race was official government policy, and some cabinet ministers actually shared certain reservations about the NATO programme.[5]

The focus of this essay is on the centre-right cabinet, led by Christian Democrat, Andries (Dries) van Agt, in the run-up to the December 1979 decisions. This fragile coalition government came to power in December 1977 and virtually from the start was bedeviled by political challenges connected with nuclear weapons. As the evidence shows, the government's views and actions were influenced by Dutch public opinion, an active and influential anti-nuclear movement, and the polarised state of Dutch politics in the late 1970s. Its NATO policies, however, also deserve to be evaluated on their own merits.

What made the position of the Van Agt cabinet so precarious? How did it seek to balance participating in NATO decision making processes, on the one hand, and maintaining majority support in the Dutch parliament, on the other? How did it seek to shape NATO's dual-track decision and did it have any success? Is there something to the charge that the cabinet was too timid in its public communications on the issue, and that it displayed insufficient leadership toward parliament? Finally, what were some of the reactions to Van Agt's policies from the NATO allies most closely involved with the dual-track decision? The research for this essay draws on newly available material from several Dutch archival collections: cabinet files, files of the office of the prime-minister, foreign ministry papers, defence ministry papers, and the papers of former prime-minister Van Agt and of former vice-prime-minister Hans Wiegel.[6] The essay builds on existing Dutch scholarship and is the first scholarly treatment in English of this question.

II. Political instability and the neutron bomb

A centre-right government was not supposed to come into being in 1977, and it only did so after a five-month-long effort to create a cabinet led by the Social Democrats (Partij van de Arbeid, PvdA) collapsed. This sudden and surprising turn of events ensured that party politics would co-determine all government business after 1977, including foreign policy.

Between 1973 and 1977, the country had been governed by a coalition government led by Social Democrat, Joop den Uyl, with the participation of four smaller parties. The most important of these were the Catholics (Katholieke Volkspartij, KVP), whose cabinet ministers included Dries van Agt. Parliamentary elections in May 1977 brought victory for the Social Democrats, who, just about everyone expected, would therefore lead a new government. However, during the negotiations with the Christian Democrats the party overreached. The Christian Democrats, led by a Van Agt bearing the scars of four years in the Den Uyl government, ultimately refused to take a minority position in a new cabinet or to accept PvdA vetoes of key candidates for cabinet posts, and Den Uyl had to abandon his hopes of another four years in power.

Instead, Van Agt quickly reached agreement with the VVD, led by Hans Wiegel. Together, the two sides had a slim majority of 77 out of 150 seats in parliament. Its actual stability was even more precarious, due to the transitional state of Dutch Christian Democracy at the time.[7]

Traditionally, the great majority of Dutch Christian Democrats were represented by three parties; the KVP, the protestant Anti-Revolutionaire Partij (ARP), and Christelijk-Historische Unie (CHU). As Dutch society became more secular and less rigidly organised according to the traditional social-political 'pillar' system during the 1960s and early 1970s, all three parties, but especially the KVP, began to lose electoral ground. Talks about a possible merger began as early as 1966, and 1977 was the first time the three ran in national elections on a joint platform connected to a single list of candidates.[8]

Ideologically the new group (it was to complete the merger into a new political party only in 1980), the CDA, was still divided. Left-leaning members, many of whom originated in the ARP, resented the fact that their new party now governed with the VVD. Six of their newly elected members of parliament declared they would not consider themselves bound to support Van Agt's government. The best they said they would be able to do was to judge the cabinet on a case-by-case basis. These six, later joined by about four more, became known as 'loyalists.' In the next four years, their independent stance constantly threatened to bring down the coalition, especially because the PvdA aimed its parliamentary strategy at winning over these loyalists.

Political polarisation therefore was the order of the day, as it had been for most of the decade. The PvdA-dominated Den Uyl government had aimed to reform Dutch society along collectivist lines, while the PvdA sought to cement its dominance at the expense especially of Christian Democratic parties. Inside the cabinet, some resistance to this line had been mounted by Christian Democrats such as Van Agt, while outside of it the VVD, led by the charismatic and energetic Wiegel, had mounted a spirited opposition. However, as the election results of May 1977 illustrated, a lot of voters approved of the left-leaning Den Uyl policies, and to many it came as a shock suddenly to find oneself governed by a centre-right government. There seemed to be opportunities, in short, for the Social Democrats to bring down the Van Agt government, maybe torpedo the CDA project in the process, but in any case return to what they considered their rightful place at the head of the government.

The Cold War immediately began to play a part in these political contests through the case of the ERRB weapon. When word got out in summer 1977 that it might be introduced into NATO's arsenal in Europe, the Dutch Communist Party (Communistische Partij Nederland, CPN) organised a protest campaign. In the May election, the party had been trounced by the PvdA, and it was in need of an issue with which to reverse its political fortunes. It also sought to restore its ties to the Kremlin, which had deteriorated under the rigidly autonomous leadership of Paul de Groot (who was removed from the leadership in August). The campaign received active support from the Soviet bloc, especially the German Democratic Republic, and it was quite successful in mobilising a wide cross-section of the Dutch population against what many considered a particularly heinous weapon, reported to kill people while sparing buildings.[9]

The neutron bomb was not popular in the incoming Van Agt cabinet either. At the same time, with the important exception of Defence Minister Rudolf Kruisinga (CDA), the government believed it ought to deal with the problem within a NATO context, instead of unilaterally announcing its opposition. The Social Democrats in parliament believed otherwise, and it appeared there were CDA politicians who agreed. In early 1978 the problem turned into the first of what was to become a string of political crises for the Van Agt government. In the Dutch fight over the neutron bomb many of the outlines of the 1979 contest over the dual-track decision were visible, from PvdA opportunism, internal CDA divisions, and widespread anti-nuclear sentiments among the population. In early March, Kruisinga, unable to fall into line with his cabinet colleagues, had to resign over the matter. Van Agt's team never got into the substance of why the Netherlands should or should not participate in a possible deployment, limiting itself to managing–unsuccessfully in the end–Kruisinga's rebellion. Cabinet minutes suggest, however, that had a substantial discussion taken place, divisions over the matter would have threatened the political survival of the new government.[10] In the case of the ERRB weapon, there would be no further crises. In April, United States President Jimmy Carter decided for the moment not to go forward with production. Still, the cabinet's failure to have a substantial discussion is yet another way in which this episode foreshadowed the cruise missile case of the following year.

The anti-nuclear campaign in the Netherlands did not die down after the neutron bomb episode. Instead, it gave new life to the Ecumenical Peace Council (Interkerkelijk Vredesberaad, IKV), which under its slogan 'Abolish nuclear weapons, first in the Netherlands', and working through numerous local groups all over the country, continued the anti-nuclear campaign. Its activities and clout increased in 1979 in tandem with the gathering momentum of NATO's development of what would become the dual-track decision. The IKV did not represent all Dutch religious groups, Christians, or Christian Democratic politicians. At the same time, a common spiritual heritage and many shared social forums ensured that the IKV was in close contact with CDA politicians, particularly the loyalists, who, virtually without exception, were deeply troubled by the nuclear arms race and determined to reverse its course. Like the IKV, they believed that the Netherlands ought to take the lead for the whole world to see. On this issue, there were other CDA parliamentarians who were sympathetic.

In the autumn, the government, aware of intensifying discussions within NATO over a response to the threat of, in particular, the growing Soviet arsenal of SS-20 missiles, sent parliament a position paper on nuclear weapons, the *Kernwapennota*. In it, it tried to balance the goal of a smaller role of nuclear weapons with alliance needs. There were no converts, however, among CDA parliamentarians, many of whom remained opposed to any new deployments in the nuclear field, something the paper did not rule out.[11]

Autumn 1978 was the time when NATO's High Level Group (HLG) for the study of the alliance's TNF was beginning to look into the question of which European member states might deploy new American intermediate range nuclear missiles should the alliance decide on such a modernisation. As a country with an existing nuclear role in NATO, the Netherlands was an obvious candidate. Because United States soundings at this time occurred at a level below that of the political decision makers, and also to maintain a voice in subsequent discussions, Dutch HLG representatives refrained from taking a position.[12] In early December, at NATO's Defence Planning Committee (DPC), Defence Minister Scholten (CDA; Kruisinga's successor), was non-committal.[13]

Things were headed in a certain direction, however; one sure to create political difficulties at home. At their January meeting in Guadaloupe, the heads of government of the United States, Britain, France, and the Federal Republic of Germany reached agreement in principle on the need for a NATO response to the Soviet SS-20s (and an arms-control initiative to go with it). Foreign Minister Chris Van der Klaauw (VVD) was unhappy with the exclusive nature of the meeting, as he told Washington's ambassador to the Netherlands, Geri Joseph. For her part, Joseph asked how 'the enormous pressure' on the government regarding nuclear issues might influence its decision making, and later enquired how the United States could help. In an indication of how the ERRB controversy a year earlier had changed Dutch debates over national security, Van der Klaauw responded that a decision to produce the neutron bomb would be 'a serious matter.' Dutch officials would reiterate this toward their American colleagues regularly, even after 1979.[14]

III. Containing threats at home and abroad

The possibility that NATO might seek to deploy new intermediate-range nuclear missiles in Europe became ever more real in 1979, as a memorandum prepared in March by the defence and foreign ministries confirmed. The memo outlined how the Soviet Union had gained the upper hand recently, leading to fears of a de-coupling of United States and Western European security interests. NATO's Nuclear Planning Group (NPG) was still studying exactly what kind of alliance response would be necessary, but thanks in part to Dutch efforts arms control would receive serious attention. Regardless, Dutch participation would be a major political decision. 'A decision about possible Dutch participation cannot, in any case, be taken if not all possibilities for arms control in the grey area have been explored carefully and exploited fully.'[15]

At their meeting on 4 April, all members of the *Algemene Verdedigingsraad* (cabinet sub-council for national security matters, AVR) recognised there was trouble ahead. Nuclear headaches just would not go away, Scholten seemed to lament. 'After all the turbulence surrounding the ERRB weapon, we are now confronted with the developments surrounding the grey area weapons.' What, he was asked by his VVD colleagues, would be his position at the ministerial NPG meeting (later in April in Miami)? Scholten said there would be three main elements: first, Dutch participation in TNF 'appears unthinkable' if ERRB weapons get introduced; second, '[i]n no circumstance can the introduction of new weapons systems lead to an increase in the number of warheads in Europe'; third, a shift in nuclear warheads from the short to the intermediate level 'could perhaps be taken as a contribution to the reduction of the role of nuclear weapons'. Asked if it would be wise to 'seek a first public confrontation' on this issue following the Miami meeting, Scholten answered that he recognised the national political problems, but that for the time being he preferred to proceed in a low-key manner. Nobody in the AVR took issue with him.[16]

Given the recent unfriendly reception of the government's *Kernwapennota* in parliament, and the growing strength of the anti-nuclear movement outside of it, this was undoubtedly wise. Exactly what NATO's final decision would be was not yet clear, nor could it be predicted with any great precision what position the CDA caucus in parliament would take on TNF modernisation. As it became clear in subsequent months that the United States in particular would like to have a decision by the end of the year, the government intensified its efforts to influence the alliance's decisions in such a way as to make the end result potentially acceptable for enough CDA representatives. On the domestic end, it sought out moderate elements of the anti-nuclear movement, especially certain religious groups. They were the government's main competitors for the attention of especially the CDA loyalists. Given the growing strength of the anti-nuclear movement, this was an uneven battle, certainly in hindsight. The battle was also inevitable, and starting in April Van Agt's team set about its thankless task with some energy.[17]

The government's strategy emerged more fully during preparations for a visit by United States vice-president Walter Mondale, on 21, 22 April. Speaking notes for the prime minister show how the neutron bomb continued to be political dynamite. They also show that the government sought a form of TNF modernisation that would make it look as if the role of nuclear weapons, and their number, was diminishing. On ERRB:

> Make clear that *internally* (within NATO) the Dutch government will resist any decision for production [of ERRB weapons], and *externally* any decision to deploy . . . make clear that any further step regarding ERRB – for the Netherlands – will be disastrous for decision making over TNF . . . make clear that with introduction of ERRB Dutch participation in *military* cooperation in NATO will be in grave danger (starting with [the activist slogan] 'nuclear weapons out of the Netherlands!').

On the missiles, the Dutch intended to bargain:

> It is too early to take any decisions. In order to enable us to do so we need to have at our disposal an overall view of on the one hand the possibilities for the TNF modernisation (weapon systems), and on the other hand those for arms control . . . it should be pointed out that it is my government's policy to reduce the role of nuclear weapons. This means that modernisation of TNF shall not even give the impression of extending that overall role but it can mean that a certain shift in accentuation takes place within the field of TNF. If that happens it is important that the number of nuclear warheads is not increased.[18]

In the meeting with Mondale, Van Agt went as far as linking the neutron bomb to the political survival of his cabinet. This was a 'losing battle,' and premature decisions could lead to a situation his government would not survive. It certainly would jeopardise support for TNF modernisation:

> The mood in the Netherlands was changing. In the past, just a small minority argued for a complete removal of nuclear weapons from Dutch territory. This group, however, was growing. In part this was a reflection of the thinking, and subsequent positions, in the Dutch churches.

Mondale responded by saying that in the United States too there was no lack of those who felt an emotional resistance against the neutron bomb or nuclear weapons as a whole. 'President Carter himself belongs to these elements.' Yet, a response to growing Soviet military strength was necessary, and the current, undetermined situation surrounding ERRB weapons 'kept a sword dangling over the Russians' heads' and hopefully would bring them to reason. Van der Klaauw returned to Van Agt's point, emphasising

> the growing emotional character of the difficulties in the Netherlands. The campaign against the neutron bomb was originally started from the side of the Communists but has since been adopted by other groups. A large majority of the Dutch parliament is worried about the notion of a new wave in the area of nuclear armaments, regardless of what form it takes.

On TNF, Van Agt kept to his speaking notes, underlining that 'modernisation cannot even give the impression that the role of nuclear weapons is being increased.' Van der Klaauw elaborated by explaining that

> there is still a majority in parliament that recognises the need for nuclear weapons, but that its preference is for concentration on a few types of weapons. For the air force, there was no problem yet, and neither was there for the Lance; nuclear artillery, however, was becoming doubtful already. It was absolutely necessary to maintain this majority, but in order to do so it was necessary to be able to show that the overall goal was a decrease, and not an increase, in nuclear weapons.

The conversation then moved on to Scholten's proposal to do away with the rotational membership in the NPG for small member states such as the Netherlands and to give them permanent seats. Circumstances had changed since the Dutch accepted this arrangement. These days, the Dutch felt very closely involved with nuclear policy.

> Hardly a week passed without the government having to answer questions in parliament about nuclear issues. It had become essential for the Netherlands to be visibly involved in the most credible way with allied decision making on nuclear weapons. There was an additional aspect of practical political significance. The present minister of defense was greatly respected in parliament. But he therefore had to be able to demonstrate his influence with the allies. On this issue, judged so important by the entire nation, he cannot really afford a defeat.

On this last point at least, Mondale was sympathetic.[19]

Soon after, Van Agt prepared to meet with a delegation from the Dutch protestant Council of Churches (Raad van Kerken, RvK), a group representing more than a dozen Protestant denominations in the Netherlands, influential in the anti-nuclear movement. His top adviser, J. P. M. H. Merckelbach, warned that on the key issue – whether disarmament should be pursued unilaterally instead of in connection to East-West military (im)balances – both sides were unlikely to agree. In part because there existed such a gap between what the government believed to be its responsibilities and the RvK's push for unilateral steps, Merckelbach suggested Van Agt offer the RvK the government's technical assistance the next time it was to write a paper on the matter. Informal contacts already existed.[20]

Along with Van Agt, Scholten and Van der Klaauw also participated in the meeting. Merckelbach was correct; the best the sides could do was to agree to disagree and to try to meet again in the near future. Van Agt and his colleagues rebuffed any suggestions for Dutch initiatives outside of NATO–or within, against alliance consensus. If one wanted to have influence, one would have to do one's part, Scholten said. 'One's influence does not increase when one distances oneself from nuclear weapons.' And the Dutch did have influence within NATO, he continued. Following a Dutch initiative in the DPC the previous year to include arms control in discussions of nuclear modernisation, the West Germans had made a formal proposal to form a high level study group for this alongside the HLG (the so-called Special Consultative Group, SG). And there was agreement that an eventual decision on modernisation would only be taken when both groups had completed their work. Scholten also mentioned his proposal to end the rotating membership in the NPG for small countries. 'Looking at the facts, the frequent charge that under this cabinet things have gotten dull within NATO is completely unfounded.'[21]

Scholten was right. Aware of the growing influence of anti-nuclear ideas in Dutch politics, the allies did pay attention to Dutch proposals and tried to accommodate them–up to a point.[22] Later that month, for example, the alliance did move toward permanent membership in the NPG for its smaller member states. On the core Dutch issue concerning TNF modernisation, however, there were definite limits. As the process moved from the study phase to decision making, the allies were unwilling to let the goal of arms control delay any decisions on production or deployment of new intermediate-range missiles. On 7 May the Dutch permanent representative to NATO had to report that the allies would not go on record on the Van Agt government's own central objective of a reduction of the role of nuclear weapons: 'no support.' The best the alliance could do here was to seek to avoid an increase in the overall reliance on nuclear weapons. Furthermore, and more directly relevant for the TNF decision, arms control considerations would not be allowed to hold up modernisation. A passage in the DPC's 'Draft Ministerial Guidance 1979' that the Dutch found objectionable would stay: 'consideration of their [TNF modernisation and arms control] relative merits should not be allowed to delay progress in taking steps necessary to assure NATO's deterrent and defense capabilities.'[23]

Scholten pledged to keep trying to get the passage removed or amended. Failing that, he promised to add a footnote stating that the Netherlands was unable to endorse it. Van Agt agreed, 'worried that by keeping the passage in, the impression would be created . . . that the NPG working group on arms control only has been established for the sake of public opinion.'[24]

The NATO ministerial council at the end of May confirmed that many allies wanted a decision by the end of the year. The Hague, however, decided to separate the process into two distinct phases: the first, dedicated to the HLG and SG studies, was ongoing; the second, political phase could begin only after the expert reports had been completed. Hence, Van der Klaauw reported to the cabinet on 1 June that he and Scholten had warned the allies that 'because it would be better for the alliance's credibility only to decide when the studies have been completed, [they] had expressed a willingness to aim for a decision already in 1979, but without being able to commit to one.' Scholten added that this was 'one of the most sensitive issues' in parliament, and one would have to await the results of a plenary debate there, likely to take place in September. In any case, 'it should be made clear to the press that the Dutch government has not committed itself in any way. The United States position is not clear. This is why the government should not take the lead with a decision here.'[25]

'Leading' with a decision was hardly the issue within NATO. If anything, the government was struggling to keep in contact with mainstream thinking on TNF modernisation, while in parliament it could never count on majority support for its nuclear policies. This, of course, was the government's real predicament. Within NATO, the government did not play a leadership role, but it was active, and it got a hearing. At home, there was much less of that. There were informal contacts with elements of the anti-nuclear movement, but there was never a government campaign to, so to speak, educate the Dutch public on TNF-related questions. The Van Agt government has been criticised for this, but in the circumstances it had good reasons for its hesitance.[26] When there had been a public confrontation over nuclear issues in recent years–over the neutron bomb, or over the *Kernwapennota*–pressure for a reduction in Dutch nuclear tasks had been strong in parliament, while the IKV-led anti-nuclear movement seemed to gather momentum every time nuclear issues were in the news. 1979 was also the year when the cabinet considered its nuclear energy policy. Here too, it was running into a very sceptical public opinion. There was talk of initiating a public debate, a guided national conversation. Scholten's take on this idea speaks volumes: this was asking for trouble, because there was no way one could control such a debate. Several of his cabinet colleagues agreed.[27]

A public debate was one thing, trying to work closely with key members of parliament, i.e. CDA politicians, another. There is little evidence that Van Agt and his cabinet developed a strategy here, thereby perhaps foregoing a potential opportunity to keep some control over the debate. Here, personalities probably were a hindering factor. The CDA leader in parliament, Ruud Lubbers, has been quoted as saying: 'Van Agt had this constitutional view that parliament was a conflicting factor, hence also the [CDA] parliamentary group, hence also Ruud Lubbers's.'[28] Lubbers's relationship with Scholten does not appear to have been close either. The defense minister may have lacked the political insight to recognise the importance of keeping the influential Lubbers fully informed of both the NATO process and his own efforts within it to get attention for Dutch views. Or perhaps he believed the risk of confidential material getting shared with too many people was too great. Foreign minister Van der Klaauw was, also by his own account, even less adept politically. It was not until fairly late in the game, August, when Lubbers began to play a central part. As it turned out, even under the best of circumstances it would have been very difficult for the government to get Lubbers on its side.[29]

In July, President Carter sent his Deputy National Security Adviser, David Aaron, to Europe 'to discuss... in detail our thoughts on how a common Alliance TNF modernisation and arms control approach can be achieved.' The work of the HLG and SG had proceeded far enough to enable NATO to achieve the necessary consensus on modernisation by the end of the year, according to the president. The Van Agt government could no longer doubt where the Americans stood.[30]

Lubbers may have heard the news through American channels also. On August 9, he had, at her invitation, a conversation with Ambassador Joseph which primarily dealt with NATO's upcoming decisions on grey area weapons. Reporting on his impressions to Van Agt, Lubbers wrote that while he had not made up his mind on the matter, politically it was going to be extremely difficult. Given his party's goal, shared by the government, of reducing the role of nuclear weapons, 'an excess of proof' would be necessary, and 'when in reasonable doubt, abstain'. If a positive decision proved to be inevitable, 'the decision to acquire the new weapons' should not be front and centre. Rather, 'it should be the other way around, with the decision to acquire as a means to autonomous [i.e. regardless of any negotiations with the Soviet Union] reductions in the total number [of nuclear weapons and tasks], and to specific negotiations to stop the "SS-20"'.[31]

The same week, Scholten did send CDA chairman Piet Steenkamp a paper outlining the reasons behind NATO's modernisation plans and the government's conditions for Dutch participation. Recent developments (SALT talks between Washington and Moscow; the Soviet nuclear build-up), Scholten wrote, had led to a situation where 'for a counterweight against Soviet power in the "grey area" one cannot automatically rely on United States strategic forces. This, however, can never be said openly, at least not by me.' Furthermore, an increased sense of insecurity in especially the Federal Republic could lead either to a new push for an independent European nuclear force, or West German accommodation with Moscow 'in the form of West German neutrality'. Chancellor Schmidt had declared that his country could not be the only European ally to deploy; Belgian prime-minister Wilfried Martens did not want Belgium to be the only small alliance member to participate. Of course, any Dutch participation would have to be in accordance with the goal of reducing the role of nuclear weapons. The allies, Scholten continued, would be more inclined to consider Dutch conditions if these served as conditions for participation in the programme. 'Necessary for all this is the presence in some form in the Netherlands ultimately of a willingness to participate.'

Scholten promised to collaborate closely with parliament in the coming months, but he only mentioned formal channels. He also claimed that the government would facilitate public debate, but his one example was support for a conference sometime in the fall organised by the Dutch Institute for Peace (Nederlands Instituut voor Vredesvraagstukken, NIVV), a meeting the group had been planning to have anyway.[32]

Did Scholten not understand that more was required? Had he not been shown Lubbers's letter to Van Agt? Already in February Lubbers had written that in response to the SS-20s NATO would not necessarily have to come up with a symmetrical response and should be willing to accept a certain 'margin of uncertainty'. The designated CDA experts in parliament, Joep de Boer and Ton Frinking (both ex-military men), with whom Lubbers collaborated closely on this matter, agreed wholeheartedly, questioning, for example, whether NATO ought to worry at all about the SS-20s. In addition, Lubbers's independent, loyalist, colleagues in parliament were coming under increasing pressure from the IKV.[33] All this threatened a divided CDA vote on TNF modernisation, and probably the fall of Van Agt's cabinet, given the VVD's insistence on Dutch participation in the NATO plans. In that case, the final merger, envisioned for 1980, between the three Christian Democratic parties into the CDA might also fail. Lubbers, in other words, was a key player in several political processes and needed to be kept close. Van Agt and Scholten did not succeed here, in spite of a series of meetings and letters between Scholten and Lubbers during the second half of September.

Scholten, together with Van Agt, met with Lubbers on 17 September to convey the number of new missiles likely to be involved with TNF modernisation (572) according to the recently completed HLG study. In a letter to Scholten the following day, Lubbers professed to be shaken by the news.

> This will be taken as a [symmetrical] reply to the SS-20. Until now I had thought hard about whether or not it would be responsible to take a limited step, in part as a warning signal to the Soviets, in part as "trigger" to get to negotiations. What threatens to come on the table now, however, is something completely different. This is not a quantitative nuance, but it leads qualitatively to a different situation. From this, I can only expect trouble.[34]

Scholten replied the next day. The government shared Lubbers's concern, but at the same time was conscious of its national and international responsibilities. Most of the letter was an attempt to explain the proposed number of new missiles, and the process that had produced it, on its own merits, and to remind Lubbers that the Special Group's study on arms control still needed to be released. The HLG and SG could only be considered together. At this moment, the government 'most certainly' had not conformed itself politically to the number of warheads mentioned in the forthcoming HLG study. But to call the HLG recommendation a symmetrical response to the SS-20, Scholten found debatable. Lubbers's conclusion that all this led to a qualitatively different situation, the defence minister found even less credible. In conclusion, Scholten professed to 'have understood clearly' Lubbers's warning of trouble ahead. He pledged to do his best, taking into account the government's own responsibilities, jointly to avoid it.[35]

There was a meeting between the two men on 21 September, followed by another letter from Lubbers. The HLG recommendation was too much, he maintained. The new missiles would be enough for an offensive strike, and compared to Soviet SS-20 deployments the aim was to restore NATO superiority. And if the aim was to promote the arms control process, 'why not limit the decision now to what you may produce and deploy in 2–3 years?' How serious would an offer for arms control talks appear anyway if NATO decided to deploy almost 600 new missiles? 'The more I think about it, I fear my phrase of a "symmetrical response" in my previous letter was actually an understatement and that the term "escalating response" will come into use.'[36]

Scholten replied the next day to remind Lubbers that having participated in the HLG study did not mean that the Netherlands had committed itself automatically to its recommendations. 'The real political phase starts now.' There already had been a good conversation with his German colleague Hans Apel, and other initiatives would follow. 'I'm not pessimistic about the Dutch negotiating position, although we still have a tough row to hoe in the coming months.' He asked Lubbers not to discuss the matter with his CDA colleagues in parliament and to speak to Van Agt and himself before taking any initiatives.[37]

Scholten wanted to know of any initiatives Lubbers might develop, but in this letter he did not offer to share information about his own diplomacy with the allies. The following month, the two men appear to have operated independently from each other. As Scholten sought to get allied support to lower the HLG's number of 572, so that the Netherlands might be able to join a final decision to produce and deploy, Lubbers developed a position paper for the CDA group in parliament (the so-called *Vertrekpunten*) which demanded that NATO only decide to develop and produce the new missiles, and take no decision on deployment, so as not to jeopardise the arms control process and the CDA's ultimate goal; zero new missiles in the West.[38]

Both men, but especially Scholten, have been criticised for leaving each other mostly in the dark about their respective activities in October. When the CDA parliamentarians published their *Vertrekpunten* paper on 30 October, it fatally undermined Scholten's efforts with the allies. The papers of former prime-minister Van Agt, however, suggest more information was exchanged between the two than is generally assumed.

Given Lubbers's communications, Scholten especially must have known that even if he were to succeed in getting NATO to halve the number of missiles it would initially deploy, as he was trying to do, CDA parliamentarians would still vote against participation in a plan to deploy. There is another letter from Lubbers to Scholten in the Van Agt papers, directly following Scholten's letter to Lubbers of 25 September and right before a summary of the Dutch negotiating position prepared for a meeting between Scholten and United States secretary of defence Harold Brown in early October.[39] This letter by Lubbers has no date, and neither does the accompanying memo in which Lubbers 'at this stage, for myself, [summarised] the matter in eight points.' It most likely indeed dates from late September, as Lubbers concludes by wishing Scholten 'a lot of success, once again, in this difficult mission.' More revealing probably is that in the letter Lubbers seems to refer to specific negotiating positions he and Scholten must have discussed together, perhaps in their meeting of 21 September, perhaps later.[40]

For example, Lubbers explains that in his memo he purposely left out 'the possibility to limit oneself right now to a replacement of the Pershings now stationed in Germany'. Also, Lubbers continued, Scholten might notice that the memo did not speak of a number (of missiles). 'You know the reason for this.' There was nothing specific in the memo about the neutron weapon either, Lubbers noted, although it could come up later in parliament. 'I will be vague now also about the Dutch nuclear tasks.' These were almost all specific issues that, as becomes clear for example from Scholten's position paper for his meeting with Secretary Brown, the government employed in its negotiations with the allies. Lubbers seems to have known, at least in broad outlines, Scholten's strategy.

Whether all this matters much is very doubtful. Lubbers's memo foreshadowed the *Vertrekpunten* where it stated: 'To avoid escalation, NATO for now will have to limit itself to the further development and possible limited production of intermediate missiles for deployment in Europe.' Lubbers warned Scholten that '[w]ith that I will not be able to guarantee success, but without it I should really expect failure'.[41]

Lubbers and Scholten appear to have known each other's positions (and predicaments) fairly well. The problem was that partly due to their personal convictions, in part because of the views of the people and groups they depended on (his CDA colleagues for Lubbers, the NATO allies and his VVD cabinet colleagues for Scholten), these positions were far apart and could not be reconciled. It is indeed unlikely that Scholten kept Lubbers posted on the progress of his diplomacy in October, and the minister certainly was blindsided by the CDA parliamentarians' *Vertrekpunten* (Scholten reportedly considered resigning).[42] Whether better coordination would have made much of a difference is very questionable, although it remains remarkable how little evidence there is of Van Agt's own involvement in these communications.

IV. Toward the 'commitment to commit'

The fact that Lubbers's *Vertrekpunten* at the end of October effectively ended Scholten's diplomacy with the NATO allies does not mean that this campaign to modify the HLG's recommendations was going well. Late September–early October Scholten, Van Agt, and Van der Klaauw had developed the government's position for what they kept calling the political phase of NATO's decision making process. (Significantly, the other members of Van Agt's cabinet were not informed.) Firstly, due to the Dutch political process, there could not be a final decision until NATO's 12 December ministerial meeting. The NPG meeting on 12–13 November in the Hague was merely a first occasion to discuss the HLG and SG reports at the political level. Secondly, ratification of the SALT II treaty (signed by President Carter and Soviet leader Leonid Brezhnev the previous June) was a condition for TNF modernisation. Thirdly, the HLG's 'proposed number of 572 warheads is politically unacceptable for the Dutch government. Political consultation has demonstrated that acceptance of this number will lead to a crisis of government (fall of the cabinet).' The three ministers would be willing to argue in the cabinet for half that number, provided the other Dutch conditions were met. A fourth condition was the start of a so-called 'shift' study to examine if an eventual increase in long range TNF weapons could lead to a smaller number of short-range nuclear weapons. Finally, the Dutch also wanted to reduce the number of nuclear tasks now performed by their armed forces.[43]

The allies were sceptical at best. Visiting with Italian prime-minister Francesco Cossiga on 13 October, Van der Klaauw and Van Agt learned that Rome would much prefer to have a formal alliance decision sooner rather than later, and that it viewed the relationship between TNF modernisation and SALT II in exactly the opposite way to The Hague: for the Italians, an alliance decision on TNF would make SALT II ratification more likely; the Dutch, for whom the arms-control side of the coming dual-track decision was paramount, believed ratification of the accord on strategic arms would make productive talks on grey-area weapons more likely. Van der Klaauw's report on the meeting had to conclude, therefore, that 'the Italian views... are diametrically opposed to ours... '.[44]

The Americans, while promising to be as helpful as possible, were not very receptive either. David Aaron stopped over on 22 October for a conversation with Scholten. It was his last stop on a tour of all the countries included with the HLG's recommendations. There was an 'emerging consensus' in NATO, and at this late stage one could not jeopardise it by making significant changes, he announced. Scholten resented being pressured:

> Several weeks ago I delivered a very clear political message to our most important ally, the United States. You yourself have decided on the itinerary of your Europe trip, in spite of our request to do it in a different order... you can't say now that there already is an emerging consensus at the political level.

On specifics, Aaron warned that making modernisation conditional on SALT II ratification would be counterproductive. The United States was willing, with some trepidation, to accommodate The Hague on a 'shift' study and on a reduction in Dutch nuclear tasks. Partly because of these concessions, however, 'I have to tell you in all frankness that we cannot take up your proposal to reduce [the number of 572] by 50%.' It would, among other things, cause 'the President of the United States to lose all respect domestically if he now came with a decision that was only 50% of the military experts' recommendation.' 'We are too far along to go back now.' Scholten could only reply that 'a very difficult situation' had now arisen.[45]

A letter from Carter to Van Agt followed on 31 October, pleading not to introduce the 50% proposal at the upcoming NPG meeting. As a gesture, Carter did offer to withdraw 1000 U.S. nuclear warheads from Europe.[46]

The day before Carter sent his letter, the CDA's *Vertrekpunten* had been made public, confirming that 50% reduction or not, there would in all likelihood be no majority in parliament for a NATO decision at this time to deploy any new missiles. Scholten would have to change his strategy. During a debate in parliament on 7 and 8 November, he indeed agreed to plead for the *Vertrekpunten* with the allies during the upcoming NPG meeting. As he could report to his cabinet colleagues one week later, there was no support for his arguments there.[47]

Following the meeting, Scholten tried again, in a letter sent to his colleagues in NATO. The differences between NATO's Integrated Decision Document (IDD, based on the HLG and SG reports) and what he had argued on the basis of the *Vertrekpunten* really was 'not as big as it may seem.' On the relationship between the production and deployment decisions:

> In both cases it will be necessary to evaluate the results of arms control negotiations and to reach a consensus about these results before the actual deployment of the new systems. Thus in neither case will the actual deployment automatically result from decisions that are going to be made at the end of this year.

And given the importance of the arms control track, Scholten argued it would be better to start with a lower number of missiles. One could always adjust it upward depending on the outcome of the negotiations.[48]

Van Agt's files contain the British reply. While understanding of Scholten's political position, it was negative. On the proposal to separate deployment and production, Defence Secretary Francis Pym quoted a former British prime minister, who used to say that 'it is unwise to cross a chasm in two leaps.' What the IDD envisages, Pym continued,

> is that we should take firm decisions now but should acknowledge that we shall be prepared to modify them later if the other side gives us solid and assured reasons for doing so. This is a fundamentally different political and negotiating proposition from the one the CDA has indicated – it requires the Russians to react positively to our arms control initiative, rather than leaving the onus on the Alliance: that seems to me to be crucial.

There were other important considerations. The point was, the alliance's process had been one of give and take for all members.

> My country has influenced the outcome: so, very clearly, has the Netherlands – the package before us in December will bear your positive imprint in many ways (the emphasis on arms control, no increase in stockpile, the concept of the 'shift' study and a firm date for it, just to take some examples).

Pym concluded: 'We must consider whether it is better for our own and Western security for each of us to be perfectly right (as we see it) in isolation, or to be perhaps imperfectly right together. The alliance is built on the principle that the latter is better.'[49]

It was a perfectly reasonable argument, and Scholten probably agreed with just about every part of it. The problem was, his party, and a significant section of the Dutch population, had decided that, in Pym's words, it had become more important to be perfectly right (in one's own eyes), if necessary in isolation. As the IKV's slogan put it, nuclear weapons had to be abolished, to begin with in the Netherlands. This reality Van Agt set out to explain on a mission to the capitals of the NATO member states designated to participate in TNF modernisation. At the moment, the Netherlands would not be able to commit itself to deploy the new missiles on its territory, even though the government did support the upcoming decision.

First stop, on 4 December, was Brussels. Van Agt explained to his colleague Martens that especially because of the divisions within his own party in parliament, unqualified support for NATO's IDD was impossible. Unqualified support would be political suicide, and his government would probably be succeeded by a left-of-centre coalition not nearly as loyal to NATO. 'The discussion in the Netherlands has intensified in recent weeks, now displaying para-psychotic characteristics, and it is virtually uncontrollable.' Because of its own position toward NATO, an outright rejection of the IDD was not an option for the government either. Given the likely alternative, the survival of his government certainly was in the alliance's interest also, according to Van Agt. Therefore, a compromise decision would have to be found, adhering as closely as possible to the IDD.

Martens said his government was feeling the pressure too, especially from the Flemish Socialists, who for their part were being influenced by the Dutch PvdA. Therefore, Martens, too, was thinking of a middle way, for example by accepting the IDD on 12 December, but to postpone full implementation in Belgium by six months. Van Agt confirmed his government had something similar in mind, except that the Netherlands would choose a longer delay. Both agreed that because one country's less than complete endorsement of the IDD could have a negative effect on another member state where modernisation was controversial, it was important to take the final national decisions as late as possible. The two prime ministers decided to time their final decisions in close coordination, probably on Monday evening, 10 December.[50]

On 6 December Van Agt traveled to Rome to meet Cossiga, and later that day he flew on to London to brief British prime minister Margaret Thatcher. After Cossiga had kicked off the meeting with a report on his parliament's endorsement of the modernisation plans, Van Agt remarked that 'his political friends would barely allow him to congratulate the Italian government with the outcome of this debate.' His own situation was very different. Once again overdramatising the situation, he explained:

> What is happening in the Netherlands tends toward a mass psychotic development, encouraged by the largest part of the press and television, who are radically tinted. This development washes over the cabinet like a wave and because it is irrational it cannot be controlled.

He proceeded to lay out his three choices, only one of which was both politically feasible (perhaps) and in the interest of the alliance. If Van Agt tried unconditionally to accept NATO's IDD, it was not a given that all his cabinet colleagues would support him. A middle way, where the Netherlands would 'grumble a little' over the number of new missiles, but then 'commit to commit' at a later time was something he would be prepared to take to the cabinet. In addition, the nuclear tasks of the Dutch armed forces would have to be adjusted downward. Van Agt realised that this would be a disappointment for the allies, but even with this approach there was no guarantee his government would survive. At their recent meeting, Van Agt continued, he had told Cossiga that he could not imagine his country would get into this position, 'because we are not a people that lets others carry the load while keeping our own hands clean. Unfortunately he had been mistaken.' Cossiga accepted Van Agt's plan, provided the Dutch supported the alliance's upcoming decision and provided Chancellor Schmidt and the Americans agreed too.[51]

London was next. Van Agt again spoke of a 'mass psychotic movement rolling like a wave over the country,' adding that his government might well fall. He next presented his three options and explained why he had opted for the 'commitment to commit.' Thatcher said she did hope that Van Agt's approach would be successful. Asked to explain the mood in his country, Van Agt, now using more nuanced language, pointed to a widespread, general aversion to all things nuclear. The opposition had focused on the TNF issue because here the government actually had a decision to make. The loyalists in Van Agt's own party had been looking for a way to replace his centre-right coalition with a centre-left one ever since 1977, and this was their chance. Also, '[t]he Dutch are a people of theologians, some more, others less. This also means that the Dutchman is a super-individualist; everyone has his own conscience that is decisive, everyone reads the Bible and has his own interpretation.' Many would prefer a Russian occupation over destruction. Thatcher remarked that this ignored 'the many who are both red and dead.' History was full of examples showing the illusion of trying to stave off destruction by not defending oneself, she added. Were the Dutch so principled that they would also reject protection by other NATO members? Also, she wondered, was the Dutch population being informed properly? According to Van Agt, 'Dutch public opinion was being manipulated greatly, not so much by the written press, but by television.' Finally, Van Agt explained how his government had pledged to parliament to advocate with the allies for the *Vertrekpunten*, particularly the idea of separating production and deployment. In response, Thatcher had the meeting's last word:

> one could not in earnest expect from the US that it produce new TNF systems without knowing whether and where these would be deployed. She believes that the allies should follow the same line as much as possible; otherwise the entire TNF discussion will end in a victory for the SU. As far as she is concerned, the prime-minister can tell parliament and the press that the UK sees nothing in the separation idea and that it is willing to defend the Netherlands, if it does not object to that.[52]

Arriving in Washington the next morning, Van Agt had some additional bad news for President Carter. The previous night, parliament had held its final debate on the TNF matter prior to 12 December. 'The outcome is far from favourable for the government or NATO. The lower house has voted that at the moment there should not be a decision on production or deployment of new TNF systems.' (This was the doing of a new opposition proposal. Lubbers had opposed it because it went beyond the *Vertrekpunten*, but ten CDA representatives, the loyalists, voted in favour anyway.)

Van Agt proceeded to lay out his 'commitment to commit' solution. Asked if that meant that his government would not oppose the upcoming dual-track decision, Van Agt replied affirmatively, but added that there would still be some 'verbal resistance' to the size of the modernisation programme. National Security Adviser Zbigniew Brzezinski objected, saying that such grumbling had nothing to do with the postponement of the Dutch decision. Carter agreed. Brzezinski added that it now appeared that the Soviet Union might, after all, be willing to negotiate over grey-area weapons, even when NATO decided to go forward. Dutch criticism of the programme would confuse the situation and possibly undermine Soviet willingness to talk. Secretary of State Cyrus Vance agreed: if the Netherlands wanted to postpone its own decision, 'it should not undermine the decision of the other allies.' Van Agt may have been thrown a little off balance by this, yet another set-back. He next chose to make a comment about the Dutch national debate, his only in this meeting, but one that was a far cry from the dramatic 'mass psychosis' of his earlier presentations that week. Instead, he sounded rather defensive: 'Without trying to apologize, Prime Minister Van Agt did want to point out that in no other NATO country was there such an intensive and widespread discussion of this matter.'[53]

After the discussion with the president, the Dutch delegation had an additional meeting with Brzezinski, Vance, and other US officials. Van Agt began by asking for confirmation that his government was not supposed to 'grumble' about the size of the envisioned TNF deployment. Vance confirmed. Brzezinski weighed in, noting that 'not the character or size of the programme, but the attitude of parliament was the reason behind the position the Dutch government believed it had to assume.' Van Agt may have decided there was little point in telling the national security adviser that inside the cabinet there were those who also objected to the number of missiles NATO intended to deploy. In any case, if the Dutch would take another look in two years, the exact number of missiles to be deployed in the Netherlands could remain open as far the United States was concerned. Van Agt next proceeded to another Dutch condition: the link between TNF implementation and SALT II ratification. Again the Americans said no. Instead, the Dutch could express the expectation that when the Netherlands made its decision in two years' time, SALT II would have been ratified. On the issue of the Dutch nuclear tasks, the Americans professed to have no difficulty with a reduction. At the end of the meeting Van Agt warned that there was no guarantee that his full cabinet was going to approve the approach he had come to Washington to present. Also, parliament could reject his government's position. If that happened, he would ask for a vote of confidence, out of solidarity with the NATO alliance. It was far from certain that he would win.[54]

Of the final stop on Van Agt's trip, the meeting with Chancellor Schmidt, no memorandum of conversation exists in the TNF file of Van Agt's papers, but published German diplomatic papers do contain a memorandum of conversation. It shows that Schmidt, too, could live with the Dutch delay, provided The Hague did not interfere with NATO's decision making process.[55]

V. Conclusion

The Dutch did not interfere, or grumble, and Van Agt's government survived the subsequent debate in parliament on 19 December, albeit by a whisker. The key point of contention was the way the government had positioned itself in Brussels, or rather, how the exceptional Dutch position had been presented to the world. The allies had insisted that the Dutch reservation not appear in the communiqué of the meeting, allied unity being essential. Instead, it appeared in a public annex to the (secret) list of decisions. For the CDA "loyalists" this was not enough. The NATO communiqué showed that the Netherlands was co-responsible for the decision to produce and deploy the new missiles if negotiations failed, a course of events these Christian Democrats had been dead-set on preventing. When the opposition moved that parliament vote that the Netherlands could not accept responsibility for NATO's decision, it appeared the government might fall. Van Agt indicated that his cabinet would not be able to accept approval of the motion, putting the ball in the loyalists' court. In the end, party interests won out: the fall of the cabinet would have handed a great victory to the Social Democrats, and it might well have meant the end for the CDA also. The loyalists showed they could, indeed, be loyal, even on nuclear issues. The opposition motion was voted down, Van Agt's government survived, and the Netherlands remained within NATO's fold on TNF modernisation, if only barely. This tenuous situation continued all the way until November 1985, when parliament finally accepted the 48 cruise missiles.

This epilogue goes a long way to answering the question as to whether a different approach by the Van Agt government, vis-à-vis parliament–and the CDA group there–could have kept the Netherlands fully in NATO's mainstream on TNF modernisation. It is very difficult to see how. Given the growing strength of the anti-nuclear movement (it was to reach the height of its influence between 1981 and 1984), any pro-active intervention by the government in the public debate could well have backfired. Communication with Ruud Lubbers could have been better, especially in October 1979 and particularly by the prime minister himself. But Lubbers was deeply sceptical himself of the need for modernisation, certainly after the HLG's numbers came out. And Lubbers, it became clear in early December (at the latest), did not really control the members of the CDA caucus.

Since the contested formation of the Van Agt government and the controversies surrounding the neutron bomb in 1977–1978 there had been too many divisions in Dutch politics, at too many levels, and on nuclear questions there had been too much pressure from within society to leave decision makers much room on what was a controversial issue in many other NATO countries too. The internal deliberations of the Van Agt cabinet examined here make this clear. Significantly, internally the cabinet often refrained from discussing nuclear weapons issues in depth, knowing that if a substantial discussion developed, fissures between CDA and VVD ministers, and also among CDA ministers, would likely reveal themselves. Van Agt usually limited these substantial discussions to himself, the defence and foreign ministers, and at times vice prime minister Wiegel. In its rare discussions with advocacy groups, the best the cabinet and its interlocutors could do was a polite agree-to-disagree. Whether the Netherlands in 1979 suffered from some kind of 'mass psychosis' or whether the country simply discussed the matter more intensely and with greater popular participation than anywhere else, it does appear that the government's position at the Brussels meeting on 12 December 1979 was the best that could be attained.

A similar conclusion seems warranted for the government's role in the formulation of NATO's dual track decision, although here the balance may be slightly more positive. As British Defense Minister Pym's letter of early December 1979 points out, United States officials demonstrated on several occasions, and published German documents confirm, Dutch concerns were taken into account by the allies. Dutch insistence on equal status for missile deployment and arms control found expression in the final decision; the alliance did commit itself in 1979 to a future 'shift' study; prior to the 12 December meeting the United States pledged the withdrawal of 1000 nuclear warheads from Europe; and there was acceptance also of a future reduction in Dutch nuclear tasks alongside deployment of the new intermediate-range missiles on Dutch soil.

The story of the Dutch role in the 'Euromissiles' crisis would continue until the end of 1985, but major themes were visible already by 1979: from growing resistance in society to nuclear weapons in general and NATO's modernisation plans in particular; to significant opposition within parliament to a possible deployment and uncertain support among Christian Democratic cabinet ministers; to sometimes irritated but often also accommodating NATO allies. Further work is needed on especially this last aspect: how were Dutch objections and reservations perceived in other countries; did the Dutch resistance inspire others in Europe to fight implementation of the dual-track decision (as the example of the Flemish socialists, mentioned by Martens, suggests), and, indeed, to what extent can the Dutch role be called unique? Placing the Dutch story more firmly in a wider international context can illuminate not only developments in the Netherlands during the crisis of détente, it can also contribute to an international history of this era.

Acknowledgement

The author would like to thank the Dutch foreign and defense ministries, the staffs at the Dutch National Archives and the Catholic Documentation Center, Radboud University Nijmegen, and especially former prime-minister A.A.M. van Agt, for their cooperation in making their respective collections available for this research. Thanks also to Maarten Brands, Ronald Havenaar, Dick van Rietschoten, Bert Steinmetz, and the two anonymous reviewers for this journal for many helpful comments.

Notes

[1] For NATO's decision making process see Leopoldo Nuti, 'The origins of the 1979 dual track decision – a survey.' *The Crisis of Détente in Europe: From Helsinki to Gorbachev, 1975–1985* Leopoldo Nuti, ed. London: Routledge, 2009. Also, more generally, Havenaar, *Eb en Vloed*, and Wiegrefe, *Das Zerwürfnis*.

[2] Laqueur, 'Hollanditis.'

[3] The various statements connected with this policy are reproduced in Van Eenennaam, *48 Kruisraketten*, 302–309. An account that assigns a special role in the discussions about the December 12 communiqué to NATO Secretary-General, Joseph Luns is: Kersten, *Luns*, 593–594. In most documents used here, the envisioned new NATO missiles–Tomahawk cruise missiles and Pershing II missiles with a range of, respectively, 2500 and 1800 kilometers–are referred to as Theatre Nuclear Forces, TNF, but at times the term Long Range Theatre Nuclear Forces, LRTNF appears. Gradually, the term Intermediate Nuclear Forces, INF, began to be used to describe these weapons.

[4] Spohr Readman, 'Germany and the Politics of the Neutron Bomb, 1975–1979'; Garthoff, *Détente and Confrontation*, chapter 25; Haftendorn, 'Das doppelte Mißverständnis'; Haslam, *The Soviet Union and the Politics of Nuclear Weapons, 1969–87*; Haslam, *Russia's Cold War*, chapter 10.

[5] For a recent account of developments in Dutch society in connection with the NATO plans see, Van Diepen, *Hollanditis*; for the domestic side of Dutch foreign policy: Everts, ed. *Controversies at Home*; specifically with regard to nuclear weapons: Everts, 'Public Opinion on Nuclear Weapons, Defense, and Security: The Case of the Netherlands.' In *The Public and Atlantic Defense*, Gregory Flynn and Hans Rattiger, eds., Totowa, N.J.: Rowman & Allanheld, 1985; the Dutch role in NATO: A. van Staden, 'De rol van Nederland in het Atlantisch bondgenootschap. Wat veranderde en wat uiteindelijk bleef.' In *De kracht van Nederland: Internationale positie en buitenlands beleid*, N.C.F. van Sas, ed., Haarlem: Becht, 1991; for Dutch foreign policy since the Second World War: Hellema, *Buitenlandse Politiek van Nederland*.

[6] A number of these documents now appear in English translation. See Van Dijk, 'A mass psychotic movement washing over the country like a wave.'

[7] See for example Van Merriënboer et al., *Van Agt*, chapter 11.

[8] Kennedy, *Nieuw-Babylon*, 184–190.

[9] De Graaf details how the campaign was coordinated between the CPN, Moscow, and East Berlin, *Over de Muur*, chapter 4; the Dutch domestic security agency (BVD) tracked the campaign, and its East European ties, carefully: Report 'Communistische campagne tegen kernwapenvernieuwing,' head BVD, P. de Haan, to Dutch Defense minister, February 6 1980, *Nationaal Archief* (Dutch National Archive: NA), The Hague, Defense Ministry 5.050.114/1954–1979/647.

[10] See the cabinet meetings of 17 February 1978: *NA 2.02.05.02, 2397*; and 23 February, 28 February, and 3 March: Papers of H. Wiegel, *NA 2.21.303, 366* and *NA 2.02.05.02, 2665*.

[11] Nederlandse Atlantische Commissie, *Nederland en de Kernwapens*, 122–127.

[12] Van Eenennaam, *48 Kruisraketten*, 30–31.

[13] Cabinet meeting, 8 December 1978, *NA 2.02.05.02, 2407*.

[14] Memorandum Van der Klaauw, 5 January 1995. *Archief Ministerie van Buitenlandse Zaken* (Dutch foreign ministry archive: ArchBuZa), *9/1975-1984/6958*. For a later episode, see the Reagan administration's decisions of August 1981 and Dutch reactions: *ArchBuZa, DPV/1983-1990/00735*.

[15] *NA, 2.02.05.02, 2927*.

[16] Ibid.

[17] Van Diepen covers the domestic debate in considerable detail. See *Hollanditis*, chapter 2.

[18] Cabinet prime-minister. *NA, 2.03.01, 9464*. (TNF speaking notes originally in English).

[19] Memorandum of conversation, Van der Klaauw to Van Agt, 23 April 1979. *ArchBuZa, apa/gs/1975-1984/1121*.

[20] Briefing paper, 2 May 1979. Cabinet prime-minister. *NA, 2.03.01, 8700*.

[21] *NA, 2.03.01, 8701*.

[22] There is significant evidence for this point in German diplomatic papers also: *Akten zur Auswärtigen Politik der Bundesrepublik Deutschland* 1979, for example document numbers 113, 303, 312, 313, 316, 321, 323.

[23] Telegram permanent representative to NATO (Barkman) to the minister of foreign affairs, 7 May 1979, on the meeting of the DPC. In AVR files, *NA, 2.02.05.02, 2928.*

[24] AVR meeting, 11 May 1979. *NA, 2.02.05.02, 2924.*

[25] *NA, 2.02.05.02, 2664.*

[26] Ambassador to NATO, Barkman, did so to Van Agt at the time. See Van Merriënboer et al., *Van Agt*, 397. Early December 1979, British prime-minister Margaret Thatcher also raised the issue with Van Agt: *Archief A.A.M. van Agt, box 41: TNF file* (Papers of A A.M. van Agt: Van Agt, TNF), *Catholic Documentation Center, University Nijmegen.*

[27] Cabinet meeting 2 July 1979. *NA 2.02.05.02, 2665.*

[28] Koster, *De eenzame fietser*, 177.

[29] See for example, Van Merriënboer, et al., *Van Agt*, 398–401; Steinmetz, *Ruud Lubbers*, 124–126. Also Van der Klaauw, *Een diplomatenleven.*

[30] Carter to Van Agt, 12 July 1979. *Van Agt, TNF.*

[31] Lubbers to Van Agt, 13 August 1979. *Van Agt, TNF.*

[32] Scholten to Van Agt, 16 August; paper to Steenkamp dated 15 August. *Van Agt, TNF.*

[33] Van Diepen, *Hollanditis*, 121–123, Lubbers quote, 122.

[34] Lubbers to Scholten, 18 September 1979. *Van Agt, TNF.*

[35] Scholten to Lubbers, 19 September 1979. *Van Agt, TNF.*

[36] Lubbers to Scholten, 24 September 1979. *Van Agt, TNF.*

[37] Scholten to Lubbers, 25 September 1979. *Van Agt, TNF.*

[38] Nederlandse Atlantische Commissie, *Nederland en de Kernwapens*, 134–136; Van Merriënboer, et al., *Van Agt*, 398–400; Van Eenennaam, *48 Kruisraketten, 72–73.*

[39] Scholten's meeting with Brown was on 5 October this position paper has a date and time, handwritten at the end: 2 October 1979, 11:10 hours. *Van Agt, TNF.*

[40] Later, Lubbers claimed not to have known of Scholten's initiatives. Van Eenenaam, *48 Kruisraketten*, 72–73, especially note 37; and Steinmetz, *Ruud Lubbers*, 126.

[41] Lubbers to Scholten, n.d. *Van Agt, TNF.* On 4 October, Lubbers also sent Scholten his draft remarks on nuclear questions prepared for the debate in parliament on the government's program for the 1980 fiscal year. Ibid.

[42] Van Merriënboer, et al., *Van Agt*, 400.

[43] Summary Dutch position TNF modernisation for Brown-Scholten meeting. 2 October 1979. *Van Agt, TNF.*

[44] Memorandum of conversation, Van der Klaauw and Van Agt with Cossiga and his foreign minister Franco Malfatti, 15 October 1979. *Van Agt, TNF.*

[45] Memorandum of conversation, Scholten-Aaron meeting, 22 October 1979. *Van Agt, TNF.*

[46] Carter to Van Agt, 31 October 1979. Cabinet prime-minister. *NA 2.03.01, 8699.* Van Agt would take until 29 November to send a reply, in which he agreed not to press the 50% demand, but in which he did argue, following the CDA parliamentarians' *Vertrekpunten*, for just a production decision now, and a postponement of the decision to deploy. Ibid.

[47] Cabinet meetings 14 and 16 November 1979. *NA 2.02.05.02, 2669.*

[48] Scholten to his NATO colleagues, 23 November 1979. *Van Agt, TNF.*

[49] Message Secretary of State for Defence to the Netherlands Minister of Defence. Accompanied by a separate paper on a possible reduction of Dutch nuclear tasks. Forwarded to the office of prime-minister Van Agt on 5 December 1979. *Van Agt, TNF.*

[50] Handwritten memorandum of conversation, 6 December 1979, meeting Van Agt-Martens, Brussels, 4 December 1979. *Van Agt, TNF.*

[51] Handwritten memorandum of conversation, 9 December 1979, meeting Van Agt-Cossiga, Rome, 6 December 1979. *Van Agt, TNF.*

[52] Handwritten memorandum of conversation, 9 December 1979, meeting Van Agt-Thatcher, London, 6 December 1979. *Van Agt, TNF.*

[53] Handwritten memorandum of conversation, 9 December 1979, meeting Van Agt-Carter (and others), Washington, 7 December 1979. *Van Agt, TNF.*

[54] Handwritten memorandum of conversation, 9 December 1979, meeting Van Agt, Van der Klaauw-Brzezinski, Vance (and others), Washington, 7 December 1979. *Van Agt, TNF.*

[55] Aufzeichnung des Ministerialdirektors von Staden, Bundeskanzleramt, 11. Dezember 1979, *AAP* 1979, 1884–1887. Handwritten summary of main points, conversations Brussels, Rome, London, Washington, Bonn, n.d. *Van Agt, TNF.*

References

Akten zur Auswärtigen Politik der Bundesrepublik Deutschland 1979. Munich: Oldenbourg, 2010.

Diepen, Remco van. *Hollanditis: Nederland en het Kernwapendebat, 1977–1987.* Amsterdam: Bert Bakker, 2004.

Dijk, Ruud van, ed. '"A mass psychotic movement washing over the country like a wave": Explaining Dutch Reservations About NATO's 1979 Dual-Track Decision'. *Cold War International History Project e-Dossier #21*, 2 April, 2010. http://www.wilsoncentre.org/index.cfm?topic_id=1409&fuseaction = topics.publications&doc_id = 606479&group_id = 13349

Eenennaam, B. J. van. *48 Kruisraketten: Hoogspanning in de Lage Landen.* 's-Gravenhage: SDU, 1988.

Everts, Ph. P., ed. *Controversies at Home: Domestic Factors in the Foreign Policy of the Netherlands.* Dordrecht: Martinus Nijhof, 1985.

Flynn, Gregory, and Hans Rattinger, eds. *The Public and Atlantic Defense.* Totowa, N.J. Rowman & Allanheld, 1985.

Garthoff, Raymond L. *Détente and Confrontation: American-Soviet Relations from Nixon to Reagan.* Washington: Brookings, 1985.

Graaf, Beatrice de. *Over de Muur: De DDR, de Nederlandse Kerken en de Vredesbeweging.* Amsterdam: Boom, 2004.

Haftendorn, Helga. 'Das doppelte Mißverständnis. Zur Vorgeschichte des NATO-Doppelbeschlusses von 1979'. *Vierteljahrshefte für Zeitgeschichte* 33, no. 2 (1979): 244–87.

Haslam, Jonathan. *Russia's Cold War: From the October Revolution to the Fall of the Wall.* New Haven: Yale University Press, 2011.

———. *The Soviet Union and the Politics of Nuclear Weapons in Europe, 1969–87: The Problem of the SS-20.* Houndsmills: MacMillan, 1989.

Havenaar, Ronald. *Eb en Vloed: Europa en Amerika van Reagan tot Obama.* Amsterdam: Van Oorschot, 2008.

Hellema, Duco. *Buitenlandse Politiek van Nederland: De Nederlandse Rol in de Wereldpolitiek.* Utrecht: Spectrum, 2006.

Kennedy, James. *Nieuw-Babylon in Aanbouw: Nederland in de Jaren Zestig.* Amsterdam: Boom, 1995.

Kersten, Albert. *Luns: Een politieke biografie.* Amsterdam: Boom, 2010.

Klaauw, C. A. van der. *Een diplomatenleven: memoires.* Amsterdam: Bert Bakker, 1995.

Koster, Adrianus. *De Eenzame Fietser: Insiders over de Politieke Loopbaan van Dries van Agt (1971–1982).* Culemborg: Van Duuren, 2008.

Laqueur, Walter. 'Hollanditis: A New Stage in European Neutralism'. *Commentary* 72, no. 2 (August 1981): 19–26.

Merriënboer, Johan van, Peter Bootsma, and Peter van Griensven. *Van Agt: Tour de Force, Biografie.* Amsterdam: Boom, 2008.

Nederlandse Atlantische Commissie, ed. *Nederland en de Kernwapens: Een studie over het Nederlands nucleair beleid, 1972–1985*. Alphen aan de Rijn: Samson, 1987.
Nuti, Leopoldo, ed. *The Crisis of Détente in Europe: From Helsinki to Gorbachev, 1975–1985*. London: Routledge, 2009, 57–71.
Sas, N. C. F. van, ed. *De kracht van Nederland: Internationale Positie en Buitenlands Beleid*. Haarlem: Becht, 1991.
Spohr Readman, Kristina. 'Germany and the Politics of the Neutron Bomb, 1975–1979'. *Diplomacy and Statecraft* 21, no. 2 (2010): 259–85.
Steinmetz, Bert. *Ruud Lubbers: Peetvader van het Poldermodel*. Amsterdam: Prometheus, 2000.
Wiegrefe, Klaus. *Das Zerwürfnis: Helmut Schmidt, Jimmy Carter und die Krise der Deutsch-Amerikanischen Beziehungen*. Frankfurt a.M.: Propyläen, 2005.

General Lyman L. Lemnitzer and NATO, 1948–69: a deferential leader

Lawrence S. Kaplan

ABSTRACT

The Supreme Allied Commander, Europe (SACEUR), General Lyman L. Lemnitzer, was an unlikely hero who rose to the challenge of France's expulsion of the North Atlantic Treaty Organization (NATO) from its territory in 1966. President de Gaulle's action forced the Alliance to locate its new headquarters in another NATO country and move 800,000 tons of military equipment out of France in less than a year's time. How to achieve this goal without irrevocably fracturing relations with France was the charge given to the Supreme Allied Commander, a man of equable temperament and – from the perspective of some of his peers – of modest talents. He lacked the authority of General Dwight D. Eisenhower, the intellect of General Alfred M. Gruenther Gruenther, and the imperious temperament of General Lauris Norstad. But against the odds he succeeded in opening Supreme Headquarters Allied Powers Europe (SHAPE) headquarters in Belgium on 1 April 1967. This essay seeks to examine his long relationship with NATO and judge how successful he was in his leadership as Supreme Allied Commander in the 1960s.

A major in 1941, Lemnitzer's talents for organisation and planning were recognised in his assignment to the War Plans Division. Within nine months he was a brigadier general, serving as General Eisenhower's assistant chief of staff in London. Specifically, he was in charge of planning the successful invasion of North Africa in 1942. In the course of this operation he developed diplomatic skills working clandestinely in Vichy-controlled Algeria. After a lesser role in the Tunisian and Sicilian invasions he served as US Deputy Chief of Staff and Chief of Staff under British Field Marshal Harold Alexander, Supreme Allied Commander in the Mediterranean.[1] General Lemnitzer was among the veterans of World War II who understood the importance of promoting a new relationship with the Old World.

Director of Military Assistance Program: 1949–50

The creation of the Brussels Pact – designated as the Western Union by Britain, France, and the Low Countries in March 1948 – was intended to show the United States that the old barriers had been breached and that Europe was prepared to link its future to a

[1]This background is drawn from biographer L. James Binder, *Lemnitzer: A Soldier for His Time* (Washington, DC: Brassey's, 1997).

50-year military alliance. Unspoken but understood were the Allies' hopes that the United States would respond with membership, or at least with a guarantee of military aid. American support had to be given clandestinely until Congress and the Truman administration were ready for an open alliance.[2]

Given Lemnitzer's diplomatic experiences in World War II and his proficiency in organisation, he served as Defense representative on a new Foreign Military Assistance Advisory Committee. In light of this background he was tapped by Secretary of Defense James V. Forrestal to be his surrogate at the Brussels Pact's Military Committee meeting in London in July 1948. He headed a group of seven officers chosen by the Joint Chiefs of Staff (JCS). They were assigned to the Western Union's (WU) Military Committee on a 'non-membership basis'. The JCS had given him detailed instructions on what he could do in talking with Europeans about a coordinated military supply programme. He was cautioned against agreeing to military arrangements of any sort that might 'unduly influence' US global strategy.[3]

Lemnitzer responded with enthusiasm not simply because he shared Europe's goals: the assignment evoked memories of his clandestine service in North Africa and Switzerland during World War II. He believed that he achieved complete anonymity in travelling to London. He entered the city in civilian clothes to conceal his identity from the press. In conversations with him years later, I found that the General remained convinced of his anonymity despite evidence to the contrary. On the day of his arrival, the London *Daily Express* reported: 'US Major General Lyman Lemnitzer, in London to advise the Military Committee on Western Union, had suggested that they set up a permanent military staff and pool all military secrets and weapons.' The paper went on to claim that the United States will 'partly arm 35 European divisions'. That the London headline was known to Lemnitzer was included in his report to the Joint Chiefs of Staff.[4]

Lemnitzer was pleased with the centrality of his position as the American in charge. For a relatively low-level US general this European reaction to his presence in their councils was a heady experience. It fitted his own belief in the importance of US military aid to Europe. He quickly acted on the assumption that US leadership was necessary to accelerate the integration of Western Union forces. And the Europeans gladly accepted the role Lemnitzer and his colleagues assigned to themselves.

Even at the first formal meeting of the Western Union's Military Committee Lemnitzer appeared to be present on more than a 'non-membership basis', despite the instructions from the JCS. He eagerly responded to the Committee's invitation to express any views he wished without having the responsibility for their conclusions. He had no hesitation about urging the Committee to move rapidly to integrate their forces, assuming that the Pentagon was as anxious as he was to aid WU's emerging Defense Organization (WUDO).[5]

---

[2]Lawrence S. Kaplan, *NATO 1948: The Birth of the Transatlantic Alliance* (Lanham, MD: Rowman & Littlefield, 2007), 67.

[3]Alfred Goldberg and Samuel A. Tucker, "Interview with General Lemnitzer", 21 March 1974, 3–4, Historian's Office, Office of the Secretary of Defense files, Pentagon, Washington, DC.

[4]*Daily Express,* 23 July 1948, 1, recorded in US Delegation to the Western Union (hereafter cited as DELWU), National Archives and Records Administration (hereater cited as NARA); Lemnitzer to Lieutenant General Albert C. Wedemeyer, JCS, 4, 23 July 1948, DELWU, NARA.

[5]Lemnitzer to Wedemeyer, 23 July 1948, DELWU 4; NARA; Steven L. Rearden, *The Formative Years, 1947-1950,* I, History of the Office of the Secretary of Defense (Washington. DC: Historical Office, OSD, 1984), 468-9.

His appreciation of WUDO's contribution was obvious. He urged the JCS to adopt the elaborate security procedures established by the Western Union powers. He reasoned that 'if US is to participate in activities of Western Union Military Committee ... it will be necessary for US representatives to have access to all committee information and documents.'[6] Here was an example of how far the US military representative would depart from the JCS instructions. In making this recommendation, Lemnitzer clarified the role he believed the United States should play in that organisation.

His enthusiasm for linkage with the Western Union was not always shared by his superiors. He had to contend with the scepticism of Lt. Gen Albert C. Wedemeyer, Army Deputy Chief of Staff for Plans and Operations, about the extent of military involvement with the Europeans. Wedemeyer had contemplated withdrawing US representation in Western Union military talks for fear that they would take advantage of America's generosity.[7]

Lemnitzer emphatically rejected the idea. The American presence had been the major factor in speeding up the activities of the Committee and its removal could seriously damage the developing Western Union structure. 'In addition' he informed the JCS, 'and without attempting to forecast what US attitude or alignment towards Brussels Powers may eventually take, I believe it would be unwise to abandon or neglect taking full advantage of the opportunity to observe and influence military planning.' Whoever succeded him as head of the US delegation must be at least a major general – his own rank. Since the heads of all the other delegations were of that rank, Europeans would have regarded any downgrading of rank to be a signal of 'waning US interest in the Western Union with consequent harmful effect on the activities of the Military Committee'.[8]

In less than two months Lemnitzer had become a vigorous and articulate advocate of America's linkage to the Western Union. It was not suprising that his zeal for entanglement would carry over to the subsequent Atlantic Alliance a year later. In the meantime, he had won his case with the JCS. When Major General A. Franklin Kibler replaced him in mid-August 1948, he was able to deepen the connections his predecessor had made. A futher indication of Lemnitzer's successful intervention was the naming of Lieutenant General Clarence A. Huebner, General Lucius D. Clay's deputy in Germany, as US representative on WU's Commander-in-Chiefs Committee in April 1949. The reluctant military establishment in the Pentagon was pushed steadily forward toward entanglement with Western Europe. No American military figure was more active in securing this commitment than Major General Lyman L. Lemnitzer.

Given the very visible role he had played in the summer of 1948, his movement from the National War College to the Pentagon in January 1949 was a natural progression. He was to represent the Defense Department in coordinating the planning of the various agencies – State, Defense, and the new European Cooperation Administration – for a Military Assistance Program (MAP). President Truman himself gave special attention to the MAP in his inaugural address on 20 January 1949, noting in Point Three the importance of 'how the United States was now working out with a number of countries a joint agreement to strengthen the security of the North Atlantic area'. The

---

[6]DELWU to Wedemeyer, 26 July 1948, CCS 092, RG 218, NARA.
[7]Wedemeyer to DELWU, 26 July 1948, CCS 092, RG 218, NARA.
[8]DELWU 9, 31 July 1948, CCS 092, RG 218, NARA.

forthcoming Atlantic Alliance would be the framework within which the MAP would operate. In that year he was appointed director of the Secretary of Defense's Office of Military Assistance. In essence, he was to be the military's key agent in the MAP.[9]

It took some time before the US military establishment appreciated the opportunity the MAP had given it to modernise the equipment of all the Services. They were able eventually to replace obsolescent items – dispatched to the European military – with more expensive and more efficient equipment. Rather than serving as the whipping boy of the Joint Chiefs, Lemnitzer became the liaison with the State Department in promoting the military-aid programme. Reciprocal assistance in the form of base rights further mollified critics.

When the bill was enacted, it had become the 'Mutual Defense Assistance Act' (MDAA), in deference to the Congressional demand that the European beneficiaries not only increase their own military capabilities, but also show evidence of their commitment by opening their territories to American air and naval bases.

The President signed the MDAA bill on 6 October 1949. The amount allotted for NATO, essentially a billion dollars, was less than the US$2 billion Lemnitzer had suggested to Rep. Carl Vinson (D-GA), Chairman of the House Armed Services Committee, but more than originally expected.[10]

Between November 1949 and October 1950 Lemnitzer was the point man in most of the problems involved in the administration of the MDAP, coordinating the military aspects of planning, programming, and logistics. His instructions were so vague that the general had to improvise appropriate ways of dealing with the European Allies. It was his job to get the programme off the ground. Inevitably, it was plagued with problems, not least of which were divisions among the armed services.

If he succeeded in managing frictions within the Defense Department and between the Allies, it was due in part to the outbreak of the Korean War in June 1950. When Lemnitzer was asked if the Korean War had not occurred, would the President have raised the defence budget ceilings and accepted an expanded rearmament of Europe, he was sceptical: 'I don't think we would ever gotten the support around the country, in the Congress, or even within the government itself, if it wasn't for the terrible war that confronted us in Korea.'[11] The US $4 billion supplement was a belated effort to undo the damage.

Lemnitzer's biographer, L. James Binder, noted that this was the figure he had proposed to Secretary Johnson upon learning of the invasion. Although Johnson ignored his memorandum, it was precisely the number Congress had approved in September 1950. In 1974 Lemnitzer told an interviewer that:

> One of the things I take as much pride in, as anything I've ever done, on my own initiative and without consulting anybody in the Pentagon, particularly the Secretary, is that I sat down and wrote a memorandum to the Secretary of Defense recommending that a supplementary request be submitted to the Congress immediately in July 1950, for a supplemental program of $4 billion, I don't know just what got into me to do this.[12]

---

[9]Lawrence S. Kaplan, *A Community of Interests: NATO and the Military Assistance Program* (Washington, DC: Office of the Secretary of Defense Historical Office), 23.

[10]Goldberg and Tucker, "Interview", 21 March 1974, 10.

[11]Maurice Matloff, "Interview with General Lemnitzer", 19 January 1984, 38, Historian's Office, Office of the Seceretary of Defense files, Pentagon, Washington, DC.

[12]Goldberg and Tucker, "Interview," 21 March 1974, 10.

As the President was leaving office in 1953, he thanked Lemnitzer for getting the Military Aid Program underway:

> He took a paper off his desk and handed it to me. He said, "I thought you'd like to keep this in your files." It was my recommendation for the $4 billion supplemental Military Aid bill with an OK-HST at the bottom.

Although Lemnitzer assumed that Johnson must have sent his recommendation to the White House, he noted that:

> 'I never got an indication from the Secretary as to his reaction to my recommendation for a $4 billion supplemental program – there was only complete silence – a thunderous silence.'[13]

The Korean War saw the climax and termination of Lemnitzer's leadership of the MAP. Under his guidance military aid to Western Europe was expanded exponentially. An additional benefit was the dismissal of Secretary Johnson in September 1950, a victim of his obsessive paring of the Defense budget at a time when enlargement was on the agenda of both the President and the Congress.

From two stars to four stars: 1950–62

George Marshall succeeded Johnson as Secretary of Defense. He was a model for the office and a man Lemnitzer esteemed as the architect of victory in World War II. Ironically, just as his devotion to the MAP and the defence of Europe was rewarded by the appointment of a Secretary who would advance his programme, he left Washington for a post at Fort Benning, Georgia, as commander of the 11th Airborne Division. At the age of 51 his new assignment turned him into a parachutist in preparation for a command assignment in Korea. It certainly meant that the dedication he had given to NATO would be lessened if not terminated, and should have been an occasion for regret. This was not the case. He welcomed the change as a long-awaited opportunity to move from a staff position, which characterised his career, to active command in a major war. In the words of his biographer: 'It is difficult to imagine him having felt anything but great happiness when he received his orders.'[14]

This reaction is understandable. No matter how devoted he was to the MAP and how proud he was of his contributions to its progress, his position was still that of a staff officer, chained to a desk. His role in Korea would be of a different order. Division command in Korea would be a vehicle for promotion.

It was. Promoted to lieutenant general in August 1952, he received his fourth star in March 1955. Lemnitzer had two tours in Korea, and the first was the more significant and satisfying. At last he commanded troops in battle, the storied Seventh Division, and did so with distinction in the winter of 1952. Three years later, he was back in Asia, this time with four stars as commanding general of the Eighth Army and US Forces in the Far East. It was the summit of his combat career, and the mementos of these experiences in Korea were prominently displayed in his Chevy Chase home.

After his Far East command was dissolved in mid-1957 and placed under UN auspices, Lemnitzer was back in the Pentagon for the next four years. There he

---

[13] Ibid., 10–12.
[14] Binder, *Lemnitzer*, 176; Goldberg and Tucker, "Interview", 14–15.

occupied increasingly influential positions where his expertise in both planning and diplomacy served him well. He was first appointed vice chief of staff of the Army on his return to Washington. He was elevated to chief of staff in May 1959, and subsequently replaced ailing General Nathan D. Twining as chairman of the Joint Chiefs of Staff in October 1960.[15]

He was a logical choice for these demanding offices. The chairman of the Joint Chiefs of Staff had no special powers of his own; he could not command compliance from his fellow chiefs. If he won it, it was through tact and convincing arguments. Whatever differences he had with the administration were often suppressed – to be revived in oral interviews many years later. Even in private correspondence he was usually a model of discretion.

But his legendary ability to work agreeably with colleagues as well as with superiors was sorely tested when John F. Kennedy succeeded Eisenhower in the White House in 1961. Lemnitzer's background and personality were in sharp contrast to the youthful, brash "Whiz Kids" chosen by Secrertary of Defense Robert S. McNamara. The new team was filled with civilians sophisticated in the use of quantitative methods and contemptuous of the old-fashioned, unscientific way the Joint Chiefs conducted military policy. Lemnitzer, in their eyes, personified all that was wrong with the Eisenhower administration.[16]

Most damaging to his reputation at the time was his seemingly passive role in accepting the doomed Bay of Pigs operation in April 1961. Although the president recognised that the plan to invade Castro's Cuba was conceived and controlled by the Central Intelligence Agency, he was disturbed that the Joint Chiefs did not alert him to the risks involved. While formally taking the blame for its failure, Kennedy nursed a grievance against the military, most notably against the chairman of the Joint Chiefs of Staff.[17]

Supreme Allied Commander, Europe: 1962–69

Given these circumstances, why did Kennedy appoint Lemnitzer as Norstad's successor as Supreme Allied Command, Europe, a position more visible under the aggressive General Lauris Norstad than it would be under Lemnitzer? One answer would be that it would follow the logical progression of Lemnitzer from Army Chief of Staff to chairman of the Joint Chiefs of Staff, to Supreme Allied Commander, Europe. Reasonable though this solution might be, it would not take into account that Lemnitzer would reach retirement at the age of 64 in August 1963. Indeed, he anticipated a post-military career in industry. The general himself recognised that it would not be desirable to have a retired officer as SACEUR. In keeping Lemnitzer on active duty, Kennedy would be setting a precedent.[18] Why would the President go to such lengths to keep him in uniform when he was hardly the model of a New Frontiersman – and a scapegoat just one year before in the Cuban fiasco?

A more satisfactory explanation would be the absence of a better choice for the post. Granted that General Earle G. Wheeler, a highly regarded leader capable of serving as

---

[15]Binder, *Lemnitzer*, 248.
[16]Ibid., 279.
[17]Ibid., 277.
[18]Lemnitzer was officially retired in 1961, and then reappointed, creating pension problems later.

SACEUR, was in place as Deputy Commander in Chief of the US European Command. But Wheeler lacked connections with NATO military figures that Lemnitzer enjoyed.

There was a candidate, however: Maxwell Taylor, who could equal if not surpass Norstad's qualifications as SACEUR. Kennedy's elevation of Taylor to the White House was evidence of his standing in Washington. Despite European concerns about his opposition to massive retaliation, Taylor was widely repected in NATO. However, Taylor turned down Kennedy's suggestion in July 1962 that he succeed Norstad as SACEUR.[19]

By ruling out other possible choices for the position, Kennedy was left with Lemnitzer, whom he knew was devoted to NATO and a familiar figure in Europe. He would be more malleable than the imperious Norstad. But his reasoning may have stemmed more from a new appreciation of the general. Despite his identification as an Eisenhower disciple and his linkage to the Bay of Pigs, Lemnitzer's ability to work with Kennedy was a counterpoint to the initial, unfavourable impression he had made on the new administration.

His engaging personality and effectiveness as military planner surfaced as a positive factor in his relationship with Kennedy during the Berlin Crisis of 1961. He earned the President's confidence en route to his meeting with Khrushchev by convincing him that the US was prepared to win any contest with the Russians.[20]

By the summer of 1962 Lemnitzer seemed to fit the requirements for SACEUR when Norstad appeared ready to retire after suffering a mild heart attack. At least this was the impression the administration leaked through a newspaper article in April 1962. Secretary of Defense McNamara underscored this point in a presumably sympathetic comment that 'Norstad had suffered a heart attack, and the long period during which had he held his post had no doubt a general effect on his health.'[21] In fact, Norstad had fully recovered from an attack that had occurred two years before. This was a more than subtle hint that the administration would be happy to relieve Norstad of his duties.

The SACEUR was too closely identified with a nuclear-defence programme that conflicted with McNamara's insistence on Europeans building up their conventional forces. Norstad had been an author of a programme that emphasised a European nuclear contribution which appeared to deviate from the Kennedy administration's policy of flexible response. Kennedy's decision to nominate Lemnitzer as Norstad's successor in July 1962 was an opportunity to remove a general too close politically to NATO's European leaders and still return to Europe a well-known supporter of the Atlantic Alliance.[22] Not least among Lemnitzer's qualifications was his willingness to abstain from the political activities of Norstad. Lemnitzer's standing in Europe was helped by the skill and tact he displayed while completing a year as chairman of NATO's Military Committee's Chief of Staff meetings.

All things considered, Lemnitzer should have been welcomed by NATO Europe. Instead, he met with a barrage of denigrating rumours resulting initially from the length of time it took for the Allies to approve his appointment. The delay was occasioned by de Gaulle's demand to interview Lemnitzer before giving his approval, an arrangement

[19]Robert S. Jordan, *Norstad: Cold War NATO Supreme Commander* (New York: St. Martin's Press, 2000), 221–2.

[20]Binder, *Lemnitzer*, 292–3.

[21]Jordan, *Norstad*, 6–7.

[22]De Gaulle to Lemnitzer, 7 February 1967, box 48, Lemnitzer Papers, National Defense University Library, Fort McNair, Washington, DC (hereafter cited as NDUL).

the general considered appropriate in light of SACEUR's position under the authority of the North Atlantic Council.[23] Nevertheless, the responses of major newpapers centred on their sense of loss of General Norstad rather than appreciation of the assets Lemnitzer brought to the office. *Le Monde* speculated that his appointment was a temporary solution until some better candidate came along.[24]

The President himself appeared to give substance to the hesitations about Lemnitzer's qualifications when he noted that his choice was 'very adequately equipped' and 'the best officer for that position at this time', statements that suggested a lack of enthusiasm on his part. He did amplify his support the next day, saying: 'We are confident that the general will carry on in the traditions of his illustrious predecessors in this assignment most vital to the security of the free world.'[25] The correction did not undo the damage.

While Kennedy's intention was to give a positive gloss to Lemnitzer's record, the Kennedy team was more patronising in describing the fitness of a soldier of the old school. Jack Raymond of the *New York Times* expressed a consensus of the Washington establishment in dismissing him as 'one of the World War II veterans with a good war record, but who were bland, passive men in Washington'.[26]

Lemnitzer's diplomatic talents and unassuming ways had their limits. These were reflected in his initial exchanges with the Secretary of Defense. When McNamara and his staff were visiting France early in his tenure as SACEUR, the Secretary asked the general to meet him at the US Embassy in Paris, which he 'thought a bit odd': 'Since they were coming to France, I felt they should come out to SHAPE.' He reluctantly accepted the invitation. In the embassy's conference room:

> I was told that they had come to the conclusion that I should reorganize the SHAPE staff. They were convinced that I should have my SHAPE staff organized into nuclear and conventional sections. I had been through this proposition in a study during my chairmanship of the Joint Chiefs of Staff, and we came to the conclusion that it wasn't feasible or desirable, and that it couldn't function effectively.

The general went on to point out: '[Y]ou can't separate a tactical aircraft that can fire nuclear or conventional weapons ... and so I said "No way".' On his return to SHAPE his colleagues were worried that he might be fired:

> I told the group that I would start reorganization of my staff if I got a directive from the Council. But I also pointed out, if I got such a directive from the Council, it would have to get another SACEUR.[27]

These were brave words, a fiery challenge to both the Pentagon and the NATO Council. One wonders if these sentiments were expressed in that language a dozen years before. They certainly reveal the feelings he had at the time – and later – but the words were not in keeping with Lemnitzer's conduct in dealing with his superiors.

---

[23] *New York Times*, 24 July 1962, 5.

[24] *Le Monde*, 22–23 July 1962, 1.

[25] 25 July 1962, *Public Papers of the Presidents, John F. Kennedy, 1962* (Washington, DC: Government Printing Office, 1963), 574.

[26] Jack Raymond, *Power at the Pentagon* (New York: Harper & Row), 287; and see also Arthur M. Schlesinger Jr., *A Thousand Days: John F. Kennedy in the White House* (Boston: Houghton Mifflin, 1965), 200.

[27] Matloff, "Interview", 24 January 1974, 10.

He had to cope with a larger issue as the Vietnam War increasingly claimed the nation's manpower after 1963. US troops and equipment were diverted to Vietnam from Europe, diluting the calibre of US forces in NATO. The strain on American resources was compounded by Secretary McNamara's long-standing objective of reducing the financial burden of NATO by basing American troops in the US and flying them over for regularly scheduled exercises. Flying the combat-ready Second Armored Division from Texas to Germany in 1963, under the name of 'Exercise Big Lift', was his response to the financial pressures. McNamara envisoned a way for an armoured division to be flown to Europe, draw supplies and equipment from depots there, and be ready to participate in NATO manoeuvres immediately.

SACEUR knew that the diversion of resources to Southeast Asia and the experimental basing of US NATO forces in Texas would have negative effects on their readiness in the event of a Soviet attack. McNamara, however, was convinced that an American division could be airlifted to Europe overnight and be ready for combat the next day. Lemnitzer did not share this confidence. He made this clear to the *New York Times* correspondent Hanson Baldwin that the 'Big Lift' would be no substitute for troops on the ground: 'While dual-basing does not reduce the troop commitment to NATO, it does degrade "in-theater" capabilities and therefore reduces our readiness to meet an attack with little or no warning.'[28]

But as a leader familiar with the problems in other theatres, Lemnitzer accepted the Pentagon's judgment without serious complaint. The reason for his compliance, he pointed out 20 years later, was that:

> We were thin all over the world, and the right thing to do was to move what we had and what we needed to where the fighting was going on. It never bothered me except that I didn't like to see our forces getting a lesser capability.[29]

Yet it irritated him when the press and many of the NATO Allies claimed that the US was weakening the organisation. He recalled that he

> bluntly told them that this was American equipment, bought and paid for and placed here to serve NATO, but there is a war on and they desperately need the equipment in Southeast Asia. We had damned well better accept giving it up until it could be properly replaced. Period.[30]

Was he really so blunt in 1963, as he remembered in 1982? There is no doubt about his fears of losing valuable human and physical assets to the Vietnam conflict. The losses did weaken the organisation, and he understood the implications. But that he admonished his colleagues in NATO in the language he cited after his retirement is unlikely. He had always recognised the key role the United States played in the military build-up of Western Europe, and said as much in the 1960s. If he was sharper in reminding the Allies of the provenance of the equipment, it may have been because of embarrassment over the situation in which he found himself in defending the Pentagon perspective.

[28]Hanson Baldwin, *Strategy for Tomorrow* (New York: Harper, 1970), 141.
[29]Binder, *Lemnitzer*, 323–4.
[30]Ibid., 324.

Despite the many obstacles in his path, General Lemnitzer felt he was able in March 1965 to call a press conference at SHAPE, the first official news conference since assuming office. It was an opportunity to talk of NATO's success in building a new mobile force as a deterrent against Soviet aggression. Although he lacked the charisma of a Taylor or Norstad, Lemnitzer's patient persistence was making progress toward assuring NATO's ability to withstand any pressure from the Soviet adversary.[31]

Supreme Allied Commander, Europe: 1966–69

The SACEUR's most significant challenge confronted him when President de Gaulle expelled all NATO forces and military installations from France.

Whether he could stand up to de Gaulle, whose ego and and authority exceeded those of Lemnitzer's American colleague, was in question in 1966, and had been since Lemnitzer's arrival on the scene in 1962. Indeed, de Gaulle's dissatisfaction with NATO long antedated the appointment of Lemnitzer as SACEUR.

De Gaulle's contentious relationship with the United States dated back to World War II, when he felt humiliated by his exclusion from the Anglo-American leadership of the West. Given this attitude when he was out of office, it should not have been a surrprise to Lemnitzer – nor to American policy-makers – when de Gaulle brusquely expelled NATO from French territory in 1966. As a newly designated SACEUR in 1962, Lemnitzer was witness to de Gaulle's provocative behaviour. Now president of France under the Constitution of the Fifth Republic, de Gaulle was even more outrageous in American eyes. He had already taken steps to detach his country from the Alliance. In carefully calibrated stages, he took France out of the Mediterranean command and removed French forces from annual military exercises in Western Europe. These actions were taken before his dramatic removal of NATO's presence from France.[32]

Lemnitzer, however, empathised with de Gaulle's mood despite disagreeing with his actions. He seemed to blame his countrymen almost as much as the French government. As late as June 1965 he complained that many Americans felt that de Gaulle's speeches were 'made for the purpose of being anti-American, and vice versa'. He added: 'I hope something can be done to reverse this trend, because it is damaging to the interests of both countries and NATO.'[33]

Nothing was done to stop the growing break between the two countries, and the responsibility, according to American 'Atlanticists', rested wholly with de Gaulle. When the final act was concluded in February 1966, a shocked Under Secretary of State George W. Ball, a committed Francophile, felt betrayed. He was annoyed with de Gaulle's exploitation of France's geographical position between Germany and the Atlantic, 'knowing that no matter how brazen his shameless flaunting of France's sovereignty, his country would be protected by American power'.[34] Ball wanted to challenge the legality of the eviction. It was ironic that US civilian leaders were more aggrieved than the military when the letter of expulsion was delivered. Lemnitzer, like

[31]*New York Times*, 17 March 1965, 3.

[32]Frederic Bozo, *Two Strategies for Europe: de Gaulle, the United States, and the Atlantic Alliance* (Lanham, MD: Rowman and Littlefield, 2002).

[33]Lemnitzer to Admiral Harry W. Hill, 22 June 1965, box 42, Lemnitzer Papers, NDUL.

[34]George W. Ball, *The Past Has Another Pattern: Memoirs*(New York: Norton, 1973), 334.

many of his colleagues, had been more willing than the State Department officials to support the admission of France into the nuclear club not only on the grounds of inevitability, but also in the interests of harmony in NATO.

If any American official had reason to harbour hostility toward the French president, it was Lemnitzer. He was summoned to an audience with de Gaulle for his approval of the appointment, and was informed that de Gaulle reportedly had never heard of him. Neither of these seeming slights weighed on Lemnitzer. He recognised that every head of a NATO state had a right to judge him.[35] De Gaulle's problems with America did not intrude on his good, if patronising, relationship with the Supreme Allied Commander. He treated Lemnitzer with unfailing courtesy as a fellow soldier, behaviour that Lemnitzer cherished. Shortly before the SACEUR's departure from Paris in February 1967, de Gaulle bestowed the Grand Cross of the Legion of Honour, along with a letter mentioning 'great esteem that I hold for you because of the eminent military qualities of whch you have given proof in the exercise of your command and the sincere friendship that our excellent relations inspire in me in your regard'. **An endnote needs to be inserted here. It should read: De Gaulle to Lemnitzer, 7 February 1967, box 48, Lemnitzer Papers, NDUL.

A trace of condescension could be found in this tribute, but not by Lemnitzer. Through the remainder of his life he would display on his lapel evidence of his pride in being so honoured by the French president. Writing to his son and daughter-in-law in March 1967, he noted that de Gaulle's decision to evict the US and NATO headquarters from France 'had nothing whatsoever to do with his feelings toward me personally. This I had always understood, because he had made this very clear in my frequent contacts with him during the past six months.'[36] Although there is no reason to doubt the accuracy of Lemnitzer's observations, de Gaulle's patronage may have been influenced by his recognition of the lesser role the general played in the American hierarchy.

If Lemnitzer had any sense of a timetable for France's withdrawal, he failed to express it. Writing to a friend, General Barkdale Hamlett, President of Norwich Unversity, on the very day de Gaulle sent his letter to President Johnson announcing France's withdrawal from the NATO military structure, Lemnitzer explained his inability to be a commencement speaker simply on the grounds of an upcoming NATO Ministerial meeting scheduled in early June.[37]

It took 10 days before the 14 remaining Allies could gather their wits and affirm the importance of NATO's survival. In a brief but clear statement they declared that: '[T]he North Atlantic Treaty and Organization are not merely instruments of common defense. They meet a common political need and reflect the readiness and determination of the North Atlantic Community to consult and act together.'[38] Though self-evident, this pronouncement was a rallying cry for the Allies. Rather than emerging demoralised by the crisis, NATO seemed almost euphoric in its realisation that it could move ahead without a military contribution from the French ally. Bohlen even detected a manic ingredient in this reaction, as if the Allies had outwitted the French by not

[35]*New York Times*, 30 July 1962.
[36]Lemnitzer to Lydia and Bill Lemnitzer, 20 March 1967, box 66; Lemnitzer Papers, NDUL.
[37]Lemnitzer to President Barksdale Hamlett, Norwich University, 7 February 1966, box 44, NDUL.
[38]Harlan Cleveland, *NATO: The Transatlantic Bargain* (New York: Harper, 1970), 106.

begging for a delay or dragging their feet – by not behaving, in short, 'in a rather bitchy fashion', which the occasion might have warranted.[39]

De Gaulle, who never wanted the Allies to remove the political headquarters from Paris, played his part in easing tensions by allowing continued operation of the oil pipeline from the Atlantic to Germany and permitting the flight of NATO planes to southern Europe. These arrangements required the use of French space – ground and air.

Subsequent negotiations between Lemnitzer and General Charles Ailleret, chief of staff of France's armed forces, resulted in contingency plans for collaboration in the event of a Soviet-inspired crisis. Lemnitzer tried to promote a sense of normality by telling Ailleret in May 1966 that: 'It will be a disappointment, of course, not to have you and the chiefs of staff of the separate French Services at SHAPEX 66 [the annual NATO exercises]. I understand your position in this matter.'[40] In return, the Allies granted France continued benefits of the NATO air-defence alert system, which the French pursued even though it epitomised the spirit of integration that de Gaulle had denounced.

The Alliance survived the absence of a French presence in its military councils. With France gone there could be progress on including participation of the smaller Allies in nuclear decision-making through the Nuclear Planning Group. And the absence of France from the tripartite Standing Group of NATO's Military Committee allowed its replacement with a new, enlarged military representative system that would guide NATO into the future from its new base in Brussels.

France paid a price for expelling the military headquarters from Paris in the form of losing that capital as the organisation's political headquarters. Brussels became the centre of both the political and military branches of NATO. To their credit the French did so gracefully, quietly moving from Paris to Brussels with their NATO colleagues.

NATO's leaders could congratulate themselves in the successful transfer of their political headquarters from France to Belgium – to Evere, a ready-made base occupied by the Belgian military, close to Brussels' Zaventem airport. The move was not difficult to manage. The international staff had no deadline to meet when Secretary-General Manlio Brosio left for Brussels in October 1966. Unlike the SACEUR who had less than a year to remove all NATO and US installations from France, and find new locations for them, the political headquarters with its national delegations could proceed at a more leisurely pace.

These ameliorating factors could not conceal the reality of the disruption the French departure caused NATO. General Lemnitzer had no reason to share the satisfaction Brosio and his colleagues displayed. De Gaulle's order required finding new quarters for a host of operations, as well as the rerouting of supplies from the Atlantic to the North Sea ports of Bremen or Hamburg. He had to cope with the lessening of the defence posture of the Alliance until new adjustments had been made. The burden of making the transition work fell on his shoulders. Where SHAPE should relocate and how to arrange the move was his responsibility. Lemnitzer was confronted with a deadline his political masters had accepted, which meant that in less than a year's time, before 1

[39]Charles Bohlen, *Witness to History 1929–69* (New York: Norton, 1973), 507–8.
[40]Lemnitzer to General Charles Ailleret, 19 May 1966, box 44, NDUL.

April 1967, he had to oversee not only the removal of his SHAPE headquarters, but also the headquarters of his American command (EUCOM) to a destination unknown. The order was delivered to the President on 7 March 1966. De Gaulle dispatched identical letters to the West German, British, and Italian heads of state two days later. By the end of the month memoranda were sent to all the Allies announcing France's withdrawal from NATO's military structure with the expectation of the prompt removal of NATO forces from its soil.[41] Lemnitzer's problems were exacerbated by further consquences of de Gaulle's directive: where to place the subordinate NATO commands.

For a time he believed he had a satisfactory solution to the problem of finding a new headquarters. This would be to take over the old Belgian military base at Evere, close to the Brussels airport. But he was denied this arrangement when the Secretary General and NATO officials claimed these headquarters for themselves. His failure to obtain the base indicated Lemnitzer's standing in both the US and NATO hierarchies. One wonders if a supreme commander with Norstad's authority or Taylor's reputation would have experienced the same treatment. In any event, when a friend asked in July 1966, he still could not say just where the base would be located because final decisions had not been made with regard to the relocation of SHAPE: 'I was unable to give them some of the specific information that they would like to have received.'[42]

Lemnitzer was frustrated: 'We do not yet know whether we will be able to go into a completed facility, or whether one will have to be built from the ground up.' This was the same answer he had given to General Alfred M. Gruenther in April when he complained 'that we have received practically no political guidance to date'.[43] He wrote to General James Collins on 29 August 1966: 'As you can well imagine, we are having a hectic time here in connection with all the things that have to be moved out of France, including our major headquarters and the enormous amount of supplies in France.' He was concerned that:

> Important political decisions are required in connection with the relocation of the various headquarters, and to date we have only one decision; i.e. EUCOM [the US European Command] is going to Stuttgart to occupy the facilities now used by the U.S. Seventh Army.[44]

Spacious and comfortable as this facility was, he felt it too far removed from his SHAPE headquarters in Belgium, near Mons on the French border.[45]

If he had reservations about Stuttgart being too far from his new SHAPE home in Casteau some 55 kilometres from Brussels, he was even less satisfied with these headquarters. Evere was always his choice. South and east of the city would be reasonable; any further distance, he felt, would limit the effectiveness of his headquarters.[46]

Try as he did, Lemnitzer was unable to secure a site that fit his specifications. He came up against political and economic obstacles with the Belgian government, and not incidentally, a lack of support from the NATO estabishment as well as from the Johnson administration. The Belgian government offered two sites far from the capital

[41] *NATO Letter*, 14 May 1966, 22–3.
[42] Lemnitzer to Robert B. Anderson, 11 July 1966, box 44, NDUL.
[43] Lemnitzer to General Gruenther, 23 April 1966, box 43, NDUL.
[44] Lemnitzer to General James Collins, 29 August 1966, box 45, NDUL.
[45] Lemnitzer to Major H. E. Simpson Jr., 26 September 1966, Family Papers, box 66, NDUL.
[46] Air Marshal MacBrien memorandum to Lord Coleridge, 26 July 1966, 'Broad Outline of the SHAPE Requirement When Relocated in Belgium', box 44, NDUL.

and unsatisfactory in almost every respect. Both were in southern Belgium in the neighbourhood of Casteau and Chievres and were government properties. Belgian officials were unwilling to consider Lemnitzer's objections. According to Count Charles de Kerchove, head of a special commission on this issue, these were the only available places large enough to accommodate headquarters the size of SHAPE's. Other possible sites were either too expensive to acquire or too time consuming to organise, given the time constraints imposed on the Alliance. De Kerchove claimed that problems building new roads and laying electric mains as well as establishing a telecommunications network would be too dificult to resolve. Moreover, the government would not consider any urban area that would be exposed to threats from the Warsaw bloc.[47] What was less publicised was Belgium's opportunity to use the development of a large NATO base as a way of alleviating the economic plight of depressed Hanau province in southern Belgium.

The SACEUR was given little choice. Casteau was preferable to Chievres since it was on the main road to Brussels. Still, he persisted in his efforts to counter Belgian objections. On 8 July he informed General Norstad that:

> I finally was able to get a small reconnaissance party off yesterday to look over some tentative sites that the Belgian Government had selected. In general, the sites were too far from the city of Brussels that it would require too much travel to reach any areas where housing might be available. This reconnaissance was useful, however, in more precisely identifying our requirements, and the Belgian officials are going to take another look at possible sites to more nearly meet our requirements.[48]

Even though Lemnitzer's protests were relatively mild as well as ineffective, Belgium's defence minister belittled Lemnitzer in the popular satirical journal, *Pourquoui Pas* for reputedly turning down his offer of Chievres or Casteau and touring the Waterloo region in search of a more desirable place. The magazine then suggested that the real reason for the SACEUR's reluctance to move to suitable quarters an hour from the capital was not the distance from the airport, but the opposition from families of senior SHAPE officers who would be unhappy living in the countryside so far from the urban life of Brussels. The journal trivialised a serious problem that bothered Lemnitzer. As late as August 1967, he lamented that housing at Casteau was still short of 1500 units, and that 1000 families, including his own, were still in France.[49]

It took six months after de Gaulle issued his expulsion orders before the Casteau decision was made. Lemnitzer was annoyed with the behaviour of his new Belgian hosts, and no less annoyed by the absence of any guidance from the NATO establishment. AS he informed former SACEUR, General Alfred M. Gruenther, in April 1966:

> I'm very anxious to bring you up to date on developments here in connection with the recent French decisions to withdraw from the military activities of NATO. While we have received practically no political guidance to date (and we cannot do much other than planning until we do receive guidance), we are intensively looking at all the problems areas (of which there are many) involved.[50]

---

[47]de Kerchove to Lemnitzer, 16 August 1966, box 44, NDUL.

[48]Lemnitzer to Norstad, 8 July 1966, box 44, NDUL.

[49]*Pourquoi Pas*, 11 August 1963, box 163; Lemnitzer to Norstad, 8 July 1966, box 44, NDUL; Lemnitzer to James Gerrity Jr., 2 August 1967, box 45, NDUL.

[50]Lemnitzer to General Gruenther, 23 April 1966, box 44, NDUL.

Four more months had to pass before the political choice of Casteau was concluded, and it is questionable how much guidance the SACEUR received in that interval.

The Pentagon itself was no more helpful in this period. Secretary McNamara operated on the assumption that the removal of France from SHAPE would be 'in no way disabling' to the military posture of the Alliance; neither the United States nor its Allies have ever contemplated a way in which falling back upon French soil through the battlefield of Germany was an acceptable strategy for the alliance.[51] McNamara's emphasis was on forward defence, which centred on the West German frontier with East Germany. In this context French cooperation could be useful but not vital for the containment of a Soviet assault.

This reasoning diminished the importance of French resources. From Lemnitzer's perspective the dismissal of French manpower required an increased commitment of men and equipment at a time when US troops in Europe were being shipped to Vietnam. Moreover, the line of NATO communication was potentially in jeopardy. The east-west flow of supplies from France to Germany had to be relocated to the north-south route in order to serve NATO forces in Germany. The Berlin Crisis of the early 1960s, however, revealed that the north-south supply line was painfully vulnerable. Even if the dislocation were only temporary, the negative impact on NATO's defence posture should have been as obvious to McNamara as it was to Lemnitzer.[52]

SACEUR Lemnitzer, unlike McNamara, could not ignore the consequences of the realignment of NATO's forces in Europe and the temptation they offered to the adversary. He had to live with them. He tried to make clear that NATO and the United States must recognise that de Gaulle's action had damaged the defence capabilities of the Alliance. In an address to the North Atlantic Assembly in November 1967, Lemnitzer expanded on this theme. He asserted that Soviet military assets remained substantial and were growing. He asked rhetorically what would happen to deterrence if the Allies reduced their term of military service, or if the United States redeployed all troops to the homeland or to Southeast Asia, and when all the Allies cut back on their military budgets? Could NATO expect to conduct an effective forward defence in the event of aggression? One response, and a grim one, would be 'the earlier employment of selected nuclear weapons'.[53]

While SACEUR's warnings and judgements were reasonable and clear, they had limited effect upon an administration increasingly preoccupied with the war in Vietnam and upon a Pentagon convinced that it had NATO's problems under control. Lemnitzer had done his duty when he called the attention of Washington and Brussels to NATO's plight. He informed former Senator Harry Darby (R-Kansas) that: 'The new headquarters will not be nearly as satisfactory from military point of view as they are in France, since political and economic considerations, rather than military, have determned the new location.'[54] But he could do no more. As a soldier, always conscious of his place in the chain of political authority, he accepted the limits of his powers.

---

[51] McNamara statement, "The North Atlantic Alliance", Hearings before the Subcommittee on National Security and International Operations of the Committee on Government Operation, US Senate, 89th Cong., 2nd, sess, part 6, 21 June 1966, 187.

[52] *New York Times*, 3 May 1967, 35.

[53] *NATO Letter*, 16 January 1968, 4.

[54] Lemnitzer to Harry Darby, 13 January 1967, box 46, NDUL.

What compensated for his many frustrations was the opportunity to undertake and succeed in a project essential to his mission, namely: the relocation of SHAPE and its subsidiaries within the time given to him. This assignment played to his organisational strengths. The many years in which he served as a staff planner in Europe during World War II, as deputy to the Commander of the Eighth Army in Korea and later as deputy the Army Chief of Staff in the late 1950s, served him well when the time came to buld a new home for SHAPE. He was given only six months to complete the task because of the wrangling over the Casteau site.

He then presided over the movement to neighbouring NATO countries of all the installations that had been in France. This involved the transportation of ultimately over a million tons of equipment and supplies in this short time period. Even more difficult was the transfer of 100,000 military personnel and their families. He admitted that he was unable to complete this task before the new SHAPE buildings opened. Four months after 1 April 1967, Casteau was still short of 1500 units. His wife and daughter had to remain in their Paris home until their new quarters were available.[55]

All told, it was a remarkable achievement and Lemnitzer's biographer L. James Binder was in awe of his success: 'That the vast bulk of NATO's assets made it to their destinations in good order and on time has to rank as one of the great military logistics triumphs of all time'[56] He might have added that no SACEUR was better prepared to succeed in this operation than General Lemnitzer.

The general revelled in his success in meeting the deadline. Writing in February 1967, he could say that:

> We are busily engaged in preparing for our relocation from France by April 1. The construction of the new SHAPE facilities in Belgium is going along quite well, notwithstanding the fact that the construction had to take place during the wintertime.

He predicted that the facility would open on 31 March 1967, in compliance with de Gaulle's demand.[57] He went on to announce that:

> [O]n the U.S. side our program is somewhat in advance of the NATO side. EUCOM will open in Stuttgart on 15 March. In addition, the movement of more than 800,000 tons of equipment out of France is proceeding ahead of schedule. As you know from experience, the handing over of facilities to the French authorities is not the least delicate of the problems we encounter.[58]

If there was a note of pride in this letter, it was deserved.

In August 1968, his sense of satisfaction was shattered by a familiar and troubling ordeal: his seeming failure to communicate to his superiors in Washington and Brussels the gravity of NATO's situation. The occasion was the Warsaw bloc's invasion of Czechoslovakia in August 1968 when the Allies appeared to accept Soviet aggression as a regrettable event, but not critical to NATO's future. His objections were ignored; the responses from the Pentagon were lackadaisical. Explanations for this behaviour ranged from the absence of policy-makers in Washington and Brussels on August vacations, to comfort from Soviet assurances that their troops on the Czech-West German borders did not pose a threat to the West.

---

[55]Lemnitzer to James Gerrity, Jr., 2 August 1967, box 45, NDUL.
[56]Binder, 330.
[57]Lemnitzer to Lieutenant General August Schomburg, 11 February 1967, box 44, NDUL.
[58]Ibid.

Just as in 1966, the SACEUR in 1968 complained that he received no political guidance in what he perceived to be a crisis. He feared that NATO appeared 'helpless, hopeless, and harmless'.[59] Nor did the JCS fill the gap. He recalled asking:

> What does the United States propose to do about this movement into Czechoslovakia? ... No one knew anything about it. It was all kind of low-key accepting of what the Russians were doing. And I thought, My God, what are the Chiefs doing? The Chiefs weren't doing anything.[60]

He was no more successful with NATO leaders. With Secretary-General Manlio Brosio in Italy:

> His deputy was the only one around; there wasn't a minister in sight. In August, everyone was on summer leave. And I made the statement to my Chief of Staff and a couple of people in SHAPE, 'That's a hell of a fine exhibition of leadership on the part of the United States and NATO. That's the worst I have seen since I've been over here.[61]

Lemnitzer's anger, as in the past, was never expressed bluntly in his communications with the Johnson administration or with the Allied military command in Brussels. Even in his private letters to friends and relatives he was restrained in his criticisms. Only after he retired did he let off steam.

In retrospect, his fears were exaggerated. The crisis passed. Lemnitzer's concerns did resonate with the Allies. Many of them found the Soviet action so repugnant that they was less reluctant than in the past to fulfill their military obligations. Moreover, according to the US Embassy in Moscow: 'The underdeveloped third world countries will have second thoughts as to Soviet connections.' Even if this was only wishful thinking on the part of American officials, it reflected a hope that Lemnitzer could share.

In Washington, Congressional pressure to bring the troops home lost momentum. And President de Gaulle, facing unrest at home in 1968, abandoned his long-held belief that a bilateral rapport with the Soviets would make NATO unnecessary. In this improved environment Lemnitzer retired after six years as Supreme Allied Commander, Europe. He took satisfaction in having met the greatest challenge to his leadership in the course of his service – the successful removal of SHAPE from France to Belgium.

Reflections

In his years as SACEUR Lemnitzer failed to secure many of the objectives he had sought. In 1966 his passionate warnings about the dangers that the Soviet adversary could bring to NATO in the wake of de Gaulle's expulsion of NATO from France did not influence the Pentagon or the North Atlantic Council, nor did the Soviet invasion of Czechoslovakia four years later. He argued persistently and cogently, if not persuasively, that the withdrawal of France from the military structure of NATO did major damage to NATO's ability to cope with Soviet aggression. In 1968, he seemed to be a lonely voice decrying the Warsaw Pact's

[59]Lemnitzer to Brigadier General Randolph T. Pendleton, 17 May 1968, box 50; quoted in Edward J. Drea, *McNamara, Clifford, and the Burdens of Vietnam, 1965–1969*, VI, *History of the Office of the Secretary of Defense* (Washington, DC: Historical Office, 2011), 509.

[60]Matloff, "Interview", 24 January 1974, 34–5.

[61]Ibid.

suppression of the 'Prague Spring' at a time when the Allies appeared to regard the invasion as a regrettable but not critical event. In both instances he failed to make the impact that arguably an Eisenhower or Norstad might have made. One may speculate that his personality, lacking the forcefulness of his predecessors, undercut his message. A habit of deference to his superiors induced him to accept what he could not change. There was no rebellion in the manner of Taylor or Gavin in Lemnitzer's response to indifference or rejection despite the soundness of his pleas.[62]

In contrast to his frustration over NATO's reactions to the Soviet threat, on 27 November 1967, he happily reported his triumph to the North Atlantic Assembly in meeting de Gaulle's deadline: 'These tremendous relocations have been completed successfully without the loss – not even for a moment of the command and control so vital to the security of the Allied Command Europe.'[63]

Yet, Lemnitzer, unlike some of his predecessors, lacked the political insights to respond to the negative implications of his achievement. Once he recognised that the Belgians would not accept any location for his headquarters outside the Mons area, his complaints about the distance from Brussels stopped. He not only accepted the reality, but determined to turn it into a victory. He succeeded in this mission, but the cost was loss of the influence the SACEUR enjoyed when he was in close proximity to the political headquarters in Paris. Lemnitzer refused to recognise that the distance between Casteau and Brussels meant that his authority would be diminished. The new International Military Staff in Brussels, replacing the Standing Committee, filled the space that the Supreme Commander had occupied in the past.

If these observations suggest flaws, they do not cast a shadow on a distinguished career. In fact, they illuminate his virtues. Lemnitzer was on the mark in his warning to the Allies and to the Pentagon against being lulled into a false sense of security through the relative ease of the move from France to Belgium. Those higher up in the chain of command were at fault for not heeding his advice in 1966 and 1968. While he may not have recognised the shrinkage of his status in Casteau, the SHAPE that he reorganised in 1967 was able to cope with the challenges of the next generation.

It is obvious that Lemnitzer did not make his reputation as a conceptualiser or as a strategist, and certainly not as a political leader. His contribution was as a manager whose organising abilities and diplomatic talents served the interests of his country and the Alliance. He spent his time in retirement as a teacher, informing a new generation of the importance of NATO to the future of the nation and the West. In appreciation of Lemnitzer's tireless efforts to inform college students about the importance of the Alliance, in 1984 Kent State University attached his name to its Center for NATO Studies. It was an honour worthy of the often unheralded services he gave to the North Atlantic Treaty Organization.

---

[62]US Embassy in Moscow to Secretary of State, 21 August 1968, *Foreign Relations of the United States, 1964–1968*, vol. 17, 247.

[63]News Release, No. 67–22, SHAPE, Belgium, 27 November 1967.

Disclosure statement

No potential conflict of interest was reported by the author.

Acknowledgement

The author's thanks to the contribution of Dr Kathleen A. Kellner, a former doctoral student at Kent State University.

The NATO-Warsaw Pact competition in the 1970s and 1980s: a revolution in military affairs in the making or the end of a strategic age?

Diego A. Ruiz Palmer

The NATO-Warsaw Pact military competition at the heart of the Cold War was also the incubator of a 'Revolution in Military Affairs' (RMA) in Europe in the 1970s and 1980s, which predates the better-known American concept of RMA of the 1990s.

Recent scholarship on NATO and the Warsaw Pact has gone a long way in unearthing and documenting the increasingly *interactive* nature of that competition and in explaining the central role that the notion of an RMA plays in helping identify salient aspects of opposing NATO and Warsaw Pact operational concepts and force developments during the last two decades of the Cold War.[1] This authoritative

[1] Dima Adamsky, 'The Conceptual Battles of the Central Front: The Air-Land Battle and the Soviet Military Technical Revolution', in *The Crisis of Détente in Europe: From Helsinki to Gorbachev, 1975–1985*, ed. Leopoldo Nuti (London: Routledge, 2009), 150–162; Dima Adamsky, 'Through the Looking Glass: The Soviet Military-Technical Revolution and the American Revolution in Military Affairs', *The Journal of Strategic Studies* 31, no. 2 (April 2008): 257–294; Dima Adamsky, *The Culture of Military Innovation: The Impact of Cultural Factors on the Revolution in Military Affairs in Russia, the US, and Israel* (Stanford, CA: Stanford University Press, 2010); Gordon S. Barrass, *The Great Cold War: A Journey through the Hall of Mirrors* (Stanford, CA: Stanford University Press, 2009); Gordon S. Barrass, 'The Renaissance in American Strategy and the Ending of the Great Cold War', *Military Review*, January–February 2010: 101–110; Beatrice Heuser, 'Warsaw Pact Military Doctrines in the 1970s and 1980s: Findings in the East German Archives', *Comparative Strategy* 13, no. 4 (1993): 437–457; Beatrice Heuser, 'Victory in a Nuclear War:

scholarship has also drawn attention to the transformational[2] influence that the Soviet concept of a 'Military-Technical Revolution' (MTR) had on American thinking in the late 1980s and early 1990s regarding the relationship between technology, operational concepts and organisational structures. In many ways, the broader American notion of RMA can be seen as the stepchild of the Soviet MTR, with the lineage between the two having been established through the technological but particularly conceptual dynamism of the Cold War NATO-Warsaw Pact competition.

An unintended by-product of this intellectual linkage between the Soviet MTR and the emerging American RMA that was revealed during the 1991 *Desert Storm* campaign has been the displacement, in Cold War historiography, of the transformational centre of gravity of the NATO-Warsaw Pact interactive competition from the mid-1970s towards the mid-1980s. In this American RMA-centred construct, the apex of industrial-age warfare on the cusp of the information age that was reached in the European theatre in the 1980s foreshadowed the wider transformations that were to follow in the next decade. This conceptual and temporal tilt towards the 1980s, however, masks the fact that the real RMA pivot in the NATO-Warsaw Pact competition happened a decade earlier. Moreover, the focus on the 1980s neglects this RMA's fundamental Cold War and European specificity.

Therefore, embedding the Cold War RMA in Europe into the wider post-Cold War RMA narrative carries with it the risk that RMA historiography could distort Cold War historiography. This risk can be illustrated by highlighting contrasting perspectives on four aspects of the relationship between the RMA narrative and the NATO-Warsaw Pact competition of the 1970s and 1980s:

Footnote 1 continued

A Comparison of NATO and WTO War Aims and Strategies', *Comparative European History* 7 (1998): 311–327; Vojtech Mastny, *Learning from the Enemy: NATO as a Model for the Warsaw Pact* (Zurich: Forschungsstelle fur Sicherheitspolitik und Konfliktanalyse der ETH, 2001); Vojtech Mastny, Sven G. Holtsmark and Andreas Wenger, *War Plans and Alliances in the Cold War* (London: Routledge, 2006); R. Craig Nation, 'Programming Armageddon: Warsaw Pact War Planning, 1969–1985', in Nuti, *Crisis of Détente in Europe*, 124–136; and Diego A. Ruiz Palmer, 'Paradigms lost: A Retrospective Assessment of the NATO-Warsaw Pact Military Competition in the Alliance's Southern Region', *Comparative Strategy* 9, no. 3 (1990): 265–286.

[2] Soviet military theorists began in the 1970s to describe contemporary changes in the conduct of warfare as a 'Military-Technical Revolution (MTR)' and the third such MTR in the twentieth century, after the 'mechanisation MTR' which followed World War I and the 'nuclear MTR' that followed World War II. Paradoxically, while these theorists assigned technology a leading role in driving revolutionary change – hence, the terminology MTR – conceptual innovation and organisational adaptation accompanied and often anticipated weapons developments in Soviet conventional force developments in Europe of the 1970s and 1980s, This was also the case for NATO, as addressed in this article. Accordingly, because the American term RMA has been widely accepted as more satisfactory than the term MTR to describe the full content of the concept of military revolutions, and its wider scope encompasses the MTR, RMA is used throughout this article as the preferred term. See, Stephen Peter Rosen, *Winning the Next War: Innovation and the Modern Military* (Ithaca, NY: Cornell University Press, 1994); MacGregor Knox and Williamson Murray, *The Dynamics of Military Revolutions* (Cambridge: Cambridge University Press, 2001); and Adamsky, *The Culture of Military Innovation*.

(i) The salience of the statements made in the early 1980s by Marshal Nikolai Ogarkov, chief of the Soviet armed forces General Staff between 1977 and 1984, and other Soviet military and academic theoreticians on the emergence of an MTR is generally attributed to their prospective and prophetic nature.[3] As such, these statements are seen as having helped lay down the conceptual background for the broader notion of RMA that was formulated in the United States nearly a decade later.

In fact, by the time these Soviet statements were made, the conceptual and organisational dimensions of a Cold War RMA in the European theatre were largely in place, in both the Warsaw Pact and NATO, and its technological applications were well under way.

(ii) The MTR described by Soviet writers in the early 1980s is often characterised as a bold conceptualisation of the implications for warfare and politics of Western, predominantly American, development of so-called 'emerging technologies' oriented primarily to battlefield surveillance and follow-on force targeting and conventional attack.

In reality, the Soviets had been integrating into their operational art and their force posture opposite NATO, since the mid-1970s, many of the operational and technological components of the MTR, which Ogarkov and others were conceptualising, notably in support of the execution of 'deep operations.'[4]

(iii) The maturation of the conceptual and organisational dimensions of a successful RMA in the 1980s has been described as lagging behind the progress of its technological underpinnings.

In fact, the reverse was, more often than not, the case. In both alliances, conceptual innovation and organisational transformation in the 1970s often ran ahead and anticipated the fielding of new generations of military equipment.[5] Starting about 1976–1977, Polish exercise planners were directed to script into their exercises capabilities that were expected to become available within the next five years, in order to test new concepts ahead of time.[6]

(iv) The United States has been faulted for neglecting the operational level of war, as well as operational art, during most of the Cold War, at least until the adoption

[3] For a review of Ogarkov's writings, see Mary C. FitzGerald, *Marshal Ogarkov On Modern War: 1977–1985* (Alexandria, VA: Center for Naval Analyses, November 1986).

[4] On the historical roots of the Soviet concept of 'deep operations', see David M. Glantz, 'The Nature of Soviet Operational Art', *Parameters* 25, no. 1 (Spring 1985): 4–6; and David M. Glantz, *Soviet Military Operational Art: In Pursuit of Deep Battle* (London: Frank Cass, 1991).

[5] The extent to which conceptual innovation in the United States Army, following the end of the Vietnam War, anticipated, rather than followed, technological development, is highlighted compellingly in Richard Lock-Pullan, 'How to Rethink War: Conceptual Innovation and AirLand Battle Doctrine', *The Journal of Strategic Studies* 28, no. 4 (August 2005): 679–702.

[6] *Relationship of Military Exercises to War Plans – 'Wiosna-69' Exercise*, 30 July 1982, classified Secret (Langley, VA: Central Intelligence Agency) CIA Freedom of Information Act (FOIA) Electronic Library, declassified and publicly released on 18 June 2012, 4.

in 1982 of the US Army's 'AirLand Battle' doctrine, in the form of an update of the FM-100-5 field manual.

In reality, the operational level of war, as well as operational art, were alive in NATO throughout most of the Cold War, with the notable exception of the period between the mid-1960s and the mid-1970s.[7]

Together, these four examples of differing perceptions illustrate how association with the broader RMA narrative of the early 1990s can cloud awareness or distort perception of the deeply transformational aspects of the NATO-Warsaw Pact competition in the second half of the 1970s.

The Cold War RMA that emerged in the Warsaw Pact and NATO in the mid-1970s stood at the juncture of an advanced form of manoeuvre warfare and what became known in the 1990s as 'network-centric warfare' – a combination of mass, fires and computers.[8] This RMA was so highly evolved for its time and structured, conceptually, on such an unprecedented operational scale that its *sui-generis* nature inescapably would create the very conditions of its demise, once the strategic circumstances that had motivated its rise had vanished with the end of the Cold War. During its last two decades, the Cold War was truly the 'Great War' of its time, all-pervading strategically and operationally, until the fall of the Berlin Wall in November 1989, and irrelevant a year later, following Germany's reunification in October 1990.[9]

[7] For an exposition of NATO operational art in the late 1950s and early 1960s, based on AFCENT-level command post exercises in the *Lion* series, see General Hans Speidel, 'Mission and Needs of NATO's Shield', *Army*, September 1960: 33–38. The decline in NATO's practice of operational art in the Central Region of Allied Command Europe (the Federal Republic of Germany, France, Belgium, Luxembourg and the Netherlands) in the mid-1960s was the consequence, in part, of the gradual engagement of the French, United States and British armies in non-traditional operations in Algeria, Vietnam and Northern Ireland, and the associated withdrawals of French forces from West Germany from the mid-1950s onwards, as well as of American and British forces in 1967–1968. It also resulted from the disbandment in 1967 of several operational-level commands, notably the headquarters of NATO's Allied Land Forces, Central Europe (LANDCENT) in Fontainebleau, France, and of the 7th United States Army in Stuttgart, Germany, following France's withdrawal from NATO's integrated military structure in 1966, in a drive to meet heightened headquarters and manpower reduction concerns. 'Reorganization of AFCENT', NATO Military Committee document MC 5/21 (Draft), 7 August 1967, Section II, Enclosure 1, classified NATO Secret (Brussels, Belgium: NATO International Staff Central Archives (NISCA)), declassified and disclosed on 1 August 2002, 12–13.

[8] On the contribution of mass to Soviet operations, see Major John G. Hines, 'The Principle of Mass in Soviet Tactics Today', *Review of the Soviet Ground Forces*, DDB-1100-307-81 (Washington, D.C.: Defense Intelligence Agency), June 1981, 1–8. The increased availability in the 1970s of automated data processing means to support the development of operational and logistical plans and of more sophisticated communications links to transmit orders gradually made the planning and conduct of complex, theatre-scale operations easier to execute, planting the seeds for the more ambitious vision of 'network-centric warfare' two decades later.

[9] The notion of the 'Great Cold War' was introduced by Barrass in his landmark book, *The Great Cold War*. To date, Barrass's book is the most authoritative strategic assessment of the Cold War and of the NATO-Warsaw Pact competition.

This questionable transferability of the RMA of the late 1970s and early 1980s in Europe to a later period, and to theatres other than Europe, helps explain the inadequacy of the Soviet Army performance in Afghanistan, as well as the operational void that the Russian armed forces, as well as the United States and other NATO armed forces, encountered, each in their own way, after the end of the Cold War, and which made them often ill-prepared for the asymmetric security challenges of a new strategic era.[10] Against this background, this article addresses how and why the Cold War RMA of the late 1970s and early 1980s was, at once, so significant in its own right during its time and became so irrelevant to the strategic age that followed it.

Cold War and post-Cold War revolutions in military affairs

The concept of Revolutions in Military Affairs, in its fullest meaning, was set out in the landmark memorandum prepared by the US Department of Defense's Office of Net Assessment (ONA) in 1992.[11] In its wake, it has become widely accepted that a genuine RMA should include four interdependent components: (i) technological change; (ii) military systems evolution, as an application of the latter; (iii) operational innovation; and (iv) organisational adaptation, the latter two being the enabling components for battlefield impact and success. Dima Adamsky has included the 'vision of future war' as the RMA's necessary propelling force.[12]

The writings of Ogarkov and his Soviet contemporaries are often looked upon as the intellectual springboard to the American RMA of the 1990s.[13] By the mid-1970s, the Soviet military, steeped in the operational lessons from the 'Great Patriotic War', notably in relation to the theory of deep operations,[14] had a rapidly-gathering and broader conceptual understanding of the evolving nature of warfare than their contemporary Western counterparts. Under an increasingly ambitious and militant Soviet military leadership, the Warsaw Pact was running ahead of NATO in integrating

[10] It is worth noting that General Makhmut Gareev has cautioned that 'in focusing military development only on conflicts and local wars, the point of maintaining a modern military is lost. [. . .] Unless we work on and improve large-scale military operations, our officer corps and all the training of the Army and Navy begin their decline.' Quoted in General M.A. Gareev, 'Applying Zhukov's Command Heritage to Military Training and Reform in Today's World', *The Journal of Slavic Military Studies* 12, no. 4 (December 1999): 100. For 15 years, between 1974 and 1989, General Gareev exercised high-level responsibilities for the operational training and readiness of the Soviet armed forces, rising to the position of a deputy chief of the General Staff. He has been one of Russia's most authoritative and prolific military writers on matters of strategy, doctrine and tactics for nearly half a century and is currently, at the age of 91, the president of the Russian Academy of Military Sciences.

[11] Andrew F. Krepinevich, Jr., 'Cavalry to Computer', *The National Interest* 37 (Autumn 1994): 30–42, and Andrew F. Krepinevich, Jr., *The Military-Technical Revolution: A Preliminary Assessment* (Washington, D.C.: Center for Strategic and Budgetary Assessments, 2002).

[12] Dima Adamsky, *American Strategic Culture and the US Revolution in Military Affairs, Defence and Security Studies* (Oslo: Norwegian Institute for Defence Studies, 1/2008), 6.

[13] Adamsky, 'Through the Looking Glass', 262–276.

[14] Richard Simpkin, *Deep Battle: The Brainchild of Marshal Tukhachevskii* (London: Brassey's, 1987).

new force employment concepts, innovative organisational schemes and new generations of weapons systems into an all-encompassing paradigm for the conduct of a strategic operation in a Theatre of Military Operations (*teatr voyennykh deystviy* or TVD).[15] Exercise *Zapad* 77 in May–June 1977 can rightly be seen as a bold application of the rapidly emerging Soviet RMA to the execution of a 'Theatre-Strategic Operation' (TSO) under the direction of an experimental TVD high command.[16]

Operational and organisational innovation, however, was by no means restricted to the Warsaw Pact. The scope and depth of NATO conceptual and force development processes, although lagging behind those of the Warsaw Pact, had become apparent operationally by 1977, in the form of a joint, land/air campaign at the operational level as the preferred approach to the execution of allied operations in wartime. Such an approach underpinned increasingly the planning of NATO's highly visible *Autumn Forge* exercises, conducted from 1975 onwards every autumn until the end of the Cold War. This new approach reached its full fruition, technologically, with the gradual fielding of a new generation of 'smart' weapons systems, munitions and sensors, a decade later, such as the Multiple Launch Rocket System (MLRS), the *Copperhead*, Search and Destroy Armour (SADARM), *Paveway* and *Durandal* munitions, and the TR-1 reconnaissance aircraft.[17]

The full maturation of NATO's Cold War RMA was reflected in the unprecedented scope of exercises REFORGER 87 and 88 and their field training exercise phase – in northern and southern West Germany, respectively – as well as the maritime exercises *Ocean Safari* 85 and 87 and *Teamwork* 88 in the Norwegian Sea.[18] However, the conceptual and organisational seeds of this NATO RMA, geared to match the

[15] John G. Hines and Philip A. Petersen, 'The Warsaw Pact Strategic Offensive: The OMG in Context', *International Defense Review*, October 1983: 1391–1395; William E. Odom, 'Soviet Force Posture: Dilemmas and Directions', *Problems of Communism*, January–February 1985: 7; Mary C. FitzGerald, 'Marshal Ogarkov on the Modern Theater Operation', *Conflict Quarterly*, Summer 1986: 50–58; Adamsky, 'Through the Looking Glass', 270.

[16] *Materials of the critique of the operational-strategic command-staff exercise Zapad-77*, TS #788301, 13 October 1978, classified Top Secret (Langley, VA: Central Intelligence Agency) CIA FOIA Electronic Library, declassified and released to the public on 18 June 2012; and Vojtech Mastny and Malcolm Byrne, *A Cardboard Castle? An Inside Story of the Warsaw Pact, 1955–1991* (Budapest and New York: Central European University Press, 2005), 406–407.

[17] For a comprehensive review of the state of 'emerging technologies' for 'deep attack' in the mid-1980s, see *Technologies for NATO's Follow-On Forces Attack Concept* (Washington, D.C.: Office of Technology Assessment, July 1986).

[18] These NATO maritime exercises simulated multi-carrier operations conducted against the Soviet Union from inside Norwegian fjords. Eric Grove, *Battle for the Fjords: NATO's Forward Maritime Strategy in Action* (Annapolis, MD: Naval Academy Press, 1991). The US-led maritime exercise *Ocean Venture* 81 in September–October 1981 was the first in a series to reassert an allied naval presence in the Norwegian Sea, north of the so-called Greenland-Iceland-United Kingdom (GIUK) gap. *Ocean Venture* 81 also contained a dedicated psychological operations (PSYOPS) dimension that contributed to the 1983 Soviet 'war scare.' See Nigel West, *The Third Secret* (London: Harper Collins, 2000), 218–222; and Benjamin Fischer, 'The Soviet-American War Scare of the 1980s', *International Journal of Intelligence and Counterintelligence*, no. 19 (2006): 480–518.

Soviet RMA, had been planted a decade earlier, often well ahead of the fielding of the technologies upon which the hopes for NATO's ultimate operational success in a conflict with the Warsaw Pact had been pinned.

The Office of Net Assessment was cognisant, as early as the late 1970s, of this confluence of RMA developments in both alliances. They heightened a new awareness that the balance of forces in Central Europe had become more dynamic and complex, more challenging to measure confidently and potentially more unstable and unpredictable. These findings were reflected in successive assessments of the NATO-Warsaw Pact balance of forces carried out by ONA under the auspices of National Security Study Memorandum 186[19], starting with a first assessment completed in March 1978.[20] By the early 1980s, ONA assessments had integrated the latest, most innovative developments in Warsaw Pact and NATO planning for a war in Europe.[21] Not surprisingly, this ever-deeper understanding of the interactive relationships between conceptual and technological developments in the two alliances during the last decade-and-a-half of the Cold War provided the indispensable intellectual background and impetus to ONA's path-breaking work in the late 1980s on the concept of RMAs. Intellectually, therefore, the American RMA of the 1990s had a direct affiliation relationship with the European theatre's Cold War RMA of the late 1970s and early 1980s.

The reach and depth of this Cold War European RMA were so all-encompassing on both sides of the NATO-Warsaw Pact competition, however, that they raise several questions regarding the standing and lasting pertinence of conclusions associated with the American RMA of the 1990s: (i) Was Soviet MTR conceptual thinking in the 1970s and 1980s, by its very nature, inherently superior to NATO's allegedly poor conceptual

[19] For an authoritative analysis of the origins of the net assessment function in the United States Department of Defense, see Phillip A. Karber, *Net Assessment for SecDef* (Vienna, VA: The Potomac Foundation, 2013). For a comprehensive review of its application, see George E. Pickett, James G. Roche and Barry D. Watts, 'Net Assessment: A Historical Review', in Andrew W. Marshall, J.J. Martin and Henry S. Rowen, eds., *On Not Confusing Ourselves: Essays on National Security Strategy in Honor of Albert and Roberta Wohlstetter* (Boulder, CO: Westview Press, 1991).

[20] To date, only a single ONA classified assessment of the NATO-Warsaw Pact balance of forces has been declassified and released to the public. Lieutenant Colonel Peter R. Bankson, *The Military Balance in Europe: A Net Assessment*, Office of the Director of Net Assessment, 1 March 1978 (Washington, D.C.: Department of Defense), declassified and released to the public on 31 December 1988.

[21] National Security Study Memorandum 186, *National Net Assessment of Comparative Costs and Capabilities of US – USSR Military Establishments* (Washington, D.C.: The White House, 1 September 1973.) For over a decade and a half, starting in the mid-1970s, NSSM-186 was the analytical framework for the conduct, under the authority of Andrew W. Marshall, director of Net Assessment in the US Department of Defense, of successive, increasingly ambitious and complex assessments and simulations of the NATO-Warsaw Pact balance of forces and competing operational strategies. A task force of analysts was assembled to conduct the NSSM-186 assessments under the direction of Phillip Karber, who exercised that responsibility with a steady hand for nearly fifteen years. By the end of the Cold War, NSSM-186 had been the most ambitious and longest-running analytical effort ever undertaken by the Department of Defense. See Stephen Peter Rosen, 'The Impact of the Office of Net Assessment on the American Military in the Matter of the Revolution in Military Affairs', *The Journal of Strategic Studies* 33, no. 4 (2010): 477–480.

record? This postulate reflects what may be an unwarranted glorification of Soviet military thinking. (ii) Can the RMA concept be depended upon reliably to guide transformation of the armed forces with a view to the planning and conduct of future operations outside the context of a competitive and interactive relationship with a relatively symmetric, determined and methodical peer competitor? (iii) By implication, is the RMA concept transferable from the European theatre, where its deeper roots lie, to extra-European theatres, where adversaries might employ forms of warfare that are not easily susceptible to RMA-inspired interpretation and disruption?

New RMAs will occur and they will probably be as unpredictable in regard to their consequences as their predecessors. Assessment of the Cold War RMA offers a guide to how far their conceptual, organisational and technological scope can reach, yet how quickly their relevance can vanish in a new strategic era.

The 1961 Berlin Crisis and the NATO-Warsaw Pact military competition

Throughout the Cold War, the military postures and operational strategies of NATO and the Warsaw Pact reflected shifting preferences and constraints between and within the two alliances, influenced by enduring geographical, historical, political and economic factors, as much as by evolving perceptions and assessments of the likely opponent's capabilities and vulnerabilities. Following the 1961 Berlin Crisis, the competition between the two alliances reflected an increasing degree of interaction that reached its apex in the mid-1980s. This ever-growing interaction was triggered by the respective strategic and operational lessons that the two alliances derived from the Berlin Crisis, which can rightly be considered as the foundational event of the NATO-Warsaw Pact military competition of the Cold War's last two decades.

For the Warsaw Pact, American firmness, awareness of *Live Oak* and NATO planning for protecting Western access rights to Berlin[22] – including large-scale allied land and air operations into the German Democratic Republic (GDR), as well as a nuclear option[23] – and the unsuitability of the Soviet Union's then prevailing military strategy for managing European contingencies, other than through prompt escalation to a strategic nuclear exchange with the United States, had combined to prevent the

[22] Circumstantial evidence, based on testimony and investigation, suggests that early *Live Oak* and SHAPE Berlin Contingency (BERCON) plans were compromised by Georges Pâques, a French civil servant working as a Soviet agent in the press service at NATO Headquarters, located at the time in Paris, before his arrest in August 1963. *Possible Compromise of LIVE OAK Plans*, Memorandum from Commander, Live Oak, General Lyman Lemnitzer, to the Washington Ambassadorial Group, classified Live Oak Secret, 20 February 1964, Live Oak file no. 58 (Freiburg: BundesArchiv-MilitärArchiv), declassified and disclosed to the public on 4 October 2005 and Pierre Assouline, *Une question d'orgueil* (Paris: Gallimard, 2012), 224.

[23] *Berlin Contingency Planning*, SGPO 29/62, 30 March 1962, classified Cosmic Top Secret (Brussels, Belgium: NISCA) declassified and disclosed to the public on 29 March 2010. For a comprehensive and authoritative assessment of the *Live Oak* organisation, see Gregory W. Pedlow, 'Three Hats for Berlin: Lauris Norstad and the Second Berlin Crisis, 1958–1962', in *The Berlin Wall Crisis: Perspectives on Cold War Alliances*, eds. John S. Gearson and Kori Schake (London: Palgrave Macmillan, 2002), 175–198.

USSR from imposing its will in Berlin. The unfavourable outcome of the Berlin Crisis for Moscow had exposed the inadequacy of the Soviet military position in Central Europe and highlighted the requirement to alter the 'correlation of forces' in the Warsaw Pact's favour, through a strategy of countervailing military power.[24] The increasing autonomy of the European theatre in relation to the central strategic competition with the United States sprang from these strategic considerations.[25]

The Berlin Crisis also exposed the desirability of embedding the Soviet Union's management of its East European empire into a collective Warsaw Pact structure that, the Soviets hoped, would be more useful politically, and more usable militarily, in crisis situations.[26] This evolution of the Warsaw Pact was reflected, starting in 1961, in the conduct of multilateral command post and field training exercises,[27] and in the adoption in 1969 of the pact's peacetime statutes.[28] Over the three decades between the 1961 Berlin crisis and the end of the Cold War, the importance of East European forces in the USSR's military strategy for a war with NATO in Europe grew steadily, despite gaps in capability and shifting concerns over reliability.[29]

At the same time, the prospect of large-scale NATO nuclear use associated with the deployment of a growing number of nuclear weapons with US and other allied forces, as well as an ever-greater awareness of the devastating consequences of any employment of nuclear weapons in Europe, prompted a growing scepticism regarding the attractiveness of nuclear use.[30] These considerations fed an increased Soviet preference for a conventional-only option.[31] It has been common knowledge for

---

[24] Soviet premier Nikita Khrushchev had pressed the Soviet military to be ready to confront NATO conventionally over Berlin. See Aleksandr Fursenko and Timothy Naftali, *Khrushchev's Cold War* (New York and London: W.W. Norton, 2006), 358–359 and 370. According to Soviet Colonel Oleg Penkovsky, who was a clandestine source of the Central Intelligence Agency, the Soviet armed forces were unprepared for a war with NATO over Berlin. Jeffrey W. Legro, 'Soviet Crisis Decision-making and the Gorbachev Reforms', *Survival*, 31, no. 4 (July–August 1989): 346, and *CIA Analysis of the Warsaw Pact Forces: The Importance of Clandestine Reporting* (Langley, VA: Central Intelligence Agency) 28 May 2013, 14.

[25] Mastny and Byrne, *Cardboard Castle*, 21.

[26] *Warsaw Pact Military Strategy: A Compromise in Soviet Strategic Thinking*, RSS No. 0007/65, 7 June 1965, classified Secret (Langley, VA: Central Intelligence Agency), CIA FOIA Electronic Library, declassified and released to the public in June 2007; and Mastny and Byrne, *Cardboard Castle*, 15.

[27] Mastny and Byrne, *Cardboard Castle*, 19; and Matthias Uhl, 'Storming on to Paris: the 1961 Buria Exercise and the Planned Solution of the Berlin crisis', in Mastny, Holtsmark and Wenger, *War Plans and Alliances*, 46–71.

[28] Mastny and Byrne, *Cardboard Castle*, 31 and 38–39.

[29] *CIA Analysis of the Warsaw Pact Forces: The Importance of Clandestine Reporting*, 33.

[30] Soviet operational research study – *Assessment of Irretrievable Losses in the Western Theatre of War in Case of Operations with Nuclear Weapons* – published in 1969, cited by Vitalii Tsygischko, in Jan Hofenaar and Christopher Findlay, *Military Planning for European Theatre Conflict during the Cold War*, An Oral History Roundtable, Stockholm, 24–25 April 2006, study no. 79 (Zurich, Switzerland, ETH, 2007), 65. From the mid-1960s onwards, Dr Tsygischko was a leading operations research analyst working for the Soviet General Staff in Moscow on the planning and conduct of a strategic operation in a theatre of military operations.

[31] James M. McConnell, *The Soviet Shift in Emphasis from Nuclear to Conventional*, CRC-490 – vols. I and II (Alexandria, VA: Center for Naval Analyses, June 1983).

several decades that Soviet field training exercises *Dnepr* and *Dvina* in 1967 and 1970 respectively included an initial, non-nuclear phase.[32] A classified document recently declassified and released to the public indicates an even earlier rehearsal of an extended conventional phase during the *Narew* manoeuvres, a Polish *Front*-level exercise conducted in 1965.[33] Other Warsaw Pact exercises in the 1970s continued that pattern.[34] Evidence from post-Cold War interviews with Soviet commanders and defence scientists, such as Gareev, reveals a well-rehearsed preparedness to fight in a nuclear battlefield, as well as a consistent policy position that the USSR would have employed nuclear weapons only in response to (anticipated) NATO nuclear use.[35]

For NATO, the Berlin Crisis also involved a fundamental reassessment, foremost by the Kennedy administration, prompted by a new awareness of growing disconnects in the Alliance's defence posture:

(a) A widening geographic and operational gap between relatively static allied force deployments anchored predominantly on the Rhine and Main Rivers, a commitment to protect allied access rights to Berlin halfway across the territories Federal Republic of Germany (FRG) and the GDR, and a higher command structure concentrated around Paris;[36]

[32] Thomas W. Wolfe, *Soviet Power and Europe, 1945–1970* (Baltimore and London: The Johns Hopkins Press, 1970), 456 and 472–473.

[33] *Polish Defense Ministry Document Concerning Experiences and Conclusions from the 'Narew' Maneuvers*, 20 January 1967, classified Top Secret (Langley, VA: Central Intelligence Agency) CIA FOIA Library, declassified and publicly released on 26 April 2012.

[34] *Soviet Concepts for Employment of Nuclear Weapons in a Conflict with NATO – Evidence from Warsaw Pact Military Exercises*, 24 March 1978, classified Top Secret (Langley, VA: Central Intelligence Agency) CIA FOIA Electronic Library, declassified and publicly released on 18 July 2012. It should be noted that, as early as 1966, the Central Intelligence Agency had identified increased Soviet interest in the conduct of military operations without the use or the early use of nuclear weapons. See *Soviet Military Theorists Reappraise Nuclear War*, memorandum CIA/RR MM 66-6, dated September 1966, classified Secret (Langley, VA: Central Intelligence Agency) CIA FOIA Electronic Library, declassified and released in March 1996, 2, 6 and 9. for an indication dating back to 1966 of growing Soviet interest in conventional operations under the threat of nuclear first use by the adversary see also John G. Hines, Phillip A. Petersen and Notra Trulock III, 'Soviet Military Theory from 1945–2000: Implications for NATO', *The Washington Quarterly*, Fall 1986: 122.

[35] 'Summary of interview with Army General Makhmut A. Gareev', John Hines, Ellis M. Mishulovich and John Shulle, *Soviet Intentions 1965–1985: An Analytical Comparison of U.S.-Soviet Assessments During the Cold War, Volume II: Soviet Post-Cold War Testimonial Evidence* (McLean, VA: BDM Federal, September 1995) 74. See also Hans Rühle and Michael Rühle, 'Warschaupakt plante nuklearen Überfall auf Westeuropa', *Neue Zürcher Zeitung*, 13 September 2008, in which they report that during the Warsaw Pact's first ever multinational exercise – *Buria* (Storm) – held in late September and early October 1961, during the tensest period of the Berlin crisis, simulated Soviet employment of nuclear weapons was executed just *three minutes before* NATO's simulated nuclear first use.

[36] The headquarters of Allied Forces, Central Europe (AFCENT) and its three land, air and naval component commands (LANDCENT, AIRCENT and NAVCENT) were located until early 1967 in Fontainebleau, France. The increasing distance – approximately 900 kilometres – between Fontainebleau and forward areas along the inner-German border where allied covering forces would be deployed in order to screen advancing Soviet forces prompted General Dr Hans Speidel, COMLANDCENT, to request in

(b) Contingency plans unsuited to manage situations other than a full-scale Warsaw Pact attack on Western Europe, even though NATO's strategic concept of 1957 had acknowledged the possibility of Soviet operations with limited objectives, such as infiltrations, incursions, . . . ;[37] and
(c) A strategy relying on prompt and large-scale nuclear use, for lack of sufficient conventional forces, that, in a crisis, risked encouraging uncontrolled and unnecessary escalation, rather than inducing restraint. As David S. Yost has aptly remarked, 'There was no real military advantage in using TNF if the Soviets replied in kind, and NATO could be left worse off than the Warsaw Pact, with great collateral damage in Germany.'[38]

Adoption of the flexible response strategy in 1967 was meant to rectify the latter two disconnects, by making NATO's responses to Soviet intimidation, coercion or aggression tailored to the circumstances of an emerging crisis or a developing attack.

After the Berlin Crisis, however, NATO's quest for a conventional capability aimed at diminishing reliance on the *early* use of nuclear weapons was postponed for over a decade by successive conventional force reductions,[39] notwithstanding the expanded

Footnote 36 continued
1960 the relocation of his wartime headquarters from Margival, near Soissons, in France, to either a former Maginot Line fort in eastern France or buildings at Trier, Germany that had been vacated in 1958 by NATO's 4th Allied Tactical Air Force, upon its relocation to Ramstein air base. See 'LANDCENT Wartime Advanced Command Post', *Headquarters, AFCENT History for 1960*, classified NATO Secret, (Fontainebleau, France: Headquarters, Allied Forces Central Europe, 24 November 1961), downgraded to NATO Unclassified, July 2013, 18.

[37] MC 14/2 *Overall Strategic Concept for the Defence of the North Atlantic Treaty Area* (Washington, D.C.: NATO Military Committee, 1957). SACEUR's Berlin Contingency (BERCON) operations plans of the early 1960s were the first plans that the Alliance had ever developed for operations for a purpose and on a scale other than general war. *Contingency Plans, Excluding General War*, MCM-165-65, 18 November 1965 (Washington, D.C.: NATO Military Committee), NISCA, declassified and disclosed publicly on 13 April 1999. Historian John Duffield astutely called attention to the fact that the reference in MC 14/2 to the risk of limited Soviet aggression can rightly be considered as the conceptual birth of 'flexible response' and Beatrice Heuser duly recorded this counter-intuitive proposition in her book on Western nuclear strategies. Beatrice Heuser, *NATO, Britain, France and the FRG: Nuclear Strategies and Forces for Europe, 1949–2000* (Basingstoke: Macmillan, 1997), 40. Gregory W. Pedlow has traced SACEUR Lauris Norstad's thinking on making NATO strategy more flexible, 'Flexible Response before MC 14/3: General Lauris Norstad and the Second Berlin Crisis 1958–1962' *Storia Della Relazioni Internationali*, 13, no. 1 (1998): 234–268.

[38] David S. Yost, 'The History of NATO Theater Nuclear Force Policy: Key Findings from the Sandia Conference', *The Journal of Strategic Studies* 15, no. 2 (June 1992): 251.

[39] These reductions included the loss of two French mechanised divisions, army- and corps-level troops, two brigades of *Nike-Hercules* surface-to-air missiles and seven fighter wings, following France's withdrawal from NATO's integrated command structure in 1966, as well as the withdrawal from West Germany, between 1966 and 1968, of a British infantry brigade and the equivalent of a US Army division (two mechanised brigades and an armoured cavalry regiment), as well as five US Air Force fighter and electronic warfare squadrons. Friedrich Wiener, *Forze Armate ed Armamenti dei Paesi della NATO* (Rome, Italy: Istituto per la divulgazione della storia militare, 1968), 84, 90 and 451–453; and Walter S. Poole, 'NATO Under Strain', *The Joint Chiefs of Staff and National Policy*, Volume IX: 1965–1968, (Washington, D. C.: Historical Division, Joint Chiefs of Staff, 2012), 336.

threat represented by the stationing of Soviet forces in Czechoslovakia, following the Warsaw Pact invasion in August 1968.[40] As Bruno Thoss has remarked, adoption of an ambitious forward defence posture oriented to defending allied territory as far forward as possible inevitably increased NATO's reliance on the early use of tactical nuclear weapons, in the absence of satisfactory conventional force improvements.[41]

Forward defence and deep operations as the pivot of the Cold War RMA

Often masked by the twists and turns of the transition to flexible response, it was the solution to the *first disconnect* exposed by the Berlin crisis, through adoption on 1 September 1963 of a forward defence posture along the FRG's eastern borders,[42] which had the most enduring impact on NATO's strategy for the rest of the Cold War, by shaping the conditions for the rise of a Cold War RMA. Once NATO had made the commitment not to yield West German (and other allied) territory under any circumstances in case of conflict, forward defence became the inalterable concept around which NATO organised its operational strategy for the remainder of the Cold War.[43]

Even though various conceptual constructs of the 1980s, such as the US Army's AirLand Battle doctrine of 1982, have often been presented as challenges to, or deviations from, forward defence, in reality they extended forward defence *forward*, by

[40] Five divisions, army and *Front*-level units, and several air regiments. See *Capabilities of the Warsaw Pact Against NATO*, Special National Intelligence Estimate, SNIE- 11-17-68, 8 October 1968, classified Secret (Langley, VA: Central Intelligence Agency) CIA FOIA Electronic Library, declassified and released to the public, no date.

[41] Bruno Thoss, 'Aims and Realities: NATO's Forward Defense and the Operational Planning Level at NORTHAG', in *Blueprints for Battle: Planning for War in Central Europe, 1948–1968*, eds., Jan Hoffenaar and Dieter Kruger (Lexington: University Press of Kentucky, 2012) 28.

[42] The commitment to forward defence across the breadth of NATO's front line, from Norway to Turkey, had been a mainstay principle of Alliance planning since its inception. In practice, enduring conventional force deficiencies had made its operational implementation impractical. For a decade following the creation of the Western Union in 1948, NATO's operational strategy in Central Europe was anchored on a firm defence on the Rhine River, as the prelude to a hypothetical counter-offensive. The build-up of the *Bundeswehr* after 1955, as well as the large-scale availability of tactical nuclear weapons to US and other allied forces from 1957 onwards, offered the prospect of conducting a mobile defence well forward of the Rhine and motivated the move to a 'semi-forward defence' posture, along the Weser and Lech Rivers, on 1 July 1958. 'CENTAG Emergency Defense Plan (EDP) 2–58', *Annual History, United States Army, Europe, 1 July 1968- 30 June 1959*, classified Top Secret, 6 July 1960 (Heidelberg: Headquarters, USAREUR & 7th Army), downgraded to Unclassified, 48–49. The transition to a full forward defence became effective on 1 September 1963. *History for 1963*, 3340/CE/AG/1149/64, 16 October 1964, classified NATO Secret (Fontainebleau, France: Headquarters, Allied Forces, Central Europe), downgraded to NATO Unclassified (Mons, Belgium: Supreme Headquarters Allied Powers Europe, July 2013) 8.

[43] For an operational history of forward defence, see Phillip A. Karber, 'In Defense of Forward Defense', *Armed Forces Journal International*, May 1984: 27–50, Helmut R. Hammerich, 'Kommis kommt von Kompromiss: Das Heeer der Bundeswehr zwischen Wehrmacht und U.S. Army (1950 bis 1970)', in *Das Heer 1950 bis 1970: Konzeption, Organisation, Aufstellung*, eds. Helmut R. Hammerich et al (Munich: R. Oldenbourg Verlag, 2006), 131–154; Helmut R. Hammerich, 'Suddeutschland als Eckpfeiler der Verteidigung Europas', *Military Power Revue der Schweizer Armee* no. 2 (2011): 34–45; and Helmut R. Hammerich, 'Fighting for the Heart of Germany', in *Blueprints for Battle*, 155–174.

engaging Warsaw Pact lead and follow-on echelons while still deployed on their own territory, ahead of, and away from, the forward edge of the battle area. Despite appearances and allegations to the contrary, these concepts remained anchored in the notion that the most strategically compelling line of defence for NATO was, for sound operational as well as political reasons, the forward line of defence situated between the Weser and Lech Rivers and West Germany's eastern borders.[44] This principle gave rise in the 1970s to the imperative of 'winning the first battle,' which endured even under the more ambitious, manoeuvre-oriented schemes of the 1980s.

NATO's adoption of forward defence in the 1960s, and the resulting repositioning of defensive positions along West Germany's eastern borders, were interpreted by the East German leadership as a reflection of the Alliance's inherently aggressive military posture and intentions.[45] From the 1960s onwards, in an almost exact reverse mirror-image of NATO's forward defence strategy, the Warsaw Pact's strategy of *deep* operations aimed at breaching and overwhelming NATO's forward defences, through fire, manoeuvre and shock.[46] Denying NATO victory in the first battle could well have spelled the difference between success and failure in the execution of the Theatre Strategic Operation. The forward momentum built into the Soviet concept of ground force echelonment, the execution of a massive, theatre-scale air and anti-air operation, and the insertion of high-speed Operational Manoeuvre Groups (OMGs) into NATO's force deployment, to spearhead operational-strategic-scale encirclement operations, were all aimed at puncturing and overwhelming NATO's forward defences and at ensuring the TSO's early and irreversible success. Conduct of a TSO became the defining theme for nearly all Warsaw Pact exercises almost through the end of the Cold War.[47]

Forward defence became, therefore, the operational pivot for the competing strategies of the two alliances and the prism through which each side arrayed the components – operational concepts, organisational schemes, and technological applications – of its emerging RMA. These converging developments prompted an unprecedented degree of interaction between NATO and Warsaw Pact conceptual and force development processes that became salient from the mid-1970s onwards. A decade-and-a-half after the 1961 Berlin Crisis, the conditions for a Cold War RMA had been set in motion on both sides.

---

44 Drew Middleton, 'Air Superiority Key to NATO Defense', *The New York Times*, 3 October 1984. The operational aspects of terrain along West Germany's eastern borders were addressed in detail in Hugh Faringdon, *Strategic Geography: NATO, the Warsaw Pact, and the Superpowers* (London and New York: Routledge, 1989), 347–385.

45 Jan Hoffenaar, 'East German Military Intelligence for the Warsaw Pact in the Central Sector', in *Blueprints for Battle*, 87.

46 Major John G. Hines, 'The Principle of Mass in Soviet Tactics Today', *Review of the Soviet Ground Forces*, DDB1100-307-81 (Washington, D.C.: Defense Intelligence Agency), June 1981, 1–8.

47 Dale Herspring has noted that, as early as 1963, Ogarkov had called attention to the over-riding importance of strategic command at the theatre level and reliance on deep operations. Dale R. Herspring, *The Soviet High Command, 1967–1989* (Princeton, NJ: Princeton University Press, 1990), 137–140.

The Soviet theatre-strategic operation and the rise of the Cold War RMA

By the mid-1970s, the Warsaw Pact's RMA was in full motion and increasingly transparent to the United States, thanks to the intelligence information supplied by Colonel Ryszard Kuklinski of Poland, Colonel Ghulam Dastagir Wardak of Afghanistan, and Soviet General Dmitri Polyakov.[48] The clandestine contribution of Kuklinski on Warsaw Pact operational concepts, command structure, and exercises, in particular, was of an unprecedented and unparalleled quality and duration.[49]

As evidenced by the nature and the scale of the *Zapad* 77 command post exercise[50], the pace of the negotiations over the adoption of Warsaw Pact 'wartime statutes'[51] and the standing-up of coalition high commands for the western and southwestern TVDs,[52] efforts to translate Ogarkov's conceptualisation of the RMA into a theatre strategic operation[53] had reached a high momentum. *Zapad 77* was described by Ogarkov as designed to test the capacity of a theatre high command to plan and synchronise the forward movement and engagement of six *Fronts* into West Germany.[54] The envisaged strategic operation also included the execution of a theatre-scale air and counter-air campaign across Western Europe and a sea-landing operation against Denmark.[55] Given the degree of mechanisation of Warsaw Pact forces in the mid-1970s and the massive scale of their logistical resupply in wartime with fuel,

[48] Barrass, *The Great Cold War*, 394.

[49] As Aris Pappas, one of CIA's leading analysts dedicated to exploiting the information supplied by Kuklinski, has stated, Kuklinski's material 'virtually defined our knowledge. It was the touchstone. It was the basic standard.' Quoted in Benjamin Weiser, *A Secret Life: The Polish Officer, His Covert Mission and the Price He Paid to Save His Country* (New York: Public Affairs, 2004), 245. Robert Gates, Director of Central Intelligence, described Kuklinski as 'one of the most important CIA sources of information on the Soviet military of the Cold War period'. Robert M. Gates, *From the Shadows* (New York: Touchstone, 1996), 238.

[50] *Materials of the critique of the operational-strategic command-staff exercise Zapad-77*, 10–15.

[51] *The Soviet Union's Control of the Warsaw Pact Forces*, SOV 83-10175CX, October 1983, classified Top Secret (Langley, VA: Central Intelligence Agency) CIA FOIA Electronic Library, declassified and released to the public on 18 June 2012.

[52] In wartime, the command element and operational staff of the two TVD high commands would have been housed in two large, purpose-built bunkers, located at Legnica, Poland, and an undisclosed location in Bulgaria. The highly secret project under which these bunkers were built, code named *Albatross*, was disclosed to the Central Intelligence Agency by Colonel Kuklinski. Weiser, *A Secret Life*, 105–106.

[53] Adamsky, 'Through the Looking Glass', 270.

[54] The command post exercise *Zapad* 77 in spring 1977 stands out as the most ambitious attempt, up to that date, since the establishment of the Warsaw Pact, to address the massive command and control and synchronisation challenges associated with the planning and conduct of TVD-scale strategic operations, in that instance in the context of the western TVD. The command post exercise *Soyuz* 78 seems to have been aimed at exploring similar challenges in the southwestern TVD. It was staged on Romanian territory, with the participation of Romanian forces, a posture that contrasts with Romania's refusal in March 1980 to sign the Warsaw Pact's new 'wartime statutes'. *The Warsaw Pact SOYUZ 78 Exercise*, TS 788321, 22 September 1978, classified Top Secret (Langley, VA: Central Intelligence Agency) CIA FOIA Electronic Library, declassified and released to the public on 18 June 2012.

[55] On the strategic importance for the ultimate success of the Soviet strategic operation of Denmark's defeat and occupation, see Christopher N. Donnelly and Phillip A. Petersen, 'Soviet Strategists Target Denmark', *International Defense Review*, August 1986: 1047–1051; and Frede P. Jensen, 'The Warsaw Pact's

ammunition, spare-parts, food and water, a six-*Front*-deep strategic operation would have involved the synchronised forward movement of hundreds of thousands of troops and tens of thousands of tracked and wheeled vehicles, with the support of thousands of fixed- and rotary-wing aircraft, across a geographically restricted theatre and into densely populated areas.[56] Indisputably, such an offensive would have been, by far, the largest military operation of all time, posing traffic control, airspace management and logistical resupply challenges on an unprecedented scale.[57] The scale of the challenge was underscored by Ogarkov during *Zapad* 77's post-exercise critique, in which he lamented the insufficient level of automated data processing means available to support the planning and conduct of such a massive undertaking.[58]

Zapad 77 also rehearsed the large-scale employment of nuclear weapons in support of offensive operations, nominally in response to but, in effect, ahead of NATO's own nuclear use, and highlighted the absolute requirement to degrade NATO's nuclear forces by conventional means before the start of nuclear operations, including by the use of 'search and destroy' teams ferried by helicopter.[59]

Despite the many shortcomings which it revealed, exercise *Zapad* 77 confirmed for the Soviet General Staff the compelling strategic logic of the TSO as the enabling mechanism for developing and applying a higher form of operational art, one at the cutting edge of modern warfare. Tellingly, when addressing air defence coordination shortcomings exposed by the exercise during the post-exercise critique of *Zapad* 77, Marshal Dmitri Ustinov, the Soviet minister of defence, stated that 'It is necessary to

Footnote 55 continued

Special Target: Planning the Seizure of Denmark', in Mastny, Holtsmark and Wenger, *War Plans and Alliances*, 95–117.

[56] The formidable density of such a deployment led assessments of a putative NATO-Warsaw Pact conflict conducted under the auspices of NSSM-186 to give greater attention to 'force-to-space' ratios, alongside 'force-on-force' ratios, and to the relative ability of the two opposing alliances to counter the actions of the adversary by delivering fire, rather than amassing force, in a precise and timely way.

[57] The vulnerability of Soviet lines of communication across Poland to attack by NATO during a conflict, notably bridges over the Vistula and Oder Rivers, is described in a 1977 Polish General Staff document outlining the scenario of a war game that was played in February 1978. *War Game Scenario – Central Europe – 1978*, TS 788269, 17 August 1978, classified Top Secret (Langley, VA: Central Intelligence Agency) CIA FOIA Electronic Library, declassified and released to the public on 18 June 2012, 23–25.

[58] *Materials of the critique of the operational-strategic command-staff exercise* Zapad—77, 44. The first large-scale use of computers in support of the planning of a theatre-strategic operation was reportedly rehearsed during the command post exercise *Soyuz* 75. Oliver Bange, 'Comments and Contextualisation of Polish Documents related to SOYUZ 75 and SHCHIT 88', CWIHP e-Dossier No. 20, (Zurich: Cold War International History Project, 20 February 2010), 4.

[59] Reliance on such heliborne teams was a recurrent theme of successive Warsaw Pact military exercises in the 1970s. See *Soviet Concepts for the Employment of Nuclear Weapons in a Conflict with NATO – Evidence from Warsaw Pact Military Exercises*, 24 March 1978, classified Top Secret (Langley, VA: Central Intelligence Agency) CIA FOIA Electronic Library, declassified and released to the public on 18 July 2012, 8 and 10.

ponder well what else should be done from an *organizational*, *operational* and *technical* standpoint to successfully resolve them.'[60]

From 1977 onwards, *Zapad* 77 became the template for successive, theatre-scale, command post and field training exercises in the western and southwestern TVDs aimed at rehearsing a strategic operation in a theatre of military operations. *Zapad* 77 was followed notably by *Soyuz* 80, 81 and 83, and *Zapad* 81 in the western TVD and *Soyuz* 78 and *Sh'chit* 82 in the southwestern TVD.[61] Exercise *Soyuz* 78 apparently replicated the aims of *Zapad* 77 in the southwestern TVD.[62] The scale and regularity of these exercises bear witness to the ambition and persistence of Ustinov, Ogarkov and Kulikov to make the Warsaw Pact a credible operational coalition, despite the bitter legacy of the Warsaw Pact's invasion of Czechoslovakia, the growing burden of the USSR's engagement in Afghanistan, and the deepening political crisis in Poland.

The establishment of high commands for the western and southwestern TVDs was accompanied by the construction of dedicated command and control bunkers in Poland and Bulgaria and the adoption of a new, unified readiness system for the transition of Warsaw Pact forces from peace to war, under the code names *Albatross* and *Monument*, respectively.[63] A comparison of the 1980 'wartime statutes' with the 1969 'peacetime statutes' suggests that the Warsaw Pact's supreme high command kept primarily training and equipment standardisation responsibilities, while the two TVD high commands would have assumed wartime responsibilities under the direction of

[60] *Materials of the critique of the operational-strategic command-staff exercise* Zapad—77, 72. Italics added.

[61] The aim of *Soyuz* exercises was, it seems, the training of senior-level staffs and field command elements in the execution of a theatre-strategic operation. Although exercises in the *Soyuz*, *Zapad* and *Sh'chit* series had been conducted from the late 1960s onwards – there is evidence that *Soyuz* exercises were conducted in the western TVD in 1969, 1974 and 1975 and in the southwestern TVD in 1973 – *Zapad* 77 marked a turning point by centralising command and control of a theatre-strategic operation in the hands of yet-to-be-established permanent TVD high commands. See *Planning, Preparation, Operation and Evaluation of Warsaw Pact Exercises*, undated, classified Secret (Langley, VA: Central Intelligence Agency) CIA FOIA Electronic Library, declassified and released to the public on 18 June 2012. On exercise *Zapad* 69, see Matthias Uhl, 'Soviet and Warsaw Pact Military Strategy from Stalin to Brezhnev', in Hoffenaar and Kruger, *Blueprints for Battle*, 47–48. On exercises *Soyuz 81* and *Sh'chit* 82, see Frank Steinert, 'Command Staff Exercise Soyuz-81', DDB-1100-329-81, *Review of the Soviet Ground Forces* (Washington, D.C.: Defense Intelligence Agency), October 1981, 1–2, and Major James Brusstar and Frank Steinert, 'Exercise Shield-82', DDB-1100-412-83, *Review of the Soviet Ground Forces* (Washington, D.C.: Defense Intelligence Agency), May 1983, 1–3.

[62] *The Warsaw Pact SOYUZ 78 Exercise*, TS#788321, 22 September 1978, classified Top Secret (Langley, VA: Central Intelligence Agency) CIA FOIA Electronic Library, declassified and released to the public on 18 June 2012.

[63] The *Monument* alert and readiness system is described in *Background Information on the Development of the Unified Wartime Command System for the Combined Armed Forces of the Warsaw Pact*, FIRDB-312/01197-83, dated 10 June 1983, classified Secret (Langley, VA: Central Intelligence Agency) CIA FOIA Electronic Library, declassified and released to the public, no date, 10–12. The *Albatross* installation in Poland is addressed in *Warsaw Pact Exercise 'Center', Far Eastern Theater of Operations, Installation 'Albatross'*, dated 8 June 1979, classified Top Secret (Langley, VA: Central Intelligence Agency) CIA FOIA Electronic Library, declassified and released to the public on 18 June 2012, 6.

the Soviet General Staff, although the division of labour between the former and the latter was kept deliberately ambiguous by Moscow, as a means to assuage East European sensitivities over the extent of Soviet domination and control.[64]

Often ahead of these command arrangements, the other constituent parts of the TSO were coming into place at a rapid pace. The introduction of the Mi-24 *Hind* attack and transport helicopter in 1977 – which had no equivalent in NATO – was accompanied with the build-up of airmobile and special operations forces (*Spetsnaz*) trained in the performance of air assault and vertical envelopment missions into the depth of the enemy, with the purpose of identifying main concentrations of NATO land forces and disrupting their movement and their defensive positions, as well as providing intelligence on the location and readiness status of NATO nuclear delivery systems.[65]

The conduct of a theatre-wide air/counter-air operation, involving six to eight massed air strikes over a period of five days, was aimed at 'pinning-down' NATO's airpower and interdicting allied air sorties, as well as degrading NATO's nuclear forces and operational reserves.[66] It led to the establishment of two air armies, headquartered at Legnica in Poland and at Vinniytsa in Ukraine, and subordinated to the western and southwestern TVD high commands, respectively. These two air armies were equipped with large numbers of Su-24 *Fencer* fighter-bombers specialised in the execution of long-range air interdiction sorties, including at night and in adverse weather conditions.

In parallel, Warsaw Pact forces were introducing rapidly into their inventory the modern assets – main battle tanks, armoured fighting vehicles, self-propelled artillery, mobile anti-tank and surface-to-air missiles, and assault bridging equipment – necessary to conduct a TSO, notably for breaking through NATO's forward defences into the depth of allied deployments.[67] During the period 1973–1983, armour production in the Soviet Union amounted to approximately 3,000 main battle tanks a

[64] *The Soviet Union's Control of the Warsaw Pact Forces*. Of note, *Zapad* 77 was directed by Marshals Ustinov and Ogarkov, while *Soyuz* exercises seemed to have been directed consistently by Marshal Kulikov.

[65] *Soviet Concepts for Employment of Nuclear Weapons in a Conflict with NATO – Evidence from Warsaw Pact Military Exercises*, 5, 6 and 10.

[66] *The 'Air Operation': The Warsaw Pact Strategy for Achieving Air Superiority*, SR 79-10137C, dated October 1979, classified Top Secret (Langley, VA: Central Intelligence Agency) CIA FOIA Electronic Library, declassified and released to the public, no date. The large scale of the envisaged massed air strikes is indicated in *Report on Visit of Polish Armed Forces General Staff delegation to USSR Armed Forces General Staff and the Combined Command of the Combined Armed Forces*, FIRDB-312/02329-80, 8 October 1980, classified Top Secret (Langley, VA: Central Intelligence Agency) CIA FOIA Electronic Library, declassified and released to the public, no date, 31. See also Phillip Petersen, 'Soviet Air and Antiair Operations', *Air University Review* 36 (March–April 1985): 36–54; and Mastny and Byrne, *A Cardboard Castle*, 482.

[67] The scale of the military build-up, from the mid-1960s through the mid-1970s, of Soviet and other Warsaw Pact forces deployed opposite NATO is documented in *Warsaw Pact Forces Opposite NATO*, National Intelligence Estimate NIE 11-14-75, 4 September 1975, classified Top Secret (Langley, VA: Central Intelligence Agency) CIA FOIA Electronic Library, declassified and released to the public on 19 June 2008, 33–42.

year.[68] By the late 1970s, the Warsaw Pact had 10,000 more tanks than NATO in Central Europe.[69] Lessons learned from the performance of the Egyptian Army during the early phases of the 1973 *Yom Kippur* War taught the Soviet Army the advantages in a war of deploying anti-tank guided missiles (ATGMs) to counter NATO armoured counter-attacks.[70] The proliferation of ATGMs with NATO forces in the late 1970s eventually drove the Soviet Army to protect its tanks with 'explosive reactive armour', rendering them in many cases invulnerable to antitank hits.[71]

Furthermore, while Soviet writings in the early 1980s gave considerable prominence to the emergence within NATO forces of so-called 'reconnaissance strike complexes,'[72] the Warsaw Pact was ahead of NATO in deploying a long-range self-propelled howitzer and multiple-rocket launcher (MRL), in the form of the 2S3 152 mm howitzer and the BM-27 220mm MRL, respectively, for deep attack. The BM-27 had a range of 40 kilometres – a range sufficient to execute effectively counter-battery fires against NATO's own deeply-deployed fire-support systems – and could deliver high-explosive conventional rounds, cluster munitions and fuel-air explosives to that end, as well as scatterable mines to prevent the forward movement of NATO armoured counter-attacks. The BM-27 was followed by the more formidable BM-30 300mm MRL, with a range of 70 kilometres, which, in addition to various types of anti-tank and anti-personnel munitions and sub-munitions, reportedly could deliver a mini-drone to facilitate overhead target acquisition of enemy positions. The BM-30 began approximating a genuine, autonomous reconnaissance-strike complex. However, it had not been widely deployed opposite NATO forces by the time of the Cold War's end.

A final step in completing the architecture of the theatre-strategic operation was the resurrection of the World War II Mobile Group in the form of specially-configured OMGs of variable scale, from division to corps-size, tasked with leading the transformation of the initial breakthroughs into operational-strategic-scale encircle-

[68] *Soviet Tank Programs*, NI IIM84-10016/DS, classified Secret, June 1985 (Langley, VA: Central Intelligence Agency) CIA FOIA Electronic Library, declassified and released to the public in October 1999, 3.

[69] Major General Paul F. Gorman, 'U.S. Intelligence and Soviet Armor', *Studies in Intelligence*, vol. 24, Spring 1980, classified Secret (Langley, VA: Central Intelligence Agency) CIA FOIA Electronic Library, declassified and released to the public in March 2004, 4. A US Army officer and a former commander of a US Army division in the V (US) Corps in West Germany, General Gorman was at the time the US intelligence community's national intelligence officer for general purposes forces.

[70] Phillip A. Karber, 'The Soviet Anti-Tank Debate', *Survival*, May–June 1975: 105–111; 'Already in Service: The 2nd Generation of Soviet Anti-tank Missiles', *International Defense Review* 11, no. 1 (January 1978): 15–17.

[71] On the characteristics of Soviet tanks and associated defensive measures against NATO's improving anti-armour capabilities, see *Soviet Tank Programs* and Malcolm W. Browne, 'Threat to NATO Is Seen in Armor On Soviet Tanks', *The New York Times*, 12 July 1987.

[72] Milan Vego, *Recce-Strike Complexes in Soviet Theory and Practice* (Fort Leavenworth, KS: Soviet Army Studies Office, June 1990).

ment operations.[73] Reportedly, the employment of OMGs was first tested in 1981, during the *Yug* 81, *Soyuz* 81 and *Zapad* 81 exercises.[74] *Zapad* 81, held in September 1981 in the western USSR, was the natural follow-on to *Zapad* 77, the four intervening years having been a period of fast-paced maturation of the TSO. Like *Zapad* 77, *Zapad* 81 was directed by Ustinov and Ogarkov, rather than by Kulikov, and involved multiple *Fronts*.[75] Unlike *Zapad* 77, however, *Zapad* 81 was a two-sided, field training exercise – reportedly the largest such Soviet exercise since the end of World War II – and included the participation of Soviet forces only.[76] Of note, the attacking forces, which simulated the Warsaw Pact, were led by General Yevgenni Ivanovskiy, who, until a year earlier had been the commander of the Group of Soviet Forces in (East) Germany and presumably had an excellent knowledge of the strengths and weaknesses of NATO forces stationed in West Germany. The defending side was led by General Stanislav Postnikov, who in 1988 replaced Ogarkov as the commander of the western TVD. Every aspect of the TSO was rehearsed during *Zapad* 81, including the commitment of a division-size OMG, although the exercise's field training dimension made actions by participants appear as excessively pre-scripted.

The employment of an OMG featured prominently again in the *Soyuz 83* command post exercise, with a three-division-strong OMG following up behind and, then, moving through the lead armies of a first-echelon *Front* into the depth of NATO's Northern Army Group (NORTHAG) area in northern West Germany.[77] Exercise *Soyuz* 83 marked, seemingly, the climax of Soviet offensive-oriented planning and, in effect, the completion of the Warsaw Pact's Cold War RMA.[78] The exercise's conduct showed a growing emphasis on initiating operations from pre-planned attack locations, with little warning, and on high-speed manoeuvre, in order to preempt NATO and negate the higher readiness and ever-improving conventional capabilities

---

[73] Christopher N. Donnelly, 'The Soviet Operational Manoeuvre Group: A New Challenge to NATO', *International Defense Review* 15, no. 9 (1982): 177–186; *The Soviet Operational Maneuver Group*, SOV 83-10034, February 1983, classified Secret (Langley, VA: Central Intelligence Agency) CIA FOIA Electronic Library, declassified and released to the public in 1999.

[74] The command post exercise *Yug* 81 is mentioned by both Beatrice Heuser and Christoph Bluth as the first exercise to include employment of an OMG. Heuser, *Warsaw Pact Military Doctrines*, footnote 42, 454; and Christoph Bluth, 'Offensive Defence in the Warsaw Pact: Reinterpreting Military Doctrine', *The Journal of Strategic Studies* 18, no. 4 (December 1995): footnote 26, 75. Oliver Bange makes reference to *Soyuz* 81. Bange, 'Comments on and Contextualisation of Polish Documents', 5.

[75] *Comments on Exercise 'ZAPAD-81'*, FIRDB-312/02950-81, 18 September 1981, classified Top Secret (Langley, VA: Central Intelligence Agency) CIA FOIA Electronic Library, declassified and released to the public on 18 August 2008, 4.

[76] Arch Shero and Richard Oden, 'Exercise Zapad-81', *Review of the Soviet Ground Forces*, DDB-1100-362-82 (Washington, D.C.: Defense Intelligence Agency), April 1982, 1–9. One can speculate that keeping participation restricted to Soviet forces aimed at protecting sensitive operational details from Warsaw Pact partners associated with the planning and execution of a theatre-strategic operation.

[77] Hans Frank, 'Die Westgruppe der Truppen (WGT)', in *NVA Anspruch und Wirk-lichkeit*, ed. Klaus Naumann (Berlin: Verlag E.S. Mittler & Sohn GmbH, 1993), 333–344.

[78] Heuser, *Victory in a Nuclear War*, 321; and Bange, 'Comments on and Contextualisation of Polish Documents', 6–7.

of NATO forces for both forward defence and follow-on forces' attack.[79] *Soyuz* 83 reflected, seemingly, an acknowledgement by the Soviet General Staff that, in the light of these new operational and technological realities, successful execution of the TSO required 'front-loading' the three first-echelon *Fronts* and reducing reliance considerably on the forward movement across Eastern Europe and subsequent engagement of the three second-echelon *Fronts*.

Soyuz 83 was followed by *Soyuz* 84 in the southwestern TVD, apparently oriented to an attack to conquer the Turkish Straits[80], and complemented by *Zapad* exercises in the western TVD in 1983 and 1984 that reportedly emphasised counter-measures against NATO's maturing deep attack capabilities and the employment of Soviet reconnaissance-strike complexes[81], as well as a short-notice attack capability that might have been used in a conflict to seize a geographically-exposed West German city as a bargaining chip.[82]

The combination of the higher readiness of East German and Soviet forces stationed in the GDR noted in the early 1980s and the OMG's emergence helps explain NATO's growing concern at that time that the Warsaw Pact might have been pursuing a combat and logistical capability to attack from an un-reinforced, 'standing-start' posture, with little warning.[83] A revised assessment by the US intelligence community in 1984 of Soviet logistical stockpiles stored in East Germany gives credence to that theory.[84] Observation of Soviet ammunition stocks in East Germany following the end of the Cold War indicated that NATO had grossly under-estimated the Warsaw Pact's capacity to initiate operations against NATO without a massive resupply effort from the western USSR.[85] In effect, in the early 1980s, the Soviet concept of 'meeting engagement' was assuming a new meaning, this time in the form of preemption of NATO's mobilisation in the initial, conventional phase of a war in Europe.

Awareness of the risk that, in a crisis, the USSR might be tempted to undertake a so-called 'standing-start' attack, with virtually no warning and a limited number of

---

79 Document no. 99, Mastny and Byrne, *A Cardboard Castle?*, 56 and 481–482.

80 Miroslav Lazanski, 'Warsaw Pact Maneuvers: How To Reach the Bosporus', *East Europe Report* JPRS-84-046 (Washington, D.C.: Foreign Broadcast Information Service), 11 April 1984, 1–5.

81 Adamsky, *Culture of Military Innovation*, 36–37.

82 'New Soviet tack seen in exercise in Germany', *The New York Times*, 14 July 1984.

83 Document no. 97, Mastny and Byrne, *A Cardboard Castle?*, 470; *The Readiness of Soviet Ground Forces*, NI-IIM-82-10012, November 1982, classified Secret (Langley, VA: Central Intelligence Agency) CIA FOIA Electronic Library, declassified and released to the public in October 1999; Graham H. Turbiville, Jr., 'Emerging Soviet Approaches to Mobilization', in *European Security Policy after the Revolutions of 1989*, ed. Jeffrey Simon (Washington, D.C.: National Defense University Press, 1991) 85; and See Sangho Lee, *Deterrence and the Defence of Central Europe: The British Role From the Early 1980s to the End of the Gulf War*, D. Phil. dissertation (London: King's College, August 1994), 116–117.

84 *Soviet Military Rear Services in East Germany*, SOV-84-10006JX, February 1984, classified Top Secret (Langley, VA: Central Intelligence Agency) CIA FOIA Electronic Library, declassified and released to the public on 14 July 2010, 1.

85 'East German Army Masked Severe Flaws Behind Scenes', *The Baltimore Sun*, 2 December 1990. On the scale of Soviet preparations, see also John J. Yureshko, 'Emerging Soviet Approaches to Mobilization', in Simon, *European Security Policy*, 85.

forward-deployed forces, in order to catch NATO forces unaware in their garrison locations or, at best, on a hasty march to their defensive positions, had driven NATO to anticipate a situation where generating a cohesive forward defence would not have been possible. Ensuring that allied forces could cope with such an extreme and fluid situation had prompted the development of specific counter-measures. These included a specific 'Counter-Surprise' alerting system, distinct from the regular, step-by-step NATO Alert System, as well as the conduct several times a year of no-notice alerting exercises, nick-named *Quick Train* in the 1960s and *Active Edge* in the 1970s and 1980s.[86]

Together with the large-scale deployment of the SS-20 intermediate-range ballistic missile, the TSO reflected a well-thought-out and deliberate strategy to defeat in a conflict the two pillars of NATO's strategy – forward defence and flexible response. This would have been achieved by overwhelming NATO's conventional defences, through a combination of an initial, knock-out blow and subsequent, relentless annihilation, and making a NATO nuclear first use and follow-on nuclear escalation, if necessary, either infeasible or unattractive. According to Soviet General Andrian Danilevich, the deployment of the SS-20 'was a breakthrough, unlike anything the Americans had. We were immediately able to hold all of Europe hostage.'[87] Half-a-century of lessons learned, and conceptual and force development rooted in the Red Army experiments of the 1930s and the experience of World War II had reached their pinnacle.

The Soviet challenge and NATO's post-Vietnam strategic renaissance

As the Soviet RMA was gathering momentum, the attention of the United States turned rapidly to the defence of Europe, following its withdrawal from Vietnam in 1973. The steady build-up of Warsaw Pact forces opposite NATO had prompted growing alarm in Washington and in Europe about the poor state of the Alliance's conventional forces and the risk that the Soviet Union might become militarily predominant.[88]

The appointment of General Alexander Haig to the position of Supreme Allied Commander, Europe (SACEUR) in December 1974, as the successor to General

[86] *Allied Command Europe Counter-Surprise Military Alert System*, RDC/46/57, classified NATO Secret, 30 January 1957 (Paris: North Atlantic Treaty Organization) NISCA, declassified and disclosed to the public in 1996.

[87] Colonel-General Andrian A. Danilevich, quoted in Gordon S. Barrass, 'The Renaissance in American Strategy and the Ending of the Great Cold War', *Military Review*, January–February 2010: 103. General Danilevich was the leader of a Soviet General Staff team that drafted the three-volume *Strategy of Deep Operations (Global and Theatre)* that in the 1970s and 1980s was the capstone document guiding Soviet operational planning.

[88] This increasing level of concern had been amplified by a succession of highly publicised studies, notably Jeffrey Record, *Sizing Up the Soviet Army* (Washington, D.C.: The Brookings Institution, 1975); General Robert Close, *L'Europe sans Defense?* (Bruxelles: Editions Arts & Voyages, 1976); and Senators Sam Nunn and Dewey F. Bartlett, *NATO and the New Soviet Threat*, report to the Senate Armed Services Committee, 95th Congress, 1st Session, 24 January 1977 (Washington, D.C.: Government Printing Office, 1977).

Andrew Goodpaster, ushered the most far-ranging transformation of NATO since General Lauris Norstad's tenure as SACEUR a decade and a half earlier. Within months of taking command at SHAPE headquarters in Mons, Belgium, Haig set in motion a bold and wide-ranging process aimed at modernising the way NATO would defend Western Europe and at challenging the momentum of the Warsaw Pact's own operational and technological transformation. The centrepiece of this conceptual revolution was a broader approach to planning and the conduct of operations on an increasingly large scale.

The starting point of Haig's transformation was a series of 'flexibility studies' that Goodpaster had proposed earlier in 1974 and that the United States had recommended that NATO pursue actively.[89] The first and most important study focused on NATO's Central Region opposite East Germany and Czechoslovakia. It was completed in time for its examination by NATO defence ministers in December 1975 and proposed 236 remedial measures to enhance the readiness and capability of Central Region forces.[90] This study became the springboard for Haig to launch an unprecedented series of four interdependent initiatives:

(i) Initiating the so-called 'SACEUR's 3Rs' programme – Readiness, Reinforcement and Rationalisation – aimed at improving the ability of Alliance forces to transition rapidly from a peacetime to a wartime posture, by means of a rigorous operational readiness evaluation and certification process,[91] expanding NATO's rapid reinforcement capacity and enhancing mutual support among allied forces to achieve a rationalized use of limited resources;[92]

(ii) Linking previously autonomous multinational and NATO exercises conducted every autumn into a single exercise series, under the name *Autumn Forge*, extending geographically from Norway to Turkey and, chronologically, from September through November;[93]

[89] *Flexibility Study*, NATO Military Committee Memorandum for the Supreme Allied Commander Europe, MCM-71-74, classified NATO Confidential, 1 October 1974, (Brussels: NISCA) declassified and disclosed to the public on 12 March 2007; and *SACEUR's Flexibility Study*, NATO Military Committee Memorandum for the Secretary General, North Atlantic Treaty Organization, MCM-76-75, classified NATO Confidential, 14 November 1975 (Brussels: NISCA) declassified and disclosed to the public on 17 March 2010.

[90] Final Report - *Study on Flexibility of NATO Forces in the Central Region (U)*, 1240.3/20-5-1/S9/75 (Mons, Belgium: Supreme Headquarters Allied Powers Europe), classified NATO Secret, 23 October 1975, declassified and disclosed to the public on 25 February 2014.

[91] *History of Headquarters Allied Forces Central Europe 1977 and 1978*, 3340/ACCGSX/0001/S2000/80 (Brunssum, the Netherlands: Headquarters, Allied Forces Central Europe), 12 November 1980, classified NATO Secret, declassified and disclosed to the public on 4 March 2014, 22.

[92] Yves Robins, 'SACEUR and the three 'Rs', *Aviation & Marine International*, no. 47 (September 1977): 11; Morris Honick, 'Haig: The Diplomacy of Allied Command', in *Generals in International Politics: NATO's Supreme Allied Commander, Europe*, ed. Robert S. Jordan (Lexington: The University Press of Kentucky, 1987), 166 and 171.

[93] *Study on Flexibility of NATO Forces in the Central Region (U)*, VII-4; and 'Autumn Forge 75', *Flight International*, 30 October 1975, 656.

(iii) Expanding the number of army and air force units stationed in the United States that could reinforce US forces in Europe, under the dual-basing concept, and participate in the army's REFORGER and the air force's *Crested Cap* rapid reinforcement exercises, as part of *Autumn Forge*; and
(iv) Consolidating previously separate American, British and Canadian reinforcement plans into a single SACEUR Rapid Reinforcement Plan (RRP), with an expanded focus from the Alliance's Central Region to the allies on NATO's flank regions (Denmark, Norway, Italy, Greece and Turkey). The initial version of the RRP was published in November 1978.[94] Development of the RRP was accompanied by the construction and funding by NATO of warehouses to store pre-positioned equipment for US Army reinforcements and of hardened aircraft shelters at so-called 'collocated operating bases' to provide protection from air attack to incoming American, British and Canadian combat aircraft. Bilateral lines of communication and wartime host nation support agreements were also concluded, to facilitate the reception of reinforcements in continental Europe and their onward movement to pre-identified wartime defensive positions.[95]

Together, Haig's measures set the conditions for NATO's own Cold War RMA to take root over the next five years.

Political support for these measures was pursued by means of a long-term defence programme, developed by the Carter administration, at the initiative of ambassador Robert 'Blowtorch' Komer,[96] and adopted by the Alliance at its 1978 summit meeting in Washington.[97] As part of the LTDP, the United States formalised a commitment to have 10 divisions deployed and combat ready at their General Defence Plan (GDP) positions within 10 days of a reinforcement decision.[98] This pledge was known as the '10-in-10' commitment.[99]

The centrepiece of this commitment was the doubling of the size of the US Army equipment stockpile pre-positioned in Europe, from three to six divisional sets, to support the deployment of a three-division-strong US Army corps – the III (US) Corps stationed in peacetime in the United States – in order for NATO to be able to counter effectively a Soviet breakthrough and penetration in the exposed NORTHAG area.[100] The equipment for the corps's three component divisions was pre-positioned

94 *History of Headquarters Allied Forces Central Europe 1977 and 1978*, 16.

95 Brigadier General Walter W. Kastenmayer, 'Reinforcements and Prepositioning', *NATO's Fifteen Nations* 27, no. 5 (October–November 1982): 38–44.

96 Bob Komer had developed the concept of a NATO long-term defence programme while at The Rand Corporation and had become in 1977 special advisor for NATO Affairs to the US secretary of defence in the Carter administration, Harold Brown.

97 Robert W. Komer, 'NATO's Long-Term Defence Programme: Origins and Objectives', *NATO Review*, June 1978: 9–12.

98 General Defence Plans, known as Emergency Defence Plans in the 1950s and 1960s, were NATO's principal war plans for conventional defence operations in the 1970s and 1980s.

99 Robert W. Komer, 'The Rejuvenation of Seventh Army', *Armed Forces Journal International*, May 1983, 54.

100 *Study on Flexibility of NATO Forces in the Central Region (U)*, III-6.

at newly constructed warehouses in northern Germany and in the three Benelux nations. In addition, starting in 1978, a US Army armoured brigade, labelled 'Brigade 75', was stationed at Garlstedt, near the city of Bremen, in West Germany's northern half, marking the first time since the creation of NATO in 1949 that US land forces had been based in that part of the country.[101] That brigade's mission was to operate as the III Corps's lead element and to establish a close relationship in peacetime with the headquarters of AFCENT, as well as that of NORTHAG and those of the latter's four component army corps.[102] As a result of these steps, the United States reinforcement capability for the Central Region alone was doubled in size for land forces and tripled for air forces.[103]

In parallel, Haig worked secretly with the French defence staff to facilitate a French contribution to NATO's forward defence operations in a reinforcement role, should France, as a non-integrated ally since 1966, decide to take part, building upon the undertakings agreed upon in successive, highly confidential agreements between French and NATO commands dating back to the presidency of General de Gaulle.[104] Together, these undertakings ensured that, once implemented, the Alliance would have available two powerful sets of reserve forces – the US Army's III Corps in the NORTHAG area and the First French Army in the Central Army Group (CENTAG) area – to counter and repel Soviet operational-strategic-scale encirclement operations aimed at isolating and annihilating NATO's forward defences. The dynamic nature of the operational competition between NATO and the Warsaw Pact was now becoming tangible and visible – in a war in Central Europe, between

[101] 'U.S. Combat Unit Set for Duty in North Germany', *The International Herald Tribune*, 22 August 1975. On the operational rationale for the establishment of the US Army's Texas-based III Corps as AFCENT's main reserve formation, see 'The Northern Army Group (NORTHAG) Stationing Concept', *1975 Annual Report of Major Activities, 1 January to 31 December 1975*, classified Secret (Heidelberg: Headquarters, US Army, Europe and Seventh Army), 15–23, pages downgraded to Unclassified on 19 January 2012; and 'Brigade 75 and the NORTHAG Stationing Concept', *1976 Annual Historical Review, 1 January to 31 December 1976*, classified Secret (Heidelberg: Headquarters, US Army, Europe and Seventh Army), 1–10, pages downgraded to Unclassified on 19 January 2012.

[102] Remarkably, a Polish *Front*-level command post exercise, *Lato* 74, conducted in June 1974, rehearsed the engagement of Polish and Soviet forces against the III (US) Corps – labelled the 'super-corps' – several years before it was committed to NATO and a decade before its equipment had been stored at pre-positioning sites in Western Europe to enable its rapid deployment in a crisis, suggesting excellent Warsaw Pact intelligence on US Army post-Vietnam planning for NATO. *Exercise Lato-74*, 20 October 1978, classified Top Secret (Langley, VA: Central Intelligence Agency) CIA FOIA Electronic Library, declassified and released to the public on 18 July 2012.

[103] General Charles A. Gabriel, 'Tactical Air Reinforcement for Europe', *NATO's Sixteen Nations* 29, no. 4: 91–97.

[104] The first such confidential agreement regulating the possible participation of French forces in NATO-led collective defence operations in the southern half of West Germany, following France's withdrawal from NATO's integrated military structure in July 1966, was the Ailleret-Lemnitzer Agreement of 22 August 1967 between the French chief of defence staff, General Charles Ailleret, and General Lyman Lemnitzer, then the SACEUR. David S. Yost, *France and Conventional Defense in Central Europe* (Boulder, CO, and London: Westview Press, 1985) 14; and Claude Cartigny, 'La France quitte les organismes militaires de l'OTAN', *Recherches internationales* 75, no.1 (2006): 146.

10 and 20 Warsaw Pact armies, subordinated to between three to six *Fronts*, would now be confronted by up to 12 NATO army corps – three West German, three American, and one each contributed by the United Kingdom, the Netherlands, and Belgium, as well as, possibly, up to three French corps – controlled by two army groups.

In his quest for an alliance that could stand up operationally to the Warsaw Pact, Haig was seconded by Generals George Blanchard and Franz-Joseph Schulze. Blanchard had taken command of the US Army in Europe and, concurrently, of CENTAG at Heidelberg in June 1975, after having headed the VII (US) Corps in Stuttgart for two years. Schulze, who had been Haig's deputy chief of staff for plans and operations at SHAPE and, in effect, his senior war planner, had become commander-in-chief, Allied Forces, Central Europe (CINCENT) at Brunssum, the Netherlands, in January 1977 (the same month that Ogarkov was appointed chief of the Soviet General Staff). Now he was Haig's major subordinate commander for NATO's Central Region (the functional counterpart of the commander of the western TVD at Legnica, Poland) and Blanchard's boss.[105]

Upon becoming CINCENT, Schulze's main focus of attention became giving the operational level of command the preeminence it had lost and developing a single, theatre-wide approach to the conduct of allied land and air operations between the Baltic Sea and the Alps. To ensure that these concepts would become a unifying theme, the subject of AFCENT's annual commanders' study period in February 1978 – *Central Fortress* 78 – was appropriately titled 'The Combined Land/Air Battle'. Chaired by Schulze, it involved all of the Central Region's land and air commanders, as well as that of General Donn Starry, at the time the commanding general of the US Army's Training and Doctrine Command (TRADOC), who briefed the audience on 'Transatlantic Views on the Land/Air Battle in Central Europe.'[106] A month later, Schulze directed *Crested Eagle* 78, the biennial Central Region-wide command post exercise designed to rehearse the execution of NATO's conventional war plans. A main focus of *Crested Eagle* 78 was the employment of the new reinforcements made available to NATO by the United States.[107] The close coincidence in time and conceptual overlap between *Zapad* 77, staged in May-June 1977 with the aim of exercising the command and control arrangements for a TVD-scale offensive into Western Europe, and exercises *Central Fortress* 78 and *Crested Eagle* 78, held less than a year later, with the aim of refining concepts, plans and procedures to conduct a joint land/air campaign to defend West Germany, is remarkable. *Central Fortress* 78 and *Crested Eagle* 78 were followed, over the next two years, by *Central Fortress* 79 and *Crested Eagle* 80. The former focused on the requirements and challenges of the complex transition from peace to wartime in NATO's Central Region and the

[105] 'Gen. Schulze new CINCENT', *Armies & Weapons*, no. 34 (April–May 1977): 23.
[106] *Histories of Headquarters, Allied Forces Central Europe 1977 and 1978*, 37.
[107] *Histories of Headquarters, Allied Forces Central Europe 1977 and 1978*, 40.

latter on the conduct of the 'covering force battle' and main defensive operations and on the employment of reinforcements.[108]

One level of command down from Schulze, Blanchard gave multi-nationality and interoperability an unprecedented impulse under a programme called 'Rationalisation, Standardisation and Interoperability' (RSI)[109]. Working successively with Generals William DePuy and Starry at TRADOC, Blanchard resurrected effectively the operational level of command and operational art in CENTAG after a decade of neglect. The US Army adopted the 'active defence' as its tactical doctrine for corps-level operations and below, but embedded this transition in a wider, concerted approach with the *Bundeswehr*, bilaterally between the two armies and at the army group level within NATO.[110] CENTAG became the framework and test-bed for bringing the doctrines of the US Army and the *Bundeswehr* closer together.

A particular concern of the German Army had been that with two German army corps – the II and III *Korps* – positioned on CENTAG's right and left flanks, a failure of the two American army corps – the V and VII Corps located, side-by-side, in CENTAG's middle position – to fight forward might force German forces to abandon territory unnecessarily, to avoid creating dangerous gaps with adjacent American forces. As Haig remarked, 'in our Central Army Group we have made some changes in our corps and division concepts for defense to get a strong, forward, initial defense. It is not logical to have one corps defending with one concept and a corps alongside defending with a different concept.'[111] Accordingly, to ensure that a high level of operational coherence would be attained between adjacent American and German corps, in autumn 1979, for the first time, CENTAG sponsored a so-called 'inter-corps coordination exercise' in the form of a field training exercise in Hesse – *Constant Enforcer* – involving the coordinated employment, side-by-side, of the III (GE) Corps and the V (US) Corps.[112]

The US Army Europe war and reinforcement plans in support of CENTAG were revised extensively, on the basis of recommendations developed for the chief of staff of the US Army that called for planning to be based on 'preparation for an intensive early battle to stop any attack within 15 days . . . A forward defense concept should be

[108] 'Central Fortress 79', *1979 Annual History*, 3300/ACCGSX/445/SO736/81, classified NATO Secret (Brunssum, The Netherlands: Headquarters, Allied Forces Central Europe), dated 1 July 1981, declassified and disclosed to the public on 23 May 2014, 50; and 'Crested Eagle 80', *1980 Annual History*, 3340/ACCGSX/258/SO0552/82, classified NATO Secret (Brunssum, the Netherlands: Headquarters, Allied Forces Central Europe), 28 April 1982, declassified and disclosed to the public on 23 May 2014, 46.

[109] General George S. Blanchard, 'CENTAG/USAREUR Interoperability - A Total Program: From the Bottom UP', *Strategic Review*, Winter 1977: 7–13; and Richard L. Kugler, *Commitment to Purpose: How Alliance Partnership Won the Cold War* (Santa Monica, CA: The Rand Corporation, 1993), 305.

[110] Major Paul H. Herbert, *Deciding What Has To Be Done: General William E. DePuy and the 1976 Edition of FM 100-5, Operations*, Leavenworth Papers, Number 16 (Kansas: Fort Leavenworth, July 1988), 61–73.

[111] G.M. Bailly-Cowell, 'Apprehension without Fear . . . : An Interview with General Alexander M. Haig, Jr, *NATO's Fifteen Nations* 21, no. 1 (February–March 1976): 26.

[112] *1979 Annual History*, Headquarters, Allied Forces Central Europe, 51.

adopted, with plans, organization, and assignments of sectors revised accordingly'.[113] Thereafter, General Defence Plans at all levels, from Army Group-level downward, reflected an unambiguous commitment to a strong forward defence and to 'winning the first battle' without trading space for time.[114] In the words of Major General Richard S. Kem, 'So, in fact, our general defense plan was being revised to reflect this doctrinal shift of fighting forward, [...] which meant, if we were going to fight forward, we had to move forward... We are no longer going to trade space for time.'[115] In his 1975 SHAPE study on flexibility, Haig reported that 'modifications of defence plans in CENTAG increased the number of US brigades deployed close to the border.'[116] In 1977, Schulze revised his General Defence Plan to ensure that the 'Covering Forces' – those closest to the Iron Curtain – would consist of a least a third of all available forces and all Central Region nations were requested to 'defend as far to the east as possible and not to trade space for time.'[117]

This revised approach was anchored on a careful identification of defensive terrain features, the widespread deployment with allied forces of helicopter-launched, vehicle-mounted and shoulder-fired antitank guided missiles, and the preparation of obstacles and pre-planned armour and artillery 'engagement zones'. Forward defensive positions were backed-up with brigade-size reserves. The US Army deployed to West Germany over 200 *Huey Cobra* attack helicopters armed with TOW antitank missiles.[118] General Kem highlighted that 'We were really redoing operating plans and redoing them in terms of not only forward defense concepts but down to the actual terrain.'[119] Upon taking command of the V (US) Corps in February 1976, Starry instituted the practice of detailed 'terrain walks' along the corps's forward defence positions, to ensure that his subordinate commanders were intimately familiar with the terrain they would have the responsibility to defend in wartime, as well as with the precepts of the army's new 'active defence' doctrine.[120]

By 1977, all Central Region allies, with the exceptions of Canada and France, had instituted the practice of conducting multi-national, corps-scale field training

[113] 'The Hollingsworth Study', *1976 Annual Historical Review* (Heidelberg: Headquarters, US Army Europe and Seventh Army, 1 January–31 December 1976), classified Secret, downgraded to unclassified, 19 January 2012, 16–17.

[114] General Leopold Chalupa, NATO's CINCENT from 1983 to 1987, cited in Hoffenaar and Findlay, *Military Planning for European Theatre Conflict*, 58.

[115] Major General Richard S. Kem, *Engineer Memoirs* (Alexandria, VA: Headquarters US Army Corps of Engineers, October 2002), 193–196. In 1976–1978, General Kem was commander of the 7th Engineer Brigade, subordinated to the VII (US) Corps stationed opposite Czechoslovakia.

[116] *Study on Flexibility of NATO Forces in the Central Region (U)*, III-8.

[117] *History of Headquarters Allied Forces Central Europe 1977 and 1978*, 15.

[118] 'I Can Move Damned Fast, Maybe Even Fast Enough for NATO to Stop a Soviet Blitz', *Time*, 11 December 1978, 40.

[119] Kem, *Engineer Memoirs*, 193.

[120] Major Aaron J. Kaufman, *Continuity and Evolution: General Donn A. Starry and Doctrinal Change in the U.S. Army, 1974–1982* (Fort Leavenworth, KS: School of Advanced Military Studies, United States army Command and General Staff College), 8 May 2012, 51.

exercises periodically, as part of *Autumn Forge*, to enhance interoperability and the ability of allied forces of various nationalities to fight together. In the NORTHAG area, the United Kingdom executed exercise *Spearpoint* in 1976, Belgium carried out exercise *Blue Fox* in 1977 and the Netherlands exercise *Saxon Drive* in 1978. The US Army's own corps-level exercises in West Germany – 'REturn of FORces to GERmany' or REFORGER – initiated in 1969 took on a new dimension. In autumn 1975, the REFORGER exercise was extended for the first time to the NORTHAG area, with US Army and, exceptionally, Marine Corps forces participating in a West German exercise.[121] Two years later, exercise REFORGER 77/*Carbon Edge* in the CENTAG area involved, for the first time together, the land forces of all of the Central Region allies.[122] General Kem observed that 'REFORGER 77, (which) turned out to be a most significant exercise and one that was the culmination of a lot of planning'.[123]

Schulze also helped ensure closer involvement of the French Army in NATO contingency planning, under the terms of the December 1978 Biard-Schulze agreement with the commander of the First French Army, which built upon the Valentin-Ferber agreement of July 1974 between their two predecessors.[124] Contingency plans were developed to cover the employment of the First French Army as a two-corps-strong, counter-attack force along two eastward-oriented operational directions, either in the direction of Fulda, to protect the approaches towards Frankfurt and the Rhine River, or in the direction of Munich, to stop a Soviet advance in the Danube valley towards Stuttgart.[125] These were two of the principal operational directions, it was believed, that the Warsaw Pact would focus on in an attempt to encircle CENTAG's American and German forces. The expanding scope of AFCENT's confidential agreements with France would have meant that, paradoxically, a French contribution to West Germany's defence in the late 1970s would have been larger in volume, and more useful operationally, than that in the mid-1960s, when France was still part of NATO's integrated military structure, but was weaker militarily.[126] Following a French-sponsored commanders' seminar – *Kellerman* 79 – held at the headquarters of the First French Army in Strasbourg in December 1979, the AFCENT staff observed that the seminar 'was the first time since

[121] *Study on Flexibility of NATO Forces in the Central Region (U)*, VII-5.

[122] Master Sergeant Dick Larsen, 'REFORGER 77: mobility systems tested as part of Autumn Forge', *NATO's Fifteen Nations* 23, no. 1 (February–March 1978): 66–72; and Diego A. Ruiz Palmer and Wolfgang Igert, Fahrzeug Profile no. 61, *REFORGER 77/Carbon Edge: Die multinationalste REFORGER-ubung der siebsiger Jahre* (Stengelheim, Germany: UNITEC – Medienvertrieb, 2014).

[123] Kem, *Engineer Memoirs*, 201.

[124] *History of Headquarters Allied Forces Central Europe 1977 and 1978*, 16; and Frederic Bozo, *La France et l'OTAN: De la guerre froide au nouvel ordre européen* (Paris: Institut Français des Relations Internationales, 1991), 118.

[125] These contingency plans were given colourful nick-names, such as *Classic Fanfare* and *Charming Gorilla*. Christian E.O. Millotat, 'Streitkrafteentwicklung, Ruckblick und Ringen um neue Wege - Ausblick', *Military Power Revue der Schweizer Armee* no. 1 (2013): 45.

[126] Diego A. Ruiz Palmer, 'Between the Rhine and the Elbe: France and the Conventional Defense of Central Europe', *Comparative Strategy* 6, no. 4: 471–512.

France's departure from NATO's integrated military structure that the 1st (FR) Army had exercised so thoroughly in a NATO environment.'[127]

In parallel, at the initiative of General David C. Jones, commander-in-chief of the United States Air Forces in Europe (USAFE) between 1971 and 1974, the US Air Force was leading a resurrection of airpower at the operational level in NATO with the re-establishment of Allied Air Forces, Central Europe (AAFCE) in June 1974, as a region-wide air command under CINCENT.[128] Jones' ambition, and that of his successor, General John W. Vogt, was to have AAFCE lead a region-wide air campaign aimed at confronting a Soviet theatre-scale air operation and, simultaneously, interdicting the forward movement of Warsaw Pact land forces.[129] 'With the creation of AAFCE, NATO (also) introduced a new theatre perspective on the use of airpower.'[130]

The standing-up of AAFCE was accompanied by a vast array of other *organisational* measures, including:

(i) The activation of a state-of-the-art, US Air Force-manned Tactical Fusion Centre, inside the *Erwin* bunker, to provide CINCENT round-the-clock with NATO-releasable US intelligence information on the readiness and disposition of Warsaw Pact forces stationed opposite the Central Region;[131]

(ii) The gradual development of an AFCENT-wide intelligence architecture, built around a first-generation network of US servers deployed in Europe under the innocuous name of 'Limited Operational Capability – Europe' (LOCE)[132] designed to make intelligence information on the Warsaw Pact available more widely;

(iii) The extension of the area of operational coverage of the United States Air Force, and its associated tactical air control system,[133] from its traditional zone in West Germany's southern half, corresponding to NATO's 4th Allied Tactical Air Force

[127] *1979 Annual History*, the Netherlands: Headquarters, Allied Forces Central Europe, 35.

[128] A NATO region-wide air command for Central Europe – AIRCENT – had last been in existence at Fontainebleau until November 1966, when it was disbanded, following the withdrawal of France from NATO's integrated military structure four months earlier, to meet headquarters efficiency requirements.

[129] General John W. Vogt, Jr., 'A Look at a New Command in the Central Region', *NATO's Fifteen Nations* 19, no. 6 (December 1974–January 1975): 57–64; and Yves Robins, 'One Year of Allied Air Forces Central Europe', an interview with General John W. Vogt, *Aviation & Marine International*, no. 27, (November 1975): 15–17.

[130] David J. Stein, *The Development of NATO Air Tactical Doctrine, 1970–1985* (Santa Monica, CA: The Rand Corporation), Project AIR FORCE, report R-3385-AF, December 1987. 24.

[131] Dan Boyle, 'C3 – the Essential Ingredient to Air Defense', *International Defense Review*, 6 (1978): 862; and Thomas C. Housman and Raymond Fuentez, *Knowledge-Based Multi-Level Secure Network Technology*, Air Force Rome Laboratory (New York: Griffiss Air Force Base, December 1993), 5–6.

[132] As LOCE matured technologically, it was renamed 'Linked Operations Intelligence Centers-Europe', before becoming the NATO Battlefield Intelligence Collection and Exploitation System (BICES).

[133] *Tactical Air Control System* (Ramstein air base, Germany: United States Air Forces in Europe, March 1980); and 'The Command Expanded the Tactical Air Control System into Northern Germany', Thomas S. Snyder and Shekia A. Shaw, *Profiles in Leadership* (Ramstein air base, Germany: Headquarters, United States Air Forces in Europe, 28 January 1992) 186.

(ATAF), to the Central Region as a whole, to match the establishment of AAFCE. Concurrently, USAFE stood up a NATO Operations Support Cell at the 2nd ATAF bunker in Kalkar, in West Germany's northern half, to facilitate the provision, for the first time, of offensive air support to the Belgian and British land forces located in the more exposed and vulnerable NORTHAG area, notably by US Air Force combat aircraft stationed in the United Kingdom;[134]

(iv) The commitment to NATO for the first time of nearly all Royal Air Force reconnaissance, fighter, tanker and transport assets stationed in Britain, through the establishment in April 1975 of a dedicated NATO air command – United Kingdom Air Forces (UKAIR) – under Haig's authority.[135]

Successive AAFCE commanders, starting with Vogt, also worked closely with their French Air Force counterparts to facilitate a French contribution to a NATO air campaign, should France decide to participate early on in the combined defence of West Germany in a war against the Warsaw Pact. Accordingly, confidential protocols were agreed upon in July 1975 and August 1976 that regulated the planning and execution of French conventional air sorties, as well as, in December 1980, the use of French airspace by the allies.[136]

All of these steps aimed at ensuring that NATO's air forces would make a strong contribution to winning the 'first battle', as part of a joint land/air campaign and at a time when NATO's ground forces had few interdiction capabilities, notably by ensuring the allocation of sufficient surveillance, air-delivered firepower and electronic warfare means to the battlefield interdiction effort against the lead armies of the Warsaw Pact's first strategic echelon. To that end, Schulze issued 'War Planning Directive No. 1 – *Battlefield Interdiction Programme*' in early 1977.[137] Over the following two years, implementation of this directive led to the identification of the most suitable target areas, within a 20 kilometre-wide band on both sides of the FRG's borders with East Germany and Czechoslovakia, for the battlefield interdiction by NATO of advancing Warsaw Pact forces.[138]

These innovative organisational steps were underpinned by the concurrent development of new NATO tactics, techniques and procedures that favoured the employment of large 'packages' of fighter, fighter-bomber and electronic suppression aircraft over the earlier, piecemeal commitment of small numbers of aircraft sorties.[139]

134 'USAFE units in Northern FRG', *Aviation & Marine International*, no. 45, June 1977, 21.

135 'Commander UK Air Forces appointed', *Flight International*, 17 April 1975, 637; Yves Robins, 'CINCUKAIR: A New NATO Command', *Aviation & Marine International*, no. 26, October 1975, 15–17; and David Miller, *The Cold War: A Military History* (London: John Murray Publishers, 1998), 296–298.

136 Diego A. Ruiz Palmer, 'French Security Policy', in Simon, *European Security Policy*, 232.

137 *History of Headquarters Allied Forces Central Europe 1977 and 1978*, 18.

138 1979 Annual History (Brunssum, the Netherlands: Headquarters, Allied Forces Central Europe), 38–39.

139 For a description and assessment of the various national impulses that triggered conceptual innovation in regard to the employment of airpower in NATO in the 1970s, see David J. Stein, The Development of NATO Tactical Air Doctrine, 1970–1985, 10–12.

The greater effectiveness and efficiency of employing limited assets in larger-scale, targeted air operations had been one of the major lessons learned by the US Air Force during the war in southeast Asia. This new *conceptual* approach to the employment of airpower culminated in the mid-1980s in the rise of 'composite air operations', involving 50–100 aircraft and designed to overwhelm the Warsaw Pact's dense air defences and inflict large-scale damage on its land forces and ground infrastructure. The concept of a comprehensive 'air campaign' that guided the employment of coalition air forces during the 1991 Gulf War had been born.

Executing a broader, more ambitious joint, land and air battle also required better training. Building on the initial lessons learned from the US Air Force's *Red Flag* live flying exercises in the Nevada desert, in 1976 USAFE stood-up at RAF Alconbury air base, in the United Kingdom, an 'aggressor' squadron trained in Soviet air tactics and tasked to challenge USAF and other allied fighter pilots during 'force-on-force' flying exercises.[140] Without a stronger theoretical grounding in the application of airpower at the operational level, however, better flying skills alone were not sufficient. Accordingly, in 1979, AAFCE established a tactical leadership programme at Jever air base, in Germany, to train allied fighter pilots in the planning and execution of complex air missions in an adverse wartime environment.[141] Periodically, the operational aptitude of allied air forces was put to the test during increasingly ambitious large-scale, live flying exercises, such as *Central Enterprise* for air defence and *Cold Fire* for ground support, in the spring and the autumn, respectively, the latter integrated into *Autumn Forge*.

The establishment of AAFCE in 1974 and the various subsequent steps prepared the ground for the stationing in the United Kingdom, in 1977, of a second wing of F-111 long-range fighter bombers, more than doubling the US Air Force air interdiction potential in Europe and its capacity to attack Warsaw Pact forces and sites deeply into Eastern Europe in a conflict, several years *before* the concept of Follow-On Forces Attack (FOFA) emerged. They also anticipated the arrival in Europe, starting in 1976, of a new generation of USAF specialised combat aircraft, in the form of the F-15, F-16 and A-10 fighters, to replace the multi-role, but aging F-4 *Phantom*.

The gradual availability of expanding numbers of combat aircraft with much greater range and payload, including the *Tornado* in the *Luftwaffe* and the Royal Air Force in Germany, revolutionised the application of airpower in NATO. It also increased considerably the requirement for reliable, near-real-time targeting information from photographic, radar and signals intelligence sensors, as well as for physical attack and electronic suppression against the Warsaw Pact's dense air defences. In response, the

[140] Yves Robins, 'USAFE gets an Aggressor Squadron', *Aviation & Marine International*, no. 40 (January 1977): 16–17, and Lindsay Peacock, 'Aggressors at Bentwaters', *United States Air Forces in Europe – Yearbook 1989*, 31–35.

[141] 'Tactical Leadership Programme', *1979 Annual History*, Headquarters, Allied Forces Central Europe, 36; and 'Allied Air Forces Central Europe (AIRCENT) Tactical Leadership Programme (TLP)', *NATO's Sixteen Nations* 40, no. 2/95 (Spring 1995): 22.

USAF deployed successively to European bases, EB-57 and F-105G in the mid-1970s[142] and, from 1979 onwards, the U-2R, SR-71, TR-1, EC-130, EF-111 and F-4G specialised reconnaissance, signals intelligence, electronic jamming and anti-radar attack aircraft.[143]

By the late 1970s, then, the completion of a specialised command and control ground infrastructure around *Erwin* and a network of other bunkers, as well as the growing emphasis in NATO's war planning and exercises on the conduct of a theatre-scale, joint land and air campaign, had created the necessary conditions for the resurrection of the operational level in the Alliance and a growing awareness of the importance of operational art. Haig and Schulze's transformational vision was being realised. In a conflict, the Warsaw Pact would confront a much more capable and prepared adversary than would have been the case just half-a-decade earlier.

Senior Soviet and other Warsaw Pact commanders were aware of this trend – which portended, if left unchecked, an adverse shift in the 'correlation of forces' against the Warsaw Pact – from their clandestine sources, such as East Germany's agent *Topaz* inside NATO Headquarters in Brussels and the Clyde Conrad spy ring run by Hungary's intelligence service against the US Army in West Germany, as well as from their signals intelligence collection activities.[144] Articles in military journals such as *Zarubezhnoe voennoe obozrenie* reflected growing Soviet acknowledgement of, and alarm at, the scale and momentum of NATO conventional force improvement, perhaps best exemplified in the annual *Autumn Forge* exercise series.[145]

The first phase of NATO's RMA in the second half of the 1970s planted the seeds for the next step in NATO's Cold War RMA. This second step involved the development, between 1980 and 1986, of operational scale concepts for: (i) the mass employment of

---

[142] A Polish General Staff document setting out the scenario for a war game in 1978 mentions specifically the RB-57 and F-105G aircraft deployed temporarily to Europe, in support of NATO's *Autumn Forge* exercises. *War Game Scenario – Central Europe – 1978*, 6.

[143] T. Malcolm English, 'Jamming Swingers' and Bob Archer, 'Reconnaissance in Europe', *United States Air Forces in Europe – Yearbook 1989*, 46–50 and 66–67; and T. Malcolm English, 'Alconbury's High Fliers', *United States Air Forces in Europe – Yearbook 1990*, 40–44.

[144] Bernd Schaefer, *The Warsaw Pact's Intelligence on NATO: East German Military Espionage Against the West*, Parallel History Project on NATO and the Warsaw Pact, November 2003. On Rainer Rupp, alias *Topaz*, see Markus Wolf with Anne McElvoy, *Memoirs of a Spymaster: The Man who Waged a Secret War Against the West* (London: Pimlico, 1998) 299–333. On the Hungarian intelligence penetration of the US Army in West Germany, see Colonel Stuart A. Herrington, *Traitors Among Us* (Orlando, FL: Harcourt, Inc., 1999); and on East Germany's signals intelligence operations, see Benjamin B. Fischer, 'One of the Biggest Ears in the World: East German SIGINT operations', *International Journal of Intelligence and Counter-Intelligence* 11, no. 2, 142–153.

[145] See, for example, Lt. Col. V. Stroganov, Lt. Col. V. Kulikov, 'Exercises AUTUMN FORGE-85',, USSR Report, Military Affairs, *Foreign Military Review*, no 5, May 1986, JPRS-UMA-86-065 (Washington, D.C.: Foreign Broadcast Information Service), 18 November 1986, 7–15. The scale of the Warsaw Pact's monitoring and awareness of NATO's military strategy, deployments and exercises was also revealed in a 1988 propagandistic publication of the German Democratic Republic's Ministry of Defence: *Militardoktrin der NATO und Ihrer Mitgliedstaaten* (Berlin, GDR: Militarverlag der Deutschen Demokratischen Republik, 1988).

helicopters to destroy Warsaw Pact armour;[146] (ii) the engagement of armoured and mechanised forces in manoeuvre warfare and the execution of a daring army group-level 'counter-stroke' operation; and (iii) the targeting and disruption of the forward movement of Warsaw Pact follow-on forces, through exploitation of 'emerging technologies' for 'deep attack.'

The bold vision of helicopters being engaged *en masse* to arrest the progression of fast-moving OMGs that would be opening the way to the completion of operational-strategic encirclement operations originated with General Ferdinand von Senger und Etterlin, Schulze's successor as CINCENT, and Lieutenant-General Charles Georges Fricaud-Chagnaud, head of the French Defence Staff's liaison team to CINCENT.[147] Their thinking was inspired by the unprecedented, but moderately successful, involvement of the combat and transport helicopters of the US Army's 101st Airborne Division (Air Assault) in the REFORGER 76 exercise in Germany,[148] as well as by persistent US Army interest in air mobility associated with the creation of an experimental air cavalry brigade in Texas.[149] The introduction of a new generation of anti-tank helicopters in the French and German armies also offered a new opportunity to explore new, innovative forms of manoeuvre warfare at the operational level.[150]

Their ideas led eventually to the creation of self-contained airmobile formations, in the form of the French Army's 4th Airmobile Division, as a component of its new *Force d'Action Rapide* (FAR), and of NATO's NORTHAG Airmobile Division, composed of helicopters contributed by Belgium, Germany, the Netherlands and the United Kingdom.[151] Although the expected congestion of Central Europe's airspace in a conflict meant that the scope for employing helicopters on a large scale would necessarily be limited and probably could not match von Senger's ambitious vision of 'air-mechanised divisions', the German Army's exercise *Kecker Spatz* in Bavaria in the

146 Richard Simpkin, *Antitank: an Airmechanised Response to Armoured Threats in the 1990s* (Oxford: Brassey's, 1982).

147 Diego A. Ruiz Palmer, 'Countering Soviet encirclement operations: emerging NATO concepts', *International Defense Review*, November 1988: 1413–1418.

148 Yves Robins, 'REFORGER 76: The 101st Is Coming', *Aviation & Marine International*, no. 37 (October 1976): 15–18; and Massimo Ferrari, 'REFORGER 76: The Screaming Eagles Descend', *Armies & Weapons*, no. 29 (November–December 1976): 2.

149 The US Army's first operational application of air-mobility was during the Vietnam War. Mark D. Sherry, 'Airmobility', in *A History of Innovation: U.S. Army Adaptation in War and Peace*, ed. Jon T. Hoffman (Washington, D.C.: Center of Military History, 2009), 117–126.

150 General Ferdinand von Senger und Etterlin, 'New Operational Dimensions', *RUSI Journal*, June 1983: 11–15; General Ferdinand von Senger und Etterlin, 'The Airmobile Division: Operational Reserves for NATO', *RUSI Journal*, March 1987: 23–30; and General Charles Georges Fricaud-Chagnaud, 'L'Armee de Terre face a ses missions en Europe', *Defense Nationale*, May 1983: 35–44. A 1977 Polish General Staff document outlining the scenario of a war game that was played in February 1978 made specific reference to the deployment with NATO forces of helicopters armed with TOW and HOT antitank guided missiles. *War Game Scenario – Central Europe – 1978*, 7.

151 General Sir Nigel Bagnall, 'Airmobile Operations in Northern Army Group', *NATO's Sixteen Nations* 32, no. 6 (October 1988): 75–79.

autumn of 1987, involving the forward engagement of the FAR, demonstrated vividly the conceptual prescience of their thinking.[152]

Manoeuvre warfare at the operational level was the focus of the US and British armies in CENTAG and NORTHAG, respectively, in the mid-1980s. In CENTAG, where terrain in the 'covering force battle' area favoured, in most places, the defence, the transition from the 'active defence' to the 1982 version of the US Army's Air Land Battle doctrine opened the way to a more mobile form of forward defence.[153] AirLand Battle tactics sought to capitalise on the greater tactical mobility, firepower and survivability of the new generation of armoured vehicles and attack helicopters – the M-1 tank and the M-2 infantry fighting vehicle and the AH-64 helicopter – to engage advancing Warsaw Pact forces at a greater range and on the flanks of their penetrations through manoeuvre and deep fires.[154] Exercise REFORGER 88 in Bavaria, involving the employment of the V and VII (US) Corps on opposite sides, marked the most evolved form of the US Army's implementation of AirLand Battle in the European theatre and can rightly be seen as a live rehearsal, three years ahead of time, of the ground offensive in Operation *Desert Storm*.

In NORTHAG, British Generals Nigel Bagnall and Martin Farndale, successive commanders of the 1st British Corps and of NORTHAG, directed their attention to thwarting a Soviet and East German advance into the easily accessible North German Plain by bringing together a British and two West German armoured divisions into a corps-size, army group reserve. Their planning envisaged that either this reserve force or the III (US) Corps from Texas, if redeployed to Europe and available for employment sufficiently promptly, would be engaged in an operational-scale 'counter-stroke' to break the momentum of a Soviet offensive.[155] Remarkably, the very year that Marshal Kulikov directed the *Soyuz* 83 command post exercise, which, as highlighted above, included the simulated employment of a three-division-strong OMG to break NORTHAG apart, General Bagnall directed a 1st British Corps command post exercise – *Winter Sales* 83 – to rehearse the concept of a counter-stroke to break a Warsaw Pact offensive apart.[156] Thereafter, reinforcement exercises *Lionheart* 84 and REFORGER 87 and their field training exercise phase – the 1st British Corps exercise *Spearpoint* in 1984 and the III (US) Corps exercise *Certain Strike* in 1987 – were staged

152 Walter Bohm and Diego Ruiz Palmer, *Kecker Spatz: Panzerschlacht in Suddeutscland* (Erlangen: Verlag Jochen Vollert, 2012).

153 It is worth noting that, despite the often heralded opposition between AirLand Battle and NATO's forward defence strategy, General Crosbie Saint, commander of CENTAG in the late 1980s, highlights the importance of forward defence and the first battle. General Crosbie E. Saint, 'A CINC's view of Operational Art', *Military Review*, September 1990: 65–78.

154 Colonel Charles Barry, 'Planning Aviation Cross-FLOT Operations', *Military Review*, January 1984: 34–45; and General Crosbie E. Saint, 'Attack Helicopter Operations in the AirLand Battle: Deep Operations', *Military Review*, July 1988: 2–9.

155 General Sir Nigel Bagnall, 'Concepts of Land/Air operations in the Central region: I', *RUSI Journal*, September 1984: 59–62; 'New Defence Concept for NORTHAG', *Jane's Defence Weekly*, May 24, 1986: 920; General Sir Martin Farndale, 'Counter-Stroke: Future Requirements', *RUSI Journal*, December 1985: 6–9.

156 Sangho Lee, *Deterrence and the Defence of Central Europe*, 34–35.

to test in the field NORTHAG's capacity to plan and execute the envisaged counter-stroke, without the American reinforcements in 1984 and with the nearly full US Army corps redeployed to West Germany in 1987.

With strengthened forward defences in place and powerful, if limited, operational reserves to back them up gradually becoming available, the remaining component of the three-part NATO shield – follow-on forces attack (FOFA) – gradually came into place in the early to mid-1980s, following the completion in 1980 of a 'Warsaw Pact Second Echelon Interdiction Study' initiated by General Bernard Rogers, Haig's successor as SACEUR from mid-1979 onwards.[157] Beyond airpower, a key enabler for FOFA was the new US Multiple Launch Rocket System, designed to fire artillery rounds, anti-armour munitions and conventional attack surface-to-surface missiles against forward-moving Warsaw Pact formations.[158] Interdiction was evolving into deep attack.

When looking back at the concepts imagined by the likes of Ogarkov, Gareev, von Senger und Etterlin and Bagnall, the boldness of their strategic vision and the scale of the endeavor involved in the Warsaw Pact and NATO RMAs of the mid-1970s to the mid-1980s become readily apparent and awe–inspiring. From the standpoint of military innovation, this was, truly, a revolutionary decade. Appreciating the full dimension of the two alliances' Cold War RMAs, however, will likely have to await that time when the most authoritative strategic planning documents – the three-volume Soviet *Strategy for Deep Operations – Theatre and Global*[159] and SACEUR's and CINCENT's General Defence Plans of the 1970s and 1980s[160] – become available for another generation of Cold War historians to examine.

The NATO and Warsaw Pact RMAs and the historiography of the Cold War

For both NATO and the Warsaw Pact, the 1961 Berlin Crisis had made the prospect of war in Europe tangible, in a physical and visible way, for the first time. In October 1961, Soviet and US Army tanks faced each other, a few hundred metres apart, at Checkpoint Charlie in the centre of Berlin. The lessons that both alliances drew from the crisis had largely over-lapping implications, most notably regarding the conventional-nuclear interface. They triggered sustained interest in the feasibility of

[157] *1980 Annual History*, the Netherlands: Headquarters, Allied Forces Central Europe, 44.

[158] General Bernard Rogers, 'Follow-On Forces Attack: Myths and Realities', *NATO Review*, December 1984: 1–9.

[159] Barrass, *The Great Cold War*, 213.

[160] The CINCENT General Defence Plan, revised and updated in 1987 under the authority of General Hans-Henning von Sandrart, who was CINCENT between 1987 and 1991, seems to have been the culmination of the effort initiated a decade earlier by General Franz-Joseph Schulze to embrace the operational level of war for the conduct of a theatre-scale land-air campaign in the Central Region. See Sangho Lee, *Deterrence and the Defence of Central Europe*, 281–283, and Guy Willis and Charles Dick, 'Beyond the Corps Battle in NATO's Central region – An Interview with General Hans-Henning von Sandrart', *International Defense Review* 22, no. 2 (February 1989): 169–170.

Warsaw Pact	NATO
A. Vision of future war in Europe	
• Contemporary version of 'deep operations' against a capable and prepared adversary, under the threat of nuclear use	• Conventional/nuclear campaign to execute a 'forward defence' against a numerically superior adversary enjoying the strategic initiative
B. Conceptual innovation	
• Theatre-Strategic Operation concept • Operational-strategic-scale encirclement operations • Air and anti-air operations	• Land-Air campaign concept • Counter-offensive operational concepts (e.g., NORTHAG 'counter-stroke') • Follow-on Forces Attack concept • Composite air operations
C. Organisational adaptation	
• TVD-level high commands • Operational Manoeuvre Groups • 'Reconnaissance-Strike Complexes'	• Army Group and theatre-level, corps-size operational reserves • Division-size air-mobile reserves
D. Technological development	
• Main battle tanks and infantry fighting vehicles with river-fording capability • Main battle tanks with 'explosive reactive armour' • Self-propelled field artillery • Longer-range multiple rocket launchers • Self-propelled surface-to-air missiles • River-crossing equipment • Armoured combat helicopters • Long-range fighter-bombers and escort fighters	• New generation of main battle tanks, anti-tank guided missiles, self-propelled field artillery and attack helicopters with enhanced capability against Warsaw Pact tanks • New generation of surveillance, target-acquisition and munition-delivery systems for 'deep attack'

Figure 1 Constituent parts of the Cold War RMA of the late 1970s and early 1980s

conducting conventional operations successfully (offensively for the Warsaw Pact, defensively for NATO), while preserving the latent option of being able to resort to the first use of nuclear weapons.

As postulated at the beginning of this article, by the late 1970s, the Cold War RMA was underway in both alliances and largely on the way to completion. It was fully embedded in Warsaw Pact force posture, war planning and ongoing weapons deployments opposite NATO, ahead of its *public* theorisation by Ogarkov and other Soviet writers. In both alliances, conceptual innovation and organisational transformation often ran ahead, and anticipated, the fielding of new technologies.

And, lastly, contrary to a widely-held view, the operational level of war, as well as operational art, were alive in NATO throughout most of the Cold War and witnessed a revival from the mid-1970s onwards (Figure 1).

However, a preference, as well as ever-improving concepts and capabilities for conventional operations, on both sides never removed, reliably, the risk that either of the opponents might be forced to have recourse to the first use of nuclear weapons, even when the attractiveness of such employment, with its high escalatory potential, was debatable operationally and politically, and its consequences on the course and outcome of the conflict unpredictable.

For the Warsaw Pact, nuclear use would have meant executing an improbable, nuclear 'meeting engagement', upon receipt of a reliable warning that NATO was about to escalate to the employment of nuclear weapons. Accordingly, the detection of an imminent NATO transition to nuclear use in the course of a general war in Europe was assigned the highest priority.[161] However, whether the Soviet Union had the technological capability to detect reliably, in the middle of a high-intensity conflict and into the depth of a theatre of operations, the preparatory steps for NATO's nuclear first use, as well as the communications means to alert promptly its own nuclear forces in order to execute the foreseen 'meeting engagement', remains unknown.[162]

Various patterns of behaviour suggest that, through the mid-1980s, the Soviet Union struggled to develop a compelling operational strategy that would have at once delivered conventional victory, while keeping the NATO nuclear threat at bay These patterns include most prominently the enduring nuclear escalation dimension of Warsaw Pact exercises that ostensibly rehearsed a conventional theatre-strategic operation, as well as the high level of genuine, if misplaced, apprehension exhibited in the initiation and continuation of Operation *RYaN*, notably in connection with SHAPE's exercise *Able Archer* 83 and the stationing in the FRG of *Pershing* II surface-to-surface missiles.[163]

---

[161] Hoffenaar, 'East German Military Intelligence', 86–87 and footnote 50.

[162] The relatively crude nature of human surveillance and intelligence collection operations undertaken as part of Operation *RYaN* suggests that the USSR might not have had a technically reliable capability to detect NATO preparations for nuclear first use at the sub-strategic level, or might not have had the level of confidence in that capability necessary to initiate promptly and execute successfully the envisaged nuclear 'meeting engagement'. Christopher Andrew and Oleg Gordievski, *Instructions from the Centre: Top Secret Files on KGB Foreign Operations, 1975–1985* (London: Hodder and Stoughton, 1993), 111–140. Soviet strategic ground and spaced-based early warning systems had a history of defective performance. See Pavel Podvig, 'History and Current Status of the Russian Early Warning System', *Science and Global Security*, 10, no. 1 (2002): 21–60.

[163] Andrew and Gordievski, *Instructions from the Centre*, 119–120 and 134–137; William T. Lee, 'The Nuclear Brink that Wasn't – and the One that Was', *The Washington Times*, 7 February 1995; Gates, *From the Shadows*, 273; Benjamin Fischer, 'The Soviet American War Scare of the 1980s', *International Journal of Intelligence and Counterintelligence* 19 (2006): 480–518; Vojtech Mastny, 'How Able Was Able Archer?', *Journal of Cold War Studies* 11, no. 1 (Winter 2009): 108–23; Arrnav Manchanda, 'When Truth is Stranger than Fiction: The Able Archer Incident', *Cold War History*, 9, no. 1 (February 2009): 111–33; Dima Adamsky, 'The 1983 Nuclear Crisis – Lessons for Deterrence Theory and Practice', *The Journal of Strategic Studies* 36, no. 1: 4–41; Paul Dibb, *The Nuclear War Scare of 1983: How Serious Was it?* (Canberra, Australia: Australian Strategic Policy Institute, October 2013); and Nate Jones, 'Countdown to Declassification: Finding Answers to a 1983 Nuclear War Scare', *Bulletin of the Atomic Scientists*,

Such tension was inherent to an operational strategy that, in a war in Europe, aimed at preventing a nuclear first use by NATO by achieving early and irreversible conventional success on the battlefield, but that could well have triggered the very large-scale nuclear employment it feared. The TSO, which encapsulated the Warsaw Pact's Cold War RMA, had reached a dead-end.

For NATO, preserving the deterrent effect of the option of first nuclear use in Europe, from peacetime through general war, including for the purposes of intra-war deterrence at the European theatre level, meant securing political endorsement of the battlefield circumstances that would prompt SACEUR to request nuclear release authority. General Rogers defined publicly those conditions as 'the loss of the cohesion of NATO's conventional defenses'.[164] That definition became the operational basis for agreement by the Nuclear Planning Group in 1986 of the 'General Political Guidelines' (GPG) that replaced the 1969 'Provisional Political Guidelines'.

The GPG infused NATO's nuclear planning with a degree of operational substance and predictability that contrasted with the ambiguity set out in West Germany's 1975–1976 White Paper on security and defence, which famously included the statement that '[t]he initial tactical use of nuclear weapons must be timed as late as possible but as early as necessary'.[165] It is highly probable that the combination of a large and capable NATO tactical nuclear capability and a seemingly very ambiguous employment doctrine had a powerful deterrent impact on the Soviet leadership and introduced considerable uncertainty into Soviet contingency planning for war in Europe. This remarkable combination prompted a drive by the Soviets to match every aspect of NATO's nuclear capability, including dual-capable field artillery, as well as a concept of operations that sought to degrade that capability conventionally, while keeping a capacity for, in effect, last-minute nuclear preemption.[166]

The West German White Paper's calculated ambiguity, however, could not disguise the uncertainty that such a formulation presented, not only to the potential adversary,

Footnote 163 continued

1 November 2013: 47–57. On Soviet perceptions of the threat represented by the *Pershing* 2 missiles, see Hoffenaar and Findlay, *Military Planning for European Theatre Conflict*, 28 and 62.

[164] 'An Exclusive AFJ Interview with General Bernard W. Rogers', *Armed Forces Journal International*, September 1983: 80; and Bob Furlong and Macha Levinson, 'SACEUR Calls for Research on a European ABM System', *International Defense Review* 2 (1986): 151. In the same interview, General Rogers also called attention to the Soviet offensive chemical weapon threat.

[165] *The Security of the Federal Republic of Germany and the Development of the Federal Armed Forces*, White Paper 1975/1976 (Bonn: Press and Information Office of the Government of the Federal Repiblic of Germany, 20 January 1976), 20.

[166] In the same way that it took some time for NATO's intelligence and maritime communities to acknowledge that the Soviet Navy's primary missions in a war with NATO were to protect ballistic missile submarine 'bastions' near Soviet territory and to support land operations from the sea, rather than to conduct an extended campaign against NATO's sea lines of communication across the Atlantic, it has also taken some time for a consensus to emerge that persistent 'nuclear play' in Soviet and Warsaw Pact operational-strategic level exercises into the 1980s represented preparations to preempt, if necessary, a nuclear first use by NATO and to conduct ensuing operations on a nuclear battlefield, instead of a presumed preference for initiating deliberately wide-scale nuclear employment.

but to NATO political decision-makers as well. Rogers's threshold sought to balance ambiguity and uncertainty more finely by giving advance notice to his political masters of the adverse battlefield conditions that, hypothetically, would precipitate a request for nuclear use. The wish by Alliance member nations to avoid such circumstances in a hypothetical conflict was also used by Rogers as an incentive to enrol their support for greater conventional force improvements.

Embedded in the 1986 GPG agreement, however, was also an awareness that the outer boundaries of the conventional improvements that NATO's Cold War RMA could be expected to deliver had been reached.[167] As General Farndale, former commander of NORTHAG, acknowledged after the end of the Cold War, if NORTHAG had expended all of its operational reserves and still lost the battlefield contest with the Warsaw Pact, nuclear use would have been the only remaining option to attempt to avert defeat.[168] The exceptional June 1982 Soviet nuclear exercise and the US exercise *Proud Prophet* of June 1983 are reminders of the ever-present risk and temptation 'to go nuclear' that both alliances had to contend with if confronted, in a war, with an adverse strategic situation and the prospect of defeat.[169] In the end, the 'nuclear genie' managed to elude even the most ambitious prospects of what the Cold War RMA of the 1970s and 1980s could have been expected to deliver in terms of conventional capabilities.

With the end of the Cold War and the dismantling of the NATO-Warsaw Pact military competition, the Cold War RMA disappeared into a rapidly receding past.[170] It was disposed of by the emergence of a new strategic age. Few traces of it subsist in Europe, even if the name *Zapad* that is given periodically to large military exercises on Europe's eastern periphery evokes strangely a bygone era.[171]

However, Russia's enduring determination to restore its military potential, following NATO's air campaign in Kosovo in spring 1999 and, more recently, Russia's illegal annexation of the Crimean Peninsula and related military performance, bring a new context to the study of the Cold War RMA of the 1970s and 1980s that exceeds its contribution to Cold War historiography. While it is still too early to determine with confidence whether the sophisticated performance of the Russian armed forces in the

---

[167] For a rare and compelling assessment of the nuclear-conventional interface, see Barry D. Watts, *Nuclear-Conventional Firebreaks and the Nuclear Taboo* (Washington, D.C.: Center for Strategic and Budgetary Assessments, 2013).

[168] Farndale, quoted in Lee, *Deterrence and the Defence of Central Europe*, 255 and 266.

[169] Mastny and Byrrne, *A Cardboard Castle?*, 55 and 462–465; Bruce G. Blair, *The Logic of Accidental Nuclear War* (Washington, D.C.: The Brookings Institution, 1993), 208; Ben B. Fischer, 'Intelligence and Disaster Avoidance: The Soviet War Scare and US-Soviet Relations', in *Mysteries of the Cold War*, ed. Stephen J. Cimbala (Brookfield, VT: Ashgate, 1999), 96; and Paul Bracken, *The Second Nuclear Age* (New York: Times Books, 2012), 81–89.

[170] On the fading of the Cold War, see Ian Gambles, 'Lost time: The Forgetting of the Cold War', *The National Interest*, Fall 1995: 26–35.

[171] The name *Zapad* 99 was given to a large live exercise undertaken by the Russian armed forces in western Russia in 1999, reportedly the largest since the collapse of the USSR in 1991. Jacob W. Kipp, 'Russia's Nonstrategic Nuclear Weapons', *Military Review*, May–June 2001: 30–32.

crisis in Ukraine earlier this year heralds the revival of the old Soviet RMA of the 1970s and 1980s in a revised, contemporary form, characterised notably by much lower levels of forces and without a coalition dimension, the emerging evidence is intriguing. Several military measures taken by Russia since its war with Georgia in 2008 seemingly reflect a deliberate execution of a well-thought-out construct that would correspond with the forward vision of RMA-inspired thinking:

(i) The establishment in 2010 of four theatre-level high commands superimposed over four large military districts;
(ii) The staging of large command and field training exercises on a regular basis, such as *Vostok* 2010 and *Zapad* 2013;
(iii) The holding of no-notice snap alert drills, such as the one executed in July 2013 in the Eastern Military District;
(iv) The procurement of new, state-of-the-art materiel, in the form of large weapons-systems, such as new generations of surface-to-air missiles, as well as advanced equipment for the infantryman.[172]

The skilful employment of soft power instruments, side-by-side with military means, also suggests the execution of a vision that is more sophisticated, and well-adapted to contemporary circumstances, than the Soviet MTR narrative of the 1970s and 1980s.

At the same time, the old and new forms of asymmetrical warfare that have emerged since the end of the Cold War, often categorised as 'fourth generation' warfare, have consigned broad swaths of the American RMA concept of the 1990s to the dustbin of history. The absence of a competitive and interactive relationship with a relatively symmetric, determined and methodical peer competitor, comparable to the USSR, over the last two decades, has largely emptied the RMA paradigm of its inspirational momentum. It has also raised the question of whether the RMA concept is transferable, reliably rather than readily, from the European theatre, where its deeper roots lie, to extra-European theatres, where adversaries might employ forms of warfare that are not easily susceptible to RMA-inspired interpretation and disruption.

Undoubtedly, new RMAs will emerge in the twenty-first century, more or less suddenly, reflecting evolving geopolitical alignments, economic circumstances and technological developments. They will likely be as unpredictable in regard to their operational and strategic consequences as many of their predecessors. Whether recent military developments in East Asia or on Russia's southwestern periphery could create, downstream, the conditions for the emergence of a new RMA warrants careful

[172] On Russia's strategic trajectory since the end of the Cold War, see Marcel de Haas, *Russia's Military Reforms: Victory after Twenty Years of Failure?* Clingendael Paper No. 5 (The Hague: Netherlands Institute of International Relations, November 2011); Roger N. McDermott, *Russia's Conventional Military Weakness and Substrategic Nuclear Policy* (Fort Leavenworth, KS: Foreign Military Studies Office, 2011); Daivis Petraitis, 'The Russian Military Reform 2005–2015, *Lithuanian Annual Strategic Review* 9, no. 1 (January 2011): 139–171; and James T. Quinlivan and Olga Oliker, *Nuclear Deterrence in Europe* (Santa Monica, CA: The Rand Corporation, 2011).

observation and assessment. Indeed, the United States military position in the western Pacific in relation to a rising China is not without some parallel with the United States's military position in Western Europe vis-à-vis an increasingly threatening USSR in the mid-1970s, but the analogy stops there. In today's security environment, it is difficult to imagine the rise of a strategic competition that could be as dynamic and interactive as that between NATO and the Warsaw Pact in the last two decades of the Cold War and that could become so structured as to incubate a new RMA with global implications.

In retrospect, the scale of the planning for a general war in Europe during the later stages of the Cold War was staggering. Its nightmarish implications in terms of the devastation that would have been inflicted, if war had come, are all too clear. It is not too daring to speculate that never had a war, which, thankfully, was never fought, been so thoroughly prepared over such a long time.

Acknowledgements

The author is grateful to Dima Adamsky, Charles L. Barry, Gregory W. Pedlow, Barry Watts and David S. Yost for their insightful comments on an earlier draft of this article. He is also grateful to Dr Gregory W. Pedlow, chief of the Historical Office at Supreme Headquarters Allied Powers Europe (SHAPE), Mons, Belgium, and Dr Andrew N. Morris, historian, at Headquarters, United States Army, Europe, Wiesbaden, Germany, for having declassified and disclosed to the public, in support of the research for this article, previously classified Allied Command Europe and US Army Europe documents dating back to the Cold War, respectively, and to Ms Ineke Deserno and Mr Nicholas Nguyen, archivist and assistant archivist, respectively, at NATO Headquarters, Brussels, Belgium, for their helpful assistance in locating relevant declassified and disclosed NATO documents. The contents of this article reflect the author's views and should not be taken to express those of NATO or NATO member nations.

Index

Note: page numbers in italics refer to figures and page numbers followed by 'n' refer to notes.